The Catholic Church in England and Wales 1500 – 2000

A biographical history
of the leading personalities and events
through the Reformation, the extinction of the
ancient hierarchy, the vicars apostolic, Catholic
emancipation, restoration of the hierarchy
and developments in the Church since
Vatican II

Compiled and edited by Paul Kennedy

PBK PUBLISHING LTD

First published April 2001

ISBN No. 1-903824-00-1

PBK PUBLISHING LTD
The Coach House, Herncliffe
Spring Gardens Lane, Keighley, West Yorkshire, BD20 6LH
Telephone: 01535 681484 Fax: 01535 691693
Colour origination by Coltec Parker Ltd, Keighley, West Yorkshire, BD21 3LG
Printed in England by The Charlesworth Group Huddersfield, West Yorkshire, HD2 1JJ

To Betty with love
and to Canon Edward McSweeney
and the late Father George Francis O'Doherty CSSp.
for their example of piety, spiritual guidance and friendship

*I am indebted to many people for help and advice
in the compilation of this book:*

Patricia Ballantyne, Blairs Museum, Aberdeen
Tony Castle, Great Wakering, Essex
Dan Chidgey, Archdiocese of Cardiff
Rev James Curry, Private Secretary to the Cardinal
Archbishop's House, Westminster
John Dove Photography
Rev Ian Dickie, Archivist, Archdiocese of Westminster
Rachel Davies, Darton Longman & Todd
Charlie Ellis, The Bridgeman Art Library
Robert E. Finnigan, Assistant Archivist, Diocese of Leeds
Tom Horwood, Editor, *Briefing,* Catholic Media Office
Rev Mgr Philip Holroyd, Hinsley Hall, Diocese of Leeds
Matthew Habron, Venerabile English College, Rome
Evelyn Harris, Harper Collins
Rev Gareth Jones, Private Secretary to the Archbishop
Archbishop's House, Cardiff
Hugh Kealy, Publisher, *The Tablet*
Rev Mgr Patrick M. Kilgraff, Rector, Venerabile English College, Rome
Rev Michael Lewis, St. Michael's, Brecon, Powys
Tom Morgan, National Portrait Gallery
Rev Dominique Minskip, Archives Office, Diocese of Leeds
Dr Alistair MacGregor, Librarian, Ushaw College
Mary McHugh, Archivist, Archdiocese of Glasgow
Rev Canon P. McKinney, Rector, Oscott College
Donald J.J. McEwen, Headmaster
St. Edmund's College, Old Hall Green, Ware
Jim McKell, Redemptorist Publications
Peter Seed, Procurator, Ushaw College
Austin Smith, Hinsley Hall, Diocese of Leeds
Rev Mgr William Steele, Diocese of Leeds
Alicia von Stamwitz, Liguori Publications, MO, USA
Rev Dr John Sharp, Archivist, Archdiocese of Birmigham
Dr Judith Stamp, Archivist, St. Mary's College, Oscott
Celia Walden, Yale University Press
W. J. Weld, The Weld Estate, Lulworth Castle
Charles Wookey, Archbishop's House, Westminster

Bill Gribbon for the location photography
at St. Edmund's College, Old Hall Green, Ware
and Archbishop's House, Westminster
and Helen Baird for invaluable assistance
in typesetting the manuscript

List of Illustrations

List of Illustrations

Contents

Editor's Note

I was drawn to the idea of producing this book some years ago after being introduced to the life and times of Bishop Challoner, by the late Bishop Gordon Wheeler. My appetite for English Catholic history revived, I discovered through other writers, a wealth of fascinating characters and peronalities who guided and strengthened the Catholic Church in England during and following the Reformation.

Much of the material used in the book originates from writers long since out of print such as Bernard Ward, G.E. Philips, E.E. Reynolds and Denis Gwynn. Their work having the advantage over earlier historians such as Thomas Edward Bridgett CSSR who researched excellent history without access to papers from the Public Records Office.

It was my original intention to seek to re-publish some of these books, dealing with the history of this period but this was not practicable. However I believe this story, centred on the hierarchy, is worth re-telling. I therefore decided to use much of the original material that gave me so much pleasure and helped me to more fully appreciate the history of the Church in England and Wales and the heroic labours of those prelates who have gone before us.

The scholarship belongs to others and they are acknowledged after each chapter. I have used the extracts from these published sources as faithfully as possible but inevitably this leads to a variation in the written style. I decided for the sake of economy not to use the source references listed in the original works, they can be traced using the bibliography.

PK

Preface

In the 1st Century, the episcopacy developed as the accepted form of government within the Church. Jesus commissioned Peter with full spiritual powers and called him to be the chief shepherd and foundation of His Church (Matt 16:13-19, Luke 22:31-32, John 21:15-19). Peter was conferred with the power of the keys and the image of Peter is one with a special measure of authority. He is portrayed as a fisherman (Luke 5:10, John 21:1-14) as the shepherd of the sheep of Christ (John 21:15-17), as an elder who addresses other elders (1 Peter 5:1), as proclaimer of faith in Jesus, the Son of God (Matt 16:16-17) as receiver of a special revelation (Acts 1:9-16), as one who can correct others' doctrinal misunderstandings (2 Pet 3:15-16), and as the rock on which the Church is built (Matt 16:18).

In the early centuries the Church comprised separate and often divided groups, each with its own leader and distinctive liturgy and custom. In the early Church all Christians referred to themselves as the newly chosen people of God. From the beginning Christinity was a lay movement, and laity held key leadership roles, presiding over communities, preaching, teaching and celebrating rituals of prayer and worship. All the Roman communities agreed together a formula to unite the Church against the threat of heresy. This led to the Roman episcopate. Peter's immediate successors, Linus, Cletus and Clement, all knew Peter personally. Their successors also identified themselves with Peter.

As the Church spread through the Greco-Roman world, it adapted itself to contemporary social, political and cultural forms and structures. It adopted the organisational divisions of the Roman Empire – dioceses, provinces – and identified its own centre with that of the empire, (Rome). By the latter half of the second century there were synods and councils and the emergence of the monarchical episcopate with a bishop governing each diocese. Under the influence of the Roman emperors who made Christianity the state religion, the leadership of the Church became hierarchical and separated itself from the ordinary people. By the 4th Century the Church was divided into three groups, clergy, religious and laity.

In the controversy with Gnosticism, defenders of Catholic orthodoxy like Irenaeus (d.200), appealed to the faith of local Churches founded by the apostles (apostolic succession), and especially the faith of the Roman Church, which was by now clearly associated with Peter and Paul. During the first five centuries, the Church of Rome gradually assumed pre-eminence among all the local Churches. It intervened in the life of distant Churches, took sides in theological controversies, was consulted by other bishops on doctrinal and moral questions, and sent delegates to distant councils. The local Church of Rome came to be regarded as a kind of final court of appeal as well as the focus of unity for the worldwide communion of Churches. The correlation between Peter and the Bishop of Rome became fully explicit in the pontificate of Leo I (440-61), who claimed that Peter continued to speak to the whole Church through the Bishop of Rome.

Pope Leo was educated in Roman law and sought to clarify the notion of papal succession in terms of existing Roman law of inheritance. Each Pope, in law, succeeded St. Peter, not the immediately preceding Pope, and thus inherited St. Peter's powers. This separated the papal office from the person holding it, so that the prestige and the authority of the papacy remained untouched by the individual failings or virtues of any particular Pope. Pope Gregory I (590-604) was the Pope that sent St. Augustine to England in 596. He also established the rules for the election and proper conduct of bishops. He enforced clerical celibacy. Gregory described himself as the 'Servant of the servants of God' this description is still used by modern day Popes.

Clerics in the medieval Church possessed one of the seven Holy Orders - porter, exorcist, lector, acolyte, sub-deacon, deacon or priest, the first four were called Minor Orders. The Sacrament of Holy Orders was only clarified in the 12th Century and recognised as one of the Seven Sacraments of the Church. Before the Council of Trent, priests received no formal training, they merely offered themselves to the Church and for a period worked as apprentice priests. Parish priests rarely preached or heard confession, the laity passively attended Mass, said by the priest in Latin. Both priest and laity took comfort from the familiar sounds of the liturgy.

The 6th Century Neoplatonic Syrian author who wrote under the pseudo-nym of Dionysius (Denys) the Areopagite, espoused the hierarchical view of the Church as participating in and reflecting the Divine structure of the universe. As there were three orders in the angelic hierarchy - One: Seraphin, Cherubim, Thrones. Two: Dominations, Virtues, Powers. Three: Principalities, Archangels, Angels - so there were three orders in the clerical hierarchy. Bishops, priests, deacons, and three orders in the lay hierarchy, religious, lay and catechumens. In this schema of understanding, higher orders influenced lower, the laity were perceived as passively receiving grace from the clergy.

Monks and religious came to be as greatly respected as the clergy, while the laity remained at the lowest spiritual level. (Ed.This is in complete contrast to the position of the laity since Vatican II. The laity have found new opportunities to be involved in the life of the Church by collaboration in parish and pastoral councils. Emphasis is now given to the importance of baptismal vocation, the universal call to holiness, the common call to build community, the common priesthood of all the faithful, and a lay-centred Church).

Preface

By the 7th Century the papacy had achieved a supreme position of prestige. Gradually the papacy acquired the status of secular as well as spiritual ruler. With the emergence of Charlemagne, the Latin Empire counterbalanced the Eastern Empire centred on Constantinople. The Pope needed to maintain this balance between East and West. However, in 1054 the disastrous split of Christendom occurred when the Western and Eastern Churches excommunicated one another. The ruthless pillage by the Crusaders in 1204 and the political intrigues at the Council of Lyons in 1274, and again at the Council of Florence in 1438-39, further exacerbated relations between East and West. The quarrel culminated in the dispute over Byzantine's claim on Southern Italy.

Over the centuries efforts have been made to heal the schism which, more than the long memory of history, now centres on the prerogatives of primacy enunciated in the First Vatican Council in 1869-70 with the Pope as head of the Universal Church. To the Orthodox, the Pope is no longer simply the Patriarch of the West but is claiming a supreme primacy with jurisdiction over the whole Church. In the last years of the twentieth century Pope John Paul II called for a great ecumenical effort to resolve the problem.

The Great Schism (1378-1417) split the Western Church, this was the low point to which the Church had descended caused by political intrigue and power struggles. Pope Martin (1417-1431) was chosen by the Council of Constance, and proclaimed that no one can appeal from the Pope to any other body or question his authority on matters of faith. In temporal matters however, he lavished wealth and land on his family. The activities of many Rennaisance Popes, their unscrupulous search for wealth and power, the building and acquisition of temporal assets reached a high point at the end of the 15th Century. This coincided with the lowest point of the papacy in spiritual prestige and authority

As the 15th Century drew to a close the Church in England was accepted by the population as the central influence of an ordered society. The public were certainly not all regular church-goers but at least they acknowledged general allegiance to the Church and to papal authority. There was enthusiasm, religious foundations were being established right up to the Reformation. There was a tremendous amount of church building and artistic expression was focused on Religion. The Church was stable and drew its stability from ancient tradition. England had two archbishoprics, nineteen bishoprics, over six hundred religious houses and about 18,000 parish churches. The more senior of the clergy enjoyed wealth and privileges, with the leaders of the hierarchy playing a central part in the business of government. The chancellor was always a cleric until Thomas More became Chancellor in 1529.

3

Despite earlier reforms, most notably the Gregorian reforms of the 11th Century, which among other reforming measures urged on all religious and clerics to end two abuses, those of simony, the buying and selling of Church offices, and clerical marriage. There was much more required of the reformers as the 15th Century ended. The invention of moveable type by Johann Guttenberg in Mainz, greatly improved the printing process, both in the speed and reduced costs of production. William Caxton established a press at Westminster in 1477 and a flood of pamphlets and books circulated both on the Continent and in England. Much of the new material printed was critical of the Church and fuelled the ideas from the early Protestant reformers.

In the previous century, John Wycliffe an Oxford theologian initiated Lollardy a movement that criticised the Church, the corrupt clergy and rejected the sacraments. There emphasis was on preaching and reading scripture which they had translated into English. Although the Protestant Reformation did not start through the actions of Wycliffe, many of his ideas were adopted by the reformers of the 16th Century.

There was much corruption in the government of the Church especially among the Roman Curia and the papacy itself which through the actions of many Renaissance Popes had scandalised the Catholic world. One of the most infamous, was Pope Alexander VI whose pontificate ended in 1503. He had nine children from many different mistresses, his most famous offspring was Lucrezia Borgia. Her reputation associated with her father and brother Cesare, has suffered, probably without justification.

Nepotism was rife and after the death of Pope Alexander who was poisoned, Pius III was elected. He was himself a nephew of Pius II, and although eager to reform the manifest abuses of the Church he was in poor health and his pontificate only lasted twenty-seven days. He was succeeded by another papal nephew, Julius II, the third papal nephew in succession to become Pope. Julius was a great patron of the arts, he commissioned Michelangelo, Bramante and Raphael to carry out many of the grand schemes in the Vatican. All this cost money and to fill the papal treasury Julius arranged a massive sale of indulgences.

Leo X who succeeded to the papacy in 1513 was the second son of Lorenzo de Medici. He was only 37 when he became Pope and still only a deacon. He spent large sums of money on extravagant schemes which was typical of his reign. He resolved his financial problems by simony and corruption. Martin Luther protested and in October 1517 posted 95 theses on the door of the castle church in Wittenberg. Pope Leo issued a bull against him in 1520 and later in 1521 Luther was excommunicated. Luther's creative theology and Protestantism paved the way for other reformers such as John Calvin and John Knox. Thomas Cranmer, brilliant architect of the Anglican

Book of Common Prayer, contributed much to the shape and structure of English speech and language.

There were Catholic reformers who had great influence on the Church, Teresa of Avila who reformed the Carmelites, St. Pius V, St. Philip Neri, St. Ignatius Loyola and perhaps greatest of all St. Charles Borromeo. In England St. John Fisher, St. Thomas More, Reginald Pole and Desiderius Erasmus also advocated reform. Crucially for the Church in England, by 1585 Elizabeth had rendered the Catholic hierarchy extinct. The effect of this action reverberates today in ecumenical efforts to heal the breach between the episcopal Churches in Britain. The Council of Trent, convened in 1545 by Pope Paul III set the framework of Catholicism until Vatican II in 1962.

Chapter One

The Church under the Tudors

THE head of the Church in England at the close of the 15th Century was John Morton, Archbishop of Canterbury since 1486, he had been in exile with Henry VII. He was a good and wise counsellor and Thomas More, who was a page in the archbishop's household, gives a good description of him in his *Utopia*. He reformed and improved the clergy of his diocese. Archbishop Morton was also noted as the prelate who checked the long standing abuse of the right of sanctuary, when rogues found the means of escape in what was intended as a means of mercy. Morton was created a cardinal in 1493 and died in 1500. He was succeeded as archbishop by William Warham a learned and skilled diplomat, trained in law and a good and holy churchman.

Henry VII was a sincere religious man influenced no doubt by his mother Lady Margaret Beaufort. His choice of bishops for the most part consisted of canon lawyers. Thomas Wolsey was chaplain to Henry VII and had gained a considerable collection of benefices before his famous collaboration with Henry VIII.

Before Henry's break with Rome, Thomas Wolsey championed Catholic orthodoxy. He was the most notorious cardinal in English history and appeared on the scene at a critical period for the Church. Wolsey was probably the most powerful figure in Europe. He was born at Ipswich of middle class parents. His father was a burgess of considerable wealth. The Church still offered the best opportunities for advancement and profit. The Wolsey's were a generation too soon for the distribution of Church loot that was to form the basis of the wealth and dynasty of many notable families. Thomas was born about 1471, educated at Magdalen College Oxford, and ordained priest in 1498. Wolsey held several offices and benefices, including the rich deanery of Lincoln, domestic chaplaincy to the Archbishop of Canterbury and finally was chaplain to Henry VII before the King died.

Wolsey used the Church, as did the six cardinals who preceded him, and indeed the majority who took orders at that time as a stepping stone to secular advancement. In this he did no more than share that misuse of the highest ecclesiastical offices which had become a well established practice. His share was the lion's share. At one time or another he held very nearly every preferment of high value in England, many of them at the same time.

When Henry VIII became King at eighteen, Wolsey, though nearly twenty years his senior was still a young man. He was well established at court, a man of affairs, with an attractive personality and an unrivalled capacity for making the most of his opportunities. Moreover, he was well off and lavish in display and entertainment, completely at home in the atmosphere of the court, not too much of the priest to disdain court extravagancies, or court vices. He was the perfect favourite for a luxurious, personable and active young King who had inherited prosperity and prestige as the fruits of the cunning and avarice of his father. Henry became King at a time of peace in England and Europe with as a consequence increasing prosperity. Wolsey became almoner to Henry soon after his succession. The two were intimate friends and Wolsey exerted great influence over the King. No prelate before or since has held such sway in England. He used his power in the State wisely, with such singular skill and ability to the advantage of his country - as well as himself.

Wolsey's position with the King became such that he was the regular channel of approach to the royal person, for both Englishmen and the representatives of foreign princes. Consequently his riches increased rapidly. As Henry grew he took more power, and Wolsey advanced with him. He was successively Dean of Hereford, York, St. Stephen's Westminster and Bishop of Lincoln in the years 1512-13. In the following year he succeeded Cardinal Christopher Bainbridge as the Archbishop of York.

By this time the King of England and his man were in a singularly powerful position in Europe. Their support was sought eagerly by the emperor, the Pope and the King of France. Never had England been in a position to interfere so effectively in the politics of Europe. Pope Leo X, who was threatend by Francis I, needed the support of Henry. He created Wolsey Cardinal-priest of St. Cecilia trans Tiberium in 1515 and, later, papal legate. Archbishop Warham of Canterbury tactfully made way for Wolsey in the Chancellorship.

With his legatine powers he could manipulate Archbishop Warham of Canterbury and frequently ignored the bishops. He disliked convocations and synods, and indeed, Parliament. He demoralised the bishops and abbots and they deeply resented the invasion of their powers. He interfered with the government of the Church in England far more than any Pope had dared to do. It was said that he rode papal jurisdiction in England to its death. This in turn reflected on the Popes whose standing in England was further weakened.

Wolsey was involved on three occasions with negotiations, backed by Henry, of becoming Pope. Despite his commanding advantage in Europe,

7

maintained by his consummate ability fired solely by ambition, he failed to gain his greatest objectives, either because, big as he was, he thought he was even bigger, or because he was never fully enough informed of the strength against him.

His wealth was increasing not only from emoluments from the courts over which he presided, but from his various Sees and other benefices, which he exchanged on a regular basis as other richer bishoprics became vacant. He also received considerable presents and pensions from Francis, and Charles. Pope Leo X granted him a yearly pension of seven thousand five hundred ducats from the revenues of the bishoprics of Toledo and Palencia in Spain. Wolsey although greedy was no miser. He spent freely as he gained wealth, he was a generous patron of literature, a typical Renaissance benefactor to seats of learning. He founded the college of Christchurch at Oxford, by papal authority, converting the monastery of St. Frideswide for the purpose. His building of Hampton Court, which he gave to the King, and his generous patronage of the arts mark him as a Renaissance figure with the Medicean touch.

When the doctrines of Luther found their way into England the Cardinal and the King actively opposed them. Henry's *Defence of the Seven Sacraments,* which obtained for him the title of *Defender of the Faith*, from the Pope, so proudly passed on to his successors, was popularly believed to have been supervised, at least by Wolsey and Bishop Fisher of Rochester, the future cardinal and martyr.

In 1525 the matter of Henry's divorce from Catherine of Aragon was broached to Wolsey. He appears to have approved of the project as suitable to his policy of strengthening the alliance between England and France by the marriage of Henry to Renee, daughter of Louis XII. By supporting the King, he would not necessarily be conniving at divorce, the King's case being that the marriage had never been valid. When Henry disclosed his determination with regard to Anne Boleyn, the Cardinal, after objection and protest agreed to support the King as usual.

Eventually his conscience began to worry him in the matter, and he told the King that though he was in gratitude, ready 'to spend his goods, blood and life' in the service of his master, yet he was under greater obligation to God, to whom he would have to give account of his judgements. Cardinal Campeggio as papal legate arrived in England to deal with the affair jointly with Wolsey. The procedure and caution exhausted the King's patience and he blamed Wolsey for the delay. The Cardinal's enemies seized their opportunity. He found himself in disgrace, lost his Chancellorship and one after another his richest offices until he was finally relegated to York.

There is reason to believe that at times he also lived fearing God. There was nothing mean about him, when he was summoned from York on a charge of treason he said that there lived not a man on earth who could look him in the face and charge him with untruth. He was ill with dropsy and travelled slowly and painfully. He got no further than Leicester, where he died at the Abbey of St. Mary de Pre. It is said that beneath his purple and fine linen, they found a hair shirt on his back and he wore a ring of iron on his arm. Whether he would, in the final analysis remained loyal to the Church against Henry along with Fisher and More had he lived long enough, is a matter of conjecture. It seems at least probable that he would.

He was the greatest and last of the ecclesiastical statesmen in England. He achieved the complete combination of clerical and secular power, but used that power so improperly, for his own aggrandisement, neglecting the greater issues, He enriched himself so much at the expense of the Church. In his intense preoccupation with his own avarice, he missed the menace to the unity of the Church. He was perhaps the one man who could have fought that menace with any chance of success.

One of Wolsey's contemporaries, John Fisher was a scholar-priest who rose in the Church not for his value to the King as a lawyer and politician, nor for his royal connections. His piety and learning alone gained him honours and preferment. He rose in the end to higher dignity than any other English cardinal.

He was born into a middle class family and received his early education at Beverley, the ancient capital and Minster town of the East Riding of York-shire. From Beverley he went to Michael House, Cambridge, where in due course he graduated Master of Arts. By 1495 he had become fellow, proctor and two years later master of Michael House. He had already a wide reputation for learning and sanctity. Having taken Orders he was chosen by Lady Margaret Beaufort, Countess of Richmond and mother of Henry VII, for her almoner, confessor and spiritual director. He was for a time tutor to the future Henry VIII. For many years the young King had a great respect for him. In 1501 he became vice-chancellor of Cambridge University and in 1504 Bishop of Rochester. The two causes closest to his heart were religion and learning.

Every writer of repute in his day bears testimony to his greatness. Vigorously and constantly he urged the need for reform in the Church, especially in the discipline and character of the clergy. No less vigorously did he oppose the reforms proposed by Luther and those doctrines which were derived from Wycliffe and the Lollards. He was nominated English representative at the Lateran Council in 1512, but did not go.

On 18 June 1529, in the Parliament chamber at the Black Friars there sat the Archbishop of York, Cardinal Thomas Wolsey and Cardinal Lorenzo Campeggio, legate of His Holiness Pope Clement VII, to judge whether it was lawful for the King to put away his wife. Beneath the cardinal legates sat

9

the chosen divines, scholars and lawyers of the realm, the Archbishop of Canterbury and many other bishops. On one side stood the counsel for the King, who were led by Dr. Sampson, afterwards Bishop of Chichester and Dr. Bell, afterwards Bishop of Worcester. On the other side stood the counsel for the Queen, led by Dr. Fisher, Bishop of Rochester and Dr. Standish previously a Grey Friar then Bishop of Asaph.

The King's case acquitted Queen Catherine of any personal offence and was based on Henry's conscientious scruples, denying all amorous considerations. He demanded of the assembled prelates, in particular of his confessor, whether he did not do this on their advice and approbation, signified under their own seals. The Archbishop of Canterbury on their behalf assented.

Bishop Fisher stood firm and refused his consent, denying that he had signed the document with his own seal. He defended the validity of the marriage between Henry and Catherine. The case was eventually transferred to Rome and the outcome was the catalyst that created the break between Henry and Rome. John Fisher stood alone among his brother prelates who for fear or favour, gave their broken spiritual allegiance to the King. He agreed that so far as the succession was concerned, the realm might legalise whom it chose. But to make the King supreme head of the Church there was no authority. The king could not ignore John Fisher.

On 17 June 1535, the late Bishop of Rochester, for at this time he had been deprived, (but now created cardinal on 21 May by Pope Paul III) appeared at the bar of the King's Bench before a common Middlesex jury of twelve, to answer the charges: "That in the twenty-seventh year of King Henry's reign, he the said John Fisher, late Bishop of Rochester, had in the Tower of London, falsely maliciously, and traitorously spoken and divulged against his due allegiance, before several of the King's true subjects the following words in English: That the King our sovereign lord is not supreme head, on earth, of the Church in England".

He had made the declaration to Rich, the King's man who had asked his opinion for the "quieting of the royal conscience", He therefore maintained that he had not made the statement maliciously and was not in consequence guilty under the statute. All of which was true.

He was condemned to a traitor's death of hanging and butchering, but at the last moment the King relented, and ordered a clean cut with the axe. Thus died the man whose life could do the King no harm. This venomous and brutal murder was typical of Henry's cruel determination to pursue his own ends. The King who had for years revered the Bishop as a father, had seen fit to give the venerable old priest the death of a traitor, though in fact, he succeeded only in giving him the death of a saint and martyr.

The year following the martyrdom of Cardinal John Fisher, Pope Paul III elevated to the Sacred College Reginald Pole, with the title of Cardinal-deacon of Sts. Nerens and Achilleis. He was aged thirty-six and not yet a priest. His mother, Margaret Pole Countess of Salisbury, was the grandaughter of Richard Duke of York and niece of Edward IV.

Reginald Pole was born at Castle Stourton, Staffordshire. He was educated at the school attached to the Charterhouse at Sheen and at Magdalen College, Oxford. By virtue of his birth, he received many benefices whilst still a young man. Although not in Orders he had probably received the tonsure. He studied at Padua, Rome and later Paris. In 1527 he was made Dean of Exeter. He lived his life as an ecclesiastic and student.

At the time of the trial of the King's first divorce case, he was in Paris. He disapproved of the divorce proceedings and wrote to the King from Paris and expressed his absolute disapproval and castigated Henry for his behaviour, for his differences with Rome and especially for the executions of Cardinal John Fisher and Thomas More. Pole went to Rome at the request of the Pope, to sit on a commission for the reform of Church discipline. He committed himself to the task of restoring the Church in England to its re-union with Rome.

At the end of 1536, the people of the North rose in their anger at the dissolution of the monasteries. By the spring of 1537 the uprising was formidable, gathering its strength from Yorkshire and Northumberland. The main rising was led by Robert Aske, a Yorkshire gentleman, though the rising in its entirety was popular and spontaneous. The people bound themselves by oath to stand by each other, "For the love which they bore to Almighty God, his Faith, the Holy Church and maintenance thereof; to the preservation of the King's person and his issues; to the purifying of the nobility; and to expulse all villein blood, and evil counsellors from his grace and privy counsel; not for any private profit, nor to do harm to any private person, nor to slay or murder through envy, but for the restitution of the Church, and suppression of heretics and their opinions". This rising, The Pilgrimage of Grace, was eventually dispersed with promises made. The King, contrary to his express word, hanged and butchered the leaders afterwards.

The Pope now published the Bull of excommunication and deposition, which had been prepared some time earlier, following the execution of Fisher and More, and he sent Cardinal Pole as legate to publish the Bull. He failed due to diplomatic difficulties with Francis I and Charles V. Two years passed and Pole tried again to persuade Francis and Charles against Henry. The King had judgement of treason pronounced against Pole and sent assassins to murder him. Although Henry failed to catch Pole, he persecuted the Pole family, executing most of them, including his mother Margaret. She was over seventy years old, kept in the Tower for two years then callously beheaded.

The Cardinal improved his position at Rome. In 1540 he was one of the three legates to open and preside at the Council of Trent. On the death of Henry VIII and the accession of Edward VI, Pole made strenuous efforts to induce the Protector Somerset and the Privy Council to reconcile England with the Holy See. Protestant doctrines were now in the ascendancy within the English hierarchy and court. Too many already owed their positions and wealth to the loot from the monasteries. Reconcilement with Rome was not possible for the present.

The debate at the end of Henry's rule was centred around images, the claims of the priesthood, clerical celibacy, transubstantiation, prayers for the dead and chantries. Among ecclesiastics, the debate was the nature of the Eucharist, the source of ecclesiastical authority and the doctrine of justification by faith.

Edward's first Parliament was convened in the autumn of 1547 extending reform still further from Henry's schismatic Catholicism. Censorship statutes were repealed and a huge increase in the production of books followed. The Protestant reformers used the medium of the printed word extensively, about 400 books were published under Somerset's protectorate, of these 160 were controversial religious titles - 159 Protestant and only one Catholic. Bishop Gardiner accused Somerset for this as the Government supported Protestant writers such as Hugh Latimer. Popular pressure was not the impulse of reform, it was the Government that decided. The preference of the monarch and the chief ministers, would ensure that secular authority determined the levels of reform. The bishops were weakend by their divergent views, Protestant theories were still being evolved, the Catholic wing separated as it was from Rome relied on the reaction of conservative prelates like Gardiner and Bonner who were imprisoned for their protests.

With Northumberland's ascendency, some thought the country would now revert to the ancient faith, however Northumberland relied on Cranmer to gain favour with the young King and Edward preferred the reformed religion. Parliament passed the Act introducing the Second Prayer Book of the reign in 1552. The liturgy established under Northumberland's aegis was followed by the Church of England for the next 400 years. The liturgical changes set out in the 1552 Prayer Book were completed the following year by forty-two articles of faith drawn up by Thomas Cranmer.

Important changes were made in the hierarchy. Following the imprisonment of Gardiner and Bonner, other Catholic Bishops, Day, Heath, Vesey and Tunstall were all deprived in 1552. Notable Protestants appointed to their Sees were Nicholas Ridley, John Ponet, John Hooper, Miles Coverdale and John Scory. With Cranmer at Canterbury, Holgate at York and Goodrich at Ely, they were an intimidating Protestant team. The remaining bishops guarding their conservatism appeared uncommitted.

The practice and outward symbols of the ancient Catholic faith had been for the most part destroyed, but the people and most of the parish clergy remained loyal to the Catholic way. This varied from one area to another, in London and Kent the reformers were successful, in Sussex and the north, especially Lancashire the people were predominantly Catholic.

Meanwhile Cardinal Pole remained at the papal court, and his position there was so high that when Pope Paul III died in 1549, he very nearly succeeded him. By the influence of Cardinal Farnese he had obtained the requisite number of votes in the conclave. When late in the evening, two cardinals invited him to appear and be acclaimed Pope, he begged to be allowed to wait until the next morning, either from humility or fear of the office. However the following morning another cardinal was proposed and elected Pope Julius III.

In 1553, Mary acceded to the throne. There was a suggestion that she should marry Cardinal Pole, as one of two eligible Englishmen. Although Mary liked Reginald Pole and had a great affection for his mother Margaret, she was sixteen years his junior, and declined the suggestion. It is unlikely that the Cardinal himself had any inclination for married life. He had lived as an ecclesiastic, though he was not as yet ordained.

Mary's caution deleted all reference to papal authority or restoration of Church property in the early statutes which repealed the anti-Catholic legislation of England. The Pope appointed Cardinal Pole *legate a latere* to England, but Mary, advised that his arrival might cause trouble, warned him not to come nearer than Brussels.

Pope Julius III chose Cardinal Pole for the reconciliation of England to Rome. Pole had lived in Rome since 1532 working for the restoration of papal authority in England. He was a reformer, he had adopted a doctrine of salvation similar to Martin Luther's justification by faith alone, but unlike Luther, Pole believed in the unity of the Church under the Pope and the need for obedience. Associates of Pole, Peter Martyr Vermigli the Augustinian and Bernadino Ochino the Capuchin both left the Church and joined the Protestant reformers in Switzerland. Cardinal Pole strove for the reconciliation of Protestant and Catholics, however when the Council of Trent decreed a doctrine of salvation different in every way to his own, Pole accepted it, but he remained under suspicion of heresy from the ultra orthodox.

Cardinal Pole was a reserved and diffident man, without ambition. From the moment of his appointment as papal legate in August 1553, he was impatient to return to England. He was determined to sweep caution to the wind in the urgent task of re-uniting England to Rome.

As Mary consolidated her position she repealed the attainder against Pole. He was conducted to England with great pomp and formally received by Philip and Mary with ample and solemn ceremony. When he arrived on 20 November 1554 after twenty years abroad he was a changed man. He had lost the wit and urbane style, and the decisive mind that made him such a favourite of Henry VIII. He was now sadder and grave in appearance, his drawn features and solemn eyes were more in tune with the ascetic churchman. He had of course been ravaged with grief over the destruction of his family and his mild manner and obvious melancholy showed his pain. He had devoted himself unceasingly to rid the Church of the corruption and greed that produced anti-clericalism which fed the Protestant movement against Rome. He now thought Divine Providence had greater work for him in England.

One major problem was the determination of lay holders of monastic and chantry lands to keep them. There were many Catholics who had purchased such land from the Crown and their position was equally unyielding. Finally Pope Julius, after much wrangling between Gardiner and Pole agreed to issue dispensation to those who possessed former Church property.

Mary desired a return to Catholic orthodoxy under the authority of the Pope as soon as possible, but complex legal measures were required especially with regard to the succession. Parliament passed the Bill repealing the Edwardian statutes that governed the Prayer Book, images and married priests. The new statutes authorised the services to be the same as they had been under Henry VIII, they also made Protestant services and the marriage of priests illegal.

The Act of Repeal re-uniting England to Rome finally passed into law in January 1555. On the following day, the Cardinal legate formally absolved "all those present, and the whole nation and dominions thereof, from all heresy and schism and all judgements, censures and penalties for that cause incurred, and restored them to the Communion of Holy Church, in the name of the Father, Son and Holy Ghost".

Bishop Gardiner on 16 January 1555 summoned eighty imprisoned preachers and urged them to recant their Protestant beliefs. The following week trials for heresy began. On 4 February the first victim, John Rogers, a prebendary of St. Paul's, was burned. Bishop Gardiner soon realised that burnings failed to intimidate Protestants and he withdrew from an active role. Cardinal Pole had opposed the Roman Inquisition when he was in Italy and argued that private expressions of doubt could be countered by "the way of charity and mildness", but support for heresy must be suppressed to save the people from heretic "wolves". Queen Mary undoubtedly believed that persecution of heretics was entirely necessary, although she had said that it should be taken "without rashness and directed against learned men who

might mislead others rather than against ordinary people". The most celebrated victims were the three Oxford martyrs. The trials of Latimer and
Ridley commenced at the end of September 1555, neither of the two men
would yield under pressure at the cross examination by Thomas Martin.
Cranmer had shown some inclination to yield, he had said that if he could be
persuaded of the papal case in any of the issues being disputed, he would
submit himself to the Pope. The Spanish Dominican theologian Pedro de
Soto was appointed by the Inquisition. He made little progress with Cranmer, and even less with Latimer and Ridley, one of them even refused to
speak to de Soto.

Consequently Latimer and Ridley went with defiance to their deaths on 16
October. The two men were burnt outside the city gate in Broad Street, in
front of Balliol College. They were led to the stake past Cranmer's prison.
Once the fires were lit, Cranmer was brought to a tower of the gatehouse to
watch what was going on, he was publicly traumatised by the dreadful sight,
tearing off his cap and falling to his knees in terror. Latimer before he died,
spoke to Ridley: "Be of good comfort, Master Ridley, and play the man. We
shall this day light such a candle, by God's grace, in England, as I trust shall
never be put out".

Cardinal Pole eventually wrote from Court to Cranmer. Pole's letter, was
in fact a full-scale pamphlet which was later put into print. Pole enlarged in
reproachful terms on the text of the sixteen interrogations of Cranmer, but
he concentrated in particular in refuting Cranmer's Eucharistic errors.
Cranmer still in shock in the aftermath of the burnings seemed receptive and
implored Pole to see him. Pole, however, rather than a face to face meeting,
wrote to Cranmer from Court on 6 November. In the letter, he bitterly re-
proached Cranmer for his history of disobedience, he also answered Cranmer's favourite theme of the incompatibility of papal and royal law. He
ended by dismissing Cranmer's views on the Eucharist and made a desperate
plea to the prisoner to save himself at this last moment: "I say if you be not
plucked out by the ear, you be utterly undone both body and soul".

Archbishop Stephen Gardiner, the Lord Chancellor, died on 12 November
he had been Cranmer's implacable enemy, although by now Cranmer was
seriously considering an appeal to a General Council, despite the legal difficulties which seemed almost unsurmountable. On 31 December Fra. Juan de
Villagarcia another highly talented Dominican friar began discussions with
Cranmer. After a few hours of dialogue Cranmer conceded that he would
not be so hostile to the notion of papal primacy if he did not plainly see the
papacy defend manifest errors. Purgatory was discussed and the two men
argued in detail about the patristic evidence. Villagarcia adjourned to mull
over Augustinian texts and returned triumphant flourishing the crucial texts

from Augustine, whose implications Cranmer admitted that he had not previously considered.

At Cranmer's request, the two men shifted their debate back to the role of the papacy, and Cranmer's cherished view of the General Council as the ultimate decision-maker in the Catholic Church. Villagarcia claimed that all General Councils had been called by papal authority. Cranmer scorned the claim, how could one say this of the first Ecumenical Council of Nicaea in 325 If that could be proved, he said flatly, "I will indeed openly affirm the Pope to have been and to be now head of the Church". After a night of concentrated reading Villagarcia came back with a handful of extracts from the *Chronia Maiora* of Isidore and the standard patristic text known as the Tripartite History. These stated that Nicaea ought to have been called by the then Pope, Sylvester I, and that Councils ought to be called by papal authority. Cranmer angrily said that these were texts in a recent edition corrupted by papists. A search was made in the college libraries throughout the University, none of them proved Cranmer's contention.

In Rome Cranmer's deprivation and condemnation was in progress. The Consistory was treated to a reading by Cardinal Puteo, the Inquisitor-General, of translations from selected highlights of Cranmer's heretical writings. Archbishop Cranmer was deprived on 4 December. The letter of deprivation and the papal Bull appointing Cardinal Pole to Canterbury arrived in London on 22 January.

Cranmer made a full appeal to a General Council. To be admissible as an appeal, his statement would have to acknowledge papal authority, but Cranmer did so with careful qualification: "Although the Bishop of Rome, whom they call Pope, bareth the room of Christ on earth, and hath authority of God, yet by that power or authority he is not become unsinnable, neither hath he received that power to destroy, but to edify the congregation". He argued the law of nature allowed appeal from his authority, and the natural final appeal was to a General Council. Cranmer, the life-long sympathiser with conciliarism, now unequivocally stated that: "It is openly enough confessed that a holy General Council, lawfully gathered together in the Holy Ghost, and representing the Holy Catholic Church, is above the Pope, especially in matters concerning faith".

He gave six reasons for his appeal. Three were about procedure. One was his own history and contradictions on papal authority, citing his previous oath to Henry VIII against papal authority in England. There followed a brief history of the position of Rome in the Church, at first "the mother of other Churches" and a shining example, then an example of corruption. From the See of Rome as it now existed, no reformation of abuses could be expected, particularly in his own case, so he repeated his appeal to what he now called "a free General Council, that shall hereafter lawfully be, and in a sure place". In a final section, Cranmer bluntly reaffirmed his adherence to his Edwardian views on the Eucharist, saying that he was accused of heresy merely because he sought to discuss sacramental theology exclusively in the terminology used by the early Fathers "in their treatises on the sacrament", and because he would not allow "the doctrine lately brought in" – namely transubstantiation. (Ed. The term emerged out of medieval attempts to resolve the conflict between seeing bread and wine as mere signs of the body and blood of Christ. The term transubstantiation itself is found only in the 12th Century and was used at Lateran IV in 1215. In response to opposition from the Reformers of the 16th Century, the Council of Trent in 1551 affirmed that the substance of bread and wine is changed into that of Christ's body and blood. Trent's use of the word was intended not to explain how the change takes place but to provide a term that describes what takes place).

Cranmer was returned to Bocardo, where he would remain until his death. Villagarcia accompanied by John Hapsfield visited Cranmer to discuss again the matter of the Eucharist. Cranmer, now physically weakend by his ordeal and in poor health, began giving way. In reply to Villagarcia's enquiry as to whether all the saints who disagreed with his Eucharistic theology would perish, Cranmer feebly replied: "Indeed I think that you can attain salvation through your faith and likewise I can mine". The statement would be unexceptional in modern ecumenical discussions, but in the polemical atmosphere of the 16th Century Reformation was a gift to a ruthless interrogator. What then said Villagarcia triumphantly, the matter of corporal presence was not a question of the essence of the faith! What then of Paul's claim in I Corinthians II that his narrative of the Eucharist was "received from the Lord"? Cranmer made no attempt to expound what he understood by "this is my body" but seemed disturbed and distressed, and declared that he had no answer.

On 24 February, the writ was issued to the Mayor of Oxford for Cranmer's burning, the date was set for 7 March. Cranmer affirmed that he anathematised Luther and Zwingli and any heresy contrary to sound doctrine, he not only acknowledged the Pope's power on earth, but also his position as the vicar of Christ. In precise detail he acknowledged the doctrine of transubstantiation, the full compliment of seven sacraments and the doctrine of purgatory. He begged for prayers, and begged that those who had been seduced by his example should return to the unity of the Church. He also repeated his submission to the King and Queen and their laws. Cranmer asked for sacramental absolution, a vital capitulation to Roman authority. Cardinal Pole was happy to grant authority for this.

Cranmer's burning was postponed from the first full weekend in March, against mounting unrest and political uncertainty. His original recantation bore the signatures of two foreigners, de Soto and Villagarcia, which added to public distrust of Spain. Cranmer had every reason for expecting last-minute clemency, he was after all, now fully repentant of his heresy and once more in perfect communion with the Church. By normal practice of canon law, he should have won his life. Yet Mary was implacable. For her, Cranmer's crimes had transcended the norms, the line which her foreign ambassador took was that "his iniquities and obstinacy was so great against God that clemency and mercy could have no place with him". She sent the provost of Eton Dr. Henry Cole, with the news that there was no hope of any further postponement of Cranmer's fate. The date set for his execution was 21 March.

Before the execution a service was held in the University Church. Cranmer processed on a rainy morning flanked by de Soto and Villagarcia reciting psalms antiphonally. The church was packed with the assembled majesty of the Church, the crown was represented by Lord Williams and a host of JP's and other local dignitaries. First came a sermon from Dr. Cole. Then Cranmer spoke amid an atmosphere of intense concentration. He had written his speech and the authorities had the text, but suddenly they realised this was not what they were hearing. Commotion was breaking out in the church, yet Cranmer persevered. He said: "And as for the Pope, I refuse him, as Christ's enemy, and Antichrist, with all his false doctrine". He was back on his old course again – "and as for the sacrament, I believe as I have taught in my book against the Bishop of Winchester" – and there the enraged officials stopped him. It no longer mattered. He had thrown down the gauntlet to Gardiner his dead rival, and he had succeeded in his task. He was pulled from his stage, in a scene immortalised in an engraving for John Day's 1563 edition of Foxe's Book of Martyrs, and he was hurried out to the stake through the streets of Oxford.

The day after Cranmer's burning, Cardinal Reginald Pole had finally proceeded beyond his deacon's orders, first to be ordained priest and then immediately consecrated as Archbishop of Canterbury. The ceremony took place in the presence of Queen Mary and in the powerfully symbolic setting of the newly restored church of the Friars Observant at Greenwich, that centre of resistance to the annulment of Catherine of Aragon's marriage. The following day, Pole received the papal pallium in the main church of the peculiar parishes of Canterbury diocese within the city of London, St. Mary-le-Bow. He was to be the last Catholic Archbishop of Canterbury.

Cardinal Pole was intent on re-invigorating the clergy, who were often poor, ill-educated, and in some cases indifferent. The laity was bewildered by the constant changes of the preceding twenty years. Pole had to rebuild the Church. Only seven of the twenty two bishops in office at the death of Edward still occupied their Sees. By the end of 1555 twelve new bishops had been consecrated, the new comers were men of the Catholic Counter-

Reformation concerned with theological endeavour. Pole wanted a disciplined clergy which could lead and inspire the laity. The bishops were directed to reside in their Sees, to preach and to supervise the religious life of the parishes. He proposed the establishment of seminaries to be attached to Cathedrals for the training of priests. Ignatius Loyola had offered his Jesuit preachers to Pole, but it was considered that a programme of intense preaching would only stir controversy.

Cardinal Carafa was elected to the papal throne in May 1555 as Paul IV. The Pope was hostile to Cardinal Pole and suspected him of pro-heretical sympathies. In June 1557 the Pope deprived Pole of his legative authority in England and summoned him to Rome to appear before the tribunal of the Inquisition on a charge of heresy. William Peto, Mary's confessor and twenty five years earlier Provincial of the Grey Friars, was now at the age of eighty created cardinal. He was imprisoned under Henry VIII and then spent the intervening years in Antwerp until the accession of Mary. He was included in the Act of Attainder against Cardinal Pole and others in 1539. He was too old for the work of a cardinal, he had retired from his old bishopric of Salisbury, to his convent at Greenwich which Mary had restored. Pole's loss of favour with the Pope was a blow to Mary, she recognised the insurmountable failure of her efforts to rebuild the Catholic Church in England. Both Queen Mary and Cardinal Pole were overawed at the outset when they encountered the physical destruction of the churches, monasteries and other monuments to Catholic devotion.

Cardinal Pole was greatly disappointed by the action of his former friend Pope Paul IV. He suffered fitful dreams brought on by a tertian fever. Queen Mary likewise was suffering from intermittent fever and melancholia and for days on end lay close to death. Early in the morning of 17 November 1558 Queen Mary died peacefully at St. James's Palace. At Lambeth, Cardinal Pole received the news of Mary's death, at seven o'clock in the evening of the same day he too was dead.

Extracts from: *The English Cardinals* by G. C. Heseltine,
published by Burns Oates & Washbourne, London.
Thomas Cranmer A Life by Diarmaid MacCulloch,
published by Yale University Press
with permission from the publisher.

19

Chapter Two

The Extinction of
The Ancient Hierarchy

WHEN Elizabeth came to the throne in 1558 she had already gathered around her a group of advisers led by Sir William Cecil (later Lord Burghley). Almost immediately they published a document *The Device for the alteration of religion in the first year of Queen Elizabeth.* This document is preserved amongst the Cottonian manuscripts.

The document by Sir William Cecil or Sir Thomas Smith sets out the full scheme in detail. Until the time was appropriate the Mass was to continue and no innovation to be allowed. "As for Her Highness's conscience, till then, if there be some other sort of prayer or memory and the seldomer Mass". The plotters anticipated that "Bishops and all the clergy will see their own ruin. In confession and preaching they will persuade the people from it. They will conspire with whosoever will attempt, and pretend to do God a sacrifice in letting the alteration, though it be with murder of Christian men and treason". To counteract these supposed dangers, it was proposed that "The bishops and clergy, being all made and chosen such as were thought the stoutest and mightiest champions of the Pope's Church, these Her Majesty, being included to use much clemency, yet must seek, as well by Parliament as by the just laws of England, in the *praemunire* and other such penal laws, to bring again in order and being found in default, not to pardon, till they confess their fault, put themselves wholly to Her Highness's mercy, abjure the Pope of Rome and conform themselves to the new alteration. And by these means well handled, Her Majesty's necessity of money may be somewhat relieved".

This plot for the destruction of the ancient faith of England was hatched before the death of Queen Mary, by those who had already transferred their services to her half sister whilst both Elizabeth and they, externally at least, professed themselves still Catholics.

Elizabeth's accession to the throne took place on 17 November 1558. Elizabeth began immediately to act on the plan detailed in the above *Device*, removing Catholics from positions of trust and putting men in their place who would help carry out the changes. In just one month after her accession on 20 December 1558, Sandys wrote to Bullinger from Strasburg the news that the Queen had "Changed almost all her counsellors and taken good Christians into her service in the room of papists". Sandys was a refugee under Queen Mary and was named a short time later by Elizabeth to the See of Worcester.

By the death of Cardinal Pole the Catholic leadership had devolved upon Archbishop Heath of York, who in addition to his archbishopric, had also held during the later years of Mary the office of Lord Chancellor. Heath's gentle character has been praised even by writers of opposing opinions, whilst his holiness allowed no grounds of accusation even to his enemies. However, beneath the gentle kindness of his nature there lay a quiet resolve in matters which concerned his conscience, for which Sir William Cecil and his fellow plotters were most probably ill-prepared. His influence over his fellow bishops is best shown by what Nicholas Sander the historian wrote of him in his report to Cardinal Morone, the Cardinal Protector of England, in 1561 of the events in England during the early years of Queen Elizabeth, Sanders writes: "They regard him as monks do their abbot".

During the reign of Henry, Heath of course had yielded like so many others, whether through weakness or through mistaken loyalties. Heath even consented to receive a bishopric from Henry and in 1540 had been schismatically consecrated to the See of Rochester, without any sanction of the Pope. Despite this, his eyes, as well as those of Bishop Bonner, who had been consecrated with him, were effectively opened by the events which followed. Even before the kindom was restored to Catholic unity under Mary, they had both proved the sincerity of their conversion by their endurance of imprisonment under Edward VI.

Heath's anxiety to make sure that his illicit reception of the episcopate had been pardoned by the Pope became apparent when he was nominated to the archbishopric of York in 1555. He had already been freed from censure by Cardinal Pole, acting as legate from Pope Julius III. Queen Mary with Pole's approval, had marked him out for the northern archbishopric, of which she conferred the temporalities on him on 26 March 1555. Pope Paul IV confirmed his nomination to that See and the Pallium was granted him on 23 August.

When the document arrived from Rome, Heath found that he was described in these simply as a cleric licensed to receive episcopal consecration, without any mention of the consecration he had illicitly, though validly received in schism. He therefore obtained from the Pope a fresh Bull of confirmation, dated 30 October 1555, in which it was expressly mentioned that "During the prevalence of the schism he had been instituted *de facto* bishop, first of Rochester and then of Worcester" and in virtue of it had "Received the gift of consecration from certain schismatical bishops". The Bull concludes: "We therefore wishing to provide for your state, so that with a pure heart and sound conscience you may preside over the said church of York decree that our aforesaid provision and appointment and our letters shall be in force and enable you to use the gift of consecration received by you, as is related, and the Pall to be assigned to you".

Thus completely rehabilitated, it was to Archbishop Heath that fell the great honour of conferring consecration upon Cardinal Pole, when appointed to the See of Canterbury in 1556.

On Queen Mary's death Heath, as Lord Chancellor, had no choice but to proclaim her successor, which he did in Parliament on the same day. However on the following day, he visited the new Queen, to resign into her hands the Great Seal knowing it would be impossible for him to remain in office under her new regime. The Seal was accepted from him by Elizabeth with outward expressions of regret, though probably with real inward satisfaction. However, she refused to release him from her services altogether, and so for a short time longer the archbishop was obliged to remain a member of the Privy Council, though from its Acts for the period it can be seen he was seldom present at its meetings and his attendance ceased altogether after 5 January 1559.

At Queen Mary's funeral service, Bishop White's outspoken denunciation of the impending changes to religion, brought down on him the anger of the new Queen and her Council. Some members of the reforming party, by whom reports of the sermon were circulated exaggerated shamefully the things that he had said. Jewel who was still abroad, wrote some weeks afterwards to Peter Martyr: "Your friend White delivered a most furious and turbulent discourse at the funeral of Mary, in which he declared that everything was to be attempted rather than that any alteration should be made in religion, and that it would be a meritorious act for anyone to kill the exiles on their return!" The Bishop was punished by the Council and confined to house arrest.

On 28 December a Proclamation was issued in the Queen's name, commanding "All manner of her subjects, as well those that be called to ministry in the Church, as all others, that they do forbear to preach, or teach, or to give audience to any manner of doctrine or preaching, or to use any other manner of public prayer, but that which is already used, and by law received, until consultation may be had by Parliament, by Her Majesty, and three estates of this realm".

The situation during the first month of the reign of Elizabeth is described in a letter written to his royal master by the Spanish Ambassador, the Count de Feria dated 14 December 1558:

"The kingdom is entirely in the hands of young folks, heretics and traitors, and the Queen does not favour a single man whom Her Majesty, who is now in heaven" (Queen Mary), "would have received and will take no one into her service who served her sister when she was Lady Mary. She seems to me incomparably more feared than her sister was, and she gives her orders and has her way as absolutely as her father did. They are so suspicious of me that not a man amongst them dares to speak of me, as the late Chancellor" (Archbishop Heath), "has told me plainly. He is a worthy person, and she knows it, but he is not in the gang and will not return to office. He tells me that if they offered it to him, he would not accept it".

In his report to Cardinal Morone, Sander relates that during the short time that the archbishop still retained his seat in the Privy Council, although no longer Chancellor, he resolved to try what could be done to save religion by appealing to the young queen in person. Sander writes: "With common approval of his brethren, that they might in no way fail in their duty, Dr. Heath, Archbishop of York, the best and wisest of all those now in England, presented himself before Elizabeth of whose Council he was still a member, either because a man so sage as he, who had so blamelessly and faithfully discharged the office of high Chancellor, could not be put aside without reflection on the Queen herself, or else in hope that by this favour he might more easily be allowed to give up the Catholic faith and be drawn over to her side. It is said then that, having obtained a private audience, and cast himself upon his knees, he with many tears, conjured the Queen, by the name of Jesus Christ, not only to lay a woman's hand upon the sacred mysteries". He reminded her that he himself had been "a bishop under her father and her brother, and archbishop and chancellor of the realm under her sister Mary", and he pleaded his own long experience of "the great harm which was occasioned to the State by the frequent changes in even its judicial laws. How much less then ought this to be attempted with regard to religion".

Sander also spoke in his report as follows; "Seeing that everything was going in the wrong direction and from bad to worse, the Bishop of Winchester, in the presence of the leading men of the whole kingdom assembled at Queen Mary's funeral, with great boldness and freedom declared that he, as bishop was placed upon a watch tower to see that the Church of Christ received no harm. That he knew, however, that raging wolves from Geneva were approaching, whom in God's name he most earnestly implored his hearers neither to believe nor to listen to, for the salvation of their own souls, and the honour of their country. So powerful was the impression made on all by this discourse, that on its conclusion one of the chief men then present declared that, if anyone should be still bent on casting himself into the infernal pit, at all events this bishop would not only be answerable, but would have done all in his power to prevent it".

De Feria in his letter to King Phillip, written on the 14 December 1558, the very day of Queen Mary's funeral wrote: "All the heretics who had escaped are beginning to flock back again from Germany, and they tell me there are some pestilential fellows amongst them".

Catholics were restrained from preaching but opportunities for doing so were allowed to their opponents, as is shown by the following from Hilles to Bullinger, on the following 28 February: "With respect to religion, silence has been imposed upon the Catholic preachers, by royal proclamation and sufficient liberty is allowed by the gospellers to preach three times a week during Lent before the Queen herself, and to prove the doctrines from Holy Scriptures".

On Christmas day the Queen made an attempt to interfere with the High Mass sung in her chapel by Bishop Oglethorpe of Carlisle. The Queen sent to tell him that he was not to elevate the Host. The Bishop replied that he had thus learnt the Mass and she must pardon him, as he could not do otherwise. So when the Gospel was read and completed, Her Majesty rose and departed.

When Elizabeth sacrilegiously attempted to tamper with the mode of offering the Mass, she was as yet uncrowned. The incident had the effect of confirming the bishops in their resolution to decline to perform the ceremony of her coronation held on Sunday 15 January 1559. Bishop Oglethorpe eventually consented to perform the ceremony. Sander wrote as follows in his report to Cardinal Morone: "The Bishop of Carlisle at length undertook the ceremony, after many of the others had been asked in vain, not as a favour of heresy, but lest, if no one should anoint her, the Queen should thereby be enraged, and made more inclined to overthrow religion".

In officiating at the ceremony Oglethorpe was not opposing the Archbishop, as Heath himself took part in the preliminaries of the ceremony. Moreover he did not lose the confidence of his brother bishops as was shown later by their choosing him for one of the Catholic defendants at the Westminster Conference.

The Dean of the Queen's chapel, Dr. George Carew, who the Queen had appointed two weeks before the coronation, had agreed to sing the Mass, partly in Latin and partly in English and further mutilating the most sacred ceremonies of the Mass, acting on the express instructions of the Queen. All the bishops including Bishop Oglethorpe appear to have retired as soon as they saw the way in which the royal chaplain was conducting the ceremony. Not a single bishop attended the magnificent banquet in Westminster Hall, which immediately followed the coronation ceremony in the Abbey.

Henry VIII and Cardinal Wolsey
by Sir John Gilbert (1817-97)
Guildhall Art Gallery, Corporation of London

Rt Rev Cuthbert Tunstall
Bishop of Durham died in prison 1559

Cardinal William Allen
English school – artist unknown
from a painting at Ushaw College
reproduced by kind permission of the Trustees of Ushaw College

R·D·THOMAS GOVLDVELL ANGL· EP· AS· C·R IN TRID
CONCIL° CONTRA HÆRETICOS Æ·I· ANGLIA CONT
ELIZABETH FIDET CONFESSOR CONSPICUUS

The Rt Rev Thomas Goldwell Bishop of Asaph

from a painting at The Venerabile English College, Rome
reproduced by kind permission of the Rector

Thomas Goldwell was the last surviving member of the ancient Catholic hierarchy in England. He died in Rome at St. Sylvester's 3 April 1585. There is a note from the Bishop of Clifton who says that in Pye's translation of Beccatelli's Life of Cardinal Pole there is a reference to a portrait of Goldwell as being in the Theatine house at Ravenna. It had an inscription: "R.D. Thomas Gouldwellus, Ep. Asaph. Trident. Concilio contra haereticos et in Anglia contra Elizabeth Fidei cofessor conspicuous". Addison mentions having seen it in his *Travels through Italy and Switzerland in the years 1701, 1702, 1703.* Fr Francis Goldie SJ told the Bishop of Clifton that Dr Gradwell, the first Rector after the reopening, came across it in a dealer's shop and bought it.   *Source: The Venerabile Vol V No 1 Oct. 1930 by David Crowley*

The Rt Rev Charles Walmesley
Bishop of Rama
Vicar Apostolic of the Western District 1764-1797
from a painting at Lulworth Castle
reproduced by kind permission of Mr W. J. Weld

The Rt Rev Bonaventure Giffard
Bishop of Madaura
Vicar Apostolic of the London District 1703-1734
from a painting at St. Edmund's College, Ware, Herts.
reproduced by kind permission of the Trustees of St. Edmund's College

Rt Rev Richard Challoner
Bishop of Debra
Vicar Apostolic of the London District 1758-1781
from a painting at St. Edmund's College, Ware, Herts.
reproduced by kind permission of the Trustees of St. Edmund's College

Rt Rev George Hay
Bishop of Daulia
Vicar Apostolic of the Lowland District of Scotland
from a painting by George Watson at Blairs Museum, Aberdeen
reproduced by kind permission of the Blairs Trust

The bishops had been necessary to Elizabeth, in order to secure her seat upon the throne by conferring on her that holy unction, which all the kings before her had received from the prelates of the Church. That done, she could safely cast them aside. Ten days later she opened her first Parliament, by which at her bidding, the laws were enacted which obliged these very bishops who had set the crown upon her head, to choose between apostasy and imprisonment till death.

On 25 January 1559, Queen Elizabeth opened the fatal Parliament which once more severed England from the Catholic Church. From the Act of this same Parliament dates also the beginning of the "Church of England as by Law established".

In comparison to the schism established by her father, where most of the bishops yielded under pressure from Henry VIII, Elizabeth's determined policy of heresy was met by a firm and consistent opposition offered it by the bishops. It is difficult to see a more striking illustration of the discontinuity between the new Church set up by Elizabeth and the ancient Church, which she endeavoured to destroy, than the fact that, for the erection of the new one, it was found necessary to extinguish the whole of the existing hierarchy. In its place a new body was created, composed of men whose teaching even upon the most sacred subjects was opposed diametrically to that of their predecessors.

The following is the account given by Il Schitanoya of the opening of the Parliament: "On the Queen's arriving at Westminster Abbey, the Abbot, robed pontifically, with all his monks in procession, each of them having a lighted torch in his hand, received her as usual, giving her first of all incense and holy water. When Her Majesty saw the monks who accompanied him with the torches, she said, 'Away with those torches, for we see very well', and her choristers singing the Litany in English, she was accompanied to the high altar under her canopy. Thereupon Dr. Cox, a married priest, who has hitherto been beyond the sea, ascended the pulpit and preached the sermon, in which after saying many things, freely against monks, proving by his arguments that they ought to be persecuted and punished by Her Majesty as they were impious for having caused the burning of so many poor innocents under pretext of heresy, on which he expatiated greatly. He then commenced praising Her Majesty, saying amongst other things that God had given her this dignity to the end that she might no longer allow or tolerate the past iniquities, exhorting her to destroy the images of the saints, the churches, the monasteries and all other things dedicated to divine worship . . . This sermon lasted an hour and a half, the peers standing the whole time, after which they went to the place prepared for Parliament".

The Bills effecting religion, which were laid before this Parliament are summarised by Fr. Bridgett CSSR in his *Queen Elizabeth and the Catholic*

Hierarchy: "A Bill for the restitution and annexation of first fruits to the Crown, are for the supremacy of the Crown, and abolition of all foreign jurisdiction, one for conformity of common prayer and administration of the sacraments, certain Bills detrimental to the temporal interests of the Church, and one for the restoring the Queen in blood. To this last no opposition was offered by any bishop. To all the others they offered a united and vigorous resistance but without effect".

Sander in his report gave a general account of the bishops in this Parliament: "Whenever any question was raised referring to religion, the Archbishop of York always protested that such questions ought to be discussed in a Synod not in a Parliament, and by bishops, not by laymen. Then the bishops, each in order said that they were of the same mind, nor did any one of them on any question ever differ from one another. After those of the archbishop himself, the weightiest speeches made on the whole subject were those of the Bishops of Winchester, Lincoln, Lichfield and Chester, who allowed no point to pass without pursuing it so thoroughly as to make it impossible to answer their speeches. The thing was indeed unheard of inasmuch as the laymen had nothing which they could say on any point, and yet, whilst they acknowledged their admiration for the talent and learning of the bishops, they always gave as their one reason for differing from them, that they understood the Queen to wish it".

The Archbishop of York delivered a speech against the Bill for conferring supremacy over the Church upon the Crown. The speech was remarkable, coming from a prelate, who in his younger days had yielded on this very point to Henry VIII and who now spoke also as proxy for the absent Bishop Tunstall who formerly had displayed the same weakness. It has an especial value as showing how thoroughly the truth had now been brought home to them as to the supremacy, which Our Lord had given, not to kings, but to St. Peter and his successors:

"First, when by virtue of this Act of Supremacy, we must forsake and flee from the See of Rome, it should be considered by your wisdoms what matter lieth therin in danger or inconvenience. Secondly, it should be considered what this supremacy is, and whether it do consist in spiritual government or temporal. If in temporal, what further authority can this House give unto Her Highness than she hath already? If in spiritual, it should be considered whether this House can grant it, and whether Her Highness be an apt person to receive the same.

"To the first point . . . if by this our relinquishing of the See of Rome there were no other matter therin than a withdrawing of our obedience from the Pope's person, Paul IV of that name, which hath declared himself to be a very austere stern Father unto us, ever since his first entrance into Peter's chair, then the cause were not of such great importance as it is in very deed.

When by relinquishing and forsaking of the See of Rome we must forsake and flee from these four things. First, we must forsake and flee from all General Councils. Secondly, we must flee from all canonical and ecclesiastical laws of the Church of Christ. Third, from the judgement of all other Christian princes. Fourth, and last, we must forsake and flee from the unity of Christ's Church, and by leaping out of Peter's ship, hazard ourselves to be overwhelmed and drowned in the waters of schism, sects and divisions".

After proving that these four things would be involved by separating themselves from the Universal Church, the Archbishop went on to deal with the second point: i.e. the nature of the spiritual government to be conferred by the Act upon the Queen. After speaking of the power of loosing and binding, which Our Lord gave to St. Peter, he continues: "It should be considered of your wisdoms whether you have sufficient authority to grant unto Her Highness this first point of spiritual government and to say to her, *Tibi dabimus claves regni caelorum.* If you say, Yea! Then we require the sight of your warrant and commission by the virtue of God's word. If you say, No! then you may be well assured that you have no sufficient authority to make her highness supreme head of the Church here in this realm. The second point of spiritual government is gathered of those words of Our Saviour Jesus Christ, spoken unto Peter in the 21st Chapter of St. John's Gospel 'Pasce, Pasce, Pasce'. Now, whether your honours have authority by this high court of Parliament to say unto our Sovereign Lady, 'Pasce, Pasce, Pasce', you must show your warrant and commission, Further, that her Highness being a woman by birth and nature, is not qualified by God's word to feed the flock of Christ, it appeareth most plainly by St. Paul on this wise saying, *Taceant mulieres in ecclesiis non anim permittitur eis logui, sed subditas ess sicut lex.*

Bishop Scott of Chester also made a speech against the same Bill: "There is alleged a provincial council or assembly of the bishops and clergy of this realm of England (the Convocation of 1534), by which the authority of the Bishop of Rome was abolished and disallowed. But first, a particular or provincial council can make no determination against the Universal Church of Christ. Secondly, of the learned men that were the doers there, so many as be dead, before they died were penitent and cried God's mercy for their act, and those that do live, as all your lordships do now, hath openly revoked the same, acknowledging their error". He then objects that such waverers cannot be trusted. He replies: "He which once has run so hastily or rashly that he hath overthrown himself and fallen and broken his brow or his shin, will after that take heed to walk more warily, as we have seen by the Apostles of Our Saviour Jesus Christ, which did all forsake Him and run away when He was apprehended by the Jews, especially St. Peter, which did thrice deny Him. And yet after, as well Peter as all the rest of the Apostles did return

27

again to their Master, Christ, and never would after, for neither persecution nor death, forsake or deny Him any more".

Despite the unanimous opposition of the spiritual Peers, the following terms of the oath were imposed by Parliament upon "all beneficed ecclesiastics, and all laymen holding office under the Crown". It will be noticed that the oath, without actually styling the Queen head of the Church, nevertheless ascribed to her alone all spiritual government, denying the jurisdiction of any foreign prelate. Without apostasy, it could not be taken by any Catholic.

"I, A.B. do utterly testify and declare that the Queen's Highness is the only supreme governor of this realm, and all other Her Highness's dominions and countries, as well in all spiritual and ecclesiastical things or causes, as temporal, and that no foreign prince, person, prelate, state, or potentate, hath or ought to have any jurisdiction, power, superiority, pre-eminence, or authority, ecclesiastical, or spiritual, within this realm".

The Act of Uniformity which was passed by this same Parliament, prohibited "The use by a minister, whether beneficed or not, of any but the established liturgy", i.e. the Book of Common Prayer. By virtue of this Act, on 24 June 1559, the Holy Sacrifice of the Mass was, as far as Parliament could do it, throughout the land abolished: "Under penalty of loss of goods for the first offence, of a year's imprisonment for the second and of imprisonment for life for the third". Moreover, a fine of one shilling being imposed "on all who should absent themselves from church on Sundays and holidays".

These two Acts were carried in the House of Lords by a bare majority of three. Parliament was dissolved on 8 May having done the work for which it had been called together.

Convocation had also assembled to lend support to the bishop's in their struggle. Sander included briefly some detail in his report to Cardinal Morone. "When the Parliament was opened the bishop's, archdeacons and archpriests (deans), assembling at the same time in Synod, were all unanimous in thinking it their duty to make clear to the laymen sitting in Parliament their minds and opinions upon certain questions. They subscribed therefore to the following resolutions. First, that they believed in the real and natural (i.e. physical) presence of the Body of Christ in the Eucharist, and this by the transubstantiation of the bread into His Body, and of the wine into His Blood, and that this is the Catholic faith, in accordance with the Gospel truth. Secondly, that they believed the Mass to be a propitiatory sacrifice for the living and the dead. Third, that they believed the Roman pontiff to be the head of the Church, and vicar of Christ. Fourth, that laymen ought not to discuss sacred questions and much less make laws regarding them". The document was signed by all members of Convocation and was sent to Parliament, but the Keeper of the Great Seal who presided over Parliament, kept the Resolutions back and never allowed them to be published.

During March and April 1559 The Westminster Conference took place between eight Protestants, Dr. Scory (Bishop of Chichester under Edward VI), Dr. Cox, Messrs Whitehead, Grindal, Horne, Sandys, Guest, Aylmer, and Jewel. Most of these had gone abroad during the reign of Mary and most of them were given places by Elizabeth in the new hierarchy which she established shortly afterwards. The Catholic argument was presented by Bishops White of Winchester, Bayne of Lichfield, Scott of Chester and Oglethorpe of Carlisle, they were supported by Doctors Cole, Harpsfield, Langdale and Chedsey.

The bishops were warned by the Council to prepare for a disputation in six days time. The articles of the Lutherans were put before them. First, it is against the express word of God and the custom of the ancient Church for the ecclesiastical offices to be performed in a language unknown to the people. Second, in the sacrament of the Eucharist the bread is not transubstantiated into the body, or the wine into the blood of Christ. Third, the Mass is not a sacrifice propitiatory for the living and the dead.

There was much disagreement regarding the dispute, the language to be used, should it be Latin or English, whether disputed verbally or in writing. Ultimately the bishops were accused of contempt, the meeting disolved and a short time later the Catholic bishops and doctors were all cast into prison. The Bishops of Winchester and Lincoln were sent in a boat as prisoners to the Tower and their goods sequesterd. The Bishop of St. Asaph escaped abroad in the last days of June.

The day after the Conference the other Catholic disputants, the Bishops of Lichfield, Chester and Carlisle, along with Dr. Cole, Dean of St. Paul's and Drs. Harpsfield and Chedsey, had been summoned before the Council which required each of them to give recognisance to the following effect: "First, to make his personal appearance before the Lords of the Council once every day. Second, not to depart the city of London and Westminster and the suburbs of London, until he shall have licence so to do. Third, to stand unto and pay such fine as shall be by the Lords of the Council assessed upon him for the contempt by him of late committed against the Queen's Majesty's order".

In this humiliating manner, these venerable dignitaries of the Church, one of whom was the very bishop who had just placed the crown on the Queen's head and whose only crime consisted in their maintenance of England's ancient faith, were forced to show themselves daily to their lay judges.

Rapid changes of religion now took place with royal visitors despatched as ecclesiastical commissioners throughout the realm, empowered to demand the co-operation of the clergy to the provisions of the Acts of Supremacy and Uniformity. Grindale replaced the deprived Bishop Bonner, and Parker who was chaplain to Queen Anne Boleyn, was made Archbishop of Canterbury. Bishop Kitchen of Llandaff eventually gave way to apostasy. By the beginning of November 1559, the deprivation of the whole hieracrchy had been effected.

The situation of Bishop Anthony Kitchen is interesting. He was born in 1477 and was professed under the name Dunstan in the Benedictine Abbey of Westminster. He studied at Gloucester Hall, later Worcester College, Oxford, which was originally founded as a Benedictine novitiate and dedicated to St. Benedict. He gained his B.D in 1525 and Doctorate in 1538. In 1526 he was elected prior of the students of his order at St. Benedict's, and in 1530 he became abbot of Eynsham, Oxford. As abbot he subscribed to the King's supremacy in 1534 and to the Articles of 1536. On the dissolution of the lesser monasteries he with eight of his brethren, surrendered his abbey in 1539 and received a pension of £133 6s 8d, with the promise of a benefice.

Kitchen was a temporiser of the worst kind. He accepted a royal chaplaincy and in 1545 was schismatically appointed to the See of Llandaff. The oath he took on his confirmation contains the fullest possible renunciation of papal supremacy. He clung to his bishopric through all the changes, did homage to Mary at her coronation, and obtained dispensation. He was the only bishop in the hierarchy who took the oath of supremacy to Elizabeth, although he dissented in the House of Lords from all the acts of restitution and reformation.

The Queen issued a commission on the 9 September 1559 in which she commanded the Bishops of Durham, Bath and Peterborough, along with Kitchen, Barlow and Scory to consecrate Parker, named by her to the archbishopric of Canterbury. The bishops refused, considering such an act as unlawful. They clearly could not take part in the consecration of a married priest, suspected of heresy, assisted by two excommunicated ecclesiastics. Joseph Gillow in his *Bibliographical Dictionary of the English Catholics* records that Kitchen at the last moment refused to act, it is thought at the persuasion of Bonner. Parker was not consecrated by bishops of the hierarchy, and moreover, the rite used in his consecration was not then the legal rite ordered by the statutes of the realm. The consecrators – Barlow, Scory, Coverdale and Hodgeskyn were not empowered under canon law for such a consecration. Bishop Kitchen died in 1563 aged 86.

It is interesting to note that in July, Parker and Grindal had been described in a royal writ as nominated bishops, and by late October Parker, Grindal and Cox were nominated to the Sees of Canterbury, London and Ely . They led the nineteen strong permanent Commission which enforced the Acts of Supremacy and Uniformity, and were given the full titles of their Sees, without having received any form of valid consecration.

The ecclesiastical commission made full use of their powers to imprison all recalcitrants. Bishops, doctors, priests and lay people were locked in the

Tower, the Fleet, Marshalsea and also committed to the cutody of the dignitaries of the new administration. A large number of prisoners were held by Grindal, apparently the chief jailer of the bishops at the Bishop of London's residence near to the old St. Paul's. The kind of treatment the new pseudo-bishops inflicted on their captives could be imagined from the sermons which at the opening of Parliament had been preached by Cox. In his sermon he had told the queen that: "For the purposes God had placed her on the throne, and given her the sword, that she might avenge the blood of His saints, extirpate the impious priests of Rome". There exists also a letter written by Cox and Grindal, addressed to the Council, in which they suggest that a priest, who had been brought before them for saying Mass, "Might be put to some kind of torment, and so driven to confess what he knoweth he might gain the Queen's Majesty a good mass of money by the masses that he hath said".

As events in England unfolded, news of the changes taking place spread abroad, any indignation felt by Catholic governments on the Continent failed to materialise into any concerted diplomatic action due to the conflicting interests of other powers.

Pope Paul IV died in the August of 1559, in the early months of Elizabeth's persecuting measures. The Queen's excommunication had been spoken of, though opposed by Philip II of Spain who hoped to marry Elizabeth. Pius IV was elected Pope on 26 December 1559 and tried desperately to persuade Elizabeth to return to the Catholic faith. Early in 1560 he sent as nuncio to England, Vincent Parpaglia, Abbot of San Salute, bearing a letter to Elizabeth dated 5 May, which was full of expressions of his affectionate anxiety for her salvation and desires "To provide likewise for her honour, and the establishment of her kingdom". The nuncio however was refused permission to enter England.

Bishop Quadra writing to the King of Spain on 25 July 1560, said: "She knows that the nuncio is coming at the insistence of the French, and in league with some of the Catholic's here, all of whom have consequently been arrested. As regards religion, she is so determined that in my opinion nothing is to be hoped for".

In his attempt to establish communications with Elizabeth, the one thing which the Pope had especially at heart, was the release of the imprisoned bishops. On 17 September the following despatch was sent to the two nuncios of Spain and Portugal, who were both with King Philip at Toledo: "Our Lord (the Pope), seeing that the nuncio, who was to have passed over into England, has found that sea more troubled and difficult than was expected, owing to the Queen's obstinacy in not allowing him to cross, has caused him to be written to that he will have to return home. It will, however, be your duty all the more earnestly to recommend those poor bishops and other imprisoned and exiled English Catholics to his Majesty, the former, that he may procure their liberation, and the latter, that he may give them some help to enable them to live".

Charles Borromeo, the Pope's nephew and recently made Cardinal Secretary of State, wrote to the nuncio in Portugal, Monsignor Santa Croce, who was still at the court of Philip: "Our Lord (the Pope) has heard with the greatest satisfaction that his Majesty still has hopes for something good with reference to the affairs of England, and that he is continuing to press the matter, and in order still more to assist and favour the intentions and resolutions of his majesty, he has caused his nuncio, the Abbot of San Salute, to be recalled, leaving now this whole undertaking to his Majesty, and continually praying God that it may turn to His honour".

This letter of Charles, later St. Charles Borromeo, shows the sympathy and deep attachment he had for the Catholics in England. The Pope sent a second nuncio to England who was to present to the Queen the Bull, which he had issued on 29 November, summoning the Council of Trent to reassemble on Easter Sunday 1561. Like the previous nuncio he was not allowed to enter England. There was a general expectation that Elizabeth would be excommunicated, but the Pope was unwilling to pronounce sentence on her, unless all other means had failed.

Cardinal Morone, at the Pope's request, sent in the summer of 1561 a letter to Viscount Montague, one of the chief Catholic noblemen still at liberty in England. He referred to the suffering and persecution of Catholics, and the imprisonment of the bishops. He speaks of the financial help sent to provide for the bishops. Also mentioned was how important the Pope considered it for the welfare of England, that Mary Queen of Scots (whose first husband Francis II of France had died not long before), should marry some Catholic prince, and since Philip of Spain objects to her marrying his son Charles, he suggests a match between her and Prince Ferdinand, son of the Emperor. He hoped this would give encouragement to English Catholics and deter the heretics from carrying out their projects".

The Cardinal continued: "Meantime his Holiness exhorts you all, and you especially who are enjoying liberty, to salute in His Holiness's own name (if in any way it can be done), those fellow-captives of yours who for the sake of Holy Church are now serving God in England both in spirit and in the body, and to exhort them to continue firmly in the course they have begun, by which means they will not only gain from His Holiness and from the whole Church the praise in this world they deserve, but they will receive in life eternal an imperishable crown from Him who will never die again and who for us underwent the torment of the cross.

"I myself, by happy reason of the affection which I ever bore to Cardinal Pole of happy memory, and by reason also of the protectorship of your nation which has, as I have said been entrusted to me, will to the best of my ability, whether in public or in private, be at the service of you all, and especially of your noble and distinguished self".

The second Parliament of Elizabeth was summoned on 6 January 1563. The increased penalties decreed by this second parliament for refusal of the supremacy oath are: The first refusal of the oath became *praemunire,* the second *high treason.* This penal Act by which the bishops might at once be called upon again to take the oath, and three months after their refusal, be ordered out to die the death of traitors, was passed despite opposition from Thomas Percy the Earl of Northumberland and Lord Montague. Nine years later Thomas Percy would suffer beheading rather than accept the new religion.

As the early years of Elizabeth's reign passed, the imprisoned bishops were reduced by the increasing number of deaths in captivity of these holy men who could have effected their immediate release by accepting the new religion. Pius V was elected to the papal throne on 7 January 1566, made it one of his first cares to set before the minds of English Catholics the sinfulness of participating in the new schismatic form of worship, in spite of the persecution that would follow if they refused to attend the Anglican services. The Pope, soon after his election held a Consistory, in which he nominated Dr. Nicholas Sander and Dr. Thomas Harding - as then the two most distinguished of the exiled English clergy - his apostolic delegates. They were charged with the commission of making known in England his condemnation of the practice of attending the newly established services. At the same time he bestowed on them full powers for absolving from heresy and schism, as well as for granting similar faculties to other priests.

The nomination of Sander and Harding, two simple priests, as papal delagates for England was the best way of showing the severity of the imprisonment of, by this date, the seven remaining faithful bishops still surviving in the country. Of these, five were held in the Tower, the Bishop of London was held in the Marshalsea and the Bishop of Peterborough was held in the Fleet. All were denied access to Mass, communion, confession, the Divine Office and books of Catholic theology. Professor G. E. Phillips, the historian and Professor at St. Cuthbert's College Ushaw, wrote in 1905: "We must not think of these first intruders into the Catholic Sees of England as if they were modern Anglican bishops, gentlemen of refinement and of enlarged and liberal minds, who, if we could imagine them in the position of unwilling jailers to Catholic bishops, would seek by every means to alleviate their lot. The first Protestant bishops were, almost without exception, the bitterest of Puritan fanatics, and they were under the express orders of the Council to seek by every means to bring their prisoners to conformity"

In February 1570 Pope Pius V proceeded at last to pronounce against Elizabeth the solemn sentence of her excommunication, which until this date had been delayed in the hope of her cessation in the persecution of the Catholic Church.

The Bull, *Regnans in excelsis,* in which this sentence was published by Pope Pius V on 25 February, declares that: "Elizabeth, the pretended Queen of England" had "unnaturally usurped to herself the place of supreme head of the Church in England, and the chief authority and jurisdiction", she had "forbidden the observance of the true religion, and embraced the errors of heretics, oppressing the observers of the Catholic faith". She had "dared to take away their churches and benefices from the bishops, rectors of churches, and other Catholic ecclesiastics, and given them to heretics". Finally she had "cast into prison the Catholic bishops and rectors of churches, where many worn out by their protracted sufferings and sorrows, have ended their days in misery".

"All this", the Bull continues, "being notorious and known to all nations, and so confirmed by the weighty testimony of very many witnesses as to leave no room for excuse, defence, or evasion, the persecution, moreover, of the faithful, growing daily greater, we cannot control our grief at being obliged to proceed against one whose predecessors have deserved so well of Christendom".

At the time of the Queen's excommunication, there still survived in the Tower four of the bishops, whom she had deposed and committed to prison. Archbishop Heath of York, together with the two Bishops Thirlby of Ely and Tuberville of Exeter who both died before the end of the same year, and Bishop Watson of Lincoln.

A list of prisoners kept in the Tower was published, probably no later than 27 May 1570, on which day Thomas and Christopher Norton were executed following the suppression of the Northern Rising. The list included four of the Norton family and was headed by the Duke of Norfolk who was executed in 1572.

The anonymous English exile who published the book entitled *A Treatise of Treasons against Queen Elizabeth and the Crowne of England* in 1573 undertook to show that the real traitors to Elizabeth were not the persecuted Catholics but her own chief minister, Lord Burghley and Sir Nicholas Bacon, his chief confidant. These two were shown for the benefit of their own interests, to have persuaded the Queen to change the religion of the country. Therefore not only having robbed her of the services of all the old nobility, plus the friendship of her natural allies, but brought upon her the excommunication of the Pope and the contempt of all Catholic nations.

A few extracts from the book will be of interest: "When you Queen, therefore, upon the first entry into her reign, had committed this government of her affairs unto some few mean and base persons, who forthwith used those few of the nobility, whom they reserved in appearance of credit, but as ciphers and signs, who, by slight devices and false persuasions did will her by the change of religion against her own affection, to separate herself from the union she was, in that part left in with the great Christian princes her neighbours and allies, who persuaded her to change all the Council and chief officers of the realm, who induced her to deprive and depose together and at once all her bishops one and other, with hundreds of the principal of the clergy besides, to hold their persons in prison ten or twelve years together, till by stink and close keeping, some sooner, some later, they are all in effect pined away, without colour of fault or desert, unless you account it a fault for a whole clergy of a Christian realm not to accept a new faith with the change of every prince, to subvert all the altars in the realm, to burn all the relics, images, and holy ornaments of Christ and his saints, to constitute a new form of public service in the church, to create herself chief ruler of the same, and by that authority to prohibit the adoration of Christ in His Blessed Sacrament, to abrogate the Mass with five of the seven sacraments, to change the form of administration of the other two, of the dregs of the vilest sort of people to erect a new clergy, and to them to give the cure of souls, with all the bishoprics and spiritual promotions of the realm, to permit them to marry, and with the goods of the Church so to enrich them, as with great endowments bestowed on their bastards, to disparage, in short time, all the noble houses of the realm, to intrude them into the possession of all the monasteries and sacred foundations of prayer or alms, to cast out of the realm all the religious of the same that would live in their order and habit."

The purpose of this book was to expose the complicity of Lord Burghley and Sir Nicholas Bacon in the influence they exerted over Elizabeth at the beginning of her reign. Also, of having prejudiced the Queen against Marian counsellors, who were replaced by others who would be compliant in the remorseless impulse to change the religion of England.

Renewed persecution was directed towards Catholics in 1574 and led to further questioning of Archbishop Heath and Bishop Watson. Their lives were again put in imminent danger, as is shown by the following letter of Antonio de Guaras to the Spanish Secretary of State, dated London 28 November:

"The Queen has appointed commissioners who are furiously examining the principal Catholic bishops and others who are prisoners or under surety, the substance of their examination being as follows. Do they recognise the Queen as head of the Church in England? To this they all replied to the same effect, although examined separately, that they did not, and that the sovereign pontiff is head of the Universal Church and vicar of Our Lord Jesus Christ. They were then asked if they recognised the Queen as sovereign, to which they replied that they did. They were next asked whether they accepted her as the legitimate Queen, to which they replied that they recognised her as sovereign, and declined to say anything more in consequence of the law. They were asked who they considered was the heir to the throne after this Queen, to which they replied, that would be shown in the royal pedigree. They were then asked what was the Universal Church of which they spoke, and to this they replied, The Roman Church, which was gathered by the Holy Ghost at Trent, and it always would be so considered by Catholics. They were examined as to their beliefs in the Holy Sacrament, and their reply was that they firmly believed in the real presence contained therein after the sacramental words had been pronounced by the priest. They said they believed in the presence, jointly divine and human, as it was upon the cross, true God and true man. They added with much constancy that he who did not believe this could not hope for salvation. They were then asked if the service in use in churches here by order of the queen was acceptable to God, they distinctly replied that it was not, as it was performed outside of the unity of the Church and contrary to sacred doctrine. To all these things they, being all Catholics, answered similarly, being ready to live or die in the truth, which they hold before men constant unto martyrdom. Each one had to sign his name to his confession for the information of the Queen and Council. People expect that severity will come from this".

Archbishop Heath's long suffering in captivity for nineteen years came to a close with his death in December 1578. Bishop Watson lingered on in prison until he died in Wisbeach Castle in September 1584. Bishop Thomas Goldwell of St. Asaph had escaped from England in 1559, he had tried to enter England in 1565 after assisting at the Council of Trent, but was foiled before he could cross the Channel by the English Government. He had been vicar general to Cardinal Charles Borromeo, but his great desire was to serve his native land. In April 1580 Bishop Goldwell accompanied Cardinal Allen to Rheims. Bishop Goldwell had been given permission to leave for England by the Pope. He was to travel with Edmund Campion and Ralph Sherwin who were chosen as the aged prelate's companions and guide on his perilous mission, however Goldwell became ill with fever and returned to Rome in August. With his death on 3 April 1585, died the last member of the ancient hierarchy.

Extracts from: *The Extinction of the Ancient Hierarchy* by Rev. G. E. Phillips published by Sands & Co. London

Chapter Three

Cardinal William Allen

WILLIAM Allen was born in 1532 at Rossall Grange, Fylde in Lancashire, the year Thomas Cranmer was consecrated Archbishop of Canterbury by authority of a papal Bull. Within two years his acquiescing with Henry VIII saw England formally separated from Rome. It was to be the destiny of William Allen to work for the reconciliation of England to Rome.

Young William was of gentle birth, allied by blood to the principal families of Lancashire. His mother was one of the Yorkshire Listers. He had two brothers, George who was the oldest son and Gabriel, who was younger than himself. He also had two sisters, Mary who married Christopher Coniers of Yorkshire and Elizabeth who married William Hesketh of Poulton a near neighbour of the Allen family.

William Allen was fifteen when he left home for the first time and went to Oxford. This was the year Edward VI succeeded his father Henry VIII. Oxford became the inspiration of his whole life, he witnessed momentous changes there during two reigns. By coincidence the college to which he attached himself, Our Lady of Oriel, was the same college to which John Henry Newman also brought such honour three hundred years later. He witnessed with horror and sadness the iconoclast's destruction of all that was popish - reredos, windows etc. The great libraries were stripped of books and manuscripts that were guilty of superstition and burned. Despite the difficulties he pursued his studies under the guidance of the Rev. Morgan Phillips, a Catholic tutor, and finally took his BA degree in 1550. In the same year he was elected fellow of his college.

When Mary acceded to the throne, Allen devoted himself to the ecclesiastical state, he took his MA in July 1554. He became principal of St. Mary's Hall in 1556 and served as one of the proctors of the University. He would have witnessed the burning of Protestant the martyrs at Oxford and later under Elizabeth, again the decimation of everything Catholic. He managed somehow to live on at Oxford for two years under Elizabeth's reign before he was forced to resign and leave the country. He crossed over to Flanders in 1561 and took refuge at the University of Louvain.

There was a growing colony of English Catholics who found refuge at Louvain. Among them Allen found such men as Thomas Harding, late regius professor of Hebrew, Richard Smith late regius professor of theology,

John Clement late professor of Greek and rhetoric who had married the foster daughter of Thomas More, William Rastell judge and printer, and
nephew of Thomas More, Nicholas Sander late professor of canon law and
the famous historian of the Anglican schism. Besides these there was
Cuthbert Scott the last Catholic Bishop of Chester and other exiles from the
University of Cambridge. These men set to work and produced a series of
powerful books in defence of the Catholic faith. The books were smuggled
into England in large quantities. William Allen threw himself into this work
and although he would have preferred a quite life of a student rather than a
controversialist.

He returned to Lancashire to recover from a fever he had contracted. He
spent some time with his family in hiding and wrote a number of manuscripts which he had published on his return to Louvain. Whilst in England
he was horrified by the practice, common under the penal laws of Elizabeth,
of openly attending the services authorised by Parliament, yet secretly following the Catholic religion.

He then determined to become a priest and on his return to Louvain in
1565, he received Holy Orders at Malines. He now felt further empowered
to attack the heresy he saw as a scourge in England.

In the autumn of 1567, Allen set out on a pilgrimage to Rome in the company of his old Oxford tutor Morgan Phillips and Dr. Vendeville the regius
professor of canon law in the University of Douay. Dr. Vendeville was a
friend of Cardinal Charles Borromeo and Phillip Neri. On the return journey
from Rome, Allen outlined his plan for a Catholic university on foreign soil
to instruct young Englishmen, not only in the arts and sciences, but in the
Catholic faith and practice. Dr. Vendeville immediately warmed to the idea
and agreed that the new university of Douay, which had recently been
founded by Philip II, would in every way be a suitable place for the foundation of such a college.

On Michaelmas Day 1568, the new college opened. Although this was a
humble venture of William Allen, it was in fact the very first seminary which
the Council of Trent had ordered to be established in the different provinces
and dioceses. The instigator at the Council of Trent who promoted this policy was Cardinal Pole. The first chancellor was an English exile Dr. Richard
Smith, formerly fellow of Merton College and regius professor of divinity at
Oxford. The professor of canon and civil law was Dr. Richard White some-
time fellow of New College. Morgan Phillips, Allen's old tutor and friend
assisted and when he died he left all he possessed as a legacy to the new college. Richard Bristow, fellow of Exeter College was another most valued
assistant, as was John Marshall, fellow of New College. More great names
joined the growing band at Douay including Thomas Stapleton, fellow of
New College and Canon of Chichester. He is best remembered for his

splendid book *Tres Thomae* (the lives of St. Thomas the Apostle, St. Thomas of Canterbury and St. Thomas More). In 1570, Allen and Stapleton were created doctors of divinity with Allen appointed regius professor of divinity at Douay. The annual stipend of three hundred gold crowns was a welcome addition to the funds of the new establishment. This funding enabled Allen to receive eight more students. Among these were three illustrous Oxford men, Gregory Martin fellow of St. John's and tutor to the children of the Duke of Norfolk. Martin is famous as the translator of the Rheims New Testament. The other two were future martyrs, Thomas Ford fellow of Trinity and greatest of all Edmund Campion.

New students began to flock to Douay from all parts of England. The fame of the learned men who taught them proved an irresistable attraction. Those who came were of every rank, age and education. Among those admitted to study theology in 1573 was Cuthbert Mayne who was to be the first martyr of the seminaries. He had been a Protestant minister and chaplain at St. John's College Oxford.

In 1575, Pope Gregory XIII donated to the college a monthly pension of one hundred gold crowns which placed the college on a secure footing, no longer dependent on the casual alms of both local and English Catholics. In the same year the Pope conferred very extensive faculties on Dr. Allen, empowering him to absolve all English persons who could not conveniently confess except in English, from all sins and censures however strictly reserved, and to dispense them from all irregularities etc. Furthermore, he was given permission to sub-delegate these faculties to other priests whom he judged suitable, that they might exercise them within the realm of England. This was necessary, as the greater part of the English bishops were already dead or in exile, while the two or three left in England were so closely confined that they were prevented from exercising their jurisdiction. Thus Dr. Allen became, as it were, the Pope's vicar-general for all England which greatly increased his influence and authority.

Writing in 1580, Dr. Allen says that, as a rule, twenty students were ordained every year, and that about the same number were sent to England. In 1575 out of ten ordained, three became martyrs, in 1576 out of eleven ordained, two became martyrs, next year out of twenty- four ordained, seven were martyrs and so the list in the college diary continues:

"The future priests were thoroughly trained in scripture. There was a daily lecture on the New Testament, in which its exact and genuine sense was carefully explained. Every day after dinner and supper, before they left the refectory, they heard a running explanation of one chapter of the Old and another of the New Testament. They then had to make a discourse of the subject that had been treated in a disputation, in this way they were also trained in controversy. They were taught to preach effectively in English for the benefit of simple folk. The Bible was read each day, thus the Old Testament was gone through twelve times and the New, sixteen times in the three years which formed the usual college course.

"They were also carefully instructed in scholastic theology, receiving two lectures every day in the *Summa* of St. Thomas, and once a week there was a disputation on five specially chosen articles of the *Summa*. Moreover Dr. Allen records: "Since all the labourers we send are employed in administering the sacraments, and above all things in hearing confessions (for the people have hardly any pastors now about them), we take care that they are most carefully instructed in the whole chatechism (of the Council of Trent) and in pastoral matters, and are not ignorant of ecclesiastical penalties and censures, or of the way to deal with their people in such cases. For we desire that there should be a real and true observance of Church discipline in that afflicted Church, and that all parts of our religion, but especially the marvellous power and authority of the sovereign pontiff, should be better known and more devoutly and purely honoured than it used to be, for it is the exceeding neglect and contempt with which this was treated by pastors and people alike that God has punished with the present miserable desolation.

"Hence everyone, before arriving at those higher studies which we have mentioned, is most carefully instructed in all the chapters of the Catechism of Canisius, and after that in the entire method of reading the Breviary and saying Mass, as well as in the way of using the Blessed Virgin's rosary with the meditations attached to it, in order that by understanding these things themselves, they may be more fit to explain them hereafter to the simple people. For experience teaches us that they are by no means to be despised, as though they were hindrances to greater studies. On the contrary, the use of them wonderfully kindles piety in everyone, and draws down God's more abundant blessings on our labours and studies. Certainly Sts. Augustine, Bede, Thomas and the like gave more time to such things than we do, and yet their studies gained, rather than suffered detriment, thereby".

The students made a special study of moral theology and discussed cases of conscience, in order to fit them for the office of confessor. They had a list of recommended books for private study. With regard to exercises of piety the students heard Mass together every morning at the early hour of five o'clock, after having already recited the litanies for the Church and the conversion of England. They confessed and received the Blessed Sacrament every Sunday and greater feast days, and nearly all of them recited the canonical hours daily. The priests celebrated Mass every day. On the feast of St. Gregory, St. Augustine, apostle of the English, and St. Thomas of Canterbury, they sang High Mass, and the laity received the Blessed Sacrament.

Dr. Allen's chief objective was to make his students not theologians, but good and holy priests who could by example and teaching lead the people of

England back to the Catholic faith. In contrast to the parish priests of old, the seminarians were trained more devoutly and diligently. They all knew of course that their mission was highly dangerous and for many, their lives would be all too short.

The Elizabethan Government faced with the flood of ardent young priests coming to England, in the spring of 1581 Parliament brought in new statutes which made it high treason "To withdraw any of the Queen's subjects from the religion now by her Highness's authority established to the Romish religion". It was also made high treason " To be willingly withdrawn as aforesaid or reconciled". To say or sing Mass was punished by a fine of two hundred marks and imprisonment for a year. To hear Mass involved the same penalty, only the fine was one hundred marks. The penalties against recusants - faithful Catholics who refused to attend the new services, were at the same time increased.

Pope Gregory XIII summoned Dr. Allen to Rome in December 1575, the Pope wished to consult him about the founding of a second seminary in Rome itself. Two hundred years earlier, John Shepherd, a merchant of London had founded in the Via di Monserrato a hospital for the reception of English pilgrims to Rome. There were in 1575, eight priests maintained by the charity set up by John Shepherd, the priests looked after the travellers who were allowed to stay for a certain number of days in the hospital, free of charge. Owing to the persecutions in England, the number of pilgrims to Rome was now very small and the Pope had conceived a plan of transferring the place into a seminary. Dr. Allen was very enthusiastic about the scheme and immediately set to work, with the help of Dr. Owen Lewis, who was later vicar-general of Cardinal Charles Borromeo. The building was transformed and adapted for use as a seminary, it was however, provided that the college should still show hospitality to poor pilgrims from England. This was the origin of the famous English College at Rome, now so well known as the *Venerable English College.* Cardinal William Allen himself rests within the walls of its church, and his name is still honoured, along with Pope Gregory XIII as its founder.

Later, because of the unrest in the Low Countries, which was instigated by anti-Spanish activities, Dr. Allen was forced to look for an alternative home for his seminary at Douay. Eventually in 1578 the armies of the Prince of Orange backed a revolution and amidst terrible destruction, the English in the town of Douay were ordered to leave. At Rheims, they received a most friendly reception and promise of support from Archbishop Cardinal Louis of Guise. The exile at Rheims was to last fifteen years before they returned to Douay.

In 1579, Dr. Allen again went to Rome, for twenty years English Catholics had suffered bitter, grinding persecution. The chief result was an extraordinary increase in their fervour. Those who had clung to the Catholic faith in spite of fines and imprisonment were ever eager to receive the sacraments and to hear Mass. The old Marian priests had dwindled by death and imprisonment and it was on the young seminary priests that the people relied on for support. Allen had to find a new source. Ever since Edmund Campion had left Douay in 1573, Dr. Allen had longed to obtain the co-operation of the Jesuits in his missionary work in England. Dr. Allen had none of the petty jealousies and small minded ambitions which hindered and marred much of the good work done in England by both regular and secular priests in the following centuries. He made no attempt to stop Campion from becoming a Jesuit, although at that time the Society had no English province. Nor did he hinder, later on, other of his students joining the Benedictine Order. With the help of Father Robert Persons and Father Ralph Sherwin, the Society gave long deliberation before consenting to the wishes of Allen. The success of the English mission with the help of the Jesuits provoked a proclamation by Queen Elizabeth. It was dated 15 July 1580 and ordered the recall of all students from the seminaries and for the banishment of all Jesuits and seminary priests from England. Parents who had sons at the seminaries were ordered to recall them within four months, under the threat of severe penalties, and then to present them to the Protestant bishop. The prohibition also forbade any money to be sent out of England for the maintenance of students or seminaries, and for anyone from leaving the kingdom without the Queen's special licence.

In response to the Queen's proclamation, Dr. Allen wrote his *Apologie of the English Seminaries*. The *Apologie* was published at Henault in 1581, this small book is considered by many to be the most remarkable of all Allen's works. He puts forward the argument that he should "With all hope, joy and comfort, to speak in our defence, and discover without disloyalty to her majesty, the wrong information that certain enemies of the Catholic Church have given up against us" Dr. Allen protested that if the Government would grant Catholics the right to exercise the ancient religion, most of them abroad would come home. But not only was this basic right refused, but Catholics lacking in the rites and sacraments necessary for their salvation, but much worse "We are forced by manifold coercion to those rites which we never knew or gave our assent to". He goes on to protest that the exiles were not fugitives for any crime or disloyalty, or for discontent "With the present civil state and polity, or for mislike of any of her majesty's ministers, whose persons, wisdoms, moderation and prudence, and manifold graces we do honour with all our hearts in all things, excepting matters incident to religion". He refuted claims made by the Government that on his visits to Rome he "Neither joined with rebel nor traitor, nor anyone or other against the Queen or Realm, or traitorously sought or practised to irritate any prince or potentate to hostility against the state".

Dr. Allen then goes on to discuss the meaning and purpose of the seminaries at some length. There is a fine passage about priests in consoling and strengthening the Catholics and restoring the lapsed:

"This they have done only by the power of the priesthood, in spiritual, silent and peaceable manner, and not with riots, tumults, or warlike concourses, they have done it, as the Apostles and other holy men did in the primitive Church, by travails, watchings, fastings, perils at the ports, perils at sea, perils on the land, perils of open enemies, perils of false brethren, fears of the laws, fears of hurting their friends, fears for scandalising the weak, by contumelies, disgraces, poverty, imprisonments, fetters, dungeons, racks, and death. A little further on Allen observes: "That in one man's memory, we have had to our Prince, a man who abolished the Pope's authority by his laws, and yet in other points kept the faith of his fathers, we have had a child, who by the like laws abolished together with the papacy the whole ancient religion, we have had a woman, who restored both again, and sharply punished the Protestants, and lastly, Her Majesty that now is, who by like laws hath long since abolished both again, and now severely punisheth Catholics, as other did Protestants, and all these strange differences within the compass of about thirty years". He then described how Elizabeth had set about destroying the old religion, how into the ancient Catholic Sees had been intruded Protestants from Geneva and shows how absurd was the idea that Parliament could validly alter the nations faith or bestow upon a temporal sovereign spiritual jurisdiction.

He ends a fine piece of reasoning by an appeal to the queen to consider the impossibility that temporal princes should rule and command the Church. He begs her that if she would not hear him, she should think of so much holy blood meekly yielded for the testimony of this truth, especially of that noble pair Cardinal John Fisher, the most learned of all the clergy of that realm for many ages and Sir Thomas More, the greatest of all the laity.

In one chapter, Dr. Allen defends the Jesuits and seminary priests who were scoffed at as masssing-priests: "So, these, lo are your masse-priests, whose harbouring is so dangerous, whose absolution is so traitorous, whose sacred joints, without respect of honour due to the order, or to degree of learning or gentry, are racked sometimes almost to death!" In this last chapter of the book he traces the parallel between the old persecutions and the present one, between the primitive martyrs and those now suffering in England. "Every time that you confess Christ's name, every wrench of any joint for it, every opprobrious scoff and scorn given by the populance when you be carried in the sacred vestments through the streets, every villainy and sacrilege done to your priesthood, every of your sores, sorrows and sighs, every of your wants and necessities, make a stronger intercession for your country and afflicted Church, than any prayers lightly in the world. And therefore, when God giveth the grace of martyrdom, it is a joyful sign of mercy, and that He will not forsake the place nor the people which he blesses with so high and rare benediction".

This beautiful book ends with a fervent exhortation to his brethren to rejoice in their sufferings for Christ, and to cherish the hope of martyrdom above all earthly rewards. He was writing of the subject nearest to his heart, and his words are full of fire which cannot but impress even the most unsympathetic reader. His arguments and exhortations however, had little effect on the minds or conduct of the persecutors, but the book did much to console and strengthen the persecuted, and to enlist the interest and sympathy of foreign Catholics on their behalf. It remains a noble monument to the genius of the writer.

The proclamation which Dr. Allen had replied to in his *Apologie* had been followed by new penal statutes of still greater ferocity. These barbarous laws, and the martyrdoms which followed from them, caused such general horror, that Elizabeth's ministers found it necessary to defend themselves before the civilised world. Burghley, therefore, composed his well known treatise *The Execution of Justice in England not for Religion but for Treason* which was published in 1583. He sought to blacken the character of the martyrs and to uphold the preposterous thesis that the persecution in England was not a religious one. Dr. Allen's response was to publish in 1584 his *True, sincere and modest defence of English Catholics that suffer for the faith both at home and abroad..* He also wrote an account of the Martyrdom of Edmund Campion, in a delightful little book called *A Briefe Historie of XII Reverend Priests,* which gives a most touching account of the martyrdoms from 1577.

In the summer of 1585, Dr. Allen became gravely ill and he was advised to try the waters at Spa. While at Spa, he was summoned to Rome by Pope Sixtus V. As soon as he could travel he left for Rome in company with Fr. Robert Persons. The Pope wanted the advice of Dr. Allen. Pope Sixtus was not inclined to let England be lost to the Church without a struggle, and he was inclined to follow the recommendation of the Crown of Spain to use force against England.

It is clear that Dr. Allen's gentle nature fell at this time under the influence of Fr. Persons the powerful Jesuit who enjoyed the greatest favour both at the papal and Spanish courts. It is to Fr. Person's influence that most historians ascribe certain actions of Dr. Allen, who was drawn into the political intrigues then formenting in Rome. He was persuaded to join with those who were clamouring for the overthrow of Elizabeth and her Government by force, since more subtle methods had failed.

Robert Persons was a fellow at Oxford, he left England and converted to Catholicism at Louvain, becoming a Jesuit in 1575. Along with Edmund Campion, he led the first Jesuit mission in England in 1580, but left for the Continent after Campion's arrest. He continued his diplomatic activity in Rouen on behalf of the English Catholics, promoting for twenty years the Spanish invasion of England and formulating ideas about a Catholic successor to Elizabeth I. His most influential writing was *The Christian Directory* in 1582, an exhortation to the way of salvation by faith and good works. From 1597 until his death, he was rector of the English College in Rome.

Perhaps it is to Persons influences that we should ascribe the letter which Dr. Allen wrote from Rome in 1587 in defence of the treachery of Sir William Stanley, who was holding the city of Doventer for the States who were in alliance with England. He surrendered his charge to the Spanish authorities and with his officers and men deserted the English service to embrace that of Spain. Dr. Allen considered that he did rightly, as the States were in rebellion against their princes, the King of Spain, chiefly on account of religion. He argued that an English Catholic soldier had no right to take part with Protestants who were rebelling against their lawful king. This indeed may be true, and it might well be argued that as the war was an unjust one, Sir William could not in justice take part in it. But it is one thing to resign a commission and to decline to fight in an unlawful conflict, and another to deliver up a charge confided to one's care.

Dr. Allen not only defended Sir William's action, but took it as an example of what might be expected to happen in England, if the Pope would send an expedition to invade the country in order to restore the Catholic faith. He implored Pope Sixtus V to undertake this work with the help of Spain and other Catholic princes, and he assured him that posterity would reckon this as the most glorious act of his pontificate. The result was the disastrous Spanish Armada, an occasion which gave emphatic proof of the loyalty of the Catholics of England, and of the short sighted folly of those who sought to restore the ancient faith by force of foreign arms.

The admirers of William Allen, and few can study his life and character without feeling for him an almost passionate admiration and affection, cannot but regret that his zeal for religion should have led him into these political intrigues. But if it is easy to blame, it is still easier to excuse him. He saw his countrymen groaning under an intolerable persecution, ever growing more ferocious, he saw his sons martyred, his friends exiled, his hopes disappointed, and the temptation to look to Catholic princes to come to the aid of their unhappy brethren in England must have been overwhelming.

It should always be remembered to his honour that Allen invariably kept his spiritual work strictly apart from his political designs. Never did he use his priests as political emissaries, or confide in them any inkling of the plans which occupied his mind. Their work was wholly spiritual, and he would not permit for a moment that any other thought or aim should mar its purity. Never once were any political correspondence, any compromising papers found in the possession of those who suffered for the faith in England. This is strikingly proved by the very acts of the persecutors, who in 1585, passed a law by which the fact of priesthood alone was made treasonable. If the Government had not well known that it was impossible to prove any treasonable intent or design against these holy priests, it would never have been driven to pass an act so ferocious and so unjust.

William Allen had never sought dignities or honours for himself, his faithful secretary and first biographer, Nicholas Fitzherbert, records that he had more than once refused the cardinal's hat when it was offered to him by Pope Gregory XIII. On 7 August 1587 Pope Sixtus V summoned the cardinals to a Consistory, and in it created William Allen cardinal of the Holy Roman Church with the title of San Martino ai Monti. His object, he said, was to console the English Catholics for the loss of Mary Queen of Scots, the heir presumtive to the throne of England.

He spent his last years in Rome, he laboured on the great work of the revision of the Vulgate which was completed and published just before the death of Pope Sixtus V. He was made Apostolic Librarian by Pope Gregory XIV. He took part in the election of four successive Popes, Urban VII, Gregory XIV, Innocent IX and Clement VIII. The Popes conferred on him the fullest possible powers over all priests working in England, he was their ordinary, their father and their chief. It is unfortunate that he clung to the last, the idea that the reign of Protestantism in England could only be a transitory one. This caused him to refrain from obtaining for the afflicted Church in England a permanent ecclesiastical organisation. If he had provided that, at least after his death, some form of hierarchy could have been established in the country.

William Allen, Cardinal of England, died on 16 October 1594. Pope Clement VIII, who had loved and favoured him in life, wept for and honoured him in death. The Cardinal of England was fittingly laid to rest in the college church of St. Thomas of Canterbury, beneath the pictures of his martyred sons displayed on the walls of that church.

In 1583, with permission of Pope Gregory XIII, an inscription was set up in the church attached to the English College in Rome to commemorate the English martyrs. The paintings by Circignani, better known as Pomarancio, were destroyed by Napoleon's troops in 1798. Fortunately for posterity, the originals were reproduced in a volume of engravings by Cavallieri in 1584.

Extracts from: *The English Cardinals* by G. C. Heseltine
published by Burns Oates & Washbourne, London

Chapter Four

The Early Vicars Apostolic

THE Catholics of England would now be without a hierarchy of any kind for almost a century apart from a very brief period of eight years (1623-1631). In addition to the civil, political and social disabilities under which they had so long suffered, there was also for them the handicap of a lack of priests and bishops. Despite repeated efforts to procure a Catholic bishop the authorities in Rome found that such an appointment would only increase the hostility of the English Government and lead to an increase in the persecution of Catholics in England.

After Cardinal Allen's death, there was no head of the clergy, and the clergy themselves were divided into two separate bodies, under different and even opposite influences. Father Persons, whose influence in Rome at that time was supreme, at first favoured a scheme for the appointment of two bishops, one to live in England the other at Brussells, so that the latter could exercise his faculties in the event of his colleague being imprisoned. He later changed his view and recommended an 'archpriest' not in bishop's orders. The first to hold office was Rev. George Blackwell, appointed in 1599. George Blackwell was a convert to Catholicism and a native of Middlesex. His jurisdiction extended over the whole of Great Britain.

In 1606, James I had an Oath of Allegiance drawn up, which he called upon all Catholics to take. It was intended as a formal disclaimer of the power of the Pope to interfere with the allegiance of the subject by excommunicating the sovereign, and characterises the 'Deposing Power', which it couples with the right to murder an excommunicated king. Some, including George Blackwell the archpriest did take it, the great majority including the Jesuits and their followers refused to do so. Rome decided in favour of the latter, but the archpriest refused to retract. His reign was short and troubled, owing to intrigues and various other causes. On 1 February 1608, Pope Paul V issued a Brief, removing him from office. He died in prison for the faith on 12 January 1613, in his sixty-eighth year. Two other archpriests were appointed, Rev George Birkhead (1608-14) and Rev. William Harrison (1615-21). George Birkhead was a native of the north of England and was born in 1549. He was ordained at Douay in 1577. He exercised his office with great success for six years. He died on 6 April 1614 aged sixty-six. William Harrison was born in Derbyshire about the year 1553, and went to Douay in 1575. he was ordained in Rome in 1577. His formal installation as the third

47

archpriest of England was effected by a Brief of Pope Paul V, dated 11 July 1615. He died in 1621, in his sixty-ninth year. However, the constant wish of the secular clergy and many of the laity prevailed. In 1623, the Holy See at last, and with some reluctance, decided to agree to the repeated requests for a bishop. However it was not a bishop in ordinary that was appointed, but a vicar apostolic. The former is one with full jurisdiction, governing a diocese and assisted by a chapter of canons, in accordance with the normal forms of Church government, while the latter is a 'titular' bishop without a diocese or chapter, and with restricted powers. Such bishops are given to a missionary country in which normal Church government does not exist. The decision to send a bishop at all to England was taken after prolonged discussions in Rome, and was the personal decision of Pope Gregory XV, against the advice of his cardinals. The man chosen was Dr. William Bishop, who was given episcopal jurisdiction over England, Wales and Scotland, a formidable and highly dangerous task.

William Bishop was born at Brailes in Warwickshire about 1553. He studied at Oxford, Douay and Rome, and was ordained in 1581. Three times he came to the English mission and three times he was arrested and banished. He came as the first vicar apostolic of all Great Britain in 1623, having been consecrated in Paris, as Bishop of Chalcedon. His jurisdiction was limited to England and Wales, by the Pope shortly after his arrival in England. He died on 13 April 1624 in his seventy-first year, having been bishop only ten months. He was succeeded by Dr Richard Smith who was from Hamworth in Lincolnshire. Born in 1568, he later studied at Oxford, Rome and Valladolid. He was consecrated bishop in Paris, on January 12 1625. During the six and a half years that he spent in England he was subject to endless troubles. Differences arose between himself and the Regular clergy over the question of the source of jurisdiction. The Pope was appealed to and decided that the regulars received their jurisdiction direct from the Holy See. The Bishop, of course acquiesced in this decision, but there continued to exist a state of friction with accusations by his enemies which led to the Government issuing a proclamation in the name of the King, demanding the arrest of the Bishop. Finally, for greater peace, Bishop Smith decided to leave the country. On 24 August 1631 he went to France and tendered his resignation to the Pope, which was accepted. He died at the English Augustinian convent at Poitou on 18 March 1655. There ensued another period of over fifty years during which England, Wales and Scotland was without a Catholic bishop.

Dr. Bishop, during his short rule, had set up a Chapter, known subsequently as the Old Chapter, consisting of twenty canons, to advise and support him, and to preserve jurisdiction in case of his death. He applied to Rome for confirmation of his act, but this was never forthcoming. The Sacred Congregation for the Propagation of the Faith, commonly known as 'Propaganda', recognised the existence of the chapter and allowed it to exercise certain jurisdiction. Propaganda, is the body of cardinals in Rome charged with conducting the affairs of the Church in non-Catholic countries. English Catholics came under Propaganda. Consequently, the vicars apostolic transacted their business in Rome through the Cardinal Prefect of that Congregation. The second vicar apostolic, Richard Smith, continued the Chapter and gave it the privilege of electing its own canons and dean, if the vicariate should remain vacant after his death. During the long vacancy that followed Dr Smith's resignation, it did exercise jurisdiction, reporting to Propaganda and issuing faculties to the clergy. Throughout the vacant period, the Chapter tried repeatedly to procure the appointment of a bishop from Rome. Several envoys came secretly from Rome to investigate the situation, and the internuncio in Paris recommended Philip Howard, the chaplain of Charles II's Queen Catherine. He was of illustrious birth, had influence with the King and led an exemplary life as a Dominican friar. The English clergy worked to nominate their own bishop and objected to Howard. The Chapter stipulated that whoever was appointed, he should be a bishop in ordinary and not a mere vicar apostolic. Howard was appointed, but only as vicar apostolic, however Charles II objected and the brief of his appointment never got beyond Paris. Eventually Howard became a cardinal in May 1675.

A few years later in 1667, the Chapter wrote to Mr. Lesley who was the agent in Rome for the English clergy, in which they expressed their great desire to have a superior from His Holiness, but that to receive an apostolic vicar is displeasing to the State and against the ancient laws of the kingdom. It was suggested by the Chapter that each member proposes three names for consideration and that the five who have the majority of votes be proposed at Rome. The five chosen were Dr. Godden, Dr. Ellice (the dean), Mr. John Leyburn, Dr. Gage and Mr. Manley. Again when the Chapter assembled in 1684 the main business discussed was the procurement of a bishop, and again a list of names was put forward. It is interesting to note, of the six names which then headed the poll, that three of them, Bonaventure Giffard, John Leyburn, and James Smith, were future vicars apostolic. The following year Dr. Leyburn was appointed vicar apostolic, despite the requests from the clergy, and supported by James II, that a bishop in ordinary be appointed.

The accession to the throne of James II had brought the whole matter of a Catholic bishop back into dispute. James, flatly refused to receive a vicar apostolic into the kingdom, and on the appointment of Dr. John Leyburn in September 1685 the King promised the Chapter that Leyburn would not be received with such a title. However the King relented, and agreed to the

Pope's appointment. The King's objections to a vicar apostolic were of a political nature, the Chapter made the most of this and put to the King, that if a vicar apostolic were appointed, the King's spiritual and ecclesiastical concerns would be exposed to the will of a foreign court, his plans might be revealed and his will thwarted, and he would be ill-served, as a vicar apostolic would be clearly devoted to the Pope. Despite the efforts of both King and Chapter to procure a bishop in ordinary, the Holy See considered that it would be highly imprudent to appoint such a bishop so long as the penal laws remained in force. It was therefore decided to revive the office of vicar apostolic which had been vacant for fifty four years.

Dr. John Leyburn, born in 1615, came from a Protestant Westmorland family and his brother was a Puritan. He was ordained at Douay where he had studied for the priesthood. He took his doctorate at the Sorbonne, and became president of Douay in May 1670. He relinquished this position in 1675, in order to accompany Cardinal Howard to Rome as his secretary and auditor. He was eventually consecrated in Rome with the title of Bishop of Adrumetum on 9 September 1685, and the following month he came to England with the papal nuncio, Archbishop d'Adda. One of the first things Bishop Leyburn changed in the organisation that he inherited, was to the six districts set up by Dr. William Bishop in 1623. Leyburn reduced these areas to four, and he chose Drs. Parret, Giffard, and Betham, who were the four most prominent of the Secular clergy, as vicars general. Dr. Betham later became chaplain to the Queen during the years of exile at St. Germains, and he had great influence in ecclesiastical politics. To assist these vicars general, Leyburn also appointed rural deans for each district. As the only bishop in the land his great task was to carry out the thousand upon thousands of confirmations around the country. During his tour of the north in 1687 he confirmed 20,859 people.

During the brief reign of James II there was at last liberty for the long oppressed Catholics. Religious orders were re-established, the Benedictines set up a monastery in St. James's Palace in addition to the one at Somerset House which had been established in the reign of Charles II. The Franciscans and the Jesuits also established houses, and Religious openly walked the streets wearing their habits. Mass was celebrated in public and in the King's presence. In 1688 the King and Bishop Leyburn petitioned the Holy See for the appointment of more bishops. The result was that England and Wales was divided up into four districts, each with its own vicar apostolic. The decree by Propaganda, granting the King's request for the three new bishops, was dated 12 January 1688, and it received approval of Pope Innocent XI on 30 January. The four districts were known respectively as the London, the Midland, the Northern and the Western Districts. Dr. Leyburn was in charge of the London District, Bonaventure Giffard the Midland, James Smith the

Northern and Michael Ellis OSB the Western. The creation of three new Catholic bishops caused a public sensation and King James made the most of it. The consecrations were carried out with maximum publicity in three separate localities, the Banqueting Hall at Whitehall on 22 April, at St. James's Palace on 6 May and at Somerset House, which in those days was a palace on 13 May.

Bishop James Smith of the Northern District had spent most of his long life at Douay, where he was educated. He lived there as a student and then as professor for thirty years, and became president of the College in 1683. After his consecration the new bishop travelled north and reached York on 2 August, where he was received with a military guard of honour, and sang High Mass. The antependium used on that occasion has been preserved at Hazelwood Castle, the Yorkshire home of the Vavasour family since 1067. There the Blessed Sacrament was without interuption reserved from Norman times. Hazelwood has a great Catholic history and the Vavasour family remained there into the 20th Century. When William Gordon Wheeler became Bishop of Leeds in 1964, the house was owned by Donald Hart, a local restaurateur, who became a friend of Bishop Wheeler. Mr. Hart agreed to sell Hazelwood back into Catholic hands on the understanding that he could remain living there until he died. Eventually the Carmalites came to Hazelwood in 1968 and it became a place of pilgrimage and retreat centre. Sadly in the late 1990's it was sold and became a commercial hotel.

Bishop Bonaventure Giffard of the Midland District was the most outstanding of all vicars apostolic between 1685 and 1850. He was born in 1642 during the reign of Charles I, and his father was killed in the Civil War. He lived on into the reign of George II, during his 92 years he lived in the reigns of eight rulers and the pontificates of twelve Popes. His family home was Chillington in Staffordshire where his family had lived since before the Norman Conquest, and was the mainstay of Catholicism in South Staffordshire. His great uncle, Gilbert Giffard was a Government spy in Queen Elizabeth's time and did immense harm to Catholics. He betrayed Mary Queen of Scots, and revealed the Babington Plot. Bishop Giffard was educated at Douay, and completed his studies at St. Gregory's College in Paris. St. Gregory's was the English College established to enable English priests to pursue advanced studies and to take their doctorate at the Sorbonne. Bonaventure Giffard was one of the first students, and after twelve arduous years he took his doctorate in 1678.

The third new bishop, Michael Ellis, was a Benedictine monk, he had perhaps the strangest career of all the forty six vicars apostolic in England. He was born in 1652, he was baptised Philip (Michael was his name as a religious). He was the third son of a Protestant clergyman, the Rev. John Ellis, who had six sons. They all had strangely varied careers, the eldest son, John, became Under Secretary of State to William III, while the second son, Sir William Ellis, was Secretary of State to William's rival, James II, in exile in France. The fourth son in due course became Protestant Bishop of Killala, and later Bishop of Meath, while the fifth son, Samuel was appointed Marshal of the King's Bench, and the sixth, Charles, was a Protestant clergyman.

As a pupil at Westminster School, Philip became a Catholic and escaped overseas where he became a Benedictine at St. Gregory's Priory, Douay, taking his vows there in 1670. At school he was known as 'Jolly Phil' and this nickname stuck with him for life. When he joined the English mission, he attracted the attention of the Duke of York (later James II) who appointed him one of his chaplains and preachers. It was James who influenced his selection as one of the three new bishops in 1688. The Revolution a few months later put an end to all his plans in England. He was imprisoned for a time in Newgate and on his release he left the country and went at first to St. Germains, were he was kindly received by the exiled James II, and then to Rome. There he became a friend of Cardinal Howard and was made an assistant prelate at the pontifical throne by Pope Innocent XII.

Bishop Ellis wanted to get back to England and govern his vicariate, which was meanwhile being cared for by Bishop Giffard, and he made repeated efforts to be allowed to return. But by 1705 he had given up all hope of ever being permitted to return to England and he resigned his vicariate altogether. He continued to live in Rome and in 1708, Pope Clement XI, nominated him to the Italian See of Segni. Despite his English origins, he proved both popular and successful. This one-time English Protestant schoolboy as bishop of an Italian diocese founded a seminary at his own expense. He governed his diocese for eighteen years until stricken by dropsy, he died on 16 November 1726.

Just prior to the Revolution of 1688 which swept away once more the liberties of English Catholics, the four bishops issued a pastoral. It was a letter of guidance appealing to Catholics that despite the long years of suffering to act with kindness to their fellow countrymen. The pastoral warned Catholics of the necessity of setting a good example to Protestants, and of having charity towards them, even those who had persecuted them. The whole document is of interest as showing what the attitude of the Church and of Catholics in general would have been, had toleration continued to be extended to them, and as illustrating their complete lack of intolerance or of hostility as regards Protestants, despite all they had suffered at their hands. Not the least interesting part of it is the section which portrays the very genuine devotion of King James, which was so marked a feature of his later years.

But the storm broke. The vested interests of a small select group, and the blind hatred and prejudice of many more, imperatively demanded that Catholicism should not be allowed to come out into the open. William of Orange with his Dutch soldiers invaded England, and betrayed and forsaken, James was driven out of the country. With him vanished the dreams and hopes of Catholics, and they were driven back underground for another hundred years. Bishop Leyburn in company with Bishop Giffard attempted to leave the country, but were arrested at Faversham and taken back to London. There each of them were confined in prison for twenty months, Leyburn in the Tower, and Giffard in Newgate, where Bishop Ellis was also confined. The fourth bishop, Dr. Smith was more fortunate, he was not arrested, but he had to retire into obscurity, and took refuge at Wycliffe Hall in Yorkshire, the home of his old friend, Francis Tunstall. He remained there for the rest of his life carrying out his episcopal duties in secrecy and disguise and in constant danger of betrayal. So ended the Catholic revival of 1685-88, a brief glimpse of sun-light between two long stretches of darkness, persecution, and dogged endurance. Apart from the faith, one thing alone remained amidst the ruin of all the Catholic hopes and plans, the establishment of all four vicariates. This endured through all the difficulties and dangers of the coming eighteenth century, without this foundation, without this organisation, it is difficult to see how the flickering flame of Catholicism could have been kept alive at all through those long weary years, known as the 'penal times', which was to last until Catholic emancipation in 1829.

Dr. Leyburn was released from prison in 1690 and he continued to live in London and to govern the London District. The government did not molest him, but following his release from prison his life was one of great poverty and hardship, until at the age of 86, he died on 20 June 1702. He had suffered much, he saw the brief years of Catholic liberty, and then disappointment as that liberty withered away and the rigour of the penal laws again imposed on his fellow Catholics.

On the death of Bishop Leyburn, it was suggested that Bishop Smith of the Northern District should succeed him, but Dr. Smith was unwilling that his name should go forward. He had no desire to be thrust into the limelight. The prospect of the London vicariate, which would make him *ex officio*, though quite unofficially, leader of the English Catholics, horrified him. In previous years he had constantly and successfully struggled to avoid promotion. He had on two occasions been suggested for the office of Cardinal Protector of England, vacant by the death of Cardinal Howard in 1694. After much correspondence between England and Rome, and to his vast relief Bishop Smith was left in peace, and his suggestion that Dr. Giffard should be moved from the Midland to the London, and the newly consecrated Bishop Witham be given the Midland District, was adopted.

Dr. Witham was one of the most prominent Catholic figures even before he was consecrated. As priest in charge at Newcastle-on-Tyne, he had been vicar general to Bishop Smith until he was sent to Rome in 1694 to be the

agent there for the English bishops. He held this post until he was consecrated bishop in 1703. He was born at Cliffe Hall in Yorkshire in 1655, and
he died in the same house seventy years later. His final promotion to the
episcopate he owed to Queen Mary of Modena (widow of James II) who
wrote to Pope Clement XI suggesting that he should be made coadjutor to
Bishop Leyburn in London. He had taken his doctorate at the Sorbonne
from St. Gregory's College, Paris in 1688, and had been professor of theology at Douay for four years before going on the mission at Newcastle.
There had long been uncertainty as to which vicariate Dr. Witham was to
rule. He himself wanted the Northern, he had originally been chosen to fill
the vacancy in the London District.

Bishop Giffard had been looking after the Western District (in addition to
his own Midlands) ever since 1688, and since the death of Dr. Leyburn in
1702 he had also cared for the vacant London District. He now became
vicar apostolic of the London District, and he held this post until his death
thirty years later.

Meanwhile there was still the long standing vacancy in the West, incredible
though it may seem, it was to remain vacant for a further ten years. This was
largely because the Secular clergy, despite their utmost efforts and although
they put forward a considerable number of names could not produce a really
satisfactory candidate. In 1703, Dr. Betham at the Jacobite court in France
made tentative efforts to get the Queen Mother at St. Germains to move on
the matter, but she waited until she was informed of the views of the English clergy. As tutor to her son, Dr. Betham acted as liaison between the
Queen and the bishops. He was violently opposed to the Regulars and could
be extremely outspoken in his references to them. Betham had always been a
strong supporter of the Queen's 'rights' in the nomination of candidates for
the office of bishop. He wrote to Gordon the new agent in Rome on 8 June:
"The Queen does not claim a right of naming apostolic vicars, but expects
none should be promoted but whom she approves of". When he found to
his horror that the Queen desired a Regular to be appointed, he wrote in a
letter to Gordon in December to tell him that neither Gordon nor himself
need stretch matters too far in this matter of keeping the Queen informed,
because she has no strict right to nominate bishops, and still less mere vicars
apostolic!

In October, 1705 Andrew Giffard was appointed by Rome as Bishop of
Cantusiensis and vicar apostolic of the Western District. Dr. Betham on 2
November acknowledged receipt of the news "with much satisfaction", and
arrangements were started for Giffard's consecration in great secrecy, in case
Parliament should get to hear of it and start a new persecution. However, to
the dismay and annoyance of his colleagues, Andrew Giffard flatly refused
the appointment, and nothing that anyone could say would induce him to

alter his decision. There followed lengthy negotiations and no fewer than eight secular priests were proposed, but Rome would not accept any of the nominations. On 10 September 1706, Bishop Smith of the Northern District wrote to Betham, in the peculiar coded method that Catholics felt it necessary to write in those days: "Old Andrew is stiff and not to be moved from his resolution. He is hardened against all that is offered, and gives no other answer but that he cannot, will not agree, to what is desired, and it appears to me, required by God and his friends. This peremptory refusal puts us hard to find out an excuse for the good man, for he will not write himself (to Rome), and to offer another way that may be acceptable to Mr. Clements (the Pope). Such is hoped may, in some measure, be Mr. Saltmarsh, who though in some particulars less qualified, yet *omnibus consideratis* is as, or more fit than any we could pitch on. But in all appearance the management of that farm will by Mrs Grace's interest, and other insinuations, be put into other hands (i.e the vicariate will be given to a Regular through the influence of the Queen Mother), and provided he be an able, good man and a good neighbour, tis no great matter who he be, or of what cote, or parish".

The affair still dragged on, not without a note of comedy at times. 'James III' and the Queen Mother were both offended because the bishops, on orders from Rome, had not told them the names they proposed for the vacancy. Despite still more names submitted, there was only inscrutable silence from Rome. 1709 and 1710 slipped away, and the Western District remained vacant, which it had been since it was set up in 1688. Then in 1711, Bishop Smith of the Northern District died, and this complicated matters more than ever. There were now two Districts vacant, the Western remained vacant until 1713 and the Northern until 1716.

The death of the gentle and much loved Bishop Smith had resulted from an illness which he contacted during his visitation of East Yorkshire during the very hot weather of 1710. This brought on a fit which was followed by severe nervous attacks for the next ten months, and after dropsy had set in he died on 13 May 1711, which was the twenty third anniversary of his consecration as bishop. This increased the activity of the higher clerical circles in England. Giffard promptly wrote to the agent in Rome, Lawrence Mayes, instructing him to propose the name of Mr. Savage. This was the alias of John Rivers who had succeeded to the title of Earl Rivers in 1712. In view of the fact that he was heir to the title, he had asked for a dispensation to allow him to marry, but this was refused. For some years he was the priest at York, but his closing years were spent in Douay and Louvain, where he died in 1737.

In August, the authorities in Rome were impatient for nominations for the Northern vacancy to be sent to them, but Dr. Giffard, after describing Smith's death as "an inexpressible losse", he explained that they had not yet sent them because they had not been asked to do so, and also because the King and Queen would take it ill. Moreover he himself did not know many of the northern clergy, and some that he could recommend would not accept. In any case, a man of private means was needed:

"This is of great moment. My brother Smith was heir to a great estate. Brother Witham has a very considerable annuity, and as my relations are none of the meanest, so I am so far supplyed as to be no burden to the Holy See. No person can live in that station with less than £100 per annum. I am sure it costs me £150 one year with another. Brother Smith has left a very large provision for his successors, but with this proviso, that he be of the Secular clergy. Besides the four vicars apostolic chosen out of the clergy (i.e. from the Seculars) have, I hope, given satisfaction to the Holy See, *portarimus pondus dies et aestus*. We have remained firm and constant in the discharge of our duty notwithstanding the continual hardships, difficulties and dangers we have been exposed to. Some of us also have been honoured with the mark of St. Paul's election and Apostleship *in carceribus abundantius*. I think therefore it will be very hard and some understanding of the clergy, if these should be succeeded by persons of another body".

In September, Dr. Dicconson, the vice-president of Douay (he became a bishop twenty nine years later) told Mayes that the "Fryor" nominated by the King was Matthew Prichard, while the two bishops had nominated Saltmarsh and Savage. Dicconson himself protested against James having any voice in such appointments, saying that English kings never had one from the time of King John to that of Henry VIII. Four days later Giffard himself told Mayes that the bishops had sent up eight names for the two vacancies. These were Drs. Jones, Saltmarsh, John Savage, Thomas Yaxley, Dr. Simon Rider, Dicconson, Edward Parkinson and Silvester Jenks. He lamented that Smith, though urged to do so, would never name a coadjutor and had died without one. Later he told Mayes: "If our masters would transfer Bishop Witham to the North and make some other for the Midlanand District, and joyn to it South and North Wales, I could manage the West well enough. But the best will be to have four out of our (secular) clergy for the four Districts". The exiled James for his part, said he had no objections to any of those proposed by the bishops, while the Holy father in Rome stressed the need of care that no one suspected of Jansenism should be appointed, especially as Douay was accused of being tainted with it. Partisan moves by both Seculars and Regulars, left Rome largely unmoved, indeed Cardinal Sacriponti stated that Propaganda thought it a matter of indifference whether they appointed a Secular or a Regular "as long as he was the best man. His merits must determine it". A doctrine that must have seemed almost heresy to the two contending parties in England.

In the summer of 1713, Dicconson reported from Douay that the Jesuits were trying to win over the other Orders to join them in their opposition to the Secular clergy, and that they had promised to get mitres for Prichard, a Franciscan and for Fr. Williams, a Dominican. Suddenly Rome at last spoke. In August Propaganda selected Dr. Jenks for the North and Fra. Matthew Pritchard for the West. James sardonicaly remarked that it was very strange that among all the nominations that he had sent to Rome, none should proceed but that which he desired should not!

Dr. Pritchard was thus the first Regular to rule in England since the Reformation. The Western District now had its own resident bishop since it was established, twenty-five years previously. Born at Craig, between Monmouth and Abergavenny, in 1669, he was therefore a native of the ecclesiastical district. He had made his noviciate at St. Bonaventure's, the Franciscan monastery at Douay, and after his ordination became a missioner at Perthyre in his native county. He was appointed vicar apostolic in 1713, but it was not until Whitsun 1715, that he could be consecrated, and the ceremony took place at Cologne. He laboured long and hard, in great poverty, to organise the Church in the West, but caution, moderation and patience were essential in that time of potential or actual persecution and no extension of the faith was then to be expected. For most of his long period in office he lived at Perthyre, and he strove to hold the balance impartially between Seculars and Regulars. However he took the side of his religious brethren in their conflict with the bishops on the subject of their faculties, and declined to sign the promulgation of the papal decree of 1745 which temporarily settled this matter in favour of the bishops. This earned him a reprimand from Rome, yet at the same time he was always fair and friendly to the Secular clergy, as even his opponents testified.

Pritchard was an ardent supporter of the exiled Jacobite royal family, which was a characteristic of nearly all Catholics at that time despite the severe political handicap which that imposed on them. He was in addition reputed to be a close friend of the Jesuits, with whom the Secular clergy were having at this time a long drawn out and bitter dispute over their attempt to win back control of the English College in Rome from the Society.

In 1715 John Stonor, then only 37 was one of the five names Bishop Giffard had sent to Rome for the Northern District along with Mayes, Rider and Dicconson. Stoner was considered by many to be too young for the episcopate. He, although intensely ambitious, did not wish to go to the North, it was on London that his eyes were fixed. Stonor's career provided a remarkable contrast between his earlier and his later years. In his youthful days he was a storm centre, and an object of anxiety and dislike to both bishops and clergy alike. But as he grew older he gradually won his way to a position of great influence in the Catholic affairs of the country and he was held in the highest esteem by all. Moreover he ruled for a period of forty years and consquently left behind him a resounding respect to his memory in the Midland District. His fame was equalled only by that of Bishop Milner a century later.

He was of high birth, being the son of Lady Mary Talbot, the daughter of the Earl of Shrewsbury, and as such he was a second cousin of the two future bishops, James Talbot, vicar apostolic of the London District (1781-90), and Thomas Talbot, vicar apostolic of the Midland District (1778-95) As a boy of twelve he entered Douay college, and six years later began to study at St. Gregory's in Paris, for the priesthood and for his doctorate. Then suddenly he gave up his plans for becoming a priest as he wanted to marry. However in the end he changed his mind again, and seven years later resumed his studies in Paris and after his ordination he took a doctorate in 1714. From then on he was very much to the fore among Catholics, and his high birth, great ambition, and undoubted abilities coupled with a forceful personality clearly marked him out for promotion. At this stage and for some years to come, he was a constant source of trouble and was deeply distrusted by his fellow clergy, even after he had become a bishop. This was in part due to his Hanoverian sympathies, but chiefly because of his undisguised ambitions and pushing, intriguing ways which earned him many opponents. He was unwise enough to become a close friend of that odd enigmatic character the Abbe Strickland, who was equally ambitious but more unscrupulous and who ended his life as Bishop of Namur. For some years these "two young doctors", as they were often called, were inseparable, and a constant source of uneasiness to the vicars apostolic, especially because Strickland had many powerful friends in high places. But as soon as Stoner found that his friendship with Strickland was harming his own prospects he dropped him completely and without pity, telling him bluntly that he must not look for any help from him in future. These two were indeed the *enfants terrible* of the period, and everyone knew they were scheming to obtain bishoprics, indeed they openly boasted about it, that Stoner will have the London District, and Strickland the North. Stoner, indeed, had become vicar general to Bishop Giffard, and the plan was that he should be appointed coadjutor Bishop of London. On all this, and the sequel, there is a great mass of letters in the Westminster archives, and a selection from some of them will make the situation clear. The first mention of the plot, which included a systematic denigration of Bishop Giffard to the Roman authorities, occurs in a letter from Dr. Carnaby, the procurator of the Paris seminary, St. Gregory's, to Mayes the agent in Rome. It is dated 9 April 1715:

"You'll wonder to have a line from me, but I think myself obliged to disclose a certain affair to you, which I had entrusted to me by your old scholar, Dr. Strickland. He is at present in Paris, and has been lately with Santini (the papal nuncio in Brussels). He says he is so much esteemed by Santini that he is resolved to have no other (than Strickland) for the Northern vicariate in Mr. Jenks' place. He pretends to have no hand in this, now if such a thing should happen, it would be of dangerous consequence. He would be topped over us, against the universal comfort of our brethren, and though a man of excellent parts, as you well know, his life has not bin so very apostolic as to deserve to be elevated to so high a dignity, nor does he seem sober and serious enough for so weighty an office. He tells me that the affair will be very soon done, and that Santini will have his Bulls (of appointment) before Whitsuntide. I hope you will do what you can to obstruct this, for he is not in the list, and by consequence would not be acceptable to the brethren. But pray let nothing of it be known. I was obliged to keep this secret, but I thought myself more obliged to open it so far as to intrust it to you. They, i.e. Mr. Stoner and he, are also endeavouring to get Mr. Stoner made coadjutor to Bishop Giffard, for which reason they lesson the good bishop's credit with the internunce as much as they can. I have reason to think that they are also making their applications that way against Dr. Witham, (Thomas Witham was president of the Paris seminary, under whom Stoner and Strickland had studied for their doctorates. For many years they waged a campaign against him in Rome, accusing him of Jansenistic tendencies, at that time a fatal accusation that ruined many a career), to have him removed from hence by orders from Rome. Whereas I think his greatest fault was over indulgence to them. You see what it is to have young men with noysy heads in a body of which they think themselves only fit to have the management and government".

On 23 July, Carnaby again wrote to Mayes:

"I had a letter from Mr Paston (alias of Henry Howard a priest in London), two days agone. He is for excluding both Strickland and Stonor from mitres, and with good reason, considering their late conduct but they are both of them mightily set upon episcopacy, which makes me think neither are fit, so I hope you'll do what you can to hinder their promotion. All people agree that come from England that Bishop Giffard is more fitt for labour than ever (Strickland and Stonor were reporting to their Roman contacts that Giffard was too old to be able to work), and in effect he does more than all about him. However he is advised to get a coadjutor by those very persons who have a mind to have all the power taken out of his hands, and placed in their own".

These intrigues had caused great resentment amongst the clergy by whom Giffard was universally loved and respected, and Dicconson spoke for all of them when he characterised the conduct of the two as "underhand and ungrateful". Even the gentle Howard deplored what had happened. He said the two had accused Bishop Giffard of being too old, incapable and irresolute, and Bishop Witham of being eaten with scruples and totally incapable of business. But he feared they would have their way, that Strickland would get the North and Stoner be coadjutor in London with all the real power, "and then what a condition our affairs will be in!".

"As for Mr. Stoner, I must confess I fear him in some measure still more (than Strickland). His great desire and endeavours he has used for his promotion, which I have known by his own letters, his beginning so soon after he came over from France, to undermine his own superior, to whom he has been so particularly obliged, his accusing one of his own body of what tends at least to Jansenism, while in his own conscience he thinks him orthodox, his doing all these things, not only without, but knowing contrary to the will of superiors, the ill-will he has incurred among all his brethren by these underhand dealings, joined to that uneasiness of temper he is always under, till he has some project in hand, and to his dislike of all the missionary functions and duties, are reasons I believe most persons would think sufficient to endeavour to hinder his promotion".

All this was confirmed by Thomas Day, a member of the Chapter in a letter of 27 August, in which he said that Giffard had never thought of taking a coadjutor and was naturally indignant at Strickland soliciting one for him from the nuncio behind his back. His two vicars general, Saltmarsh and Stoner, were privy to all this in secret, but a certain Mr. Hesqueth informed Giffard of what was afoot, whereupon Giffard called Saltmarsh and Stoner into his room and made Hesqueth repeat his story. He then asked them whether they had told Strickland to do this, and they had to admit it, whereupon "This being all they had to say, he gave them such a warm and vigorous reprimand that they knew not which way to look". Giffard flatly refused the suggestion of the nuncio that he should have Stonor as his coadjutor, said he had no need of any coadjutor, and added that Strickland was totally unfit to be bishop of the North.

"This whatever I have related that concerns Bishop Giffard, I have from his own mouth, and the rest from Mr. Hesqueth. Thus Mr. Saltmarsh and Dr. Strickland judged Dr. Stonor the fittest person for coadjutor to Bishop Giffard at present, and for his successor hereafter, and Mr. Saltmarsh and Dr. Stonor judged Dr. Strickland the fittest person for a bishop in the North. Thus they divided the nation between them, and it may be presumed that Mr. Saltmarsh was not to remain un-preferred, if this design had taken effect. Could an attempt of this nature, in two young inexperienced persons, just stepped into the vineyard, proceed from anything else but an unparalleled ambition, joined with an uncommon degree of blind and headlong presumption and from a violent desire for revenge".

It is of interest to give Bishop Giffard's own defence, as written by him to the agent in Rome, as it includes an interesting picture of the conditions of the time. Writing on 15 October 1715, he says:

"If my letters have not reached you it is not my fault. Our circumstances are such that all our letters are opened and often times stopt. This I have experienced in the various letters I have written to Mgr. Santini. Notwithstanding all the pains I have taken they have been intercepted. I hear that two of our clergy have reported to him (Santini) that it was necessary to give me a coadjutor, although this ought not to have been done without my knowledge and consent. The reasons alleged by them, as I hear, are these: One, that I am too old; two, that I neglect my flock and pastoral duties; three, that I attend to, and am fit for nothing else than to say my prayers.

"As to the first, it is true that I am now in my 73rd year, but I thank God I am yet strong and enjoy better health than when I was only 30 years old. As to the second, they ought to have specified in what particulars I neglect my duty. I make my visitations in the country, as far as the circumstances of the time permit, and the houses of Catholics are open to receive me. As to the obligation of preaching, called by the Council of Trent the peculiar duty of a bishop, it is notorious that I never neglect it on Sundays and Festivals, where circumstances allow me to do it. In London it cannot always be done, but in the country I never omit it. I confirm whenever I am desired, and on these occasions I give them a preparatory discourse, and sometimes I have done this three times in a day and in three different places. In London I have no chapel of my own, but I am at all times ready to perform this duty when wanted, and when it can be done without exasperating the government. While I was under the roof and protection of the Venetian ambassador I gave confirmation once a week, if wanted, and always gave a discourse on that sacrament, which I have also done in the chapels of other foreign ministers. The last time I did this in the house of the Envoy of Florence, Mgr. Bianchini, the domestick prelate of His Holiness, and Count Bardi, were present, who can testify to the vigour which they may have noticed in my voice and gestures while I preached. Almighty God has given me such strength and such consolation in seeing the fruit produced by my preaching, that I can in truth say with the apostle: 'Woe to me, if I preach not the Gospel'. The dangers which continually hung over me in London, and which obliged me in the space of nine days to change my lodgings seventeen times, have forced me to take shelter in the house of a gentleman in the country where, having more liberty, I expounded the Gospel every Sunday, and besides make a discourse to those who receive confirmation. As to my other pastoral duties, hundreds of persons can testify that, not having either carriage or horse, I go on foot from house to house, and to visit the sick and the dying, giving such instructions as the case requires.

"As to that part of my duty which regards the government of my flock, for many years I have been burdened with the care of three parts of this kingdom, and not being able to visit them all in person, I have caused my vicar general to report to me the state both of priests and of the people, and have used such diligence in sending back the instructions and directions which were wanted that without the assistance of a secretary, I have many times sent off ten letters in a day. (He adds how he has corrected erring priests) and that the necessary expenses though considerable have been well laid out, notwithstanding that I have been obliged on that account to deprive myself not only of the conveniences, but also of some of the necessities of life.

"If I be taxed of vain glory in the recital of these good deeds, I will avail myself of the apostle's apology: 'I have become foolish, you have compelled me'. I do not pretend to be free from all fault, God forbid I should be guilty of any such presumption. In the meantime, whenever their Eminences or His Holiness or Mgr. Santini shall make me acquainted with those neglects of my duty of which I have been accused, either I will justify myself by a modest reply, as far as truth allows me, or I will submit with all humility to their correction.

"If I were not afraid of being taxed with folly for saying so much of myself, I might say a great deal of the labour of so many long and painful visitations, and of the sermons and instructions given to my flock. Much I might add of my sufferings in divers prisons, and of the prosecutions I have undergone for the space of twenty seven years, without ever abandoning my flock, to whom I have constantly given all that consolation and assistance which the times and circumstances permitted. But I am now drawing up an account of my pastoral administration from the day of my consecration to the present time, and I have determined to submit it to the Congregation of Propaganda, when I will resign myself entirely to its disposal. And if it be thought of advantage to this poor Church that I be removed from the pastoral charge of it, I shall have more pleasure in being eased of it by Pope Clement XI, than I had in receiving it from Pope Innocent XI. P.S. It will probably be some time before you receive this as I am at present in the country, where few opportunities occur of sending letters. All by the post are opened. Before I left London I was in imminent danger of being apprehended. The officers had entered the house where I was, so that I was obliged to affect my escape by a back door. I have been particularly careful not to interfere in political affairs of state, so that whatever I shall have to suffer will be purely on the score of religion".

A month later Bishop Giffard received a breve from Propaganda in highest praise and commendation of himself, his sufferings and constancy, and his labours for religion, which was signed by Cardinal Sacriponti, the Prefect of Propaganda.

Dr. Stonor was promoted to the episcopate in September 1715, an event which greatly upset many. His 'breves' were made out for the Northern District, but this arrangement was soon cancelled, and it was understood he was to go to the Midland District. It was decided to postpone his consecration, on account of the recent Jacobite rising. Several priests had recently been arrested, including Fr. Plowden, who was a close friend of Stonor. On hearing of the promotion, Mayes received a warning from Dr. Witham in Paris: "If Strickland be promoted, he and Stonor will govern all, and dispose of all posts as they please. You may expect to decamp for one".

These and similar fears appeared to be justified when in March 1716 (i.e. before his actual consecration) Stonor obtained from Rome a 'Brief of Inspection', a cause of much subsequent trouble, empowering him to administer the London District in the case of the absence, illness, or disability of Bishop Giffard, but not otherwise. Naturally this greatly offended the aged bishop, and it was also hotly resented by most of the clergy. It showed where Stonor's ambitions lay, and though in fact he was never given the opportunity of putting the brief into execution, yet it was not till some seven years later that his persistent hopes of getting the London District eventually faded away. By then Dr. Giffard had secured first Henry Howard and after Howard's death, Benjamin Petre as his coadjutor with right of succession. It is however fair to let Dr. Stonor speak for himself on this matter of the brief. Here then, is what he wrote to Dr. Robert Witham of Douay on 5 June 1716, from Paris where he was about to be consecrated:

"Hnrd. Sir, . . . I must begin with what sticks most to my heart. I find that the affair of the Brief of Inspection has taken air. All I know is that this discovery is not come from me. And I cannot believe it is come from you. In all appearance tis now also known to Bishop Giffard and to the Brethren in England. I cannot say that some such thing as this Brief was not necessary, though a very unfit person has been pitched upon for the employment. All who will impartially consider both my temper and the circumstances of my future together with the present situation of Catholick affairs in England will easyly be persuaded that neither the inspection nor the vicariate are agreeable to my inclination, much less that they are the effects of my solicitations and intrigues. But whatever be my own private judgement and inclinations, I don't see how I can well decline the burden that is thrown upon me, and tis no less visible that the Holy See will not let a decree which it has been so long a-weighing and considering, be easily set aside.

"On the other side, tis cruel to think of causing a new division, and giving a new subject of scandal to the Catholicks of England in these unhappy times. I flattered myself that I had pitched upon the expedient which would have prevented all such ill effects. But those measures have been besides what now are to be taken. I see no others but what your prudence and public

63

spirit made you to suggest at first, viz. that you yourself would be pleased to intimate this brief to Lord Bishop Giffard and the brethren, and use your interest and credit with them to make them satisfyed and pleased with the contents of it. The proposal I made of having kept a secret amongst us three, and which proposal I likewise made to the internunce is a sufficient pledge of my designs of peace and quiet in regard of the body of priests and laity, and respect and tenderness in regard of him whom I look upon as my chief, Bishop Giffard. I shall look upon myself as abundantly satisfyed, if, as to what relation I shall have to his District, he'l treat me in the same manner as he would do a grand vicar in whom he has confidence, or, if you will, a suffragan that depends entirely upon his orders.

"If the apologies I can make for my past behaviour can not yet induce him to declare me innocent of ever having injured him, the submissions which I am ready to join to these apologies ought at least to obtain his favour by way of pardon, and now that everything is settled. . . to forget what's past. I know there are prejudices against me, and there will be need of all your zeal and prudence to bring this matter to an amicable composure. These preventions are so strong that it comes from (here the word in the manuscript is indecipherable) that some persons have entertained a design *quale nec inter gentes auditum est,* viz. to inform against me and cause me to be delivered up to the Government. God Almighty pardon them. I heartyly doe. All I can say is that whatever complyance and condescension charity can prompt to, and verity will allow of, I shall be always ready to exhibit on my side. And however others may be effected or behave towards me, I shall never but upon the last extremyty and the evident call of my duty make use of high and authoritative means".

Dr. Witham was in no way placated by the above letter, he was in addition totally against Stonor's desire that Catholics should renounce the Stuarts and take an oath of allegiance to George I. On this subject Stonor was also at variance with his brethren. Despite the controversy, Dr. Witham departed for the North, and Dr. Stonor took his place in the Midlands. The storm of indignation caused him to keep a low profile, and it was at this time that he severed his past connection with Strickland. There was an uneasy truce between Stonor and his clerical brethren who were still suspicious of him. In reality, apart from his overweaning ambition, Dr. Stonor had many admirable qualities, and his later career as a bishop, after he had shed his youthful indiscretions, was of great value to the Church in England. He had a very clear mind and a firm will, as well as great energy, so that it is not surprising to find that for very many years he was the leading spirit amongst the bishops.

It is interesting to compare these early aspects of Bishop Stonor, in order to give a true picture of the man as he then was, and also of the period, but it would be unfair to leave it at that, for when he matured he presented a very different picture. Indeed there is a very remarkable contrast between the young ambitious, intriguing cleric and prelate of the period 1714-25 and the dignified, wise, and widely influential bishop of his later years. It is difficult to believe they are the same man. For at least twenty years of his life his was the preponderating influence in English Catholic affairs, and in matters affecting the bishops it was generally he who took the initiative, largely because it happened that none of his episcopal brethren sought the limelight or were anxious to lead. For (to glance ahead at those years) Bishop Petre of London was extremely retiring by nature, and his coadjutor and successor, Bishop Challoner, was also humble and self-effacing, while Bishop Prichard was too far away in the West and out of touch with affairs, even if he wanted to act prominently. In particular Stonor took the lead in the matter of the very long drawn out dispute between the bishops and the regulars, which was settled first by the Decree of 1745, and then by the brief *Apostolicum Ministerium* of Pope Benedict XIV. After quitting London he lived at Heythrop, Oxfordshire, placed at his disposal by the Earl of Shrewsbury (his relation), and at his family estate Watlington Park in the same county, and sometimes at Stonor Park.

Bishop Giffard had named Henry Howard as coadjutor with right of succession to the London District to prevent Dr. Stonor from getting that position. The exiled pretender 'King James III' added his recommendation with the result that eventually Howard was appointed coadjutor with the right of succession by a Brief dated 30 September. The letter did not reach England until the end of November, and to the grief of all Henry Howard died on 22 November without ever having heard of his appointment. Bishop Giffard immediately chose another coadjutor, Benjamin Petre, the youngest son of a wealthy Essex family. The matter was held up by the death of the Pope in June 1721, it was eventually carried through despite the dismay and vehement protests of Petre. Stonor made vigorous protests to Rome, as he had done on the appointment of Howard, telling Mayes that it was due to his Hanoverian leanings which had offended James, and also it was a slur on him on the part of the Pope.

If Dr. Stonor hankered after the London District the very opposite was the case with the man who actually obtained it. Surely never did anyone receive the episcopate so unwillingly as did Benjamin Petre (save possibly the two Talbot brothers of the next generation). Petre belonged to that branch of the family which resided at Fidlers in Essex where they owned a large estate. He came in fact, of a very rich family - a fact which was not altogether unconnected with his appointment. He was the youngest son of John Petre, the holder of the estate, and he was also a relative of the famous Jesuit Father Petre, so prominent at the court of James II. After his ordination as a priest,

Benjamin became for a time tutor to the ill-fated Earl of Derwenwater who was eventually executed for his share in the Jacobite rebellion, but was a little over forty years of age when Bishop Giffard applied to Rome for him as coadjutor. His consecration took place on 11 November 1721. The answer to the question, why did Giffard select him as coadjutor is given by the bishop himself in his letter of application to Rome. He gives three reasons: (1) He was of ancient and noble family. (In those days this carried very much more weight, for in the eighteenth century, as in previous centuries, the aristocracy were given vastly more respect, almost veneration, than they are given today). (2) He had been educated at Douay, both as a boy and student for the priesthood, and that, from the point of view of the Secular clergy, was the hallmark of suitability. (3) He was wealthy. A very good reason in those days when there were no endowments and but a scanty, poverty-stricken flock. Nothing was said about learning or ability or experience. Petre came to fear that he had been chosen merely for those very reasons which had in fact influenced Giffard, and this caused him agonising scruples. Furthermore, fifty years later one of his successors in the London District, James Talbot, had precisely the same fears, and with equal justification, for he had the same three qualifications and the same reluctance to trade upon them.

The adjectives used by Dr. Burton in his book on Bishop Challoner, to describe Bishop Petre were "Gentle, pius, humble, timorous and affectionate". This was the man whose lot it was to govern the chief vicariate in England, to be the nominal head of the English Catholics, and to have to face all the dangers and complications of those troubled times. We cannot be surprised that the man shrank from such a task, and yet the further surprising fact is that although he himself in his letter to Rome touches the very depths of self-criticism and disparagement, yet strangely enough everyone else, despite his inactivity and indecisiveness, speaks of him in terms of highest praise. Obviously there must have been real merit in him, and much firmer character than one can assess at this distance of time.

Be that as it may, having been forced by great moral pressure to undergo his consecration, he at once set about seeking his deliverance from a position which he had never desired and greatly feared. As early as November 1722, he wrote both to Mayes and to the Pope himself, asking to be allowed to resign after only one year as a bishop. Mayes responded with a long letter, supporting and encouraging Petre but refused to submit the petition to the Pope. These appeals by Bishop Petre to be allowed to resign and return to his desired role as a "humble missioner" continued for some years. Yet despite his scruples and lack of self confidence Witham told Mayes in 1728: "Though Bishop Petre makes great complaint of his heavy burden, and has writ strange letters of his own incapacity to the nuncio at Brussels, and to

Propaganda, yet at the same time (he) acts with a great deal of fervour and firm zeal, instructs every Sunday to the satisfaction of all that hear him, keeps good order in all the Ambassador's Chapels, keeps under him the Irish priests and Regulars, who thereupon make all the complaints they can about him, tho without reason".

The bishop was indeed a puzzling character. On the face of things his extreme diffidence and his hatred of public attention and of active occupation seem to mark him out as quite unsuitable for his position, especially in those stormy and difficult days. In fact he appears to have been of little practical help to Bishop Giffard, and when he himself succeeded to the vicariate he obtained a coadjutor (Dr. Challoner) as soon as he could and then promptly retired to his family estate in Essex for the rest of his life, leaving the active control of the London District to his coadjutor. Even so he received expressions of high praise from those who ought to know. Perhaps the only reason Dr. Giffard originally chose him and consistantly refused to allow him to resign was to block Stonor, or even a Regular from being appointed in his place. If not, then Bishop Petre remains a complete enigma.

Extracts from: *The Early Vicars Apostolic of England* by Dom Basil Hemphill OSB published by Burns & Oates, London

Chapter Five

Catholic Life in Penal Times

IT is difficult for the modern reader to realise the conditions of life for Catholics during the long, weary penal times, but some knowledge of them is necessary for an appreciation of the difficulties and labours of the bishops and clergy.

What of the daily life of the bishops? Inevitably that of the vicar apostolic of the London District, living as he did in cheap and obscure London lodgings and concerned mostly with the slum districts of the city, differed considerably from that of his three colleagues in the country. The other three vicars apostolic, like the vast majority of the clergy, lived in the country houses of the Catholic nobility and gentry, and whose generosity was the mainstay of the Catholic missions up and down the land. For there were no public chapels in those days in the towns, and hence the faithful tended to congregate in the neighbourhood of the large Catholic houses in which alone they could practice their religion. A very great debt is owed to those old Catholic families in all parts of the country, the more so since they themselves were almost crushed by penal taxation for the crime of being Catholics, were systematically ostracised by their Protestant neighbours and were excluded from all public service under the Crown. No career was possible for them or their children, while in addition they were persistently fined large sums of money for refusing to attend the Protestant churches. But in spite of all these disabilities and sufferings they for the most part, despite some apostasies due to the economic and social causes already mentioned above, endured for generation after generation with a loyalty and a courage that is beyond all praise. In their houses then, the bishops found refuge and from them they were able to govern their Districts and to make their constant tours of inspection. It is a strange and moving picture that they present to the modern eye, and one can but marvel that the Church, persecuted and driven underground, in such circumstances survived at all in England.

The bishop of the London District, even though his District stretched as far west as Dorset, always lived in London excepting those periods of special danger when he had to flee to some refuge in the country. He was exposed to the danger of arrest and imprisonment far more than was the case with his provincial brethren. It has already been mentioned that Bishop Giffard was imprisoned many times, and narrowly escaped on several other occasions, he himself wrote: "The continual fears and alarms we are under is something worse than Newgate. In one prison I lay on the floor a considerable time, in Newgate almost two years, afterwards in Hertford jail, and now daily expect a fourth prison to end my life in". To another correspondent he wrote: "Where to get a lodging in London, such as I may admit people with security, and transact business, I cannot tell. I do all I can, and suffer a great deal, having no certain abode, but forced sometimes to change lodgings four times in a week, and once lodged at four different places in four days time. One poor garret is a palace, cathedral, table of audience, dining room, bedchamber and often kitchen too. I thank God, this is my glory and my joy. I would not change my condition for that of the greatest cardinal".

Similarly, Bishop Challoner used to preach in an Inn with an unsavoury reputation in Holborn, for he had no chapel, and the congregation sat around him at table, each member being supplied with a pipe and a mug of beer, in order to disguise what was really going on. Except in the chapels belonging to the foreign embassies, Mass was said only with the greatest secrecy, generally at dead of night and in an obscure attic to which entrance was gained only after a secret password had been given. Small wonder, then, that Bishop Challoner, writing to a newly appointed bishop (John Hornyold of the Midland District) whose humility made him shrink from such an honour, remarked: "After all, prelacy in our circumstances has nothing in it to be coveted but the benefit of more labour and trouble and the opportunity of serving a greater number".

This secrecy in carrying out the functions of the Church and the work of the clergy was essential throughout the eighteenth century, just as much as it had been for the previous one hundred and fifty years, owing to the ever present need of not fanning into flames the smouldering hatred of the ancient Catholic religion which was liable to flare up at the slightest provocation. Naturally it was essential for priests to conceal their real occupation and consequently to adopt the dress of laymen, and indeed it was not until after the restoration of the Catholic hiererarchy in 1850 that the wearing of clerical dress became general. One has but to recall the Gordon Riots which broke out as late as 1780 in furious protest against the measure of relief, meagre though it was, which was given to Catholics by the first Relief Act, to realise how deep seated and unreasonable, was the distrust and hatred of the Church amongst English Protestants, and the great need for caution on the part of Catholics.

One form which this caution took was the use of aliases by the clergy, very many of whom were known by two or even three names. Another was the code-writing so common at the time, of which some examples are given elsewhere in this book. A few instances of the aliases may be mentioned here. The Pope was often referred to as Mr. Abraham, or sometimes as the Old Gentleman, Catholics in general were mentioned in letters as Mrs Yaxley's family, Queen Anne was Mrs Hobbs, Bishop Giffard was Cousin Bona, Bishop Diconson was Mr Eaton, Bishop Williams was Thomas Rogers and Bishop Challoner signed himself J. Fisher. Bishop Smith of the Northern District had at least four aliases of which the most commonly used was Tarlton. The Jesuits were sometimes called Birlies or Etiamites, while Rome was nearly always Hilton, and a District and its clergy were the bishop's wife and family. Bishop Smith was always particularly guarded in his letters, so that some of them are by no means easy to understand even with a knowledge of the coded language.

The saying of Mass was of course a criminal offence, punishable by the severest penalties, and so for a very long period it could only be done in the utmost secrecy. Here is a contemporary description of such a Mass which was written by a Mrs Marlow about the year 1771. (This account was printed in Dr. Burton's pamphlet on Bishop Talbot, CTS Tract No.49):

"We started from our lodgings about five in the morning, to be present for the first time at a Catholic religious service, or at prayers, as it was generally called, for the word Mass was scarcely ever used in conversation. We arrived at a public house in some back street near the house in which Mr. Horne (the priest) resided. I felt rather frightened seeing some very rough looking people as we passed through the entrance, tho all were very quiet. We hurried past them, but I could not help clinging to Marlow, having an undefined fear of what was going to happen. We mounted higher and higher. At the top the door of a garret was unlocked and we saw at the far end what seemed a high table or long chest of drawers with the back turned towards us. A piece of carpet was spread before it by a young man, who pointed us to our seats. In a few minutes the door opened, and the Venerable Dr. Challoner, accompanied by Mr. Horne and another priest entered the garret, the door of which was secured inside by an assistant, who then unlocked some drawers behind what, I found, was to be used as an altar, and take out the vestments and other things for the service.

Soon after we heard the door-key turned and several rough footsteps entered the garret, some gentle taps and words were exchanged between a powerful looking Irishman who kept his post close to it, and those outside, which were passwords of admission. The key was again turned each time anyone entered, and just before the bishop vested himself to say Mass, bolts were drawn also, and no one else could pass into the garret. In the meantime the young man had prepared all that was needed at Mass, taken from behind what was used for an altar, which was covered with a white linen cloth. A crucifix and two lighted candles were placed on it and in the front was suspended a piece of satin damask, in the centre of which was a cross in gold lace.

When all was over, I heard the door key turn once more, and all the rough footsteps leaving the garret. The Bishop having un-vested, remained kneeling before us while the people departed. The two priests assisted by the young man replaced the vestments, candlesticks, and all that was used at Mass, behind the altar, locking all up carefully, and leaving the garret an ordinary one in appearance as before".

The same need for unobtrusiveness influenced the appearance of the Catholic chapels when, later on, a few were built. Until the passing of the Relief Acts towards the end of the century there were no public chapels, other than those in foreign Embassies, but when they were eventually built they were as concealed and obscure as possible, generally in back streets and with no external sign of their sacred character. Even inside their appearance would surprise the modern Catholic. There were no side altars, largely because it was not used to say Mass daily, there were no confessionals, for confessions were heard in the priest's lodgings. There were no statues, and processions were quite unknown, as also were votive candles and tablets. It is hardly necessary to add that the Stations of the Cross, as well as Benediction, were also never to be seen. Gradually all these things began to appear, chiefly as the result of the influence of the French emigre priests, after the French Revolution had broken out, but they were long regarded with suspicion by English Catholics as being 'Continental abuses', and it was not until those who had been brought up under the penal laws had died off that the new generation learned to adopt such things whole heartedly and eventually to take them for granted.

Catholic centres existed because of the location of local Catholic gentry and the faith had almost died out in the towns. Unhappily quite often such families either died out, moved away or even apostatised. The faith was dwindling steadily in those dreary days, but though many fell by the wayside under tremendous economic and social temptations held out to them to conform to the established religion, yet very many more held fast, and they kept the flame alive until the coming of the 'new people' whom Bishop Challoner had foretold. These were the people of the cities, the industrial classes of a later age, together with those of the Oxford Movement and of the Irish immigration of the nineteenth century.

It may be well to give at this point a more detailed account of just what were the powerful inducements to the Catholic nobility and gentry to turn Protestant, in other words to outline some of the penal laws. Some of these have already been mentioned. From as far back as the reign of Elizabeth I, it was high treason, with the punishment of hanging, drawing and quartering, "For any man who is proved to be a priest to breathe in this kingdom" and a later, rather milder statute of William III condemned any priest convicted of exercising his priestly functions to perpetual imprisonment. It was also high treason to reconcile anyone to the Church. Under both William III and Queen Anne, many of the most savage enactments were passed, and at the time we are considering, (the reign of George I) Bishop Stonor reported to Rome that the chief hardships endured by Catholics were (1) Exclusion from all places of trust and profit in the State, so that Catholic families have no way of repairing their losses nor others of acquiring fortunes (2) The Act of 1700 allowing a Protestant next-of-kin to dispossess the Catholic heir of estates, and making Catholics unable to acquire landed property by gift of purchase (3) The double land tax applied only to Catholics (4) The confiscation of all property given for the support of priests . Thus the State "Contrives to starve those whom it ceases to persecute". He added that there was reason to fear that sequestration of two-thirds of all Catholic property, which had recently been threatened, might soon become law. The Act 1 Geo. 1, c.50, appointed a commission "To enquire of the estates of certain traitors and popish recusants, and of estates given to superstitious uses, in order to raise money out of their security for the use of the public", and by 9 Geo. 1, c.18, £100,000 was to be assessed on Catholics above 18 years of age, over and above the double assessment of the land tax. For the rest, the laity were cut off from public life and debarred from sitting or voting in either house of Parliament. In addition to the disabilities mentioned by Stonor above, they were forbidden to keep arms. They could be deprived of any horse worth more than £5, they could not hold office in the army or navy, or practice as a barrister, doctor or schoolmaster, they could be fined if they sent a child to be educated abroad, and there were also heavy fines for non-attendance at the Protestant church. Thus in effect they were forced to live the life of recluses, shut away on their estates, with no outlet for the activities and ambitions of the younger sons. In addition there were severe penalties for performing or attending any Catholic religious service, and for educating their children as Catholics at home. Well might Burke declare that the penal code "Was a complete system, full of coherence and consistency, and as well fitted for the oppression, impoverishment and degradation of a people and of the debasement in them of human nature itself, as ever proceeded from the perverted ingenuity of man". The verdict of Charles Butler, the celebrated lawyer of the mid eighteenth century, was that the penal laws "Depressed Catholics so much below their legitimate rank in society that they hardly entered with the look or attitude of free men into the meetings of their Protestant neighbours. Such was their situation, to avail myself of Mr. Burke's strong but just expressions, that they not only shrank from the frowns of a stern magistrate, but were obliged to fly from their very species, a kind of universal subserviency that made the very servant behind their chair the arbiter of their lives and fortune".

It is true that many of these laws were not enforced as time went on, but they were always liable to be put into force at any time, and so long as they remained on the Statute Book Catholics could have no peace of mind and no security. Even after the passing of the first Relief Act in 1778, Joseph Berrington the well known priest of the time wrote: "Shall I sit down satisfied because the good humour of a magistrate chooses to indulge me, whilst there are laws of which any miscreant has daily power to enforce the execution? My ease, my property, and my life are at the disposal of every villain, and I am to be pleased because he is not at this time disposed to deprive me of them. Tomorrow his humour may vary, and I shall then be obliged to hide my head in some dark corner or to fly from this land of boasted liberty. It is surely better not to be, than to live in a state of such anxiety and dreadful uncertainty"

It should be remembered that Catholics were forced to live in this condition for three centuries. Is it any wonder that they became a people fleeing the light, of whom little was known and of whom the wildest and most absurd stories was believed? The reign of George II was the first since the Reformation in which no fresh laws were enacted against Catholics, yet in that reign were many prosecutions of Catholics for the practicing of their religion and the smouldering hatred and fanaticism found its outlet as late as the Gordon Riots of 1780. Even after the passing of the second Relief Act in 1791, which swept away most of the penal laws, all chapels had to be registered and the clergy had to take the oath of allegiance, no chapel could have bell or steeple, cassocks or habits could not be worn out of doors, and still no Catholic might sit in either house of Parliament or vote at elections, or be a judge or barrister, and the army and navy were still barred to them. Catholic marriages still had to be held in Protestant churches, and Catholic funerals were forbidden. Actually the first *repeal* of the penal laws did not take place until 1844, for the Relief Acts of 1780 and 1791 had not repealed the laws but merely made exceptions to them, allowing further latitude. The laws still remained on the Statute Book, and anyone denying the spiritual supremacy of the king was still liable to forfeiture of all goods, and if the offence were repeated, to punishment by death for high treason.

It is small wonder if, anyone enduring all this for generation after generation, a few families fell away and conformed to the State Church, but the great majority of English Catholic families who maintained their fidelity to the Catholic faith following the Reformation held fast during penal times. They were the 'hard core' on which the bishop depended, from this fact arises another peculiarity of seventeenth and eighteenth century life, the strange position of the clergy in relationship to the landed families. As already explained, it was these families who formed the backbone to the system, for on them the clergy had to rely for financial support. Each Catholic country house would have its own resident priest, and this priest was chosen and appointed, not by the bishop of the District, but by the head of the family, and upon this patronage depended the success of the mission. Neither bishop or priest could afford to offend such a patron, and so the squire or nobleman chose his own chaplain without reference to the bishop, so that the latter frequently did not even know where a given priest might be. A further result of this was that the priest came to be looked upon merely as an employee, and in fact was very often employed in a purely secular position such as estate agent or secretary. Much therefore depended on the personal character of the landowner as regards the treatment received by a priest, and if the former were autocratic or harsh the priest's lot was extremely unenviable. He could be dismissed by his employer without any reference being made to the bishop, and sometimes he even had to wait at the altar before starting Mass until his employer should say to him, 'Mr. . . you may begin'.

Of course this subservient position also served the very necessary purpose of helping to conceal the fact that any priest was living there. The liberty and possibly even the life of both priest and employer depended on the authorities being unaware of the presence of the priest on the estate. Partly for reasons of security, and partly in order to gain a means of a livelihood, many priests were forced to take up purely lay occupations. In some cases none but the squire and a mere handful of the faithful would have any idea that an apparent layman whom they had known for twenty or thirty years was in reality a priest. Then too, many of these families had special ties with one or other religious Order and so always chose their chaplains from those Orders. This practice was on the one hand sometimes a cause of irritation amongst the Secular clergy who were thus debarred from these positions, and on the other hand a source of difficulty for the bishop who, of course, had no control over the movement of the Regulars. This custom and general control exercised by lay patrons was never questioned either by clergy or by the vicars apostolic, all realising the special rights possessed by the laity by reason of the great service they performed for the Church by making the missions possible at all. In the curious circumstances it is remarkable that disputes and difficulties were not far more frequent than they actually were. But it will be realised that the bishops had considerable difficulties in these matters, and had to exercise much patience and tact, and the more so since they themselves were generally dependant on such a lay patron for their own board and lodging.

The position was made worse for the clergy by their extreme poverty, for few were those who had private means. Yet as a rule a priest had to keep a horse and groom, since he usually had to say two or three Masses at places far apart on Sundays, and therefore had to undertake long rides fasting. However generous the laity might be the fact remained that even the great

Catholic Lords were themselves very hard hit by the penal taxation and fines. In the eighteenth century their lot was made worse by the penalties inflicted on those who were in any way suspected of being concerned in the Jacobite Risings of 1715 and 1745. In fact the extreme poverty of the English Mission continually prompted appeals to Rome for financial help, but not much was forthcoming. Even the bishops needed much help, although most of them had private means, even if they required this mostly in order to keep their priests out of the debtor's prisons for not being able to pay for board and lodging. In this matter the London clergy were in a much worse plight than their brethren in the country who mostly lived with the local land-owner. Thus in 1702 the English agent in Rome was instructed to apply for a subsidy for the bishops, but this was not forthcoming owing to lack of re-sources in Rome itself and great expenses incurred through a recent earth-quake. There were endless demands on the scanty resources of the bishops, both from indigent priests and even from the laity. Dr. Giffard stated in 1722 that he gave away three-quarters of his own patrimony and of gifts he received. By 1720 Bishop Witham, despite his very considerable annuity, was sadly lamenting his extreme poverty which was such that he could not even pay his share of the salary due from the bishops to their agent in Rome. Lawrence Mayes, the agent, was in great embarrassment from the non-payment of his salary. On protesting to Giffard he was told that Witham could not afford it, but that Stonor of aristocratic birth and comparative wealth should be able to, since he could keep many servants. Mayes threat-ened to resign saying he could not carry on without financial assistance, and hoped that someone "with a better purse than I" would do the job. But in spite of his threats, Mayes continued to be agent in Rome until his death twenty years later, after having performed for forty years in that office in-valuable service to the English bishops.

What of the rank and file clergy? What sort of men were these clergy? Gen-eralisations can be misleading, and the clergy were of many varying types, just as they are today, but on the whole in those days they inevitably suffered from the defects produced by their special mode of education. Necessarily all priests had to be educated overseas, since nothing in the nature of a seminary could possibly exist in England at that time. Even long after the more savage features of the penal laws had ceased to be inflicted, so that the chances of execution or even imprisonment had become slight, those laws were still on the Statute Book and might be enforced at any time. It was therefore still illegal to bring up a child in the Catholic religion, or even to send him abroad for the purpose, let alone to train him for the actual priest-hood. So it followed that during their formative years the English clergy were inevitably completely out of touch with their compatriots. Most of them spent at least twelve or fourteen years in the English seminaries on the

75

Continent, (Douay, Lisbon, or Rome for the most part), first as schoolboys and then as students for the priesthood, and so when in due course they returned in secret as priests to this country they were cast in a very definite mould. At the same time their long segregation from the ways of ordinary life inevitably meant they were lacking that polish as well as that knowledge of contemporary affairs and familiarity with secular branches of learning that were to be found in most of their acquaintances in England. What they lacked in this respect many of them made up for by their holiness and zeal, but at the same time these defects undoubtedly did to a considerable extent hamper them in their work by making an unfavourable impression on the laity.

Complaints on the issue of the lack of polish and secular knowledge on the part of the clergy abound in the letters and manuscripts of the time, not merely from the laity but from the clergy themselves, and especially from the bishops. Bishop Giffard, Bishop Stonor and Bishop Challoner, to name but a few, frequently lament the unsuitable type of man turned out by the ecclesiastical colleges, and methods of reform in the system of training, with suggestions that more suitable candidates should be chosen, were constantly put forward by various vicars apostolic. For instance in an official document drawn up in 1737 by either Bishop Petre or his coadjutor Bishop Challoner, entitled *Praesens Status Missionis Anglicanae,* the language employed is very outspoken. After saying that the leakage caused by the apostasy of so many was largely the fault of the landed gentry (for reasons already mentioned), the document goes on to say that the clergy are even more greatly to blame, and that there could be many more conversions if there were suitable priests. Many have no zeal for souls, but seek their own ends, many are rough and ignorant and give scandal. The remedies suggested are greater care in the selection of candidates for the priesthood, reforms in the administration of the colleges abroad, especially Rome and Valladolid, that these colleges should only have students who have been sent by the vicars apostolic, and that the course of studies should be better adapted to the English mission. The opinion of Joseph Berington, was similar: "Our priests in their general character are upright and sincere, but narrowed by a bad education, they contract early prejudices which they very seldom afterwards deposit. Moderately skilled in the Latin and Greek languages, they know nothing of their own, nor do they sensible of their manifold deficiencies till it be too late to attempt improvement . . . A priest is seldom seen in the company of Protestants. The Catholics he is told to herd with either are unable to improve him, or if able, are seldom willing. Contracted in his circumstances, he has not the means of drawing information from books, and unfashioned in the forms of elegant life, his company is not asked for. Thus denied all occasion of improvement, if his native disposition will allow him, he soon sits down sullenly contented and looks no further. If he ever had ambitions disuse will in a short time lay them asleep, and at 60 he will be found the same man as at 25. It is the complaint of our gentry that priests are rough and unsociable, they would be less so, perhaps, if their patrons were less proud, less ignorant, and less imperious. On both sides are faults which should be corrected".

Elsewhere the same writer sums up the Douay clergy: "They are open, disinterested, religious and laborious, steady in the discharge of their duties, fond of their profession and emulous of supporting the character of primitive clergymen, but they are austere in their principles, confined in their ideas, ignorant of the world, and unpleasant in their manners"

All that does not amount to much in the way of condemnation, it boils down to little more than a lack of culture and freedom from worldliness, the latter of which, at any rate, is no bad thing. We have to remember too, their extreme poverty, and the hunted or at least, the obscure lives which they had to lead. It should not be forgotten that these men had in many cases sacrificed bright prospects of a worldly life in order to become priests, and were therefore motivated solely by supernatural zeal. The Catholic Church was at least spared the snare spread for the Church of England in that it provided no enticing bait of a comfortable living for a younger son who never professed to have a religious vocation. For the priest, his occupation was necessarily a spiritual vocation, for it offered no sort of worldly career or prospects whatever. Still the fact remains, that the vicars apostolic were for generations much disturbed by the deficiencies in the training given to aspirants to the priesthood, and made no bones about roundly saying so on many occasions.

Bishop Stonor, although opposed by his brother bishops, did endeavour to introduce Irish clergy. The president of Douay wrote to Rome and indicated that there were about 400 Irish priests in Paris alone. That was probably more than the total number of both Secular and Regular priests put together in all England. Yet the few Irish priests who did get into England were unwelcome to the bishops. Bishop Giffard writing to Mayes in 1708 referred to the Irish Regular priests in London and tried to have them stopped. The Church in the eighteenth century was composed almost entirely with the dwindling remnant of the English Catholics.

There were about 65 priests living in London in 1685, that was of course during the brief reign of James II, and includes Regulars as well as Seculars. It is surprising to find a letter to the Pope, dated 1704, stating that there were then 100,000 Catholics in England with nearly 100 priests. This is certainly an exaggeration as regards priests. Dr. Betham told Mayes two years later that there were about "four score thousand" Catholics in England, adding "they are rather increasing, than lapsed, since we had bishops" and he estimates the number of priests to be only 400, made up of 250 secular priests, 70 Jesuits, 40 Benedictines, 30 Franciscans, 12 Dominicans and a few Carmalites. Forty years later, Bishop Challoner reported to Rome that the London District numbered 25,000 with 60 priests, excluding regulars, and said there had been no perceptible change in the past 30 years. The same figure was given by his successor, Dr. Talbot, who however said they were diminishing and that four-fifths of them were in London, with the remainder scattered over ten counties. The priests then numbered about 130, of whom half were Seculars, and two thirds of them were in London. Indeed under this bishop the number of missions, priests and laity steadily fell (not through any fault of his), and complete extinction before very long seemed inevitable. So how did the figures drop that Joseph Berington in 1780 estimated that there were only about 56,000 Catholics in all England and Wales, distributed as follows. The London District 25,000, the Midland District 8,500, the Western District 3000 (with less than 50 priests), and the Northern District 20,000 (with 167 priests). As the population at this time was about six millions these figures mean that Catholics numbered well under one per cent of the whole.

Berington wrote just as the position of Catholics was at its worst. It was the nadir of Catholicism in England. From then on matters began to slowly improve with the passing of the Relief Acts, and the numbers began steadily to increase. The tide had begun to turn, and the inherent Divine vitality within the Church was again beginning to tell, so much so, indeed that although only scanty relief had been given, yet when Bishop Douglass of the London District died in 1812 the Catholics in England were estimated to be 400,000.

In the Western District the story was worse, but that District had always lagged far behind the others. Although the West had fiercely resisted the Reformation and in the later sixteenth and early seventeenth centuries was noted for its Catholicity, the picture had gradually but radically changed, largely owing to the tragic shortage of priests. This situation could not be remedied, and the faith almost died out in those parts, and the area was later captured by a militant nonconformity. In 1773 Bishop Walmsley reported to Rome that there were only 750 Catholics and nine priests in all Wales, and only seven public chapels. In 1802 there were only two Catholics in Cardiff, and the report by Bishop Collingridge (1809-1829) stated that in 1813 there were but two missions in Wales, Brecknock and Holywell.

In the Northern District, matters were very different. It had all along been the most Catholic part of the country, and in 1787 Bishop Matthew Gibson gave the total for his District as 33,685, with 141 priests half of them Seculars and half Regulars. No less than 23,000 of them were in Lancashire. It is curious to discover that in Lancashire the average flock for each priest was 371, while in Yorkshire it was 117. In the Midlands, which comprised fifteen counties, Catholics numbered less than 15,000 in Bishop Milner's time (1803-1826), and as he himself said "It is a long way from Ipswich to Oswestry".

During the first half of the eighteenth century, one of the greatest problems for Catholics was that of deciding what their attitude was to be towards the rival houses of Stuart and Hanover. This was no theoretical matter, on the contrary it was intensely practical, for it seemed at one period that the whole future of Catholics and their religion was involved in it. There was no doubt where the loyalties and affections of the great majority of Catholics lay, but could they afford the luxury of sentiment or must they bow to the stern facts and thereby ensure their survival and the preservation of their worldly goods? It was a cruel dilemma, and it is not surprising that great passions were roused.

All the vicars apostolic of the period, save one, were ardent Jacobites, and so also were the great majority of the clergy and laity. The last Stuart King was an ardent Catholic, he had greatly ameliorated the lot of the downtrodden Catholics of his kingdom. In the end he even forfeited his throne for his devotion and fidelity to the Catholic Church. It should be said also that in his attempt to remove legal embargo from Catholics, it was not at the expense of his Protestant subjects, he wanted freedom of conscience for his people in the choice of their religion. Catholics saw him as the lawful King and could not support the usurping Dutch William, or enthuse over the German Protestant George.

The one exception amongst the bishops was Dr. Stonor, he took the coldly realistic view of the matter. Putting aside all question of sentiment and romantic attachment to the Stuarts, he held in a word that the Stuarts were finished with, that they had no prospect whatever of regaining the throne of England, that Catholics had therefore nothing to hope from them, and that consequently it was madness for them to penalise themselves and probably ruin the prospects of the Church in England for the sake of mere sentiment. The matter was too serious for that, and if they wished to escape utter ruin the English Catholics must face facts and come to terms with the all powerful Hanoverian Government. His case was a strong one and to modern eyes eminently reasonable, but in the early years of the eighteenth century it appeared to his fellow Catholics to be utterly scandalous and treasonable. To them the words 'the King' always meant the exiled James II, and after his death, it meant his son 'the Chevalier', while 'Her Majesty' was Mary of Modena, wife and widow of James II, and mother of 'James III'. It was to the exiled court at St. Germains that they looked for guidance, and in ecclesiastical affairs, as appears frequently in these pages, the Queen Mother and young Chevalier had powerful influence. They expected to be frequently consulted by the vicars apostolic. Naturally this state of affairs made Catholics more suspect than ever in the eyes of the English Government, and the years which immediately followed the Revolution of 1688 were marked by the passing of some of the severest of the penal laws. The Rebellion of 1715 did not help matters, and it was this state of affairs that forced Bishop Stonor to take action.

In view of the failure of the Rebellion, Stonor maintained that whereas in the past it had been best for Catholics to keep quiet under accusations so as not to add fuel to the fire, now the case was different owing to the political charges levelled against them by reason of 'the 1715' and because of the greater severity of the Government. Therefore he said; "We should publicly apologise for the past, or rather swear for the future all that we can prudently think may give satisfaction to the Government and conscience will allow". He thought that Catholics should express willingness to take a simple oath of submission and non-resistance, the oath of allegiance to George I, and the oath of abjuration (of the Stuarts). He rejected of course, the Oath of Supremacy and the Test Act, neither of which any Catholic could take. It was the Oath of Abjuration that was the really bitter pill for most Catholics, but Stonor held it to be essential for them to take it.

Almost to a man the Catholic leaders, clerics and lay, totally disagreed with Stonor. Many thought the oaths would only divide Catholics and would not appease the Government, they agreed with Bishop Giffard that no good had ever yet come to Catholics by approaches to Parliament, and that in any case it would be no help to them to take these oaths so long as they did not renounce and deny the power of the Pope to dispense the faithful from oaths they had taken. He argued that nothing less than this denial would satisfy the Government, and this denial they could not make. Here indeed was a very great crisis, for Catholics were threatened with complete ruin. Stonor thought that the Government would not press the matter of the Pope's dispensing power if Rome allowed Catholics to take the oath of abjuration. Rome therefore, he said, should give definite instructions as to what is or is not lawful, for the ruin of the great Catholic families must be averted. The letters of erroneous conscience in Catholics should be broken and punctilios (about loyalty to James) exploded. Rome did not in fact allow Catholics to take the oath of allegiance and of not acting against the Government, but it would not permit them to deny the Pope's power of dispensing from oaths. Stonor's proposals only aroused greater anger in his opponents, and while recognising the good sense of the one, we can hardly do other than admire the determined loyalty and honour of the other.

Stonor thought that "We ought to be ready to lay hold of any occasion of trying even a doubtful remedy" in view of the gravity of the occasion, and in view of the permission given by Rome to take the oath of allegiance and non-resistance, Bishop Giffard and Bishop Prichard wrote to Propaganda regarding the scruples thus raised amongst Catholics. They asked four questions: (1) Whether by swearing fidelity to George they did not deny that anyone else had a right to the throne? (2) Will it not give grave scandal if Catholics swear fidelity to a Prince of a hostile religion, while non-juror Protestants refuse to do this and maintained their fidelity to a Catholic sovereign (James)? (3) If Catholics hear of Protestant plans to restore James (e.g. by the non-jurors), are they bound to reveal these to the Government? This seems clearly to be demanded by the oath of allegiance. (4) If James invaded England, and George orders Catholics, by virtue of their oath, to join in the war against James and to kill or expel him, are Catholics bound to do this? The oath seems to oblige it.

In February 1717, Robert Witham expressed his annoyance that Mayes had written to the effect that he had nothing to say against Strickland. Witham said he would change that opinion when he heard that, in addition to other superiors, the three bishops were opposed to the oaths. Meanwhile the bishops awaited the reply from Rome to the above *Dubia*. When it came, it made no mention of the questions asked, but expressed the sympathy of Rome for the plight of English Catholics and said that Rome had urged foreign powers to order their envoys in London to do all that was possible to mitigate the persecution. In addition Rome sent a subsidy of five hundred scuti for the needs of Catholics. In May, both Ingleton and Stonor reported a slight easing of the tension. The danger of a new persecution by reason of the Rebellion seemed to have passed, owing to assurances given by Catholics to the Government. However they still have to register their estates, with a view to extra taxation being levied on them, and there is no real prospect of relief.

So matters remained the same until two years later, when Strickland suddenly took a sensational step. In June 1719, he tried to force the hand of Rome and of the English Catholics by drawing up for presentation to the Government a list of conditions on which, he suggested, the Government should agree to have mercy on Catholics. He went so far as to propose to the Government that if Catholics, including the bishops, should not agree to these conditions they should be arrested. This is an extraordinary episode and almost unbelievable coming from a would be prelate, but the facts are in the Westminster Archives in papers copied from Secretary Cragg's manuscripts in the library of the Marquis of Buckingham at Stowe. This astonishing document headed *Papers relating to a Scheme for inducing English Catholics in general to become by degrees truly and heartily well affected to His Majesty's Government*. The document declares that a delegation of influential Catholics must inform the Pope that if English Catholics are to be saved from utter ruin he must agree to four conditions. His decree allowing the Oath of Allegiance to be taken must be published and made known to all (hitherto it had been 'held dormant' by the nuncio at Brussels, Mgr. Santini). The office of Protector of England must be taken from Cardinal Gualterio, "the Pretender's publick and declared Agent", and be given to some one not obnoxious to the English Government, he must revoke the *Indults* given to the Pretender for the nomination of the Irish bishops, and must promise "To govern these missions without any communication, direct or indirect, with the Pretender. Lastly, any cleric accused of any offence by the Government shall be recalled by his superior. 'As the Emperor has engaged to bring the Pope to these terms, it will be necessary to send also a proper person to him with a letter to desire his meditation in this affair. It would suffice if these letters be subscibed by the Duke of Norfolk, Lord Stafford, Lord Montague and Lord Walgrave for the nobility, and by Sir John Webb, Mr. Charles Howard, Mr.Stonor, and Mr. Arundell for the gentry".

The whole plan was to force Catholics to give up James under threat of putting the penal laws into full execution. That Strickland a Catholic ecclesiastic should advise the English Government to arrest Dr.Giffard is surely unpardonable. In the event after a dramatic meeting at Strickland's house at which feelings and words ran high, the three noblemen refused to sign the document. We are irresistibly reminded of William Cecil or Walsingham in the reign of Elizabeth I. The same day Bishop Giffard wrote a letter giving an account of an attempt to arrest him that morning and of his escape through the back door. Bishop Stonor was the 'proper person' designated in the above plan for taking the proposals to the Emperor, his was the figure standing in the shadows behind Strickland, and for his part in the affair he was threatened by Rome with disposition from his vicariate, but this made no difference to his attitude. He was convinced that he could win Parliamentary favour for the Catholics without prejudice to religion, and at the cost of merely taking the Oath of Allegiance. After saying that Norfolk, Shrewsbury, his brother Stoner, and the Duke of Powis had signed, he gave his view by saying that he and Strickland had got nearer to success than had anyone since Elizabeth I. However, he thought the foolish attitude of many Catholics, precluded any relief being gained this year, although he stated that he would try again later. He held that his duty to religion came before his duty of loyalty to the Stuarts, and indeed if the two were in conflict he was of course certainly right.

Fortunately for Catholics, at this critical juncture public attention was suddenly distracted from them by the excitement of the South Sea Bubble and its eventual disastrous collapse, so that they were not for the present further molested. The crisis passed, and no more was there any talk of embarrassing oaths - until the question of relief and emancipation arose many years later. By that time Jacobitism was long since dead and buried, so far as practical Catholic politics were concerned. Of course the second Rising of 1745, inevitably brought fresh anxiety to Catholics, all the more so since the attempt came so near to success. Once again they were faced with the painful dilemma and many a Catholic family was divided on the subject. But by then two generations had passed since the Revolution of 1688, and many of the younger people did not feel the same obligations towards the Stuart cause. Moreover in London the powerful influence of Bishop Challoner was exerted to restrain Catholics from joining Prince Charles, for he was very sceptical of the chances of success and he dreaded the inevitable severe reprisals which would fall on Catholics in the event of failure. Douay College was still extremely Jacobite, and soon after the Battle of Prestonpans its president, Dr. Thornborgh, wrote to Mayes, who was now very old but was still in charge of the agency in Rome: "Our news from Scotland has hitherto been very good, and we are in great hopes, and pray daily that heaven may prosper the just army of our glorious Prince, whose praises are in everybody's mouth. Besides our daily prayers for his success we sing a solemn High Mass at least once every week for the same intention".

When the Highlanders reached Derby in December all Catholics were ordered to leave London, and something approaching panic seized London and the court, and this very fact made the anger and suspicion against Catholics all the more intense when the danger had begun to recede. After the failure of Charles was manifest, persecution flared up, the prisons were full of Catholics, houses were searched over a wide area, and schools and chapels, even the embassy chapels were closed, while many people were tried for their lives and some executed. Catholics feared the worst, and they appealed for the intercession of foreign powers. Challoner himself tried to inform the Pope by a roundabout means, through a letter to a merchant in Antwerp, asking him to forward it to a M. de la Vacquerie, which was presumably a code name for somebody at Douay, as the letter was sent there, and later to Mayes in Rome. Dated 12 September 1746, it ran: "Sir, This is to let you know that your friends here are very much alarmed with the apprehension of a storm, that they are told by knowing people is gathering, and will break and fall upon them at the next meeting of Parliament. They are the more surprised at this, because they did not expect it, having given no just occasion for it, but on the contrary, having behaved remarkably well in the late troubles. This comes therefore to desire two things of you, the one that your prayers and those of other servants of God, you would endeavour to prevail with the King of Kings to deliver us, and to change the hearts of our enemies. The other, that you would with all convenient speed (for there is no time to be lost) acquaint Mr. Abraham (the Pope) by the means of Mr. Lawrence (Mayes), or otherwise, with the danger that threatens us, that he may make without delay the best interest he can at Vienna, Turin, etc., to divert by their mediation here the blow we apprehend".

Next day Alban Butler wrote a similar letter to Mayes to the same effect, but pointing out that it was necessary to distinguish between joining the Prince and being Catholics "Otherwise the Queen of Hungary will not stir". But slowly the storm died down, no new penal legislation was passed, and Catholics gradually settled down again. It was the last occasion on which a serious persecution of Catholics in England seemed really imminent.

Meanwhile, to resume chronological sequence, Bishop George Witham in the Northern District was growing old, and was extremely infirm. Already in 1715, a year before his transfer from the Midland District to the North, he had asked to be allowed to resign. There was a lack of unity amongst the vicars apostolic which prevented them in presenting one candidate to replace Bishop Witham. It is also curious that the secular clergy in those days so often had difficulty in producing a really strong candidate. Dicconson was proposed time and time again for vacant bishoprics but was constantly rejected by Rome, because he had (quiet unjustly) been accused of Jansenism, however in 1720 he became vicar-general to Bishop Stonor. In April 1725 Bishop Witham sent one last appeal to Rome, naming no one, he simply asked that a regular should not be appointed. Six days later the bishop was dead.

In the midst of all the speculation and proposals, news came of the appointment to the Northern District. The actual appointment came not, as was usual, from Propaganda, but from the Pope himself. He chose Fra. Dominic Williams a Welsh Dominican, who was prior of Bornhem in Flanders. Born in 1661, Bishop Williams was 64 at the time of his elevation, and he had the distinction of being not only the sole Dominican English vicar apostolic, but also the only regular to govern a vicariate other than the Western until the coming of Ullathorne more than a century later. Like his fellow regular, Bishop Prichard of the Western District, he was a native of Monmouthshire and also like him, he had been professor of Theology in the college of his Order (in his case that of St. Thomas Aquinas at Louvain). There he had four terms of office as rector, while in addition he had also twice been prior of the monastery at Bornhem, and twice provincial of the English province of the Dominicans, which position he occupied at the time of his elevation to the episcopate. Bishop Giffard and Bishop Stonor wrote to Rome in an attempt to have the appointment reversed, but the Pope remained firm in his determination to send the Bishop to England and on 11 July 1726, the Pope, himself, as a mark of special favour, consecrated him bishop in Rome.

The opposition to the appointment, coupled with the fact that the new Bishop was penniless, and that, as a Regular, he could not profit by the endowment of the Northern bishopric left by the late Bishop Smith for the use of Secular bishops, made it impossible for Dr. Williams to leave Rome for a considerable time. Two and a half years after the death of Bishop Witham his successor took ship from the Low Countries and landed on the Northumbrian coast. It was not an inviting prospect that lay before him, and one cannot but feel great sympathy for Dr. Williams. A stranger to his District, unasked for and unwanted, knowing no one and not even knowing where to obtain shelter, with his pockets practically empty and not even a travelling companion, the new vicar apostolic may well have felt forlorn. None the less he at once made a favourable impression on his critical flock. Bryan Tunstall (the same who had sheltered Bishop Witham and had reported his death) gave the news of his coming to Mayes on 26 December 1727: "Mr. Williams is at last come to us, and of a Regular, I always thought we could not have a properer. He landed at Shields and our Mr. Gibson (the priest) of Newcastle conducted him to Durham, where he remained about three weeks in an Inn. Our brethren and others eat with him mostly there, and took care to make the reckoning to him. But he seemed a little balked not to have a private lodging found him, but I know not anyone there qualifyed for that purpose. Dr. Rigby from Wycliffe went to pay him respects, and made him cousin D. Tunstall's compliments to him, with an invitation to pass the Holydays (the Christmas season) at his house. I have great hopes he will be easie with us, and we with him. He does not seem to be desirous of meddling with our private affairs, and in a dispute about some little matter given to him as his due, referred the matter immediately to Dr. Rigby's decision. He (Williams), upon his arrival as he had done before from Paris, confirmed all cousin George Witham's grand vicars".

Thus from the start the new bishop displayed tact and consideration. Dicconson (who was his eventual successor in the bishopric), writing twenty years later, told Mayes that Dr. Williams had himself told him that he landed in England "So well supplyed with the *unum necessarium* for this world that being landed he had not sufficient to pay off all he owed for his passage oversea, nor did he know (as he said to me) whre to go and find reception, till my good patron at Wycliffe, hearing how it was, sent over to him with an invitation to come and reside with him till he could otherwise be provided. Where being well entertained for five months, he had time to think of gathering subscriptions etc., from the Padri (the Jesuits) and the Benedictines. Afterwards he lived in the house of a very worthy gentleman, Sir Edward Gascoigne, gratis". The good patron at Wycliffe was Mr. Tunstall, this family had already sheltered Bishop Witham for some years, and Bishop Smith before him. As Dr. Dicconson calls him his own patron, it would therefore seem that four successive bishops of the Northern District were indebted to this family for hospitality".

Sir Edward Gascoigne had two houses in Yorkshire, one of which was Huddlestone Hall, six miles from Pontefract, and the other Parlington Hall, where Bishop Williams consecrated the chapel in 1733, dedicating it to the Transfiguration of Christ and to St. Benedict. The Gascoignes had strong Benedictine connections. One relative, Francis Tempest had been superior of St. Edmund's, Paris, and in July 1709 was elected Abbot of Lambspring, as well as president of the English Benedictines. An Abbess of Cambrai (Stanbrook) was a member of the family. The bishop at once set about visiting his District and was especially assiduous in confirming the people, in his first year he confirmed 1,379 persons.

Two of the four vicars apostolic were Regulars (Williams in the North and his Franciscan colleague, Prichard, in the West), while the other two vicariates Giffard of London was now 84 and his coadjutor, Bishop Petre, was constantly seeking permission to resign. Bishop Stonor was *persona grata* with most of the clergy at this time. There was constant lack of unity between the bishops, although we should remember how seldom it was that any of the bishops met each other. The distances involved, the slowness and discomfort of transport in those days, and the poverty of the bishops, all told against such meetings. In fact throughout the whole of the penal times there is no record of any organised or regular gatherings of the vicars apostolic. The majority of them must never have seen any of their colleagues, and this naturally handicapped efforts towards unity of outlook or policy.

In 1731, the indomitable old Bishop Giffard had at last to take to his bed. He retired to the convent of the Institute of Mary at Hammersmith. The Order was founded by Mary Ward, and he had been for many years devoted to this community. In England there was only one other convent, the Bar convent at York, all religious houses being illegal, it is extraordinary that these convents were able to exist at all in those days of persecution. The real nature of the houses were of course a close secret and the nuns never wore religious dress. The nuns at Hammersmith greatly venerated the aged bishop and were glad to be able to look after his last days. Early in 1733, he was now 90, he became very feeble and continued to deteriorate, he said his last Mass in the convent chapel on the Feast of Corpus Christi. He lay peacefully in the chaplain's house at Hammersmith, and continued there for nine months. He passed his 91st birthday and still he lingered. How his mind must have travelled back in those days of quite waiting. Back perhaps, to his boyhood days at Douay in the time of Oliver Cromwell, to his first chaplaincy in the house of Sir John Arundel at Lanherne in Cornwall, to that strange interlude when he was president of Magdalen College, Oxford, and then on to the wonderful scene of his consecration as bishop in the Banqueting Hall in Whitehall in those brief spacious days of James II. After that, the long weary, dangerous years, forty five of them, of his hunted and hidden episcopate under William III, Queen Anne, George I, and George II. It was during these last months that, on 26 September 1733, he made his last will. That done, he had the happiness of being able to devote himself entirely to his spiritual affairs, to commune with God, and to prepare for the end that was now close at hand. It came at last on 12 March 1734, he had been a bishop for forty six years.

In the following year the English Secular clergy made an effort to put an end to the Jesuit control of the English College in Rome. There was as usual disunity among the bishops, and much in-fighting as to who was or was not supporting the Jesuits. In the autumn of 1736, Dr. Prichard set out on his unprecedented journey to Rome, (no ruling vicar apostolic had left England for Rome, and none did again until Bishop Milner, nearly a century later). Stonor accused Prichard of going to Rome to aid the Jesuits claim. Prichard on his journey passed through Douay and Paris protesting at both places that he was no agent of the Jesuits. Dining at St. Gregory's College in Paris, the Bishop declared that the sole object of his journey was to obtain a subsidy from Rome to relieve the terrible poverty of his vicariate. Nothing came of Prichard's meetings in Rome. Dr. Dicconson left for Rome in the spring and arrived there on 13 May 1737. He reported that he had been warmly welcomed by Mayes who was in poor health, he also reported the 'lamentable' condition of the English Mission. He said the Mission never had less than 300 secular priests and sometimes 400, but now only had 156, of which the great majority were educated at poverty stricken Douay, far more than those produced by the Jesuits at richly endowed colleges. The affair of the control of the English College languished, and Mayes in despair suggested a compromise, by which Italian Jesuits should be substituted for the English Jesuits then in charge. In the end the whole matter petered out.

Bishop Williams after fourteen years in charge of the Northern District, was a very old man. The end came for him at 4 a.m. on Holy Thursday morning, 16 April 1740, at Huddlestone Hall, six miles from Pontefract, the house of his patron Sir Edward Gascoigne. The body was taken some four miles to the historic chapel of Sir Walter Vavasour at Hazelwood, between Leeds and York, where his tomb may still be seen. Now at last, the man whose name had so often figured on the *terna* of candidates was to be promoted to the episcopate. Almost thirty years earlier Dr. Dicconson had been suggested by Bishop Giffard for the Northern District. For all those years he had been considered eminently fitted for the episcopate, and it was unfortunate that he had to wait so long, by the time he was appointed he was 71 years old.

Edward Dicconson was the fourth son of Hugh Dicconson of Wrightington Hall, Lancashire, and was born in 1670. He entered Douay as a boy and was eventually professor there from 1708 to 1720, and for the last six years of that period was vice-president to Dr. Witham. From there he went to the English Mission where he was chaplain at Chillington, Bishop Giffard's old home in Staffordshire. A man of great ability, he always stood very high in the estimation of the clergy, but unfortunately he was afflicted with a stammer which prevented him from preaching. At this time he also became vicar-general to Bishop Stonor, and his administrative experience was doubtless enlarged by his four years in Rome on the affair of the English College, which afforded him an insight into Roman methods and procedure. He was consecrated at Ghent on 19 March 1741, after which he departed for England. The previous vicars apostolic of the Northern District had lived in either Northumberland or Yorkshire, but Dicconson was a Lancashire man and he transferred his headquarters to that county, settling at his family home at Wrightington.

The coming of the 1740's brought two new bishops on the scene, both of them as coadjutors, one to the Western District and the other to the London District. In the West, Bishop Prichard had let it be known for some time that he wanted help. It was generally expected that he would secure another Franciscan as his coadjutor, but in fact the Holy See turned again to the Benedictine Order and selected the Prior of St. Gregory's monastery in Douay, Dom Lawrence York. The new bishop-elect was a Londoner by birth, having been born there in 1687 during the brief reign of James II. As a boy he had gone to St. Gregory's for his schooling, and there he became a professed monk in 1705, and a priest in 1711. Ten years later he became Prior of St. Edmond's Priory in Paris. (this is the community which is now at Downside), for the usual term of four years, and then was chosen to fill the same office in his own monastery at Douay for the next four years (1725-1729). Afterwards he came over to the English Mission and was given charge of the Mission at Bath. It was eleven years later that he was consecrated bishop on 10 August 1741, at Douay. As coadjutor he continued to live at Bath, his chief, Bishop Prichard, always lived in Monmouthshire. When the Jacobite Rebellion broke out in 1745 the event had unpleasant consequences for Bishop York. A certain anti-Catholic bigot saw an opportunity for making trouble for the Bishop, he forged a letter which purported to be from Prince Charles to Bishop York, which conveyed the Prince's thanks for the help and encouragement given to the rebels, with a promise of the bishopric of Carlisle in return for the services he had rendered. This letter was taken to the mayor of Bath, who although realising that the letter was a forgery, he suggested that it would be prudent for the Bishop to retire from Bath for a time. This Dr. York did, but was soon able to return from his exile.

Bishop Prichard died at Perthyre on 22 May 1750 at the estate of the Powell family with whom he had lived for so long. He had been 37 years a bishop and had reached the age of 81. His tombstone may still be seen under the communion table of the local Protestant parish church at Pertyre. The death of Bishop Prichard automatically made Dr. York vicar apostolic of the Western District. In 1756 he wanted to have a coadjutor and put forward the name of fellow monk Charles Walmesley. Rome had instructed the bishops to name two Seculars and two Regulars for the vacancy, but Dr. Stonor suggested to the other bishops that they should refuse to name any Regular, and this idea had the approval of both Bishop Petre and his coadjutor Bishop Challoner. The names put on the *terna* by the bishops were Charles Howard, James Talbot, (later vicar apostolic of the London District) and Christopher Stoner. In the event it was Walmesley who was appointed. The attitude of the bishops in this matter may well have been influenced by the recent issue of Pope Benedict XIV's famous Bull *Apostolicum Ministerium* of 30 May 1753, which at last put an end to the very long standing dispute between the bishops and the Regulars over the question of the rights of the Regulars, and which reinforced the Decree of 1745 on the same subject.

Bishop Stonor was instrumental in obtaining the decree. In 1753 Stonor with advancing age petitioned for a coadjutor, he chose Challoner's friend Rev. John Hornyold. Bishop Stonor was imperious and autocratic, he was an aristocrat of the old school and remained so to the end. He felt he belonged, by right of birth, to the governing class and in his later years he was sometimes accused of writing or saying hard things or of acting in a dictatorial manner, but no one ever questioned his honesty or dignity. Described by Dr. Burton in his *Life and Times of Bishop Challoner* as "The indomitable old vicar apostolic of the Midlands", and as "imperious, autocratic and masterful". He was certainly in his old age an impressive figure. Born in 1678, he died at Stonor Park (Kirk says he died at Heythrop) on 29 March 1756, and is buried there.

In this chapter we have come across the word Jansenism. What is Jansenism and how did it come about? In the period between the Fourth Lateran Council and the Council of Trent, the theory of mortal sin developed. The name mortal was used because it required penance before one could receive Holy Communion. The definition of mortal sin developed further until it no longer was connected to the Sacrament of Penance and Eucharist, it became synonymous with eternal damnation. Confessors and penitents tortured themselves in scrupulously categorising the number and types of sins and the circumstances that may or may not alter them. The confusion about the possibility of sacrilegious confession and communion was the abiding fear of life, death and salvation.

From the middle of the 17th Century the Latin Church developed a religious fear. Through the legacy of original sin man was corrupt and was inclined to evil. They regarded God as fearsome and who hated sinners. Everyone became obsessed with death, judgement and hell. The ensuing moral rigorism created fear in everyone, priests refused absolution and the laity developed an aversion to Holy Communion.

Laxism crept into the Christian way of life which led to a rigorous reaction, becoming excessive, mainly through the teaching of Cornelius Otto Jansen (d.1638). He had written a book, the *Augustinus* when he was rector of the University of Louvain. This work dealt with the doctrine of grace in St. Augustine. Jansen, a learned but mis-guided professor, who died as Bishop of Ypers, constantly doubted his salvation and believed God to be an awful and despotic diety. Jansen focused on the most pessimistic of Augustine's theories that free will does not exist, human beings are incapable of doing good, grace alone acts, moreover, Christ did not die for everyone. God arbitrarily chose certain privileged souls to whom he grants salvation and to no one else. Jansen's friend and accomplice Jean du Vergier de Hauranne, the abbot of Saint-Cyran (d.1643) introduced this tragic Christianity to his penitents, the nuns of Port-Royal-des-Champs near Paris. Jansenist morality centred on the belief that the only source for Christian life is tradition, that is to say Holy Scripture interpreted according to the simple rules of the Church fathers, and above all St. Augustine. The source of Jansenist morality was biblical, patristic and mystical, excluding all reason and experience. Jansenism caused great anxiety and people were obsessed with the requirement of angelic purity, resulting in a fearful withdrawal from the sacraments.

When *Augustinus* was published the Jesuits of Louvain protested vigorously. Rome's repeated condemnation of Jansenism in 1641, 1647, 1653, Pope Innocent XI's condemnation in 1690 and ultimately with the papal Bull *Unigenitus* in 1713, only caused the Jansenist theory to spread like wildfire throughout Europe. Owing to the liberties of the Gallican Church of France, the Roman decree was ignored. Bishops, seminary teachers and confessors thought it heir duty to treat sinners harshly. Sex between spouses, for example was declared sinful unless it was justified by the intention to procreate. The recommended remedy for sinners was to refuse absolution and consequently communion.

Antoine Arnauld the author of the famous anti-eucharistic treatise *On Frequent Communion* (1643) caused a massive desertion from Holy Communion for a century and a half in Europe, in spite of the tradition of the Council of Trent. St. Alophonsus Liguori who in Italy, with his gentle theology, was one of the most successful opponents of Jansenism wrote: "There is nothing that so ruins souls and the Church as error disguised by the specious rigour of evangelical perfection. These evildoers are chiefly Jansenists. They are more dangerous than Luther because one can be taken in by their false pretences. Above all, one must beware of Antoine Arnauld. He will sell holiness. While he appears to seek purity and perfection for admission to Communion, he has no other aims than to separate the faithful from the sacrament, the only cure for our weakness". Alphonsus taught that: "Jesus Christ alone received the Eucharist worthily because God alone is able worthily to receive God. The consensus of the Doctors is that it is better to commune every day out of love than to abstain out of respect". 1

Against the numbing influence of Jansenism their flourished, between 1625 and 1690, three saints, John Eudes, Claud La Colombiere and Margaret-Mary Alacoque, who between them brought and taught to the Church devotion to Our Blessed Lord in His Sacred Heart. St. Margaret-Mary experienced the Divine Presence continually over a period of some years. In 1673 her devotion to His passion was rewarded with the first of the revelations. She said Our Lord told her that the love of His Heart must spread and manifest itself to men and women by means of her, and that He would reveal the treasures of its graces through her, His chosen instrument and the disciple of His Sacred Heart. During a period of about eighteen months the apparitions continued at intervals, explaining and amplifying the first revelation. She said Our Lord told her that His Heart was to be honoured under the form of a heart of flesh, represented in a way now familiar to Catholics throughout the world. This was to be done by frequent loving communion, especially on the first Friday of each month and by an hour's vigil every Thursday night in memory of His agony and desertion in Gethsemane.

The final revelation was made within the octave of Corpus Christi in 1675, when Margaret-Mary recalled Our Lord saying: "Behold the heart which has so much loved men that it has spared nothing, even exhausting and consuming itself in testimony of its love. Instead of gratitude I receive from most, only indifference by irreverence and sacrilege and the coldness and scorn that men have for me in the sacrament of love". Then He asked that a feast of reparation be instituted for the Friday after the octave of Corpus Christi, now the feast of the Sacred Heart. 2

(1) Extracted by permission of the publisher from *Moral Choices*
The Moral Theology of St. Alphonsus Liguori by Theodule Rey-Mermet C.SS.R
translated by Paul Laverdure Copyright © 1998 Liguori Publications
Liguori, MO 63057, USA
(2) Extracts from: *Butlers Lives of the Saints* edited by Herbert J. Thurston and
Donald Attwater published by Thomas More Publishing, Allen, Texas USA
Extracts from *The Early Vicars Apostolic* by Dom Basil Hemphill OSB
published by Burns & Oates, London

Chapter Six

Bishop Richard Challoner

THE same year, 1741, that saw the consecration of Bishop York to the Western District, brought about that of Dr. Challoner as coadjutor in the London District. With him we meet probably the best known of all the vicars apostolic, and certainly one of the greatest. He was born at Lewes of Protestant parents on 29 September 1691. His father, Richard Challoner was a wine cooper by trade and a Puritan dissenter by creed. In his youth he mixed with men who had lived through the Civil War and Commonwealth and their puritanism had descended the generations unabated. His mother, whose maiden name was Grace Willard, was like her husband a native of Sussex. She was only twenty two years of age when her son was born and was still quite young when her husband died. She was fortunate in finding a home for herself and her son in the house of Sir John Gage where she worked as a maid. Sir John Gage was the head of a notable Catholic family and in these surroundings Grace Challoner and her son became converted to the Catholic Church.

The Gage family had owned their estate at Firle since the time of Henry VI. Through all the changes of religion the Gage family always remained staunch Catholics. In the time of Queen Mary, Sir John Gage was Lieutenant of the Tower of London and superintended the execution of Lady Jane Grey. In the following reign of Elizabeth one of his grandsons was beheaded for aiding the cause of Mary Queen of Scots. During the Civil War the family sided with the Royalists and the Governor of Oxford was Sir Henry Gage who was killed at Abingdon. The family supported the exiled Stuart family and some of the Gage relations lived at St. Germain's assisting the exiled Catholic King. One member, Dr. Gage had been a few years earlier, president of the English College at Douay. A strong sense of Catholic tradition influenced the young Richard Challoner.

Mrs Challoner became housekeeper to another well known Catholic household, the Holman's of Warkworth. George Holman was a convert to Catholicism and had inherited the estate from his father in 1669, his wife was the daughter of the martyred Viscount Stafford. Lady Anastasia was deeply attached to her father, whose execution in consequence of the plots and intrigues of Titus Oates, although regarded by Catholics as martyrdom, was none the less a public and shameful death. George Holman had died in

1698, and when Mrs Challoner arrived with her son the estate was run by Lady Anastasia despite the fact she had five young children.

In this tranquil and stately English home Richard Challoner passed from childhood to boyhood. Here his earlier impressions of the Catholic faith were deepened and he came under the influence of John Gother the chaplain at Warkworth. This saintly priest, one of the leading priests of his age, undertook the education of Richard and his remarkable personality impressed itself strongly on the youthful Challoner. When he worked in the London Mission, Gother used the name Mr. Lovell to protect his identity. On the accession of James II he wrote extensively and was considered among the best of Catholic apologists.

In these favourable times he joined Andrew Giffard and Christopher Tootell, uncle of Hugh Tootell, who is better known as Dodd the historian, in opening a Catholic chapel in London. When James was exiled, Catholics again fled from persecution and John Gother became chaplain at Warlworth. This was the master from whom the young Richard Challoner learnt the faith and practice of the Catholic Church and whose memory he held in affectionate reverence throughout his life. Gother was appointed president of Lisbon College in 1704, but before they parted, he had arranged for Challoner to be sent to Douay to be educated for the priesthood. Sadly John Gother died at sea on his way to Lisbon.

Richard Challoner remained at Douay from 1705 to 1730. Ordained priest in 1717, he was vice president of the College three years later and won his Doctorate in 1727. He left for England in 1730 and the rest of his laborious life he spent in London, (except for a brief exile at Douay in 1737-38 owing to perecution in England). In 1738, Dr. Witham, president of Douay, died and Challoner was chosen to succeed him, however Bishop Petre intervened, declaring that he must have Challoner as his coadjutor in the London District. A lengthy correspondence followed between the interested parties that wanted Challoner. In the end Bishop Petre got his way, and he himself consecrated Challoner at the convent at Hammersmith on 29 January 1741.

Challoner began his long period of episcopal activity in London, for although it was not until 1758 that the death of Bishop Petre made Challoner vicar apostolic, in reality he governed the London District for all intents and purposes from the day of his consecration. Bishop Petre left practically everything to him and he himself retired to the country for the remainder of his days. Bishop Challoner's effective rule of the District lasted forty years and they were years which contained not a wasted day or an idle hour.

While Challoner was beginning his ministry in London, far away in Rome another great priest was drawing near the end of his days. Mgr. Lawrence Mayes had become agent in Rome of the English bishops as long ago as 1706. He was born at Yarm in Yorkshire in 1673 and was educated at Douay from the age of 14, and continued there as a student for the priesthood. Later he became professor of divinity until he took up his post in Rome which he was to fill until the end of his life. His success in that capacity was marked by his appointment as a protonotary apostolic in 1721, and it is of interest that in 1727 he was preceptor to the Young Pretender, Prince Charles. He had vast experience of Roman ways, routine and etiquette, had known many Popes and multitude of Roman prelates. Through his hands had passed all the most important and most secret business of the English bishops. In 1748, at the age of 75, he was ready to hand over his charge into younger hands and to give another the benefit of his   experience. He died on 23 August 1749.

Christopher ('Kit') Stonor was an ideal successor to Mgr. Mayes and had been carefully trained with a view to succeeding to the post since his first arrival in Rome as a student twelve years earlier. Nephew of Bishop Stonor and grandson of Lord Teynham, he had entered St. Gregory's College, Paris in 1739, after concluding his studies in Rome. In 1748 at the age of 36, he returned to Rome as assistant to Mayes, from whom he took over before the end of the year. He in his turn, was to hold that post until his death 47 years later.

On succeeding as vicar apostolic, Dr. Challoner's first duties were to arrange the obsequies of his predecessor and to settle his affairs. The burial service of Bishop Petre, according to the law in England, took place in public according to the rite of the Church of England. Requiem Masses were said in many other secret places performing in subterranean fashion the last rites and dirges for the dead prelate. There was also another pressing piece of business, important above all, which had to be carried out at once. Only a short time earlier, Propaganda had sent instructions to the vicars apostolic in England, reminding them of the necessity of making provision for the government of their Districts in case of death. Dr. Challoner sent the names of three priests, whom he thought worthy. Two, were the younger brothers of the Earl of Shrewsbury, James and Thomas Talbot, and William Walton.

The two Talbots were only 33 and 32 years old respectively, but were already distinguished by many qualities which made them likely to be good bishops. They had been together for the greater part of their lives, and were so alike in character. Both rejected the advantages of their high birth to serve as ordinary priests. There lives were marked with a deep personal piety and their share of any family posessions was lavished on the Church and the poor. They had no awareness that they had any special use and both had a humble distrust of public attention. The spiritual nature of their personalities endeared them to Bishop Challoner, but he was also alive to the advantage which both brothers would derive as bishops from their extensive patrimony and from the respect and deference with which men of such rank were then generally treated. The matter was entrusted to Christopher Stonor the agent in Rome. Besides approaching Propaganda in the ordinary way, he sought formal approval and assistance of the exiled Stuart King. This was probably the last of the episcopal appointments in which the royal rights of the House of Stuart were recognised by the Holy See. The matter was quickly arranged, and by Brief dated 10 March 1759, the elder brother, James Talbot was appointed to the See of Birtha *in partibus infidelium.*

In the summer of 1759, Bishop Challoner became very ill. His strength had been strained to breaking point, and now he was seized with an illness so serious that recovery seemed unlikely. None of his biographers have told us the nature of his illness. Barnard tells us that from the very beginning of the illness "He utterly relinquished all cares and concern for this world, and would not so much as hear even of any business, but committed it all to his nominated coadjutor and successor, and to his vicar general". For nearly three months he lay, resigning himself to the will of God, and maintaining close and unbroken union with Him in prayer.

Gradually he returned to good health, and although still weak, on the 24 August he consecrated James Talbot bishop. He was assisted by Dr. Francis Petre, vicar apostolic of the Northern District. Dr. Challoner was now entering his seventieth year, and was glad to have the assistance of his young coadjutor. He now spent the rest of his life almost entirely in London, the long tiresome country journeys were undertaken by Bishop Talbot. He would work every day at his London lodgings on administrative duties, receiving visits of his poor flock and filling up any spare time in compiling or translating books.

He presided at regular conferences of his priests, he always began by the usual invocation of the Holy Spirit, and then addressed the priests for half an hour to kindle in their minds the fire of divine love, and zeal for the salvation of their neighbours. Most of the clergy led good and holy lives, but there were some who were a source of scandal. Dr. Challoner found that his chief anxiety arose from the administration of the English College in Rome. The Jesuits, he said, were not sufficiently careful in refusing admission to improper persons, and far from dismissing unsuitable candidates, they allowed people to be ordained as secular priests who would have been refused admission to the Society. He wrote to this effect on 9 October 1759, to Christopher Stonor in Rome. A few months later he wrote again:

"The mission has long groaned for want of labourers to gather in the harvest, which in many places might have been very great, if we had proper workmen, in efficient number. But our misfortune is, and has been for a long time, that our labourers are but few, in proportion to the number we formerly had, and of these few a great part are of little or no service to the mission, yea rather of very great disservice. As to the source of this crying evil, in looking back, for these fifty years and more, we find our infelicity in a great measure owing to the want of being supplied, in proper manner, from that which ought to be our principle resource, as being so near the fountain head of religion, and withal so well endowed, I mean the college in your city. The number of missioners from thence, for these fifty years, has been far short of answering the revenues of the house, but this is not our greatest grievance. A great part of them that have been sent, have either been wretched fools, or scandalous livers, and several of them have even fallen from the Church".

Dr Challoner felt so intensely about this that he sought the support of the vicars apostolic of the Northern and Midland Districts to request the Pope to put the government of the English College into different hands. However, nothing came of this and the Jesuits continued to direct the college until the suppression of the Society in 1773. There were a number of instances when priests who had disgraced both themselves and the Church, gained chaplaincies with the foreign embassies in London. Challoner fought hard amidst some diplomatic difficulties. That such priests could obtain officially recognised ecclesiastical positions was clearly an abuse, yet the ambassadors were not bound to consult the bishop in appointing their chaplains. Accordingly he wrote a strong letter to the agent at Rome on 27 October 1760, complaining that unsuitable persons were "with excessive facility" appointed chaplains to the embassies "at the request of ladies or others incapable of a correct judgement. The loss that thence ensues to our holy religion", he continues, "is all the more notable, because the chaplains of the foreign ministers are, generally speaking, the only priests to whom Catholics can have recourse for the administration of the sacraments. It would be a great service done to religion, if our patrons in Rome could prevail upon the Catholic courts, which maintain public chapels in this city, (and especially under present circumstances, those of Bavaria and Venice) to give orders to their respective ministers to receive as their chaplains only persons recommended, or at least approved, by the vicar apostolic, and not to oblige him under such moral compulsion to give approbation to persons whom he deems unsuitable for that sacred office. The intension of these Catholic powers in maintaining here public chapels and salaried chaplains is certainly to keep up the exercise of the Catholic religion, and to procure the salvation of souls in the best way possible. And so they ought with equal zeal to support the authority of the ecclesiastical superiors, and take united counsel with them in the choice of proper persons to be entrusted with the care of souls".

On the whole however, the embassy chapels were conducted by the foreign ministers with proper consideration for the needs of the London Catholics. Challoner was instrumental in formalising the rules of these chapels, an undated copy of rules laid down probably for the clergy of the Sardinian chapel start by ordaining that chaplains are in the first place to obtain approbation from the bishop. The rules throw some light on the customs of the time, thus we learn that the last Mass on Sunday began at twelve, and that the notice for the week were read either before or after Mass or just before the Offertory, that on Sunday afternoons Vespers and Compline, followed by the Litany of Our Lady, were said at three o'clock, and that permission was given for Benediction, which on more solomn feasts was to be given by the head chaplain. And that when engaged in the chapel or sacristy the chaplains were always to wear cassock and surplice.

There was a crises late in 1759, the Sardinian embassy chapel, the chief place of worship for London Catholics, was burned. It was thought the inconvenience caused would only have been temporary, as the chapel was certain to be rebuilt. However, the ambassador decided it was a good opportunity to consider his own convenience and move the embassy nearer the court. In doing so he would be transferring the chapel to a part of London where another Catholic chapel was situated, thus depriving a large number of Catholics in and about Holborn of their facilities for Mass and the sacraments.

The situation was critical, and on 6 May 1760, Bishop Challoner wrote to the agent in Rome begging the Holy See to represent the matter directly to the King of Sardinia. "We are under a necessity now of applying to our friends with you to use the best of their interest with the court of Turin upon another head. You have heard, tis likely, of the chapel in Lincolns-inn-fields being burnt down by accident (Nov.30.1759), a dreadful loss for our people, it being the best known, the most frequented, and the most commodiously situated, for the body of Catholics, of all the chapels in town (the rest being mostly at the court end, and just upon the skirts of the suburbs) so that this chapel has been for above these fifty years the chief support of religion in London. The present minister, like the rest of those gentlemen, wants to be near the court, and therefore seems willing to lay hold of this occasion, and instead of furthering the rebuilding of the old chapel, to which he appears averse, or taking any effective means for establishing another, which might be equivalent in the same neighbourhood, he plainly discovers a design of letting time and opportunity slip, and then engaging his court to remove their chapel to a part of the town, where it would be of no use to the publick, and thus to abandon this neighbourhood, with infinite detriment to religion. Now we are quite convinced that the King is too religiously inclined, (of which we have had some late proofs, in the regulations he made for the chapel a little before the fire) to suffer the removal of his chapel, from a place where it has stood so long, with so much honour to his Majesty and profit to the publick, to a place where it would be of little or no service.

And therefore we make no doubt, but that upon the whole being properly represented to him from your parts, he would presently give orders for the fixing his chapel where it was, or at least in that same neighbourhood. For it would almost ruin religion in this capital to have it removed!". Ultimately the Bishop prevailed and the chapel was rebuilt on its former site.

The clergy conferences were held usually each week. The objectives were to discuss difficult cases of conscience which might occur and of encouraging younger priests to keep up their theological studies, but above all, of fostering a zealous, apostolic spirit among the whole body of the clergy. For the guidance of priests attending these conferences he drew up the following rules: "Regulations agreed upon by certain clergymen desirous to dedicate their labours to God in the London mission:

(1) Our first care shall be to endeavour to labour for our own sanctification. In order to do this we will allow ourselves, every morning, at least one half-hour for mental prayer and one quarter of an hour at night for the examination of conscience, and we will once a year make a spiritual retreat for eight days.

(2) We will neglect no opportunity of labouring for the conversion and sanctification of our neighbours, and we will particularly direct our daily prayers and sacrifices to God to bless our labours in this kind with success. We will also put ourselves and our flocks under the protection of the ever Blessed Virgin, and of the Saints, more especially of the Saints and Martyrs of this nation and often beg their intercession.

(3) We will endeavour to perform all our functions with an edifying gravity. We will always begin them with an invocation of the Holy Ghost, and particularly in hearing confessions we will keep ourselves as much as we can in the presence of God and frequently aspire to Him that He may enlighten, direct, and assist us in that difficult employment.

(4) When we shall be desired to go to the poor that are sick, we will never decline it, but if it shall happen that some other call of the same, or a more pressing nature will not suffer us to go ourselves, we will take care to procure some other proper person to go in our place, and neither will we content ourselves with once or twice visiting such as we find dangerously ill, but we will diligently attend them till they either are out of danger or die, and we will pray for them.

(5) We will have particular regard to the instruction of those under our charge and allow at least one hour in the week for catechizing children, exhorting all parents, masters, etc., to be diligent in sending them on these occasions. We will endeavour to instil into these young minds the fear and love of God, earnestly exhort them to diligence in prayer and teach them how to pray, how to hear Mass, how to prepare for confession etc.

(6) With regard to all under our care, we will as much as we can promote their frequenting the sacraments and strive to push them forward towards Christian perfection.

(7) We will endeavour to turn our common conversation, as much as may be, to edification. We will avoid all unbecoming levity, and all familiarity with persons of the other sex, neither will we frequent public houses without necessity.

(8) We will spend our evenings, as much as possible, at our lodgings, so that we may be found by those who shall want us for the sick, or be in the way for such as shall come for instruction etc.

(9) Whenever we are to treat with anyone, especially in spiritual matters, we will first, within ourselves, adore God, invoke Him, and then salute the Guardian Angels of the persons whom we treat with. In giving counsel, returning answers, or determining cases, we will also make a short pause to consult God, and in matters of greater importance or difficulty, we will take more time to consult superiors.

(10) We will exercise ourselves according to our ability, both in the corporal and spiritual works of mercy, and particularly we will endeavour to comfort the afflicted and to reconcile those that are at variance.

(11) We will prudently examine such penitents as we have reason to apprehend are bashful and fearful concerning such sins as they might otherwise through shame, pass over in their confessions, but in this we will use great discretion that we may give no occasion of sin to ourselves or them, or teach them sins they knew not before, we will also inculcate the sad consequences of bad confessions.

(12) In the administration of Baptism and in other public functions, if there be any number of persons present, we will take occasion to explain the ceremonies of the Church, and make some little exhortation to Christian piety suitable to the capacity of the auditory.

(13) We will exact nothing for our functions from the rich, and take nothing from the poor, and we will labour to remove far from us the love of filthy lucre.

(14) We will procure as much as we can, that all things about our altars be clean and neat, and that the wine for the august Sacrifice be genuine, and we will observe with all diligence the ceremonies prescribed by the Church, as well in saying Mass, as in the administration of the sacraments.

(15) We will marry none under age, without the consent of their parents, nor any that have not been first at confession, nor those that we know nothing of.

(16) We will procure Confirmation as soon as opportunity will permit for such of our penitents as have not been confirmed.

(17) We will meet once every week to encourage one another to the obser-vance of these rules, and to confer together about difficulties occurring. And the first meeting in every month we will read over these rules.

Bishop Challoner made a point of attending these conferences himself and addressing all the priests in attendance. He was emphatic that the clergy should be possessed of the true spirit of their vocation. He laboured with incredible zeal and took great pains to inspire them both in his private in-structions and his public conferences.

Challoner was a man of first rate talents and learning, yet he made little account of such talents in the choice of his missionaries, compared with the edification of their lives and their zeal for saving souls. He preferred a preacher of ordinary talents, with a great share of piety, to another of the most commanding eloquence, who was less devoted to the love of God.

In addition to his duties to his District, Bishop Challoner wrote or trans-lated many books and tracts, despite his advancing years. In 1761 he was struck again with a recurrence of a serious illness, He withdrew from all ac-tive business and turned from the world that he might die in close and unin-terrupted union with God, but again he recovered and never again until his death twenty years later was he incapacitated by grave sickness.

On his recovery he redoubled his spiritual fervour, having been face to face with eternity he valued still more the Sacrifice of the Mass and if any day it happened that he could not say Mass he was left unhappy and miserable all day.

He was determined to found a school for the education of boys whose par-ents were in more confined circumstances. Challoner knew that the need for such an institution was great. However the difficulties were immense, Catho-lics were debarred from buying land, and even when suitable premises were found, popular prejudice made it very difficult to obtain a lease. Two efforts, one in Buckinghamshire and another in Wales, both came to nothing. A third attempt was made, and in January 1762, the school was opened at Betley, near Newcastle-under-Lyme. A year later a lease was obtained from Lord Ward of Sedgley Park near Wolverhampton, who later had to defend his action in Parliament, and the school began its long career with eighteen boys. Among the Sedgley Park boys - or 'Parks' as they were called in those early years, were John Milner, the future bishop and Newman's 'English Athanasius', John Bew, future president of Oscott and afterwards of Old Hall, Roland Broomhead, the first 'Parker' to be ordained priest, John Philip Kemble, the great actor and Stephen his brother, John Eustace afterwards known as the author of the *Classical Tour in Italy,* and John Kirk, whose collections of papers and biographical sketches form one of the most impor-tant sources of information about Catholics of the eighteenth century.

The last twenty years of Bishop Challoner's life brought him little peace with challenging difficulties which taxed the saintly prelate to the limit. The Society of Jesus had entered upon its period of decline, in 1759 it had been expelled from Portugal. On 6 August 1762, the Parliament of Paris decreed its dissolution throughout France, the closing of its colleges and confiscation of its property. Unfortunately so far as the already strained relations between the English Seculars and Jesuits were concerned, these colleges included that of St. Omer which had been founded by Cardinal Allen and Robert Persons in 1584, for the education of English youth. The English Seculars were determined that they should carry on the college in place of the Jesuits.

Bishop Hornyold wrote to Dr. Green, president of Douay, on 22 December 1762: "The noise and clamours there are among us on account of the taking possession of the college at St. Omer. The good Fathers and their friends and many Catholics are shocked by it. They look upon the taking away that house from the Jesuits to be unjust and of course unjustifiable in us to receive it. I see plainly that keeping it will be the cause of everlasting jarrs and so totally destory the peace of the mission".

Ten years later the loss of St. Omer was merged in the greater trial of the suppression of the Society by Pope Clement XIV, and another twenty years saw St. Omer and Douay and the ex-Jesuits' new home at Liege also swept away by the fury of the French Revolution.

But while it raged the controversy was bitter and divided not only Secular from Regular but the laity also into two camps. The most notable thing about the whole matter, as it is seen over two hundred years later, is that all the actors in the drama seem to have been drawn into it against their will, and to have played reluctant parts, urged on by a sort of fateful necessity. Given the circumstances, it is difficult to see what course the Secular clergy could have taken other than that which they adopted, yet this course, once taken, with its attendant circumstances, it was not easy to see how the Jesuits could have avoided feeling as strongly as they did. The parties concerned realised this, and therefore the leaders on either side made considerable allowances and showed forebearance on the whole. It was chiefly among their respective supporters that bitterness and recrimination arose with bitter hard words spoken and written. Bishop Challoner's attitude alone is a striking commentary on the delicate nature of the situation. His innate love of peace and spirit of conciliation gave him sympathetic insight into the difficulties of either side. At first he was a warm supporter of the Jesuits in their troubles and he realised keenly the injustice which they were suffering at the hands of the Parliament of Paris. Eventually, however he was compelled by the logic of events to support the course of action and he approved of the transfer of St. Omer to the Seculars.

In 1764 there was a sudden rise in the persecution of Catholics. For as far back as most Catholics could remember, though subject to continual restriction and harassing disabilities, they had been free from anything approaching active persecution. The Government was tolerant, and public opinion was averse from the enforcement of the penal laws. It seemed as though the enactments against priests were over, and that the clergy, if they exercised ordinary prudence and self-restraint, had nothing to fear from the law. The reign of George II was the first since the Reformation, except for James II, in which no law was enacted against Catholics.

Common informers discovered that Catholics might be a lucrative field of operation, the no-popery section of the populace rallied to their support. Challoner wrote to Dr. Stonor shortly before Christmas 1765: "We are under a kind of persecution, raised by some, under the pretence of stopping the growth of popery, which is but imaginary, but in effect to revenge themselves on the papists, for Mr. Phillip's *Life of Cardinal Pole* at which some bishops have taken great offence, but we hope the storm will quickly blow over".

There is no clear record of how many cases in which proceedings were taken against priests, they must have been considerable. An Irish priest John Baptist Maloney was tried at the assizes at Croydon on 23 August 1767 "For unlawfully exercising the functions of a popish priest, and administering the Sacrament of the Lord's Supper to divers persons, after the manner of the Church of Rome, where he was convicted and received sentence of perpetual imprisonment". Fortunately after a few years his sentence was commuted to banishment.

It may well be imagined what distress and anxiety Bishop Challoner suffered during these repeated attacks upon his coadjutor and his clergy, and how he must have longed for a quieter state of things. But he was now growing too old to hope, and when the first suggestions came from which a Bill might be introduced for the relief of Catholics, he was very alarmed at the very idea , He thought it likely to result in nothing except the stirring up of yet fiercer emnity against the disheartened little body who were now only too thankful if they were simply left alone.

In 1767 Challoner brought out the last of his own books, a short Bible history. With the exception of pastorals and brief instructions, he wrote no more. At the age of seventy-six he probably felt that his strength must be husbanded, and that the administration of the District and the affairs which claimed his attention from so many quarters were as much as he could hope to grapple with. Despite his age his faculties were still alert, and his power undiminished. He played a dominant part in important matters until his ninetieth year. At this period he was actively concerned with the affairs of the English Colleges in France, Spain and Portugal, the administration of the

Catholic missions in Pennsylvania, Maryland and the West Indies, and the chief charge of Catholics in England. Having outlived his own generation, he was the object of unique deference and regard from clergy and laity alike. The other bishops looked to him for advice and direction, regarding him as the depository of long years of experience. When to all this was added the veneration which his sanctity inspired, we can understand something of the reverence in which he was held.

Incredible as it may seem in our present day, Bishop Challoner had responsibility for the American territory held by Britain. The territory was vast, but owing to the fact that the exercise of the Catholic religion was forbidden by law in all the colonies of the mainland except Maryland and Pennsylvania, it was not so extensive as might appear. In Pennsylvania - a province almost entirely in the hands of Quakers - Catholics were so generously treated as even to be allowed a public church in Philadelphia. In Maryland, as was natural, the Catholics were even more numerous, for it was originally a Catholic colony founded by Lord Baltimore. Incidentally, the Catholics of Maryland were later to suffer for their generosity in giving civil and religious liberty, for it became a place of refuge for Episcopalians who were persecuted by Puritans in New England, and for Puritans who were persecuted by Episcopalians in Virginia. When the Protestants gained the ascendancy they prohibited Catholic worship.

Bishop Challoner could not serve personally the thirteen thousand Catholics in Maryland and Pennsylvania, the priests that served them were Jesuits. In addition there were large numbers of Catholics in the West Indies. He appealed to Dr. Stonor the agent in Rome to speak with Cardinal Castelli to appoint a vicar apostolic for the American colonies so that Catholics could receive the Sacrament of Confirmation. The situation was also complicated since the outbreak in 1756 of the great colonial war between England and France which coincided with the Seven Years' War on the Continent. The Peace of Paris, signed in 1763, by which England was to keep her conquests in America, including Canada as well as several more of the islands, then posed the question as to whether Bishop Challoner's faculties covered these new acquisitions. Ultimately it was arranged by Propaganda that with the exception of Quebec, Challoner was to have jurisdiction over all territory ceded to England by the Treaty of Paris.

This is how these matters remained until the end of Bishop Challoner's life, greatly to his dissatisfaction, for he fully realised that under the circumstances, he could not possibly carry on the administration properly. The mainland missions were so well conducted by the Jesuits that they gave him little cause for anxiety. However the islands were in a condition that required personal knowledge which he could not acquire at so great a distance. The question bristled with difficulties as there were Irish Catholics in the ancient possessions and French Catholics in the newly acquired territory. Eventually Propaganda appointed Fr. Benjamin Duhamed, a French Capuchin as Challoner's vicar general.

Following the suppression of the Jesuits in most European countries, it followed that they were eventually suppressed in America. It was in the same year that the Boston men rose to fling the tea from the East India Company's ships into the waters of the harbour. On 4 July 1776, the Declaration of Independence of the United States of America was issued. Thus the Catholic Church in America began to be free and heralded the birth of the great American hierarchy which now holds sway over lands far more vast than England ever possessed there. It was a curious fact that King and Parliament had lost their power in America, but one obscure Englishman still maintained an authority which was recognised there. Bishop Challoner continued to issue his faculties and dispensations for the benefit of Catholics in America. It was not until some years after his death that the Jesuit John Carroll was consecrated first bishop of Baltimore by Dr. Charles Walmsley then senior vicar apostolic in England.

Two years before the Declaration of Independence in America, Bishop Challoner obtained a privilege from Rome on which he had long set his heart. This was for the restoration of the festivals of the more renowned English saints, so that their offices might once again be celebrated in their native land. By decree dated 26 July 1774, the Holy See gave permission for the restoration of twenty two festivals:

19 January St. Wulston, 1 March St. David, 2 March St. Chad, 20 March St. Cuthbert, 3 April St. Richard, 19 May St. Dunstan, 25 May St. Aldhelm, 8 June St. William, 22 June St. Alban, 7 July Translation of St. Thomas, 15 July Translation of St. Swithin, 17 July Translation of St. Osmond, 31 August St. Aidan, 3 October St. Thomas of Hereford, 10 October St. Paulinus, 12 October St. Wilfrid, 25 October Translation of St. John of Beverley, 3 November St. Winifred, 14 November Translation of St. Erconwald, 16 November St. Edmund, 17 November St. Hugh, 5 December St. Birinus.

Another incident of interest to record was the decree of the Holy See reducing the number of Holydays of Obligation observed in England, and substituting in place of the fast observed on their vigils the Wednesday fast and abstinence in Advent. Until that time English Catholics had observed, when possible, all the ancient Feasts of Obligation, including all the festivals of the Apostles, Monday and Tuesday in Easter week and some other days. In reality, it was rarely possible, especially in the case of poorer Catholics, to whom the precept of abstaining from servile work on such days was out of the question. There ensued all the disadvantages attaching to a disciplinary law which cannot be generally obeyed. These difficulties were greatly reduced by the decree dated 9 March 1777, which reduced the Holydays of

Obligation to twelve, and also transferred the fasts attached to the vigils of the suppressed feasts to the Wednesdays and Fridays in Advent. Three of the twelve, the Annunciation, Easter Monday and Whit Monday have long since been abrogated, and one, the feast of the local patron, never seems to have been observed.

In 1778 when the Government was in the midst of the American war and was threatened with a war on the Continent as well, the urgent need for soldiers brought the question of some form of relief from the penal laws, in order that Catholics could enlist. Sir John Dalrymple was sent to find out what might be done, to enable the Scottish Catholics of the Highlands to be recruited into the British army. He obtained an interview with Bishop Hay who on 18 February 1778, returned a written reply to his questions. He enumerated three impediments which he considered would be necessary. First the repeal of the laws against all those who say and hear Mass, secondly, a repeal of the statutes which allows the Protestant seller of an estate to take it back from the Catholic purchaser without returning the price paid, and those which enable the Protestant heir to take the estate from the Catholic proprietor, thirdly, the abolition of the religious references in the attestation oath, so that recruits should be required only to swear fidelity to the King and obedience to the laws of war.

These terms are important as they became the basis of all subsequent negotiations. Sir John Dalrymple obtained letters of introduction to Bishop Challoner and some of the leading laymen. On Dalrymple's return to London, he showed Bishop Hay's reply to the Prime Minister, Lord North, and to the only other two members of the Cabinet who were aware of the negotiations, Lord George Germain, Secretary of State for the Colonies, and Lord Suffolk. Initially Bishop Hay declined to send introductions to the English Catholic laity and suggested Dalrymple meet first of all with Bishops Challoner and Talbot, the latter being the brother of the Earl of Shrewsbury. Talbot was absent from London and Dalrymple's interview with Challoner was not very successful. He found the bishop "Old and timid and using twenty different questions". Doubtless it seemed to the old man of eighty-seven a strange and bold step for Catholics to take any sort of public action. The terrible scenes which took place two years later, during the Gordon Riots, proved in the event that his timidity or indeed prudence was justified.

Dalrymple was equally unsuccessful with other leading Catholics and seemed to be making no headway at all among English Catholics. Then by chance he met the man whose energy gave an impulse to the movement among the laity which went far to carry it through to its conclusion. This was William Sheldon, a young lawyer of Gray's Inn, who had been educated at St. Omer under the Jesuits. He was thirty four years of age and had the hopeful vigour and initiative required to lead so new a departure as a movement among Catholics for their relief. He was well qualified for the part he took, being a man of ability and resource. From the first he was convinced that this was a matter not so much for the bishops and clergy as for the laity. He turned the direction of affairs into other channels, to such purpose that, from this time until the Act had been passed, neither Bishop Challoner or his coadjutor were again consulted in the matter.

However, the laymen in their negotiations had overlooked one question, that of the Marriage Act, whereby all Catholics had by law to be married by a minister of the Church of England. Challoner felt that Parliament should grant full liberty of conscience for the private exercise of religion. After further consultation with Bishop Hay and his own coadjutor, they came to the conclusion that the surest way was to ask for free toleration. This view the three prelates expressed in a joint letter which they addressed to Lord Petre and the Committee which had been set up to negotiate with the Government: "My Lord, Considering of how great importance it is not to lose the present favourable opportunity of getting something essential done in favour of religion, and how much the time presses to come to a resolution, we beg leave to present our sentiments to your Lordship and the Gentlemen of the Committee on this occasion, and are of an opinion that the most effectual and speedy way would be to ask for the present, at once, a free toleration of religion in private, without any mention of particular grievances. This it appears to us, would be more easily granted, and appears a reasonable demand. It would effectually secure our persons and property against our enemies, it would require no length of time for the Parliament to come to a determination upon it. Whereas asking a repeal of particular statutes must draw out the matter to a greater length, and perhaps not be finished this session of Parliament. This is in fact, the basis of all the rest, and all other particular points can afterwards be considered and decided at leisure. The obtaining of this secures the whole, although nothing more should be done for some time. Whereas any particular repeal without this, is doing nothing at all to the main affairs, and if any change of circumstances should put a stop to the doing more, it's just leaving us where we are.

"We therefore may earnestly recommend to you my Lord and the Gentlemen of the Committee, to consider seriously what we here propose, and hope upon reflection you will find this the most proper ground on which to proceed in this affair".

The letter was signed by the three bishops, Challoner, Talbot and Hay. It is interesting to note that in the original transcript, crosses are prefixed to their names. The episcopal usage had not been customary since the Reformation and the extinction of the ancient hierarchy, but Bishop Challoner and his coadjutor resumed it in the first document issued by them after the Act had been passed. Challoner did not intervene again until the Committee requested his sanction for the oath of allegiance which they had drafted in the Bill.

Meanwhile Sir John Dalrymple met William Sheldon on 2 April. Dalrymple explained the three points suggested by Bishop Hay, and pointed out that he had communicated the whole affair to Dr. Challoner, who was alarmed at the idea, and feared the jealousy of the dissenters and a consequent persecution. Sheldon himself gives the sequel: "I strongly opposed any application to our clergy in temporal matters, the English Roman Catholic Gentlemen being quite able to judge and act for themselves in these affairs, and that my opinion was they would most heartily concur, but to make sure I would wait upon those in town. I called on the Duke of Norfolk, Earl Shrewsbury, Lord Petre, Sir Robert Throckmorton, Mr. Constable of Burton, Mr. Fermor, Mr. Maxwell Constable, Mr. Errington, Sir Edward Swinburne, Mr. Wright, Mr. Englefield, etc. They generally concurred heartily, a few demurred, but would follow the opinion of the majority of the body. It was decided to call a meeting by issuing the following card - "You are desired to meet the Roman Catholic Gentlemen now in Town at the Thatched House Tavern in St. James's Street, on Thursday the 9th instant at 12 o'clock, to consult on matters of general consequence to yourself and them". But this card being deemed by some imprudent, the following was agreed to - "Your company is desired on some particular business at the Thatched House Tavern on Saturday the 11th instant at 12 o'clock, and to dine at the half hour after four if agreeable. April 8th 1778".

On 11 April the meeting at the Thatched House took place. Lord Petre took the chair, and the resolution to address the King was passed. The address was written by Edmund Burke, and was signed in person or by proxy by 207 of the leading Catholics, Lord Linton signing on behalf of those in Scotland. At this meeting there appeared too, the first signs of dissension that later was to become serious. Bishop Hay, who accompanied Lord Linton to the Tavern, being refused admittance, Sir Robert Throckmorton bluntly remarking, "We don't want bishops".

On 1 May the address was presented by the Earl of Surrey, Lord Petre, and Lord Linton, and was favourably received. The question then arose as to what should be asked for in the Bill, and after some discussion it was decided to ask simply for the repeal of the Act of William III, the chief provisions of which were the grant of £100 to every informer who secured the conviction of a priest, bishop or schoolmaster, and the disability which prevented any Catholic from inheriting or purchasing land and rendered him liable to forfeit his estates to the next Protestant heir.

A vital provision of the proposed measure was that its benefit was only to extend to those who took a special oath of allegiance to George III, and it might have been thought that on this point, at least, the vicars apostolic would have been consulted, but Lord Petre and his colleagues were anxious to prove to the Government that in temporal matters they were independent of the clergy, so they proceeded to draft the Bill including the terms of the oath without any reference to the bishops. However it was not until the terms of the proposed oath had been settled between the Catholic Committee and the Government that the bishops were consulted.

On 14 May, Sir George Savile moved for leave to introduce the Bill. On 20 May it passed the third reading, and two days later was carried to the Upper House. On 1 June, after having been passed by both Houses without a division and with only a few amendments, it passed the third reading, and on 3 June 1778, received the royal assent.

The practical effect of this first Catholic Relief Act, though very limited, was yet considerable. All the Catholics of England could once more legally inherit and purchase land, no longer need they fear that they would be dispossessed by the nearest Protestant heir. In addition the bishops and clergy were freed from danger of prosecution by any common informer who wished to earn a hundred pounds. They were no longer liable to imprisonment for life, and if the supreme penalty of high treason still remained hanging over their heads, this was by virtue of Acts which might safely be regarded as obsolete, and which it would be impossible to enforce. All these benefits were open to any Catholic who within six months after the passing of the Act or after coming of age should take the prescribed oath of loyalty to King George.

Bishop Challoner issued a Pastoral Letter dated 4 June 1778 to the Catholics of the London District. In the letter he refers to the letter of St. Paul (1. Tim.ii) which instructed that all Christian pastors make supplications, prayers, intercessions and thanksgiving (Eucharists) for all men, Kings, and all in high station and authority. He specifically "required that all and every one of you should offer up your most ardent prayers to the Almighty for our most gracious sovereign, King George the third, and his Royal Consort, Queen Charlotte, and all the Royal family. . .this being the duty which by the law of God all Christian people owe to their respective sovereigns".

A two-fold price remained to be paid. In the first place, it induced a deep jealousy and resentment which, two years later, burst out into bloodshed, and incendiary rioting In the second, the Catholic laity of England had for the first time since the Reformation asserted themselves and acted independently of the clergy. Moreover, they had been successful, and it was not to be expected that, having once exercised power, they would forego further efforts. From Throckmorton's "We don't want bishops" it was but a step to intervening in matters with which the bishops were appointed to deal. The result was a long and disedifying struggle between ecclesiastical authority and lay independence before mutual confidence was again restored.

Bishop Richard Challoner

Bishop Challoner, old and frail and very wise from long experience of men and things, foresaw the coming dissension. In the diary of Bishop Douglass, written nearly twenty years after Challoner's death, there is a passage which refers to the refusal of the Catholic gentlemen to admit Bishop Hay to their meeting: "Bishop Hay, dining with Bishop Challoner, told him of the affront he had received from Sir Robert Throckmorton. Bishop Challoner paused, and then spoke of their disregard for their clergy, and that many of them would fall off from their religion. Bishop Hay lamented this, because as they supported priests and chapels, religion would suffer by their apostasy. On which the bishop again paused, then said 'There will be a new people'. This was considered by Bishop Hay as a prediction of what would take place in a few years". In both instances his prophecy was to be fulfilled.

Bishop George Hay had been a key figure in negotiations with the Government, acting as a close advisor to Bishop Challoner, but also chiefly concerned about the welfare of Scottish Catholics. Ultimately the Catholic Committee made a resolution to negotiate with the Government for a separate Act in regard to English and Scottish Catholics.

George Hay was received into the Catholic Church as a young man after graduating as a medical doctor. He came to London intending to go on a voyage in the Mediterranean as a ship's surgeon. He met Bishop Challoner, who was so impressed with his character that he took particular interest in him. The Bishop persuaded Dr. Hay that he should explore his vocation to the priesthood. While the young Dr. Hay was a sea, Bishop Challoner arranged with Bishop Smith at Edinburgh to keep a place for him at the Scots College in Rome. George Hay studied in Rome until his ordination in 1758. Eleven years later he was appointed coadjutor to Bishop Grant and consecrated Bishop of Daulia in 1769.

The new Bishop immediately set about the task of increasing the number of priests and students for the priesthood. He wrote to Bishop Challoner for help and received £1000. A great friendship developed between the two bishops through their correspondence, although it was to be almost twenty-years before they again met face to face in London in 1773. They agreed that after the death of either, the survivor of the two should celebrate Mass three times a week for the repose of his friend's soul as long as he was able to do so. It is recorded in Bishop Hay's biography that he continued faithfully to his agreement for the rest of his life.

The passing of the Relief Act immediately caused a re-occurence of anti-Catholic feeling, and this was deliberately fostered and systematically organised throughout England and Scotland. At the beginning of 1779 a Bill to relieve the Scottish Catholics which was similar to the English Act of the previous year was introduced into Parliament. Immediately the campaign began to bear its fruit. On 2 February rioting began in Edinburgh, when the chapel house in Chalmer's Close was plundered and burnt down. The provost and magistrates did nothing, and the Catholics and their houses were left to the violence of the mob. In the midst of the destruction Bishop Hay arrived from London and meeting large crowds as he was making his way to his house enquired of a woman what it was all about. She replied: "Oh, Sir, we are burning the popish chapel, and we only wish we had the bishop to throw into the fire" whereupon the bishop tactfully withdrew.

Even before the Edinburgh riots, the Scottish Committee of Protestant Interests had resolved "to come to the aid of their brethren in England", and they were in regular correspondence with some of the Protestant activists in London and after a meeting in February at Coachmaker's Hall, Foster Lane, the Protestant Association developed. Branches were formed all over England. In a little while the Association was ready, as it announced, to act against "the enemies of God". In December it elected a president, Lord George Gordon.

On Friday 2 June 1780 a vast number of Protestants had assembled at St. George's Fields, where sixty years later, the Catholics of London were to build the great Cathedral church of St. George. Contemporary accounts speak of 20,000, 50,000, even 100,000. Walpole states that the procession which formed did not exceed 13,000. They converged on both Houses of Parliament where members of both Houses suffered considerable maltreatment. Twice during the afternoon and evening attempts were made to force the doors. Repeatedly shouting "A repeal! A repeal! No Popery!"

The mob dispersed away from Parliament, marching to the Bavarian embassy in Golden Square, burst in and wrecked the chapel. They also went to the Sardinian embassy in Lincoln's Inn Fields, where Challoner had often preached, and repeated the destruction. Over the next few days houses were targetted and burned and in many cases pulled down in whole or in part as well. The rioters searched for Challoner, but he escaped and was protected by Mr. Mawhood. The forces of disorder which are ever dormant in great cities had been awakened, criminals and ruffians saw their opportunity in the scenes of arson and plunder which the religious fanatics had started. From this point onwards the riots became a flood of anarchy in which Lord George Gordon and his Protestants were overwhelmed and swept away. The attack was on law and order, and civilisation, and from six o'clock on Tuesday evening until the following Thursday London was at the mercy of the mob. The Bank of England was attacked on two occasions, each time the mob was repulsed by a force of soldiers at the Royal Exchange. Much of London was in flames. Horace Walpole stood on the roof of Gloucester House watching the fires. Next morning he wrote: "I own I shall not soon forget the sight I saw from the top of Gloucester House. I remember the Excise and the Gin Act, and the rebels at Derby, and Wilkes's interlude and the French at Plymouth, or I should have a very bad memory, but I never till last night saw London and Southwark in flames".

When the distillery was sacked the climax of horror was reached. The casks were staved in and the multitude began to drink the raw spirits. A great stream of liquor poured down into the street gutter, and was taken up by bucket-fulls and held to the mouths of all who would drink. The inflammable spirits also fed the flames into which drunken wretches staggered blindly, only to fall helpless and be burnt alive. Some died merely from the effects of the non-rectified spirits, and not only men, but boys and even women with children in their arms, lay prostrate in the street to be trampled on by the crowd. A young chimney sweep of sixteen was found dead with forty guineas in his pockets. Others wandered about half-stupefied were crushed under masonry falling from the blazing buildings.

On Wednesday evening, a council had been held at Buckingham House, at which the judges as well as the Privy Councillors attended. King George himself presided, and explained that the soldiers could not act because no magistrates could be found to read the Riot Act. Nedderburn, the Attorney-General, who throughout the whole disturbances had maintained a bold front, and who had fortified and barricaded his own house so as to offer armed resistance to the rioters, spoke out boldly while the Ministers wavered. He stated that in his judgement, when a mob was engaged in a felony no delay or formality was required by the Riot Act or any other law if there were no other means of restraint. The King agreed, a Royal Proclamation was therefore at once issued, warning all well disposed persons to keep within their dwellings, and empowering the military to repress the riot by force.

By Friday morning quiet was restored, but the national ignominy could not be complete without a shameful epilogue. The organisers of the riots escaped, but the Government, which had quailed before the strong, took its vengeance upon the weak. "A score have been tried, and most of them condemned", Walpole wrote to Mann. "They are apprentices, women, a black girl, and two or three escaped convicts. And these Catilines, without plan, plot, connection, or object, threw a million of inhabitants into consternation, burnt their houses about their ears, besieged the Parliament, drove it to adjourn for ten days, and have saddled the capital with ten thousand men". Later he writes to the same correspondent: "Dissatisfaction grows again on the continuance of the camps, and on the number of boys that have been executed for the riots, for the bulk of the criminals are so young that half a dozen schoolmasters might have quashed the insurrection. A capital blazing, and held in terror for a week by so contemptible a rabble, will not tell well in story".

He was right. Two women were hanged on Tower Hill, two cripples in Bloomsbury Square. There was the case of the fourteen year old Richard Roberts, hanged in Bow Street for his share in pulling down the house of Sir John Fielding. Standing on the scaffold, he made his speech, as was his privilege, saying that "He was never before guilty of any bad crime, nor did he think or know the danger his life was in when he committed that for which he suffered".

Bishop Challoner remained in Mr. Mawhood's house at Finchley. On Tuesday 13 June, Bishop Talbot came to dine with him and to report on conditions and affairs. The provinces had suffered too but not to the extent of the damage in London. At Bath, Bishop Walmesley's house was burnt, and with it all the archives of the Western District. The chapel at Hull had also been destroyed, but there were no further losses outside London. There were many cases of great hardship, with many Catholic families having lost there homes and all possessions. Likewise there were businesses which had suffered in the fires. Several people had become deranged through their experiences of terror, Bethlehem hospital alone received nine such cases.

The autumn brought tranquillity. Catholics soon recovered their confidence when they realised that no recurrence of the disturbance was likely. Parliament did not allow itself to be coerced into repealing the Relief Act. Challoner was now in the last months of his life, he remained at 25 Gloucester Street, tended by the devoted care of his priests, Joseph Bolton and John Lindow. On 5 October there was one solitary Confirmation recorded, it was the last entry in that list of Confirmations which he had kept throughout the forty years of his episcopate, and which shows that ten thousand Catholics had rceived that Sacrament from his hands. On 30 December Mr. and Mrs Mawhood came to make their confession to him, and this is the last recorded act of his ministry.

He sat down to dinner, on Wednesday 10 January, as was his custom in the company of his priests, he showed no signs of illness, but just as he ceased eating, his right hand suddenly fell from the table. Fr. Bolton realised something was wrong and moved closer to the bishop. Challoner's head sank on his right shoulder, but he was able to utter the word "Palsy", and to bring with his left hand a piece of paper which he put into Fr. Bolton's hand. Pointing to his pocket, in which lay some money which had that morning been given to him for the poor, he murmured "Charity". It was his last spoken word. He died just before 1 p.m. on Friday 12 January, 1781, and was buried in the chapel at Milton House, Berkshire, the home of Mr. Briant Barrett, who was devoted to the bishop. In this chapel the bishop had often celebrated Mass. There is no account of what took place at the burial except the curiously worded, yet altogether kindly and sympathetic entry of the Anglican Rector in his church register.

From this we know that the coffin was carried into the village church on Monday, 22 January, where the Church of England burial service was read over it by the Rev. James George Warren, then Rector of the parish. Yet Dr. Challoner was buried as a Catholic bishop. He had been obliged to live in secrecy and in hiding, disguised as a layman, and keeping the knowledge of his sacred office from all except his own flock. But now the need for concealment was over, a thing of the past, and on the coffin plate the inscription read: "Rt. Revd. Doctor Richard Challoner, Bishop of Debra, Died Jan. 12, 1781, aged 90, Requiescat in Pace.

The clergyman wrote in his register: "Anno Domini 1781, January 22 buried the Reverend Richard Challoner, a Popish Priest and Titular Bishop of London, a very pious and good man, of great learning and extensive abilities".

Dr. Talbot, in announcing Bishop Challoner's death to his flock wrote: "We have lost one who manifestly led the life of an angel" and Milner preaching at Winchester on the Sunday after the Bishop's death, said: "When on every occasion I represent Bishop Challoner as a saint, I say no more of him now after his death than all who knew him have said of him during his life". As if by common consent, the Catholics of 1781 spoke of their prelate as "The Venerable Bishop Challoner".

A critical time was beginning for the Catholic Church in England, and he had already seen signs of coming trouble. It was not likely that even he could have averted the contest between the bishops and the laity that was to come.

In the time of Cardinal Griffin, and at his instigation, the body of Bishop Challoner was re-buried in Westminster cathedral.

Extracts from: *The Life and Times of Bishop Challoner* by Dr. Edwin Burton
Bishop Challoner by Michael Trappe-Lomax
both published by Longman Green & Co. London

Chapter Seven

The Catholic Revival

FOLLOWING the death of Bishop Challoner, English Catholic hopes for any improvement in their situation reached its low point. Any hopes of the restoration of the Catholic faith for generations linked to the Jacobite cause had completely vanished. There seemed to be no possibility of any sort of Catholic revival, apathy and the sense of hopelessness, drained the spirit of some and a continual decline in the number of English Catholics ensued.

Following the first Relief Act of 1778, Catholics hoped to achieve further toleration by the Government and the repeal of the penal laws. Leading Catholics had as there objective complete Catholic emancipation. The Act of 1778 abolished some of the restrictions imposed on Catholics, there remained however a large number of disabilities to which Catholics were subject. These were listed in a letter sent to Mr. Pitt by the Catholic Committee in 1788. The list is not complete, as for many years some of the laws had been allowed to lapse. The list are those disabilities which Catholics were actually harassed at the time:

"(1) Catholics are prohibited under the most severe penalties exercising any act of religion according to their own mode of worship. (2) They are subject to heavy punishments for keeping schools, for educating their children in their religious principles at home, and they are also subject to heavy punishments for sending their children for education abroad. (3) They are made incapable of serving in his majesty's armies and navies. (4) They are restrained from practising the Law as barristers, Advocates, Solicitors, Attorneys or Proctors. (5) They are obliged on every occasion to expose the most secret transactions of their families, by reason of the expensive and perplexing obligation of enrolling their deeds. (6) They are subject by annual acts of the legislature to the ignominious fine of the double land tax. (7) They are deprived of that constitutional right of English freeholders, voting for County Members, they are not allowed to vote at the election of any other member, they are therefore absolutely unrepresented in Parliament. (8) They are disqualified from being chosen for a seat in the House of Commons. (9) Their peers are deprived of their hereditary seat in Parliament, and their clergy for exercising their functions are exposed to the heaviest penalties and punishments, and in some cases to death.

Bishop Walmsley of the Western District was considered to be the most prominent figure among Catholic ecclesiastics of that day and was the senior vicar apostolic. He was consecrated bishop in 1756, and he had ruled the Western District since 1764. He came from a well known Lancashire family and was the eleventh of twelve children. He was educated by the Benedictines, first at Douay and afterwards at St. Edmund's Paris where he joined the Order. He was a mathematician of international repute. The Government consulted him on the calculations necessary for the adoption of the Gregorian calendar in 1752. He was a Fellow of the Royal Society and belonged to similar philosophical societies in Berlin, Paris, and Bologna. Yet he lacked the ambition to pursue a career in which he could have attained real eminence. He much preferred the seclusion of his monastery, where he eventually became Prior. He was summoned to Rome in 1753 as Procurator General and during his stay in Rome he was chosen as coadjutor to Bishop York.

Bishop Walmesley lived a quiet life at Bath, he experienced the violence of the mob during the Gordon Riots when his house and all his books and papers were burnt. He adopted a spirit of retirement and reserve, like most Catholics of the time he asked only to be left in peace to practise his religion undisturbed. He was sympathetic with those who were afraid that repeal of the penal laws would lead to further trouble. He shared the view of other prelates that if Catholics could freely associate with their fellow Protestant countrymen, then Catholic practices would falter and more families would leave the Church.

The fear was especially real in the case of gentry families who had provided centres which kept the faith alive and supported chapels and priests. At this time it was estimated that the total number of Catholics in England was bout 60,000 or about one per cent of the total population. The Rev. Joseph Berington wrote *The State and Behaviour of English Catholics from the Revolution to the year 1780* in which he states: "The principle cause of diminution are the loss of families by death, or by conforming to the Established Church, the marrying with Protestants, and that general indifference about religion which gains so perceptibly among all ranks of Christians. When a family of distinction fails, there seldom continues any conveniency either for prayers (Mass) or instruction, the neighbouring Catholics soon fall way, and when a priest is still maintained the example of the Lord is wanting to encourage the lower class particularly to the practise of their religion. I recollect the names of at least ten noble families that within these sixty years have either conformed or are extinct, besides many commoners of distinction and fortune.

"We are at this day but eight peers, nineteen baronets, and about a hundred and fifty gentlemen of landed property. Among the first, the Duke of Nor-

folk, the Earl of Shrewsbury and the Lords Arundell and Petre are in possession of considerable estates. But the Earl of Surrey, the eldest and only son
to the Duke of Norfolk, having lately conformed, the large possessions of
that noble and ancient family will soon fall into Protestant hands. The eldest
son of Lord Teynham has also left the religion of his father. Among the
Baronets are not more than three great estates: Sir Thomas Gascoigne has
also this year taken the oaths, of the remaining commoners, with an exception of four or five, the greatest part have not on an average more than one
thousand pounds per annum in landed property".

The   concern of the bishops was understandable. The Catholic families
were the real back bone of the Church in England. Despite real penal hardships they generously endowed missions, and gave unstintingly to works of
charity. The sanctity of their personal lives is shown most vividly when we
consider that practically all who were called to priestly or religious vocation
came almost exclusively from the old Catholic families.

Bishop Poynter in his apologetical pastoral letter, written in 1815 writes of
them: "With what patience the English Catholics have suffered privation of
their civil rights on account of professing the Catholic religion, with what
piety they have adhered, and still do adhere, in the midst of the greatest
grievances, to the ancient faith and the holy Apostolic See, with what liberal-
ity have they contributed out of their private property to the support of the
public burthens of religion and charity! Let (anyone) look into a list of the
principle Catholics and into the number of those who residing neither in
London nor in any principle town support at their own charge, either wholly
or partially, Catholic clergymen and the expenses of their chapels and thus
procure the comforts of religion to be administered not only to themselves
and their families, but to numerous Catholic congregations in the country
residing in the neighbourhood of their mansions, let anyone, I say, consider
and reflect on this, and then declare whether the English Catholics do not
deserve the praises which I and other vicars apostolic have with a common
voice given them in our pastoral instructions"

Outside London, centres of Catholic activity whether at the stately homes
of the aristocracy, or gentry, or in towns, were real missions. They were the
centres from which the people from the surrounding area could be minis-
tered to. Catholics were scattered far and wide. In most cases the priest had
to keep a horse, so as to reach the outlying areas. He would often serve two
Mass centres miles apart, which required him to make a long ride, fasting,
every Sunday. Dr. Kirk writing in 1786: "It is not so common a thing now to
say two or three Masses a day as in some years past. When there is a riding
mission the priests goes one Sunday to one, and another to another, tho'
some still say two once a month, or once every indulgence". Dr. Kirk was at
that time at Sedgley Park, which was not ordinarily a 'riding mission', never-

theless he was at that time supplying at Lichfield every Sunday, which involved riding sixteen miles before his second Mass.

The clergy lived in great poverty. A gentleman's chaplain would receive £20 a year as his personal salary. A missioner who had to support himself and his servant, and sometimes to keep a horse, would be fortunate if he had an additional £20. Even allowing for the difference in the value of money between then and now, these figures indicate a very low income on which to live.

From 1781-1790 the vicar apostolic of the London District was Bishop James Talbot, his younger brother, Bishop Thomas Talbot, was in charge of the Midland District. They were brothers of the fourteenth Earl of Shrewsbury, and had been brought up in all the seclusion and isolation characteristic of the homes of the Catholic aristocracy of the period. James Talbot was unable to face with success the difficulties which preceded the passing of the Catholic Relief Act of 1791, and would have been still more unable to lead during the rapid expansion of the Church in England which took place in the nineteenth century. The greater part of his life was spent in days when the penal laws asserted their full force. He will always be specially reverenced by Catholics as having been the last priest to be brought before the courts under those laws. He was tried at the Old Bailey at least twice in the year 1769 and 1771 for the sole offence of having exercised his ecclesiastical functions, and was only acquitted for want of evidence.

James Talbot was born in Shrewsbury House, belonging to his family, at Isleworth, in 1726, the fourth of five sons, and after his baptism he was confirmed in infancy by Bishop Bonaventure Giffard, according to a custom then not uncommon. He was educated along with his brothers at a Catholic preparatory school at Twyford, near Winchester. At the age of twelve years, James and his younger brother Thomas were sent to Douay, where they went through the whole course. At the end of the philosophy course, the two brothers made the 'Grand Tour' in company with the Rev. Alban Butler, the learned author of *The Lives of the Saints,* They were absent for over a year, returning to Douay in 1748, the two brothers entered together on the study of theology, and on 19 December 1750, James was ordained priest. In 1755 he returned to England and the following year he was formally proposed for a bishopric as coadjutor to Dr. York of the Western District, but Dr. Walmsley OSB was appointed following the tradition that a Regular had always governed that District. Three years later Bishop Hornyold of the Midland District petitioned for James Talbot as his coadjutor. James was unwilling as ever to accept and the bishop begged the Pope to command him by the virtue of obedience not to refuse. He likewise wrote to Prince Charles Edward Stuart, then living in Rome to beg him to use his influence in favour of the appointment. The negotiations, however were not successful, Bishop Hornyold did not obtain a coadjutor until 1766, by which time James Talbot was already established in London. His brother Thomas was finally commanded by the Holy See to accept the post.

James Talbot was permanently attached to the London District as coadjutor to Bishop Challoner. He was consecrated at Hammersmith on 24 August 1759. During the following twenty years James Talbot acted as a most loyal assistant, being only too glad to occupy a subordinate position, and to devote himself to works of charity. Considering their small numbers, the Catholics of London were very active in the support of charities. The Aged Poor Society, founded in 1708, was suspended for a time after the Gordon Riots, but was afterwards revived. The Benevolent Society, with like aims, was founded in 1761. Another society called the Beneficent helped young Catholics to obtain apprenticeships in various trades. There were numerous others all doing good works.

Quite a feature in the lives of English Catholics of those days was the strictness with which they kept the laws of fasting and abstinence. In this respect Bishop Talbot's sympathies were in accordance with his family traditions. Yet curiously enough, it was during the years when he was vicar apostolic that important relaxations had to be made in the ecclesiastical laws. Up to this time a custom had existed of keeping every Friday of the year (except during Paschal time) a fast day, as an act of intercession for the conversion of England. This was beginning to be felt as a serious hardship, and one of Bishop Talbot's first acts on becoming vicar apostolic was to petition for the abrogation of the law. His petition was successful, and from 1781 Friday became a day of abstinence only. With respect to Lent, however, he made a great effort to preserve the strict discipline. The law still held good prohibiting meat from Ash Wednesday until Easter. A dispensation had been granted for several years, allowing it three times a week except Passiontide, but in 1782 Bishop Talbot made an effort to prevent this from becoming a fixed and regular arrangement, by withholding the dispensation. He explained his reasons in his Lenten Pastoral in a few words:

"As after mature deliberation" he wrote, "we can see no special reason this year for a general dispensation, for eating flesh meat on certain days, and lest the too frequent repetition of such dispensations should enervate the discipline of the Church in this regard, we think ourselves obliged to confine them to the following articles".

He proceeds to give a dispensation for eggs and cheese, except on Ash Wednesday and the last four days of Holy Week, and ends as follows: "As to those whose health or other circumstances seem to require more indulgence, we exhort them to be careful not to deceive their pastors by false allegations, as this would be only deceiving themselves by rendering the dispensations void"

Seven years after this, however, in 1789, Bishop Talbot once more granted a dispensation for meat, and though he was careful to guard against the supposition that it was intended to make this an annual arrangement, in point of fact it proved to be so, for this was his last Lent, and his successors always granted the dispensation.

The reasons which induced Bishop Talbot to grant the leave in 1789 are given by him in his Lenten Pastoral as follows: "There never was, perhaps, a time when the necessities of the poor were greater. And as the last frost, in which many poor persons perished through distress, has destroyed almost all the vegetables, on his account and others the following leave is granted in the London District, but so as not to be made a precedent for other years.

"As these indulgences are granted merely for necessity, we hope they will not be abused for the indulging of sensuality. And as it has become so often of late years necessary to give leave for meat, we have thought it better to restrain the leave for eggs, that as we cannot keep all, we may keep at least as much as we can. And we think it cannot be deemed a hardship to refrain from eggs, when meat is allowed. It may indeed be some inconvenience in great entertainments, but these it is our desire, as it is our duty, to discourage in Lent".

Among the difficulties encountered by Bishop Talbot, the greatest was the long and bitter disputes between the English bishops and some of the leaders of the Catholic laity which formed such an unpleasant feature of this period of our history. It is difficult to define the causes of such anti-clerical spirit in the Catholic body, or to explain that otherwise good and devout members of the Catholic laity could have been at heart so disloyal. Yet it cannot be denied that there had grown up amongst them an undefined sense of distrust of their spiritual rulers, and suspicion that the bishops were taking too strict a view of the position of Catholics. There was undoubtedly a feeling that the accepted attitude of dependence on the Holy See was incompatible with the national aspirations and duties of an Englishman. It was even questioned whether the penal laws themselves had not been, at least to some extent, due to the unreasonable attitude assumed by the Catholics of former days. When as the century wore on, and times became easier, the vicars apostolic began to exercise their jurisdiction, the jealousy evoked in the minds of the laity, if not excusable, was at least understandable. They had long assumed as their obvious right that they could appoint or dismiss their own chaplains, including those who served the missions endowed by them. They had asserted this in so many words during the differences between the bishops and Regulars in the first half of the century, and had not been contradicted. Dr. Walmesley writing to Dr. Gibson on 12 January 1796, expressly lays down that the laymen should be allowed to nominate the priests to serve the missions supported by them. When therefore the vicars apostolic began to interfere with the nominations, even to the extent of requiring to be informed of any changes, and refusing faculties to those whom they deemed unworthy, the laymen resented it as an unwarranted interference. Moreover, as in the course of time the barriers of the penal days were gradually broken down, so that the Catholics became able to mix more with their fellow-countrymen, they began to realise in a way which had not before appeared to them with such force, that they were as foreigners in their own country. They asked themselves whether this position was a necessary consequence of their principles, whether a foreign education was in reality an unavoidable accompaniment to the profession of their faith, and whether the instinct of hostility to the executive government begotten of long persecution, was either necessary or even justifiable in their own day. They carried this reaction to extreme lengths, adopting an exaggerated attitude of respect towards the civil power.

It is probable also that the fact of that generation of Catholics having grown up just at the time when adherence to the cause of the Stuarts was on the wane, and gave place to avowed loyalty to the existing Royal Family, had an appreciable effect in developing this frame of mind. Their loyalty to the House of Hanover had been confirmed by the oath enacted as an accompaniment to the Relief Act of 1778, which oath all of them had taken. Moreover, a committee of laymen had taken a leading part in the negotiations which led to the passing of that Act, though owing to the rapidity with which it went through the two Houses and other reasons, they did not come into prominence. It was natural that when the political situation held out a prospect of further relief, the laymen should expect to take the lead. They did so again by appointing a Committee from their number, who set to work with their minds full of their new and enlightened opinions, as they themselves considered them.

The reaction from the Jacobitism of their forefathers soon led the Committee to greater lengths than would easily be believed. In their anxiety to be loyal to the constitution, some of them adopted an attitude of subserviency towards the Established Church which appeared strange indeed in professed Catholics. Coupled with this, and closely allied in tendency, was their leaning towards the principles commonly known under the name Cisalpine, a name which a little later they were proud to adopt for themselves. In their desire to disclaim sympathy with Ultamontanism, they often proceeded to extremes, and used words of disrespect towards the Pope himself, and towards what they styled papal pretensions, which would have been looked for rather in Protestants than in Catholics. The chief questions in their minds was of course the action of the Popes in the days of Elizabeth and after the famous Bull, *Regnans in excelsis,* by which Pius V released Englishmen from their allegiance to the Queen. The subsequent history of the Armada, and other attempts to bring about the re-establishment of the Catholic religion in England by political means, and bound up closely in their minds with such events was the consideration of the generally intolerant attitude of the Church in the Middle Ages. Also the reaction of the eighteenth century against what is sometimes still designated under the vague term of the Methods of the Inquisition, a reaction which found expression in Italy in the well known Synod of Pistoia in 1787 which was condemned by Rome in 1794.

The appointment of the Committee did not wear any objectionable appearance. Many of the most loyal of the clergy shared the opinion that the existence of a committee of lay Catholics was desirable, perhaps even necessary, to guide the counsels of 'the body', as they commonly termed the English Catholics in their struggles for emancipation. The personnel of the Committee seemed all that could be desired, all were members of the old Catholic families, and were well known for their excellence in private life and their fidelity to the Church. In justice to them, we must believe that their intentions were good, and that they did not realise how far their opinions would develop, or where they would lead them. They were, of course, conscious of want of agreement between themselves and the vicars apostolic, and they must have foreseen that there would be difficulties in front of them before they could fully assert themselves, as they evidently hoped to do. They thought that the fault was not entirely on their side, and they were confident that their method of action was the only one that would win for Catholics that further toleration which they sought for.

The active members of the Committee were few, three or four at most. The others followed them, as did their supporters among 'the body' outside their number, trusting to the opinions and methods of their leaders, but having only a partial knowledge of the details of the case. The leaders among the laity were Lord Petre and Mr. Throckmorton, and in a lesser degree Sir Harry Englefield. Later on, at least one of the three clerics who were afterwards added took an active part in their councils.

The man who had the most influence of any one in their proceedings was not, strictly speaking, a member of the Committee at all, but their secretary, Mr. Charles Butler, the distinguished lawyer of Lincoln's Inn. In private life Charles Butler was religious and devout, even Dr. Milner, his unrelenting opponent, admitted that he might with truth be called an ascetic. He was married to a daughter of Mr. Eyston, of Hendred, by whom he had a small family. His only son died young, his two daughters survived him. He rarely entertained visitors, leading a life of seclusion and study, within his house in Red Lion Square. With a great taste for the liturgy, he was a regular attendant at the London churches, and only regretted that the circumstances of Catholics at that time prevented the proper celebration of Church functions. Every day of his life he recited the Office of the Blessed Virgin, and he was at all times ready to throw himself heart and soul into any work for the good of religion. Yet with all this, he identified himself with the action of those who held views which can hardly be described as less than unorthodox. While ever professing the greatest respect for his episcopal superiors he often acted in opposition to their wishes, and although his extensive learning usually enabled him to persuade himself that he understood the true issue better than they, and that his action was justified, nevertheless at times he could go to extreme lengths.

From what has been said, it will be seen what a valuable ally Butler was to the Committee. He was then in the full vigour of manhood, thirty-five years of age, and already a lawyer of repute. His extensive learning, both ecclesiastical and secular, was placed at their disposal, and his acquaintance with the first lawyers of the day enabled him to obtain legal advice and assistance of the highest authority, while his personal influence helped to secure for his party a hearing from men of standing. He kept all the minutes of the meetings throughout with strict formality, and whenever clerical assistance was required, he was able to supply it at his own office.

It has often been asked why the vicars apostolic allowed the Committee to proceed so far as they did before interfering, for their first united action in definite opposition to it was not until October 1789, when the Committee had been in existence over seven years. To this two answers may be given. In the first place, the main object of the Committee was one with which they were in sympathy. Bishop James Talbot used frequently to urge the desirability of having a committee of laymen to represent officially the interests of Catholics, and more than once he restrained those who would have written in strong opposition to them, lest the Committee should cease to act and should dissolve. In the second place, those who were the leading spirits of the movement were in private life, as has been said, most edifying and self-denying men. The prosperity of Catholic works, such as the establishment of missions or the building of chapels, which were at this time beginning to rise throughout the country, depended almost entirely upon these very men. Most of them had chapels of their own, with missions attached, which they supported with their own money. They were not afraid to threaten the withdrawal of such support, which would have caused many innocent persons to suffer. It is natural to find the vicars apostolic hesitating to precipitate such action.

It must also be admitted that the bishops were not all of one mind. Two of them, Dr. Walmesley and Dr Matthew Gibson, became at an early stage strongly opposed to the Committee. The two Bishops Talbot were for a long time undecided, being afraid of injuring the general peace of the Catholic body, and trusting to their personal influence as a sufficient restraining power on the Committee, though more than once they had to protest against their action. Another consideration to be remembered is that the bishops lived far away from each other, and the means of communication were slow and expensive, so that to other difficulties we must add that of isolation. Two or more of them would occasionally meet when staying at the same country house, but in arranging for a regular conference of the four vicars apostolic in 1789, they took a step which had never before been taken, and we can understand how it was some little time before they realised the necessity of so extreme a measure as this would have appeared to them.

But, in truth, the bishops were too charitable, as the event showed. They could not believe that men so excellent in private life would ever go to such lengths as the members of the Committee in fact did. Had they seen at the beginning how far they were likely to drift, they would certainly have interfered earlier. The best key to their actions is to be found in following the details of the Committee's work. These observations, though far from being a complete account of the state of affairs, may at least help us to understand the mutual relations between the bishops and the laity at this time, without which it would be impossible to estimate the significance of much of the action on both sides.

The meeting at which the Catholic Committee were elected, called by Butler a 'general meeting of English Catholics', was held on 3 June 1782, at the chambers of Mr. William Sheldon, in Gray's Inn Square. He had been secretary to the previous committee, appointed in April, 1778, which had long ceased to act and had indeed only acted for a few weeks, but had never been formally dissolved. The first motion was therefore to dissolve it, after which the meeting elected a new committee in its place.

Five members of the new Committee were elected at the meeting. Lord Petre, Mr. Hornyold and Mr. Stapleton obtained a majority of votes, three others, Lord Stourton, Mr. Throckmorton and Sir Edward Swinburn, came next with an equal number each, and on a second ballot being taken the first two of these were chosen. The Committee was subsequently completed by representatives chosen from each ecclesiastical District. The Northern, which was practically two Districts, having double representation. The following were chosen: London District - Sir Henry Englefield, Midland - Mr. William Fermor, Western - Lord Clifford, Northern - Sir Carnaby Haggerston and Mr. John Townley. A proposition was put forward that the Committee should include some representatives of the clergy, to be chosen by their own body, but this was completely rejected. At the conclusion of the general meeting, the Committee held their own first meeting, and elected Mr. Charles Butler as secretary. Bishop Milner was ready to oppose the Committee from the outset, and had he had is own way, he would have declared open war with them. Writing in 1820, he dates from this time the beginning of "that system of lay interference and domination in the ecclesiastical affairs of English Catholics which has perpetuated disorder, divisions and irreligion among too many of them for near the last forty years".

It has been customary among those who wish to discredit the authority of the Committee, to question the representative character of the meeting at which they were originally chosen. The Rev. Charles Plowden says that "they were elected only by a part of the Catholic gentry and clergy, and of course can be said to represent only them". Husenbeth, in calling it "a meeting of certain Catholics", no doubt had the same idea. In the official minute book of the Committee, which is preserved in the British Museum, we find that the meeting consisted of thirty persons, each belonging to a family of distinction It undoubtedly represented a large section of Catholics, but so small a number could hardly be considered the representatives of the whole Catholic body. In a sense this position was accepted by the Committee themselves, for we find that Lord Petre objected to Mr. Weld of Lulworth finding fault with their action on the plea that, as he did not concur in electing them, he had no concern in what they did.

Nevertheless, it would be a mistake to suppose that the Catholic meetings were in any way limited to those who held views in accordance with those of the promoters. Notices were sent out far and wide, and as time went on the meetings became well attended. The proceedings of the Committee at first achieved very little. One of the first objectives was to plan for procuring the Catholic ecclesiastics in England to be formed into a regular hierarchy by the appointment of bishops in ordinary instead of vicars apostolic. The Committee felt that if bishops in ordinary were appointed, nominated from the clergy, the Government would feel that Catholic bishops would have less dependence upon Rome, therby making it easier for Catholics to obtain further religious and political relief.

Dr. Milner expressed his opinion that the whole of the discussion and suggestions from the Committee was most improper, and that the comments made in the circular which had been sent to the bishops on the subject contained a series of assertions highly derogatory to the spiritual government of the vicars apostolic. He said that the members of the Committee could only be excused from the intention of schism by their ignorance of theological matters.

From the tone of the letters of the bishops to each other which have been preserved, it would appear that they too thought the action of the Committee improper though they did not go so far as Dr. Milner. On the main question they were not agreed. Bishop James Talbot wrote to Bishop Walmesley: "Ye proposed application seems evidently superflous, if it does not defeat its own end. For if 'tis ordinary powers they would apply for, we have it already. If ye Titles, English ones would displease Government more than our old

Asiatic ones, my opinion is that you had much better drop the scheme entirely". His brother Bishop Thomas Talbot, took a somewhat different view, regarding the proposal as "very useless, but free from reasonable objection". He even wrote to the Committee that he considered it would be "rather a desirable thing". Bishop Walmesley expressed his strong opinion against any change, but Bishop Matthew Gibson was frankly in favour of the proposal. "Though we certainly enjoy more extensive and ample powers than Ordinaries, yet they are delegated and restrained as to their direction, and if Government be desirous of our being appointed Ordinaries, and the measure should succeed, it will give a sort of legal sanction or establishment to us and to our inferiors".

The Committee concluded that the bishops were not supportive and as a consequence they dropped the proposed change. It is interesting to note that seventy years later when the restoration of the hierarchy was at last achieved the objective was the very opposite of that which the Committee had in mind. Wiseman wished to bring the Roman spirit to England, and to unite English Catholics more closely with the centre of unity. The Committee, on the other hand, wished to weaken the influence of Rome, and to emphasise the national characteristics of the Church in England. Milner says that the chief point to which they took exception was the recurrence to Rome whenever a new bishop had to be appointed. This, however, would not have been changed by the bishops becoming Ordinaries, and the very few who went to such lengths as to object to the appointments being made by Rome, would have considered themselves competent to establish their own hierarchy without petitioning the Holy See at all.

The more moderate members of the party had various objections to the system of government by vicars apostolic, some of them being matters of sentiment. They did not like being ruled by those who were nominally bishops of foreign sees, and the idea of English Catholics being immediately subject to direct representatives of the Pope was distasteful to them. They felt, even if they did not openly say, that an apostolical vicar must be to some extent foreign in his ideas and methods. The remedy seemed to be to nationalise them in name as a step towards nationalising them in fact, and so to distance their contacts with Rome.

It may be doubted whether the measure they proposed would in fact have had this effect. From their answers quoted above, we see that the vicars apostolic themselves were not of this opinion, nor was Mgr. Stonor, who quoted the experience in the case of Ireland as proof to the contrary, for although the Irish had a regular hierarchy, their affairs were carried to Rome quite as much as those of the English. Both Mgr. Stonor and the vicars apostolic are far better qualified to judge on such a matter than the Committee, for they were familiar with the actual working of ecclesiastical affairs. To the modern reader it appears incredible that the leading laymen of the time felt they had such assurance to take it upon themselves to form a judgement on a question of purely ecclesiastical government, but we should attribute this to the long custom which had engrained in them the habit of looking upon themselves as practically the directors of Catholic affairs.

Although the first major proposal of the Committee had come to nothing they soon had plans for future action. Bishop Walmesley writing to Bishop James Talbot on 15 December 1785: "I am informed, but I cannot say with full authenticity, that at a meeting soon to be held by the Catholic Committee a new oath is to be proposed, formed and so worded as to exclude the Pope's spiritual jurisdiction in this kingdom. They want, as I am told, to change vicars apostolic into Ordinaries, in order to diminish our dependence in spirituals on the See of Rome, and by degrees to shake it off entirely, likewise to take off the abstinence of Saturday, to reduce Lent to a fortnight before Easter, and to have the Liturgy in English. Probably this intelligence is exaggerated, though some little share of it I have heard myself from the mouth of one of that Committee. However, nothing will be, I suppose, absolutely attempted without the concurrence of the vicars apostolic, for so they promised publicly, as I was told, at the last general meeting. It is proper for us to be on our guard".

The bare suggestion of such a scheme as is here outlined seems outrageous coming from any one professing to be a Catholic. No doubt those who went at all within measurable distance of these proposals were few in number, and the Committee received the support of many who would never have thought of going to such extremes.

Because of the unsettled state of the political parties, the Committee did very little for a year or two. The long and docile ministry of Lord North, which had passed the first Catholic Relief Act, came to an end early in 1782. This was followed in quick succession by those of Lord Rockingham, Lord Shelburne and the Duke of Portland, none of which proved long-lived. Before the end of 1783, the Duke of Portland's ministry also came to an end, and William Pitt became Prime Minister at the age of twenty-four. It was not, however, until after the general elections of 1784 that Pitt found himself supported by a majority in the House of Commons, and at the head of a ministry that lasted almost unbroken for over seventeen years. This ministry was destined to pass the next measure for Catholic Relief.

Before the Committee had time to communicate with the Government, a reason of a different nature arose which induced them further to postpone their action. This was the marriage between the Prince of Wales and Mrs Fitzherbert, which took place privately at the end of the year 1785. This gave rise to a delicate situation which made it undesirable to raise the Catholic question for the time being. For both by her birth and by her previous marriages Mrs Fitzherbert was closely connected with the old Catholic families. She was a daughter of Sir Edward Smythe, of Acton Burnell, in Shropshire, and her early years were spent at his seat at Brambridge, near Winchester, where the family then resided. While still young she was sent to the school of the 'Blue Nuns' at Paris, where she remained for several years. On the completion of her education, she returned to her home at Bambridge, where there was a chapel in the house, and she continued to live as a strict Catholic following the rigid pattern which was then in vogue.

At the age of seventeen, Miss Maria Smythe was introduced into society. She was a girl of unusual beauty and very attractive and possessed a remarkable strength of character. She quickly attracted general attention, and before the year was out, she was already engaged to Mr. Edward Weld, of Lulworth Castle, a widower of foty four years of age, whose first wife, a daughter of Lord Petre, had died three years before. The marriage was celebrated early in 1775, within the year he died, and three years later his widow was married a second time to Mr. Thomas Fitzherbert of Swynnerton in Staffordshire. On his death in 1781, she found herself a widow for the second time at the early age of twenty five. After this for a time she lived in retirement at Richmond, but in the season of 1784 she opened her house in Park Street, which she had inherited from Mr. Fitzherbert, to her friends and it soon became a well known fashionable resort.

Very soon Mrs. Fitzherbert came under the influence of the selfish and profligate Prince of Wales. It is said that his devotion to her was the one redeeming feature of the prince's character, and it required a real devotion to overcome all the difficulties which stood in the way of the union on which he had set his heart. At first Mrs. Fitzherbert resolutely refused her consent. She refused even to see him, and decided to go abroad to escape his attention. Before she left, the prince staged a faked suicide attempt by stabbing himself, and sent emissaries to say nothing but her immediate presence would save his life. She came, and eventually a kind of pretended marriage ceremony was gone through, the prince placing a ring on her finger, but on her return home she knew that no real marriage had taken place, if for no other reason, because she was not a free agent at the time, and immediately she started for the Continent. The prince sent continual letter to her by special couriers and gradually her opposition was worn down and in the end returned to London. They were married privately at her house in Park Street, the ceremony took place on 15 December 1785, before a clergyman of the Church of England.

Of course the marriage was not legal, although according to Catholic theology it was valid. This was because the laws of the Church invalidating such marriages form part of the decrees of the Council of Trent, which had never been promulgated in England. It was not until legislation under Pius X that the law was altered in England. Had the marriage become public knowledge, the position of the prince would have been made very difficult. The truth was officially denied more than once in the House of Commons, on one occasion by Fox himself the prince's close friend. The details of the marriage were shrouded in mystery until long afterwards.

The Committee had now almost run its course and they had done very little, however during the last six months before their dissolution, a question arose which brought them into prominence in a disagreeable manner.

The question concerned the property of the ex-Jesuits. It appeared that they had sold a mission in the North of England, with some houses and land attached, to the Benedictines. Bishop Matthew Gibson contended that the ex-Jesuits being now Secular priests, had no power to part with one of their missions, and he reserved the right to place a Secular priest there later on. His contention was corroborated by a decree of propaganda dated 15 July 1786, in which it was expressly laid down that the property formerly belonging to the Jesuits was not to be alienated, and the vicars apostolic were called upon to see that the prohibition was observed. The fact that Bishop Gibson quoted this brief was made the subject by ex-Jesuits that in allowing Rome to interfere in temporal matters he was violating the oath which he had taken under the Act of 1778. The matter was taken up by the Rev. William Strickland, president of the Liege Academy. The following extract from his letter to Bishop Thomas Talbot, dated 8 February 1787, will give an idea of what he thought on the subject:

"I am sorry to observe that recourse has been had to the Congregation de Propaganda Fide on the subject. By the Oath of Allegiance we have declared in the clearest terms that we do not admit in this kingdom any foreign jurisdiction in temporal concerns, it is therefore with great surprise that I now find the authority of that tribunal brought to limit us in the disposal of our temporals.

"I have taken the opinion of a lawyer, on whose integrity and prudence I can rely, and he assures me that if any person should have been convicted of applying to the tribunal, or executing any decree issued from thence on a subject of this nature, even when Catholicity was the established religion of this country, such person would have been liable to the severest censure of our laws, and to the penalties of praemunire".

The lawyer to whom Dr. Strickland refers was Charles Butler, hence the next stage of the proceedings followed only too naturally. Dr. Strickland did not succeed in obtaining satisfaction from the bishops, he therefore appealed to the Committee to help him. They were not slow in taking the matter up, and immediately wrote a letter to each of the vicars apostolic: "My Lord, We, the Gentlemen of the Catholic Committee, having heard a report of a decree having been obtained from the Propaganda relative to the disposal of the temporalities of the late body of Jesuits in England, think it our duty to lose no time in requesting your Lordship to inform us of the truth of such a report. We hold ourselves fully justified in making full enquiry into this business, as it immediately and most seriously affects the honour and very existence of the Catholic body at large in this country, the receiving any Bull or decree from the Court of Rome on matters of temporal property being not only in direct violation of the Oath we have all lately taken, but in breach of the statutes of Praemunire and Provisors, both passed in Catholic times, for the security of the liberties of the English Catholic Church. We most earnestly hope that from your Lordship's answer we shall happily find the present alarm we feel to be ill founded".

To this letter Bishop Walmesley answered that he had not heard of any decree such as that mentioned. When he received a copy, however, he appears to have been somewhat alarmed, and to have regretted the action of Propaganda, which he attributed to their not understanding the state of things in England. In this he appears somewhat oversensitive, for the question was really purely an ecclesiastical one. There was no intention of disposing of Church property, the only question was, who were the representatives of the dissolved Jesuits, to whom the administration of their former property would belong. To this no one could answer better than the power which dissolved them, that is the Holy See. The two Bishops Talbot returned civil answers, evidently wishing to avoid being involved in a matter which did not concern their districts. Bishop Gibson, for whom the letter was primarily intended, at first took no notice of it, but eventually at the urgent request of Bishop James Talbot, he sent the Committee an explanation of what had occurred. He based his action on the general ecclesiastical law, quoting the instructions of Bishop Challoner in the London District, and Bishops Petre and Walton in the North, at the time of the suppression of the Jesuits. He added that the Decree of Propaganda was indeed opportune, for it officially confirmed his action. On receipt of this letter, the Committee wrote in a satisfied manner, and even with some cordiality.

Despite this, however, the matter continued to be discussed. Bishop Gibson complains that it was loudly said in London that he had broken his oath. When the Committee issued a printed address to the English Catholics before their dissolution, they returned to the charge, and even contended that Church government by vicars apostolic at all was an infringement of the statutes of Praemunire and Provisors. This address received much criticism and it defines the time from which Catholics began to be definitely divided into two parties, those who supported the Committee and those who were opposed to their whole attitude. It was the beginning of the long and tedious struggle between the Committee and the bishops.

The main purpose of the address was to secure for the Committee their own re-election. Although they had in fact achieved very little in the past five years they were hopeful for the future and wished to lay before the Catholic public their aims and the current situation. The main aim, as before, was to procure the restoration of the hierarchy. The reasons they gave for considering this of urgent importance were severely criticised by Milner and others. On this point the Committee wrote: "At present we are governed by four bishops who are appointed under the denomination of vicars apostolic, from which quality they derive their sole authority. They are appointed by the Court of Rome, without any election either by the clergy or laity, their power is curtailed or enlarged at the will of the Court of Rome, and revocable by the same Court. This necessarily creates an appearance of dependence on the Court of Rome, which generally represented to be much greater than it really is. But we beg leave to observe that the ecclesiastical government by vicars apostolic is by no means essential to our religion, and that it is not only contrary to the primitive practices of the Church, but is in direct opposition to the statutes of Praemunire and Provisors, enacted in times when the Catholic was the established religion of this country, (Ed. The statute of Provisors was intended to limit the Pope's power of nominating to English benefices, Praemunire concerned papal jurisdiction. Both statutes were passed in the reign of Edward III, 1351 and 1353 and re-enacted under Richard II, 1390 and 1393), and when you reflect that it is the duty of Christians to make the discipline of their Church to conform as near as may be to the laws of their country, your Committee doubt not but you will concur with them in thinking that it is incumbent on us to use our endeavours to procure the nomination of bishops in ordinary. Your Committee think it would be needless to point out to you the advantages which would result from having pastors thus chosen by the flock they are to teach and direct, and in conjunction with which they would be competent to regulate every part of the national Church discipline. Your Committee trust that you will concur with them in thinking it necessary to appoint a certain number of your body who may be entrusted to co-operate with your clergy in taking the most effectual means to free them and us from our present defective system, and establish the Church government in a manner more conformable to the general practice of the Christian religion".

Again the modern reader will see at once that the Committee here take up a very extraordinary position with a definite schismatical tendency. The other measure advocated by the Committee was the setting up of a school that would offer a system of education more in keeping for those destined for civil or commercial life. This brought them onto safer ground, and although opinions varied as to the wisdom of the scheme, there was no way to fault the proposal on ecclesiastical grounds.

The general meeting was held on 3 May 1787, and the Committee were duly re-elected for a further term of five years.. The members remained the same except that Sir John Lawson and Sir William Jerningham had replaced Mr. Thomas Stapleton and Mr. William Jones. Charles Butler was re-appointed secretary.

In some areas notably in Bishop Gibson's district, the feeling against the Committee was growing daily, caused by random talk which some members indulged in when propounding their own views. Amongst other things Mr. Throckmorton put forward the extraordinary proposition that Catholics might lawfully take the oath of supremacy. He said in effect that the Catholic authorities had interpreted the meaning of the oath too rigidly, and that it was capable of being understood in a sense that was not inconsistent with Catholic doctrine. He later published his own explanation: "The oath requiring us to deny in a foreign person any jurisdiction of power, ecclesiastical or spiritual, within this realm it becomes essentially necessary to know what the precise meaning of these words is. If by the word spiritual is meant any part of that Divine commission which is acknowledged to be given by Christ to His Church, it is evident that we cannot take the oath. But as the same word has often been used in a sense of much greater latitude, so as to extend to persons vested with an ecclesiastical character, and to tribunals which are really civil as well in their authority as in the nature of the causes on which they decide, if the meaning be only to deny to any foreign person such authority or pre-eminence it is evident there can be no religious ground of refusing the oath".

Sir John Lawson wrote saying that the matter is one for the bishops, not for laymen to discuss, but giving his own opinion that the words of the oath of supremacy are wholly incompatible with Catholic principles. "We have already", he adds, "taken an oath that any kingdom ought to be satisfied with. We have sworn as much as ye oath of Supremacy contains, except as to ye Ecclesiastical and Spiritual authority. If our principles are to be frittered away piecemeal, let those look to it who propose this scheme".

In the meantime, the Committee began to press on the two measures which they had put in the forefront of their programme, the appointment of diocesan bishops in place of vicars apostolic, and the establishment of a good school on this side of the Channel. On the first of these the bishops had indeed already given their opinions some four years before, and the bishops were not all of one mind on this issue. The Committee hoped that with further time and consideration, the bishops might gradually come round to their own views, which they believed to be shared by the general body of the clergy.

In fact the Committee's proposal was viewed with apprehension by many, especially among the clergy. The school would of course have been illegal, but the experience of Old Hall Green and Sedgley Park and a few other such like establishments gave reason to hope that the law on this matter would not be enforced. Many of those who had been educated at Douay and at other foreign colleges, were much attached to these, and apprehensive of anything that might impair their efficiency. Thus Bishop Walmesley writes: "The new school upon the extensive plan of the Committee, I suspect, will prove prejudicial both to the colleges abroad and to the mission here".

In the same sense, but in more forcible language, the Rev. Thomas Eyre, who was afterwards president of Crook Hall and Ushaw, wrote from Hassop on 13 June: "I hate the very idea of it. It is evident to me that a secret blow is aimed at Douay College, and I am fully convinced that the preservation of religion in this kingdom has been hitherto chiefly owing to that house, whatever hurts it must prejudice the other, and even was that not to be the case, I can never approve of a scheme which would prevent a great number of our young people from ever acquiring a practical (if I may so call it), and ocular information, conviction and demonstration of the universality, respectability and prevalence of their religion over the several new-fangled, pied patched and piebald sects and sections, which under the general name of Protestants (a glove which fits every hand from the claws of Lucifer to the rat that eats a hole in your wainscote) are spreading desolation over, or more properly speaking are tearing up Christianity, root and branch".

The feeling against the Committee soon became very strong, and eventually led to a formal protest against their action. This was organised chiefly by Sir John Lawson, of Brough Hall in Yorkshire who had recently been elected a member of the Committee The protest is so important as a testimony to the solid orthodoxy of the Catholics of the North, that it is worth while giving it in full:

"To the Committee of English Catholics - My Lords and Gentlemen, In answer to your circular letters of 1787, we wish to state to you that we are satisfied with your resolution concerning our Church government so far as it has been agreed 'to instruct a Committee to consult with our vicars apostolic, and in case of their thinking it proper, to co-operate with them'. We are of opinion that the laity ought not to be judges in such business, and we shall be dissentient from any step to forward ye proposed alteration that has not received ye full satisfaction of our present bishops.

"With respect to ye resolution of ye meeting of May ye 3d, that it would be beneficial to ye Catholics at large to establish a school for ye education of youth intended for civil or commercial life, we find ourselves under the necessity of withholding our consent to that measure, and we esteem our present schools in England and our establishments abroad amply and fully sufficient and adequate to ye education of our Catholic youth. We are far from being convinced of ye supposed deficiency in our present system of education. Frequent applications are made to our foreign colleges to receive youths of persuasions different from our own, intended for civil and commercial life in this country, who would be numerous there, were the heads of our Houses inclined to receive them. It is hence fair to suppose that our Protestant countrymen entertain a more favourable opinion of our foreign education, even with a view to civil and commercial life, than some of our own body are willing to allow it. we cannot help remarking that our foreign colleges are now placed on a more enlarged system. In hopes of meeting ye ideas and wishes of ye catholic laity. Accounts and writing and the English and French languages are there made a more considerable part than formerly of education, and we cannot entertain an idea that the rising generation educated in this country will be more respectable than by a continuation of ye present improved plan.

"We apprehend a new school in this country, such as is proposed in your letters may be a means of preventing several of our young men from embracing ye ecclesiastical state of life so essentially necessary to ye Catholic religion, and we fear any impediment thrown in ye way of our present colleges, so as to deprive them in ye whole or in part of their youth, will be a step very prejudicial and must in time tend to increase much our want of churchmen. We are grounded in our apprehensions that our foreign colleges may suffer much from ye success of ye proposed new school, by that part of your letter of ye 10th of April in which you say you are not without hopes that ye school 'by rising as circumstances will permit from its infant state to a degree of eminence, shall in future times be adequate to all purposes, more advantageous to religion, and to ye body of Catholics, than ye present foreign school establishments'.

"The idea of our present foreign places of education being rendered unnecessary and given up, seems to us big with fatal consequences, for should any commotions on religious matters at a future day take place in this country, which is within the line of possibility to happen, our school establishments here might probably be the first sacrifice of contending parties, and in such a situation we should then be destitute of the asylums we are at present in possession abroad, and having this apprehension in view, we shall ever deem it highly imprudent to part with them.

"We think our young men, whose inclinations may lead them to embrace a clerical state of life, will certainly be debarred from being educated in this country, from the advantage which every college abroad affords of seeing the full and publick exercise of our religion, without which the education of our ecclesiasticks would in that respect be confined, and this advantage we cannot allow to be uninteresting to ye laity.

"We may add that the students in our foreign colleges are placed at a distance from objects of dissipation and bad example, so much complained of in the public schools of this country, and we deem it a matter of extreme difficulty to guard against this objection in any extensive plan of education proposed to be set on foot in England.

"We have only further to state, that we cannot consider the penal laws remaining in force against us a dead letter. Prosecutions upon the unrepealed statutes have taken place in ye County of York since ye Act of Parliament passed in favour of ye Catholics, and as long as we are loaded with such shackles, we cannot subscribe to ye idea of viewing such laws with indifference. We are willing to hope that an erasure of them from ye statute books is ye great object to which the Committee intend to direct their endeavours".

Fifty one signatures follow, including representatives of all the chief Catholic families in the North of England - Haggerston, Maire, Silvertop, Clavering, Witham, DeTrafford, Stanley, Blundell, Riddell, Charlton, Selby, Bedingfield, Gage, Constable, Gibson, Strickland, Vavasour, Eyre, Tempest, Stapleton, etc.

This protest was read at the general meeting of Catholics at the Freemason's Hall on 15 May 1788, when the chairman, Mr. Throckmorten, gave what he considered as the Committee's answer, point by point. Nevertheless, the protest seems to have had considerable effect, for we hear nothing more of the proposed school for several years afterwards. At the same meeting Dr. James Talbot, Bishop Charles Berington, the new coadjutor of the Midland District, and Rev. Joseph Wilkes, a Benedictine monk, were all elected by a ballot . Sir John Lawson said that he was greatly pleased to read the names of such respectable characters which had been added to the Committee, but wished that a clergyman from the Northern District had been included at the same time. However the clergy were not allowed to choose their own representatives, these were nominated by the lay members, who naturally chose such as they knew to be disposed to their own way of thinking.

The new Committee wasted no time in establishing communications with the Government. Pitt was by this time all powerful and the political situation appeared to favour the pursuit of further legislation favourable to Catholics. Mr. Fermor who was a personal friend of Pitt discussed the possibility with him of getting a motion passed through Parliament. Fermor asked Pitt which of the three constitution modes he would consider preferable, they were, (1) by an address to the King, (2) by a petition to Parliament, (3) by a motion in the House of Commons. Pitt would not give an answer and asked for more time. Eventually, after a period of three months, Pitt consented to see Fermor with any others as a formal delegation from the Catholic body.

Lord Petre, Sir Henry Englefield and Mr. Fermor were received by Pitt on Wednesday 9 May. The following points were drawn up by the Committee, as a guide for the deputation in their interview with Pitt: "To endeavour not to lose the present session. If asked what our present wishes are, to press our wishes for the Army, Navy and Bar. Rather to hear what Administration may chuse to give than to make proposals of our own. If the Test is objected which excludes from the Army and Navy, then to express our wishes for those advantages which the Dissenters now enjoy, and from which we are excluded". Mr. Butler also prepared a number of observations on the legal questions raised.

The substance of Pitt's answers can be given in the words in which the members of the deputation reported them to the Committee the same afternoon: "Mr. Pitt said that Government will make no objection to the business relating to the relief of the English Roman Catholics being brought before Parliament early next sessions. But, he observed, if moved this session, it will be impossible to carry the measure to a conclusion, and of course it must lay over till next year. This, Mr. Pitt is of opinion, will not be a favourable circumstance to the Catholic cause, as it will prevent Government from preparing the minds of some of the leading interests in this country previous to the bringing on of a measure of such importance. He also desired Catholics to furnish him with authentic evidence of the opinion of Catholic clergy and Catholic universities with respect to the existence or extent of the Pope's dispensing power. That though the relief prayed for appeared simple and clear, yet many parts of it involved great and weighty considerations for Government to determine upon. He observed that whatever was conceded to the Roman Catholics, the Protestant Dissenters must also enjoy. He concluded by saying that although Government strongly wished that the subject might not be moved this session, yet it was left to the Catholics to consider whether they should run the risk of the consequences attending its laying over until next year. Mr. Pitt repeated several times that he hoped the Roman Catholics would be assured that the present adjournment of their business to next session did not arise merely from motives of delay, but Government seriously intended to consider their situation, and wished to grant them relief which in prudence they could adopt".

The Committee met shortly afterwards to discuss the provisions for the proposed Catholic Relief Bill which Charles Butler drafted. In essence this was to obtain repeal of all the statutes of recusancy, and those that prevented Catholics from serving in the Army, and Navy, or from practising the Law with full liberty to enjoy their property. The other issue which Pitt had placed before the deputation was the need to clarify Catholic belief as to the Pope's dispensing power. All this appeared to be unecessary and Bishop Walmesley who wrote to Charles Butler: "the answers returned from abroad to the queries you sent if satisfactory to Mr. Pitt, that is well. I don't see what further service they can be, our answers to them were given in the Oath of 1778".

The next hurdle was the famous Protestation. When this was published it carried no title or heading and there was some slight descrepancies between the various printed editions. The following is taken from copies circulated for the purpose of obtaining signatures:

"We whose names are hereunto subscribed, Catholics of England, do freely, voluntary and of our own accord make the following solemn declaration and Protestation.

"Whereas sentiments unfavourable to us as citizens and subjects have been entertained by English Protestants, on account of principles which are asserted to be maintained by us and other Catholics, and which principles are dangerous to society and totally repugnant to political and civil liberty, it is a duty that we, the English Catholics owe to our country as well as to ourselves to protest in a formal and solemn manner against doctrines that we condemn, and that constitute no part whatever of our principles, religion or belief.

"We are the more anxious to free ourselves from such imputations because divers Protestants who profess themselves to be real friends to liberty of conscience, have nevertheless avowed themselves hostile to us on account of certain opinions which we are supposed to hold. And we do not blame those Protestants for their hostility if it proceeds (as we hope it does) not from an intolerant spirit in matters of religion, but from their being misinformed as to matters of fact.

"If it were true that we, the English Catholics, had adopted the maxims that are erroneously imputed to us, we acknowledge that we should merit the reproach of being dangerous enemies of the state, but we detest those unchristianlike and execrable maxims and we do severally claim, in common with men of all other religions as a matter of natural justice, that we, the English Catholics, ought not to suffer for or on any wicked or erroneous doctrines that may be held by any other Catholics, which doctrines we publicly disclaim, any more than British Protestants ought to be rendered responsible for any dangerous doctrines that may be held by any other Protestants, which doctrines they, the British Protestants, disavow.

"(1) We have been accused of holding as a principle of our religion that Princes excommunicated by the Pope and Council or by authority of the See of Rome may be deposed or murdered by their subjects or other persons.

"But so far is the above-mentioned unchristianlike and abominable position from being a principle that we hold, that we reject, abhor and detest it, and every part thereof as execrable and impious, and we do solemnly declare that neither the Pope either with or without a General Council, nor any prelate, nor any priest, nor any assembly of prelates or priests, nor any ecclesiastical power whatever can absolve the subjects of this realm or any of them from their allegiance to his majesty King George III, who is by authority of

Parliament the lawful king of this realm, and all the dominions thereunto belonging.

"(2) We have also been accused of holding as a principle of our religion that implicit obedience is due from us to the orders and decrees of Popes and General Councils and that therefore if the Pope or any General Council should for the good of the Church command us to take up arms against Government, or by any means to subvert the Laws and liberties of this country, or to exterminate persons of a different religion from us, we (it is asserted by our accusers) hold ourselves bound to obey such orders and decrees, on pain of eternal fire.

"Whereas we positively deny that we owe any such obedience to the Pope and general council, or either of them, and we believe that no act that is in itself immoral or dishonest can ever be justified by or under colour that it is done either for the good of the Church, or obedience to any ecclesiastical power whatever. We acknowledge no infallibility in the Pope, and we neither apprehend nor believe that our disobedience to any such orders or decrees (should any such be given or made) could subject us to any punishment whatever. And we hold and insist that the Catholic Church has no power that can directly or indirectly prejudice the rights of Protestants, inasmuch as it is strictly confined to the refusing to them a participation in her sacraments and other religious privileges of her communion, which no Church (as we conceive) can be expected to give to those out of her pale, and which no person out of her pale will, we suppose, ever require.

"And we do solemnly declare that no Church or any prelate or priest, nor any assembly of prelates or priests nor any ecclesiastical power whatever hath, have, or ought to have any jurisdiction or authority whatsoever within this realm, that can directly or indirectly affect or interfere with the independence, sovereignty, laws, constitution or government thereof, or the rights, liberties, persons or properties of the people of the said realm or of any of them, save only and except by the authority of Parliament, and that any such assumption of power would be an usurpation.

"(3) We have likewise been accused of holding as a principle of our religion that the Pope, by virtue of his spiritual power, can dispense with the obligations of any compact or oath taken or entered into by a Catholic, that therefore no oath of allegiance or other oath can bind us, and consequently that we can give no security for our allegiance to any government.

"There can be no doubt but that this conclusion would be just if the original proposition upon which it is founded were true, but we positively deny that we do hold any such principle. And we do solemnly declare that neither the Pope nor any prelate or priest, nor any assembly of prelates or priests nor any ecclesiastical power whatever can absolve us or any of us from, or dispense with the obligation of any compact or oath whatsoever.

"(4) We have also been accused of holding as a principle of our religion that not only the Pope, but even a Catholic priest has power to pardon the sins of Catholics at his will and pleasure, and therefore that no Catholic can possibly give any security for his allegiance to any government, inasmuch as the Pope or a priest can pardon perjury, rebellion, and high treason.

"We acknowledge also the justness of this conclusion, if the proposition upon which it is founded were not totally false, but we do solemnly declare that on the contrary we believe that no sin whatever can be forgiven at the will of any Pope or of any priest or of any person whomsoever, but that a sincere sorrow for past sin, a firm resolution to avoid future guilt, and every possible atonement to God and the injured neighbour are the previous and indispensable requisites to establish a well-founded expectation of forgiveness.

"(5) And we have also been accused of holding as a principle of our religion that 'faith is not to be kept with heretics', so that no government which is not Catholic can have any security from us for our allegiance and peaceable behaviour.

"This doctrine that 'faith is not to be kept with heretics' we reject, reprobate and abhor, as being contrary to religion, morality and common honesty, and we do hold and solemnly declare that no breach of faith with any person whomsoever can ever be justified by reason of, or under pretence that such person is an heretic, or an infidel.

"And we further solemnly declare that we do make this Declaration and Protestation and every part thereof in the plain and ordinary sense of the words of the same, without any evasion, equivocation or mental reservation whatsoever.

"And we appeal to the justice and candour of our fellow citizens, whether we, the English Catholics, who thus solemnly disclaim and from our hearts abhor the above mentioned abominable unchristianlike principles, ought to be put upon a level with any other men who may hold and profess those principles".

Such is the remarkable document which was the cause of so much heat and discussion among Catholics then and for long years afterwards. To the modern reader the tone is not a little startling, revealing as it does an all-pervading influence of what is commonly known as Cisalpinism. The Oath of 1778 had already shown a tendency in that direction on the part of English Catholics. For example the Oath of 1778 contains nothing about papal infallibility, while in the Protestation of 1788 the doctrine is repudiated in strong and almost offensive terms. It is true, indeed, that the infallibility of the Pope had not been defined, and was consequently not an article of faith. It was however commonly held in Rome, and in ultramontane countries generally, so that the vehemence with which it was denied was, to say the least, unseemly. In England, there were some who held the dogma, however they equally had no scruple in disclaiming it as an article of faith.

The Catholic Committee had now to obtain the signatures of the Catholic body to the Protestation. It was important to persuade a few influential persons to sign at the outset, so that others might be led on by their example. They naturally began with the clergy, then they approached the vicars apostolic, with a letter written by Charles Butler to each of them, adding the names of the priests who had already signed it. On the same day as he wrote the letters, he called on Bishop James Talbot and obtained his support. The other two vicars apostolic, Bishops Walmesley and Gibson, were known to be averse to the whole proceedings, yet they also eventually agreed to have their names attached.

The Protestation was eventually signed by over 1,500 Catholics of whom 240 were priests. (At that date Joseph Berrington estimated the number of priests in England at 360).

The preparation of a Bill for Parliament on so comprehensive a subject as Catholic relief was a work which required a great deal of considered judgement. Charles Butler took nearly four months to complete the first draft. He submitted this to Hargrave, the distinguished Parliamentary lawyer, who took even longer to revise it. He completed the final revision on 24 March 1789.

This completed Bill was never introduced into the House, although the Committee had it printed. In subsequent stages of their controversy with the bishops they laid stress on this draft, as the only one that could be properly called their Bill. This was not without reason, for it was free from most of the objections which disfigured the Bill which later replaced it.

It was hoped that the Bill might have been passed in the session of 1789, but the arrangements for its introduction were delayed by the 'illness' of the King, which began in the autumn of 1788. Mr. Butler, in a letter to Bishop Walmesley, says plainly that when it became known that George III was out of his mind, and that Parliament was about to appoint his son Regent, it was considered that the introduction of a Bill on a purely domestic question would be out of taste. But there was in fact a further and more important reason for delay, for it was well known that in the event of the Prince of Wales becoming Regent, Pitt's ministry would have come to an end. On the first news of the King's malady, Fox hurried home from Italy, where he was enjoying a holiday, and while the Regency Bill was passing through Parliament, he occupied himself in allocating the different posts of the ministry which he confidently expected to be called upon to form.

Fox had pledged himself to the principle of religious toleration, and whenever the question was raised, whether in or out of Parliament, he was always on the side of the Catholics. He was however a personal friend of several of the members of the Committee, notably of Sir Henry Englefield and Mr. Throckmorton, so that had he found himself in a position to bring in a Catholic Relief Bill he might easily have fallen entirely into the hands of that party. In the event, he never found himself in that position, for while the Regency Bill was going through its final stages, news came that the King was recovering, and so Fox's hopes were thwarted.

Prayers in thanksgiving for the King's recovery were ordered by the vicars apostolic, each in his own District. A point of interest is illustrated on the state of Catholic affairs at that time by the fact that the official addresses of congratulations to the King and Queen were drawn out not in the names of the bishops, but in those of the laymen. They were passed at a general meeting of Catholics at the Thatched House, on 21 March 1789, and signed by Lord Petre as chairman. Bishop James Talbot complained that they would not even allow him to attend the meeting. "The Church is excluded", he writes, "and therefore I have never been summoned, though I had some title as a gentleman, and could have given them some useful information relative to an application lately made by us". There was also a solemn High Mass of thanksgiving, which was likewise arranged by Lord Petre and others, though they did in this case consult with Bishop Talbot, a fact which afterwards brought forward more than once as evidence of their anxiety to show respect to their ecclesiastical superiors. The Mass was celebrated by Rev. Thomas Hussey, at the Spanish Chapel in York Street.

The recovery of the King gave Mr. Pitt a new lease of office, and seemed after all a possibility of the Catholic Bill being taken through Parliament that year. The negotiations which followed are shrouded in some obscurity. The Committee led Catholics to understand that at this stage the Protestation was presented to Parliament with the names of the signatories attached. It afterwards appeared, however, that although Pitt had it in his possession for a time, before being formally presented, it had been revised in the form of a petition. The petitioners being described as the 'Catholic Dissenters'. The petition was presented to the two Houses of Parliament simultaneously on 9 May. On 18 May Lord Stanhope brought his own Bill into the House of Lords, and it was thrown out. The similar Bill in favour of the Protestant Dissenters introduced into the House of Commons had shared a similar fate ten days earlier, though by a narrow majority.

The period of the most recent negotiations covered about two months. During that time a completely new Bill had been drafted, plus a new oath, and no consultation whatever had taken place with any of the vicars apostolic, apart from the brief discussion with Bishop Talbot.

The new draft began by removing certain disabilities in an absolute manner, and then enumerated exceptional cases in which the restrictions were to be retained. It was made illegal to "found, establish or endow any Religious Order or Society of persons bound by religious or monastic vows" there were other equally unacceptable clauses. However a far more serious objection was made to the description "Protesting Catholic Dissenters" to those who would take the new oath, and those who refused the oath were to be designated as "Papists".

If matters had stopped there, perhaps we might have considered that the Committee had made out some kind of case for themselves. When, however, the word 'protesting' was prefixed to the title, the position was changed, and it is difficult to escape the conclusion that they wished to be associated with much of the sentiment that was common with Protestants. It is true that the real origin of the word protestant was that its first inventors protested not against Catholic tenets, but against religious toleration. The name was first given at the Diet of Spires in 1529. The popular belief identified with the term since then, is a protest against Catholic doctrine and practice. It was in this sense that the Committee found the name congenial to their own opinions, and thought it would mark them off in the popular mind as abjuring many of the doctrines of popery which were considered especially obnoxious.

The Committee were well aware that the bishops had only signed the Protestation with reluctance, and that a large number in the North, and indeed throughout the country, had been opposed to its language and tone. The present aim of the Committee was to try and force their opinions on all Catholics, under penalty of leaving those who refused to accept still liable to the old penal laws. Their objective was that in this way they stood a better chance of obtaining the repeal of the penal laws.

The delay in introducing the Bill had a very fortunate effect, for it gave the bishops an opportunity of examining the proposed oath. Bishop Walmesley wrote to his brother bishops on 10 July 1789 pressing for a meeting to discuss the whole situation. Because of the illness of Bishop James Talbot, the meeting was fixed for 19 October at his house in Hammersmith.

In the meantime, the promulgation of the proposed oath had given rise to much controversy, and threatened to create a downright schism among Catholics. The supporters of the oath were the more noisy party, consisting of all those who were favourably disposed towards the Committee and including a certain number of the clergy in London and the Midlands. In the Northern and Western Districts almost all the clergy and the majority of the laity were on the opposite side. A meeting of thirty priests was held in Lancashire, who unanimously condemned the oath, and Bishop Gibson issued a circular prohibiting anyone in his District from taking it.

When the vicars apostolic met, they went straight to the business in hand, they did not consult with the Committee at all. Six bishops were present, the four vicars apostolic and the coadjutors of two of them, the other two hav-

ing no coadjutor, were each allowed to bring with them a theological advisor.
Dr. Gibson brought Rev. Robert Banister, a well known priest in the North,
while Bishop James Talbot brought Milner. The meeting lasted four days,
perfect unanimity prevailed, and the following resolutions were passed by
the bishops:

"(1) That they do condemn the new oath lately printed, and declare it
unlawful to be taken. (2) That they judge the Oath of 1778 sufficient, and
that it contains in substance all that can be desired to ascertain our civil allegiance. (3) That they condemn the oath as unlawful, without adding specific
qualifications. (4) That they resolve to send an encyclical letter to the faithful
notifying to them the condemnation of the oath, and signifying that they
ought not to take any new oaths, or sign any new declaration in doctrinal
matters, or subscribe any new Instrument wherin the interests of religion are
concerned, without the previous approbation of their respective bishop. (5)
That they declare the new appellation or denomination 'Protesting Catholic
Dissenters' to be highly objectionable. (6) That the clause in the Bill not to
educate any child a papist is pronounced not admissible. (7) The clause in
the same Bill not to educate any child of Protestant parents a 'Protesting
Catholic Dissenter' is also declared to be inadmissible. (8) The clause 'that all
uses, trusts and dispositions, whether of real or personal property, which
immediately before the passing of the Act shall have been deemed superstitious, or unlawful, shall continue to be so deemed and taken', the four vicars
apostolic wish it to be suppressed".

The members of the Committee were not slow to observe that the action
of the bishops was a new departure. In the case of the Protestation, they had
at least discussed it with them, but in the present instance they had met, discussed and condemned the oath and other parts of the proposed Bill. Moreover, they had expressed their determination in peremptory language, ending
with the command, "to these determinations we require your submission".
This was equivalent to a declaration on the part of the bishops that they
were the leaders in ecclesiastical matters, and that the time had now come
for them once and for all to assert their position.

The Committee were both alarmed and angry. They could not afford to
have an open rupture with the vicars apostolic, their only chance of avoiding
a contest was to reach a compromise, in order to pacify the bishops from
day to day while the business proceeded. This led them to a course of action
which made the situation continually grow more difficult and complicated.

Their first act was to try and induce the bishops to postpone the publication of the encyclical, in order to allow an opportunity for the difficulties
between them to be eased. Mr. Hornyold called on each of the bishops still
in London, both Bishops Talbot consented to a delay on the understanding
that the Committee would set themselves to amend the oath. Bishop Gibson

also agreed to a delay, under the impression that all his colleagues had done so. Bishop Walmesley had already left London and a letter was sent to him at Bath, but it arrived too late and the encyclical was promulgated by him. When Bishop Gibson discovered his mistake, he at once published the encyclical which was read in the churches in the North before the end of November. The effect of the hesitation on the part of the two bishops was to destroy the appearance of strong united action. Bishop Walmesley wrote to the Bishops Talbot begging them to delay no longer and join with their fellow bishops and withdraw their signatures from the petition.

The Committee met on 19 November and on succeeding days to consider the situation. They considered it impossible to agree to Bishop Walmesley's request to have his and the other bishops signatures withdrawn from the Protestation, as the document had already been in the hands of Mr. Pitt and others and thus was now a public document. They also drew up a reply to the encyclical of the vicars apostolic, which was dated 25 November.

Besides being sent to all the vicar apostolic the letter was also printed and circulated, and with it a manifesto of the Committee addressed to the Catholics of England, giving their account of the whole history of the origin and progress of the negotiations as to the Protestation and the oath. The pamphlet comprised fifteen closely printed pages and was bound in a dark blue wrapper, which acquired the name of *The Blue Book*. It was not published, but copies were freely distributed.

Bishop Walmesley considered the issue of the *Blue Book* as an act of defiance calling attention also to the fact that only seven out of the thirteen members of the Committee had signed it. He attributed its publication mainly to the indecision of the two Bishops Talbot, and once more wrote begging them to publish the encyclical as they had agreed at Hammersmith but without result.

Bishop Thomas Talbot replied to Bishop Walmesley, and although worried about the possibility of a schism between English Catholics on the subject, stated that both he and his brother believed that the request of the Committee to postpone the encyclical was reasonable and thought it ought not to be refused. They considered the declaration by the Committee to endeavour to procure an alteration of any objectionable clauses sufficient reason for them to hold back their encyclicals.

Bishop James Talbot was now in failing health. The atmosphere of strife and contention which surrounded the last years of his life were uncongenial to his nature. He could not cope with the difficulties with the Committee. For years as coadjutor to Bishop Challoner, and for the past nine years vicar apostolic his ordinary life, his administration of his District and his passion for works of charity found full scope for his saintliness.

Despite the holiness of his private life, Bishop Talbot was never qualified either by temperament or by natural gifts to hold a position which involved taking the lead in public action, still less so at a time of difficulty, when vigorous measures were called for. This he would have been the first to admit. His naturally retiring disposition had been emphasised by his own personal history. The position in which he was placed during the last nine years of his life was a constant trial to him. He was convinced that he had been appointed vicar apostolic only for the two reasons that he was highly connected, and had a certain private income, and that he was unfit for the position was evident to all.

During the first four years that he ruled the London District, Bishop Talbot continued to live in his lodgings in Little James Street, Bedford Square. In 1785 he moved to Hammersmith and lived in the house of the convent chaplain. He was frequently absent for long periods, as he visited the whole of his District every year, and travelling in those days took up much time. Latterly, his health was visibly failing. His memory had become defective, and he had lost so many teeth that his speech was noticeably affected.

In 1787 his eldest brother, the Earl of Shrewsbury died. Bishop James Talbot received some benefit under his brother's will, and as was to be expected, devoted it all to charitable works. The Bishop survived his brother less than three years, and in that period he put in hand various good works. He completed the purchase of the property at Old Hall Green, and enlarged the school, building additions at the north and south ends. He also allocated further sums to the support of the missions and other good works, such as providing for spiritual welfare of Catholic prisoners. He also built a number of chapels and churches in London, an important building was the church near St. George's Fields, the precursor of Pugin's well known church which became the cathedral of the diocese of Southwark. The old church was often referred to as the Borough Chapel.

In early January 1790, Bishop Talbot's illness had so increased that it became evident that he had not much longer to live. He told his confessor, Rev. John Lindow, that if it pleased God to restore him to health, the first use he would make of it would be to take stronger measures against the laymen who were trying to usurp the functions of bishops. However he became gradually worse, and after receiving the last rites from Rev. John Lindow, calmly awaited his end. His deathbed was peaceful and saint-like. Dr. Milner was present, and preaching to his people the following Sunday, described the scene:

"We beheld him five days ago with mixed emotions of grief and admiration. In the very pangs of death, with an open brow and a placid countenance, waiting for the happy moment that was to consign him to his reward, after having fought the good fight, run his destined race, and preserved the faith. Who that contemplated this scene could have avoided crying out with him who had the happiness of being witness to it: Let my soul die the death of the just man, and let my latter end be like unto his".

Bishop James Talbot died at Hammersmith on Tuesday 26 January 1790. He was buried in the Baynard vault, in the parish churchyard. As no public Catholic funeral was at that time possible, it was customary to read the Catholic burial service before the body was removed. The only prayers at the burial itself consisted of the Protestant service, which was read by the clergyman. In many cases a Requiem Mass was offered for the deceased, but it was always entirely separate from the funeral, usually not even on the same day. In the case of Bishop Talbot, a High Mass of Requiem was sung at each of the four chief embassy chapels in turn, at which the clergy and laity were invited to attend.

It was almost a century later that his remains were translated from Hammersmith, and placed in their present resting place in the chapel cloister at St. Edmund's College. No better place could have possibly been found than the College which was built as an extension on his own humble school at Old Hall Green. The second funeral took place on 25 April 1901, and the ceremony and circumstances brought into sharp contrast the Catholic Church in England in the preceding century. The public procession up the college drive, the Requiem and other rites in the beautiful Gothic chapel of the college, were surroundings which would not have been thought possible at the time when Bishop Talbot ruled the London District. In the presence of the professors and students of the college, and of several representatives of his own family, his remains were placed in their last resting place.

It is regrettable that we are unable to learn more of the inner life of one whom we cannot but regard as a really remarkable man, who through his very retirement and humility exercised a widespread and lasting influence on Catholic affairs. So far as can be ascertained, he never sat for a portrait, as anyone else in his position would have done, and we are ignorant of his personal appearance. His whole aim in life seemed to be self-effacement. The few letters of his which remain, reveal a man of large-hearted charity, of boundless sympathy with the fallen and the unfortunate, and of the most tender personal piety. With all his weakness of character, and even timidity where public action was concerned, James Talbot, the last confessor of the faith in penal England, has left us an example of heroic charity and patience in the darkest days of English Catholics when the hope for the future was unknown among them, which those of later and more hopeful times should never forget.

While Bishop Talbot lay dying, Catholic England was working itself up into a ferment over the question of the oath. Not even a temporary cessation deemed necessary out of respect for his memory when he died. Meetings continued to be held and pamphlets to be printed without intermission. Bishop Gibson of the Northern District issued a vigorous pastoral against the Committee dated 15 January. Bishop Walmesley had issued a similar one before Christmas in answer to the Committee's letter published in the first *Blue Book*. Both pastorals were written in strong partisan language, such expressions as 'glaring misrepresentations' and 'glossed over with remote interpretations - a groundless pretence - a far fetched shift - delusive but no new artifice' all occurring freely throughout.

The Committee had already begun to realise that their only real chance of success lay in arranging some sort of compromise with the bishops. A conference was organised and the Committee invited the bishops. Bishop Gibson however bluntly declined all further dealings with them. He was laid up with gout, and therefore unable to come himself, and he refused to send a deputy. Bishop Walmesley was more obliging and came with his coadjutor Dr. Sharrock. Bishop Thomas Talbot came and Dr. Berrington, being a member of the Committee came as a matter of course. The meeting was fixed for Wednesday 3 February and great anxiety was felt as it was the first time the vicars apostolic had ever been face to face with the Committee.

During the meeting, despite the objections from Bishop Walmesley, some small amendments to the proposed oath were agreed. It was evident that the two vicars apostolic who were present were not of the same mind. In addition there were some who would have voted for the oath but were not present, in the majority of cases they had not even heard of the meeting, for no invitations were issued. In reality therefore the opinions of Catholics on the question of the oath was far from unanimous. In the meantime, public affairs dictated that the Catholic question was postponed, seen by many and especially Bishop Walmesley as a special providence, for had the Bill run its course that year, there would have been no one to organise any opposition to the oath as it then stood.

At the annual general meeting of English Catholics, held on 6 May there was little business to transact. Bishop Thomas Talbot was elected a member of the Committee in place of his deceased brother, this being no doubt intended as a compliment, in recognition of his kind attitude towards the Committee. It was also agreed at the meeting to go on with the Bill in its present state.

Parliament was dissolved on 20 June. As a result of the general election in the autumn, Pitt continued in power, with an increased majority, and in the session of 1791 the Catholic Relief Bill was introduced into the House. By that time Bishop John Douglass had been elected vicar apostolic of the London District, and the Catholic body were in a position to make their voice heard independently of the Committee.

There was no recognised method of procedure for electing a new vicar apostolic. For many years the Stuart claimant to the throne continued to exercise his privilege of nomination. From 1765 the election of the English bishops was left entirely in the hands of the Congregation of Propaganda. In the London District there had been no election during a vacancy within living memory, the last one had been in 1703. In the majority of cases the reigning vicar apostolic applied during his lifetime for a coadjutor, who succeeded immediately after his death. There was some doubt how to proceed. By the Constitution of Benedict XIV, then in force, the vicar general of the deceased bishop became administrator during the vacancy and accordingly that position was assumed by Rev. James Barnard.

The situation became more complicated by the action of the Committee. Immediately on the death of Bishop Talbot, they saw their opportunity. If only they could succeed in obtaining the transfer of Bishop Berrington to London as the new vicar apostolic, the influence and power of their party would be permanently established. Under ordinary circumstances it would have seemed a very popular appointment. Being an Essex man by birth, Bishop Berrington naturally belonged to the London District. He had been chaplain at Ingatestone Hall, and was well known to the majority of the London clergy.

On Thursday 18 February at the conclusion of the Requiem for Bishop Talbot at Lincoln's Inn Fields, the clergy adjourned to 4 Castle Street to hold a meeting to select nominations to send to Rome. Thirty nine priests were present, and twenty one others voted by proxy, making a total of sixty priests represented, almost all the priests in the District. At the beginning of the meeting the Rev. James Barnard announced that in Bishop Talbots will dated 2 August 1788, he had requested that Rev. Richard Southworth, of Brockhampton should be recommended to Rome for his successor . He also added that at a later date Bishop Talbot had communicated with Rev. John Douglass with a view to obtaining his appointment a coadjutor with right of succession. They then proceeded to their 'election' and chose Bishop Berrington by thirty nine votes out of sixty. Two other names were added as the result of further voting, Rev. John Douglass and Rev. Peter Browne.

Important steps were also taken by the laity to secure the same end. Immediately after the clergy meeting, the Committee prepared a letter to Cardinal Antonelli, Prefect of Propaganda, which they were fortunate enough to be able to forward that very evening, for it was the day for the foreign mail, which went then only once a week. Rev. Barnard's report did not go until the following week, and the Committee had every hope that being first in the field they would secure their wishes.

Cardinal Antonelli, after receiving the recommendations of both the laity and clergy, wrote to the vicars apostolic asking their advice. However,

Bishop Gibson's gout returned to him in an aggravated form, and after a short illness he died at Stella Hall, on 19 May 1790. The state of the English Catholics was now critical indeed. There were only two vicars apostolic left, it became a matter of the most urgent importance that the nominations to the two vacant Districts should be hastened forward with all possible speed.

The late Bishop Matthew Gibson had left a sealed envelope containing his recommendation as to his successor. It later transpired that the person whom the late bishop wished to recommend was his brother Rev. William Gibson, the president of Douay. His election was decided by Propaganda at their meeting on 19 July. In the London District after much correspondence between Rome and England the appointment of Dr. John Douglass was made on 22 August, but was held back until finally confirmed on 15 September. There was considerable anger among the Committee members and both clergy and laity. Opposition to Dr. Douglass seemed at first likely to spread. However, just as it was beginning to assume serious proportions, the whole movement suddenly collapsed owing to the unexpected action of Bishop Berington, who with straight forward common sense repudiated all pretension to the post of vicar apostolic.

Both new vicars apostolic were consecrated at Lulworth Castle the home of the Weld family. Bishop Gibson was consecrated by Bishop Walmesley on 5 December. Bishop Douglass was consecrated on 19 December, by the newly consecrated Bishop William Gibson.

John Douglass was born at Yarm in North Yorkshire in 1743, his family appear constantly in the Recusant Rolls. At the age of thirteen he was sent to Douay. He became Professor of Humanities at Valladolid, and also taught philosophy in the English College there. In 1773 he came to England and was appointed to the mission at Linton and subsequently York.

In February 1791 Parliament met and there was some hope that a Catholic Relief Bill was confidently hoped for early in the session. The bishops knew that some communications were passing between members of the Committee and the Government, but no information was given to the bishops. The Committee did not wish to be shackled by the interference of the bishops in their dealings with ministers and preferred to let the plans of the Government reach a stage when interference of any kind would be difficult, if not impossible. The bishops therefore had no alternative but to act independently of them.

Bishops Gibson and Douglass, on their arrival in London, about the middle of January, promulgated the second condemnation of the oath, in the terms agreed with Bishop Walmesley. Charles Butler wrote inviting Bishop Douglass to a conference on Tuesday 26 January. This came too late as the encyclical was read on Sunday 24 January. The encyclical letter reiterated the bishops previous condemnation of the proposed oath and warned that none of the clergy or laity should take any new oath. They also emphasised that the Committee had no right or authority to determine the lawfulness of oaths or declarations or other instruments whatsover concerning doctrinal matters, and that this authority resides in the bishops, they being, by Divine institution, the spiritual governors in the Church of Christ, and the guardians of religion. The letter ends: "We shall here conclude with expressing to you our hopes that you have rejected with detestation some late publications, and that you will beware of others which may appear hereafter. Of those that have been published, some are schismatical, scandalous, inflammatory and insulting to the Supreme Head of the Church, the Vicar of Jesus Christ."

Bishop Thomas Talbot did not sign the encyclical, the reasons he gave in a letter to Bishop Gibson, was that as he had condemned the Bill once he saw no reason to condemn it a second time. He perhaps was also slightly inconsistent as he said that in any event he could not condemn the document as he had not seen it. He also pointed out that the offensive tone was due to the "persons in administration who required that form of words, which perhaps our condemnation will not compel them to alter".

In the meantime, the Committee had recognised that the encyclical of the bishops was a direct attack on them, and they set themselves to work to answer it. The introduction of the Bill was expected within two or three weeks, and it was important, they thought, to counterbalance the effect of the encyclical before its introduction. During the next few weeks excitement reached fever pitch leading to action and language ever to be regretted.

The Committee arranged a meeting with the two vicars apostolic, Bishops Gibson and Douglass for 8 February. The bishops wished to bring with them several of their clergy as theological advisors, but the Committee refused to agree with this. As a compromise they agreed that Rev. James Barnard could accompany the two bishops. They met in Charles Butler's chambers. As soon as they arrived it became evident they were not to be received in any spirit of conciliation. The members of the Committee at once began putting questions to the bishops which criticised their action, Charles Butler wrote down their answers. It looked as though the bishops were undergoing cross-examination at a court of law, the questioning and arguments lasted for over two hours. Finally, Bishop Gibson rose to his feet and declared that all this argument was of no importance, the question was - would the Committee or would they not submit? There followed a bitter exchange, with signed written statements being issued and yet finally the meeting broke up without having achieved any definite result.

On returning home, the bishops decided to summon a number of the most prominent clergy to discuss what had taken place. The great majority of the clergy were against the lawfulness of taking the oath, they showed themselves anxious to stand by the bishops, and expressed their loyalty to Rome.

From the very beginning it must have been evident that the two parties were hopelessly unable to understand each other, and that the uncompromising attitudes assumed by both precluded any prospect of a settlement.

To the modern reader, sympathy would naturally be on the side of authority, perhaps feeling some indignation at the insults offered to the divinely constituted rulers of the Church. At the time there was a large number of Catholics who although admitting that the Committee showed disrespect or worse to the episcopal character and that their methods in order to gain their own ends were not always straight forward, resented the implication that members of the Committee were men devoid of principle or religion. There was open war between the Committee and the bishops just at the moment when the Catholic question was about to come before Parliament - and the anti-episcopal party had the ear of the Government.

The Committee issued a *'Manifesto and Appeal'* which was addressed to the vicars apostolic. The language used exceeded all the previous letters of the Committee, it remains a record of the scandalous lengths to which the party allowed themselves to be driven during the heat of contest. The *Manifesto and Appeal* is described by Milner as a "stunning complication of profaneness, calumny, schism and blasphemy". The whole document was in fact so bad that it did more good than harm to the bishop's cause, by alienating public sympathy from the side of the Committee.

There was a bitter dispute between Bishop Walmesley and Rev. Joseph Wilkes, who was considered to be the author of the *Manifesto*. This continued for several years and was to agitate the English Catholics and became the chief cause contributing to the bitterness of feeling between laity and the bishops for a generation.

The Catholic Relief Bill came before Parliament on Monday 21 February 1791 as "A Bill to relieve upon conditions and under restrictions, persons called Protesting Catholic Dissenters, from certain penalties and disabilities to which papists, or persons professing the popish religion, are subject". The motion stood in the name of Mr. Mitford. No more interesting period could be found in all the long history of the House up to that date. Pitt and Fox, as leaders of the Government and Opposition respectively, were at their best. The Speaker was Mr. Addington, who afterwards succeeded Pitt as Prime Minister, and among the statesmen in connection with the Catholic Bill are such familiar names as Edmund Burke, Windham, Dundas, Sir Archibald McDonald, John Mitford and Wilberforce.

As soon as the bishops had news that a Bill was before Parliament, and that it included the oath in the form passed at the meeting of February 1790, they immediately wrote to Thomas Weld begging him to use his influence with Mr. Pitt, who was his personal friend, and to persuade him to amend the Bill. On the evening before the introduction of the Bill, the bishops sent an invitation to the Committee to co-operate with them to obtain the consent of the Government to substitute one of the two oaths - that of the Act of 1788 or the Irish Oath of 1774 - in place of that in the Bill. They met in a cordial spirit, although yet again the bishops became dissatisfied with their own oath and submitted further commendations. Finally John Mitford refused to bring in the Bill unless the old oath remained unaltered.

The Strangers Gallery in the House was crowded. John Mitford stood up to propose the introduction of the Bill. His speech was mainly devoted to explaining the difference between Protesting and non-Protesting Catholics. He said that popular prejudices must be attended to and asked that Catholics should be allowed to practice their religion in peace.

Fox spoke next. Toleration in religion was, he said, the right of all, and with respect to the alleged reasons for the penal laws - the dangerous opinions of Catholics - he did not believe in their existence. The real origin of the laws was the fear of the Pope's power. In the reign of Charles II they had been actuated by a fear of getting a popish king. These fears were legitimate in their day, but all ground for them had now vanished. The Pope had no power, the idea of a popish king was out of the question, and for a popish Pretender, if there were Jacobites enough left to go and look for one, where would they find him? He pointed to the Act of 1778 and to the state in Ireland since their Act in 1774 as proof of the peaceable behaviour of Catholics. To plead the Gordon Riots as a reason against the Bill, would be equivalent to condemning Catholics to penal laws in perpetuity. He asked also, what right the House of Commons had to decide in matters of religion. Some thought that the Pope was infallible, some that a General Council was, but who ever thought that the House of Commons was infallible? He was glad to learn that the dissenters were in favour of the Bill. Personally he objected to Methodist doctrines more than to Roman Catholic, but there were many good men who held one or the other. The tyranny of a majority was the hardest form of tyranny, and in moving his amendment, he pleaded for universal toleration.

Edmund Burke, who spoke next, enlivened the debate with the bright humour characteristic of his nationality, and ridiculed any fear of the danger of Popery. In any case he asked, why was the oath under the Act of 1778, which the Catholics had all cheerfully taken, now deemed insufficient? Why heap up oath upon oath? He had not heard lately that the Pope was going to invade us, or that he was active in rebellions or revolutions. He admitted that in the past England had suffered at the hands of Popes. Pope Julius Caesar had conquered the whole land, Pope Claudius had been less successful, Pope Domitian and Nero had visited us by their legates. It was the duty of the State to make its citizens happy, how could a Catholic be happy, if every magistrate was an inquisitor, and if he was liable to be hanged, drawn and quartered merely for his religious opinions?

Pitt then proceeded to speak on behalf of the Government. He appealed to Fox to withdraw his amendment, at least for the present, as it would interfere with the passing of the Bill. Leave was eventually given, without division, for the introduction of the Bill.

Milner at the time the Bill was before Parliament continued to circulate handbills, speaking on behalf of the vicars apostolic, the majority of the clergy and therefore the laity, putting forward objections to the wording of the oath. This caused a long lasting dispute with Charles Butler, at their last meeting which was very heated, Butler closed it abruptly by saying to Milner, "I wish you well, but I desire never more to see your face". Milner subsequently resigned his agency of the vicars apostolic to Francis Plowden the lawyer, and returned to Winchester. Rev. Charles Plowden had returned to Lulworth, he wrote from there on 21 March testifying to the work that Milner had done. "I hear our friend Mr. Milner is retired, and however much he is abused, he has certainly the merit and comfort of having yielded essential service. He has frightened the Committee from their first plan, and he has spread information through the Parliament. I hope his active service may be properly represented at Rome".

The Bill was read for the third time on 20 April and then sent to the House of Lords. The first reading took place on 3 May, without debate. The peers proved friends of the vicars apostolic. At the request of Bishop Walmesley and Bishop Douglass, the second reading was postponed several times and did not eventually come on until 31 May. The vicars apostolic would now prefer the Bill to be dropped rather than that it should pass in an unacceptable form.

Communication was also opened up with the Anglican bishops, whose influence in the House of Lords on a question which was chiefly religious might be expected to be decisive. Milner wrote a very carefully reasoned letter, containing a precise explanation of the parts of the oath objected to, and sent copies to the Bishops of Hereford and Salisbury, with both of whom he had a slight acquaintance. Bishop Walmesley summoned up courage and wrote to Dr. Moore, Archbishop of Canterbury, and begged Bishop Douglass to do the same. Dr. Moore had, like most of his contemporaries, anti-Catholic prejudices from early education. The Anglican bishops as a body were no more favourably disposed, their position and antecedents had necessarily brought them face to face with the Catholic position at one time or another. In deciding against the Catholic Bill, we need not be surprised that they should have imbibed prejudices in a greater degree than others. The vicars apostolic saw in the attitude of the Anglican bishops who were determined to reject the Bill as the easiest way out of their difficulties with the

Committee. Bishop Walmesley's letter to the Archbishop of Canterbury, the day before the second reading was to be moved represents apparently the highest hopes of the vicars apostolic at that moment:

May 30, 1791

"My Lord, The senior of the Superiors of the English Roman Catholic clergy takes the liberty to address Your Grace on the present interesting occasion. A few persons of our Committee, called the Catholic Committee, lately presented a Bill to Parliament, now pending in the House of Lords, containing an oath which three of us (of four Superiors) disapproved as ambiguous in some expressions, and as clashing in some articles with our religious principles. This as Your Grace sees, does not affect our allegiances to Government, which is truly constant and sincere, and we fully pledged it by the oath we took in 1778. The oath in question, My Lord, relates to conscience, in which I am persuaded Your Grace would not restrain us. Probably the refractory and indecent protests of the Catholic Committee made lately and printed against us have reached Your Grace's knowledge, and which I presume you freely condemn. The spirit of unbounded liberty prevailing in this philosophic age cannot certainly be agreeable to Your Grace. Some amendments have indeed been made and admitted in the above mentioned oath, but still it is not such as to meet with our approbation, nor have we any apparent hopes of its being made religiously unexceptionable. I therefore entreat Your Grace to procure the suppression of the present Bill, which favour will remove my pressing anxiety, and will be at the same time a signal proof of Your Grace's readiness to vindicate the rights of Episcopacy.

I am, with confidence in Your Grace's protection,
Your Grace's very humble servant,
Charles Walmesley

The Catholic bishops despaired of being able to procure the amendment of the Bill, and now definitely wished to see its rejection. When, however, their prospects seemed hopeless, help came from an unexpected quarter, from one of the Anglican bishops themselves. This was Dr. Samuel Horsley, the Bishop of St. David's, and one of the most prominent members of the bench. Joseph Berington drafted a letter for Bishop Douglass to sign, and conveyed it personally to Dr. Horsley. The letter simply contained a request for assistance in the crisis, Dr. Horsley responded with such a positive effect it exceeded the highest hopes of the vicars apostolic. His speech in the House of Lords was long afterwards spoken of by Catholics as having turned the scale in their favour.

Dr. Horsley is described by contemporaries as a small man, of very dark complexion, with a determined expression, and a deep sonorous voice, and his words were listened to attentively. "My Lords," he began, "with great charity for the Roman Catholics, with a perfect abhorrence of the penal laws,

I have my doubts whether the Bill for their relief that has been sent up to us from the Lower House comes in a shape fit to be sent to a committee. My Lords, it is not my intention to make any express motion to obstruct the commitment of it, if I should perceive that measure to be the sense and inclination of the House, but I have my doubts, which I think it my duty to submit to your Lordship's consideration.

"Fixed as I am in the persuasion that religion is the only solid foundation of civil society, and by consequence that an establishment of religion is an essential branch of every well constructed polity, I am equally fixed in another principle that it is a duty which the great law of Christian charity imposes on the Christian magistrate to tolerate Christians of every denomination separated from the Established Church by conscientious scruples, with the exception of such sects only, if such there be, which hold principles so subversive of civil government in general, or so hostile to the particular constitution under which they live, as to render the extermination of such sects an object of just policy. My Lords, I have no scruple to say that the opinions which separate the Roman Catholics of the present day from the communion of the Church of England are not that dangerous complexion".

Having clearly declared his opinions as to the present time, Dr. Horsley proceeded to admit as a Protestant of that day naturally would, that there had been times when he said that "the towering ambition of the Roman clergy, and the tame superstition of the people, rendered the hierarchy the rival of the civil Government, the triple mitre the terror of the Crown, in every State in Christendom". He said that at the time of the Reformation, the breach with Rome had excited a spirit of intrigue among the adherents of the papacy against the internal Government, which rendered every Roman Catholic, a disaffected, or at best a suspected subject. But those times were now past, "the ambition of the Roman pontiff, by the reduction of his power and his fortunes, is become contemptible and ridiculous in the eyes of his own party. . . . The extinction of the Stuart family leaves the Roman Catholics of this country no choice but the alternative of continuing in the condition of aliens in their native land, or of bringing themselves under the protection of her laws by peaceable submission and loyal attachments to the existing Government.

"My Lords, this Bill is to relieve the Roman Catholics from the penal laws, under the condition that they take an Oath of Allegiance, Abjuration and Declaration, the terms of which oath the Bill prescribes. The Bill will therefore relieve such Roman Catholics as take this oath, and none else. Now, My Lords, it is, I believe, a well known fact that a very great number, I believe I should be correct if I were to say a very great majority, of the Roman Catholics scruple the terms in which this oath is unfortunately drawn and declare they cannot bring themselves to take it. The majority of Roman Catholics who scruple this oath are not papists in the opprobrious sense of the word, they are not the Pope's courtiers more than the gentlemen of the Roman Catholic Committee, who are ready to swear allegiance to the King, they are ready to abjure the Pretender, to renounce the Pope's authority in civil and temporal matters, they are ready to renounce the doctrine that faith is not kept with heretics, and that persons may be murdered under the pretence that they are heretics as impious and unchristian, they are ready to renounce the doctrine that Princes excommunicated by the See of Rome may be deposed by their subjects, but this deposing doctrine they scruple to apply the epithets of impious, unchristian and damnable. My Lords, they think that this doctrine is rather to be called false than impious, traitorous than unchristian, they say that the language of the oath should not be adorned, figured, and implied, but plain simple and precise".

Dr. Horsley next proceeded to discuss the authority of the Pope. He pointed out that if the Pope's supreme spiritual authority were allowed, some indirect interference with the civil Government would in certain cases inevitably follow. For example, such authority was incompatible with the English Law which constituted the King as head of the Church, and even with the validity of Anglican ordinations, so that Catholics looked upon him (Dr. Horsley) as not being a bishop. This of course is an error, the question of Anglican Orders stands on a totally different footing from that of papal claims. It is well known that Catholics commonly believe in the validity of the Orders of the priests of the Greek Church and even the Coptic Church of Abyssinia although their Church is not in communion with Rome. Dr. Horsley accepted that Catholics could not abjure these principles, the most that they should be asked to swear should be that they would never act upon them to the prejudice of the state, and never do anything that would be constructed as hostile to the Government or Constitution. This they already had done in taking the Oath of 1778, and were willing to do again.

It was true, he added, that the Catholic Committee did not admit that the oath bore the meaning which was objected to. That he would not argue beyond saying that it contained things which he himself, as a Protestant, would refuse to swear. The Catholic Committee, however, in denying that meaning, avowedly accepted the spiritual supremacy of the Pope just as fully as the others did, contending that the oath as it stood was not incompatible with such acceptance. Thus the contest was one of words. Both parties were equally loyal. Whatever could be alleged against the bishops could with equal truth be alleged against the Committee. There was absolutely no reason to favour one party rather than the other. He said that the dispute between them had been carried on at first in terms of moderation, but as time went on, the two parties had grown heated, and hard words had been used on both sides. "The scrupulous Catholics" he said "speak of the writings on the other side as schismatical, scandalous and inflammatory, the Catholic Committee charge the Catholic bishops with inculcating principles hostile to society and Government, and to the Constitution and laws of the British. My Lords, these reproaches are unmerited, I think, on either side, but thy are for that reason stronger symptoms of intemperate heat on both sides". He pointed out that this Bill, if passed, could not but inflame the quarrel, for the leaders of the Committee would have others at their mercy. "My Lords, I shudder at the scene of terror and confusion which my imagination sets before me, when under the operation of this partial law, should it unfortunately receive Your Lordships' sanction, miscreants or base informers may be enriched with the fortunes our gaols may be crowded with the persons, and our streets may stream with the blood, of conscientious men and of good subjects".

In conclusion, Dr. Horsley expressed his regret that the legislature was not content with the oath of 1778, but as it appeared that they were not, he was afraid that the Bill was incurable. Nevertheless, rather than that the Catholics should suffer, in the event of this Bill being rejected, he would pledge himself to bring in another the following year, which should be so drafted as to relieve, not one party or the other, but the whole Roman Catholic body.

The speech of Dr. Horsley produced a great effect on the House of Lords on account of his evident sincerity and earnestness, but likewise caused a feeling bordering on dismay among Catholics throughout the country. The sight of a Protestant bishop openly proclaiming the disputes between two sections of the Catholic body could not but fill them with shame. The Committee themselves, perhaps realising that they were in some measure answerable for this state of affairs, tried to throw the blame on Milner. They contended that the handbills, which had been circulated among the members of Parliament, had provided the matter for Dr. Horsley's speech, which was they said, practically a repetition, "with very little variation", of his handbill. Milner himself tells us that his letter to the Bishops of Hereford and Salisbury supplied Dr. Horsley with one of his main arguments.

The acute crisis was over. The idea of two Bills had been abandoned, and since Bishop Horsley's speech, the Lords had been practically unanimous that the oath must either be amended so as to be acceptable to all Catholics, or be set aside and another substituted. In the end the Irish oath was used subject to only a few modifications to form. The Bill was read the third time on Tuesday, 7 June and returned to the Commons, who probably had not enough interest in it to discuss further. They simply accepted it as it stood, with all the Lord's amendments. On Friday 10 June 1791, the Royal Assent was given, and the Bill became law, and came into operation a fortnight later. The day on which the new Act came into force made it possible to celebrate Mass publicly in England. By a remarkable coincidence, this was the actual anniversary of the day on which, two hundred and thirty two years before, Queen Elizabeth I had prohibited the Mass.

The Catholic Church in England had in fact now passed its low water mark and was beginning to expand. Churches had been built before the Act came into being, now according to the new Act, these chapels could be rendered legal and the celebration of Mass in them permissible. Two formalities were necessary, the chapels had to be registered and the clergy to take the oath about which there had been so much discussion. The oath could be taken either at Westminster or at any of the Quarter Sessions, the majority of the London clergy took it on the same day, early in July. They went to Westminster in a body numbering over forty, headed by Bishop Douglass himself.

With respect to the chapels, there was a curious proviso in the Act forbidding the celebration of Mass in any building with a steeple or bell. The further restriction that the doors of the Catholic chapels were not to be "locked, barred or bolted" shows that a strange suspiciousness still surviving that they might be used for treasonable meetings. Catholics had been so accustomed to keep the doors locked during Mass, to guard against the intrusion of 'informers', that on more than one occasion they fell into serious trouble by infringing this regulation.

A "Roman Catholic Ecclesiastick" would forfeit all benefit under the Act, if he should "exercise any of the rites or ceremonies of his religion, or wear the habit of his order" in any other place. It was under the corresponding clause of the Emancipation Act of 1829, that the Eucharistic procession was prohibited by the Government in September 1908. Parliament wished to inhibit any display of Catholic rites outside the places licensed by the Act. Likewise the clause was designed to prevent a priest appearing in the streets in his cassock. From the time of the passing of the Act, High Mass, and even Pontifical High Mass, became rapidly more common. Public sermons were definitely permitted in all registered chapels, as well as at those of the embassies.

Every member of the congregation was also theoretically bound to take the oath in order to share the privileges of the Act. The legal obligation of going to church was not abolished, and it was only such Catholics as had taken the oath who could fulfil that obligation by going to Mass at a registered chapel. In fact, however, very few laymen went through that formality. It has been estimated that not more than 5,000 did so, and this number included the clergy. The chief reason no doubt that so few took the oath was that there was a fee of two shillings attached to the taking of it. Many Catholics who drove to Mass availed themselves of the legal privilege by which those who were "driving to church" on a Sunday were excused from paying toll at the turnpikes.

The ordinary chapel of the period would appear to us now plain and even bare. On the walls there would be perhaps one or two pictures of sacred subjects, but the only decoration was centred around the high altar, which was then the only altar. The taste of the day did not lend itself to ecclesiastical art, compared to the ornamental displays of later Victorian church decoration and adornment, led by Pugin and others, the chapels were perhaps more austere than post Vatican II church decoration of the late twentieth century. Nevertheless there was a simplicity which inspired devotion, and in later times caused Cardinal Manning to assert that there was no place where he could say his prayers so devoutly as in one of the old Catholic chapels of England.

The arrangements of the benches was also very different from that which we see today. It was regarded as an axiom that anyone who required a seat must pay for it. In the space known as the 'body of the church' there were no seats of any kind until well into the nineteenth century, and then only the roughest possible forms, without backs. Those who could afford to pay went either into the 'enclosure' in front, or in one of the galleries, in all of which places seats and kneelers were provided. There was no font, the baptismal water was kept in the priest's lodgings, it was only gradually that regular presbyteries, or 'clergy houses', as they were then called, came into existence. After the passing of the Relief Acts, confessionals were erected in several churches, but the priests had become so accustomed to hearing confessions in their own rooms, that many of them continued to do so, and it was a long time before the use of confessionals became general.

In London Bishop Douglass, when at home would wear his pectoral cross openly, which was considered a great advance on previous custom, but no one ever thought of wearing a cassock, except in church until much later. When assisting at High Mass, he used his full pontificals, including mitre and crozier, which again was a great advance on previous practice.

Outside London we find already the beginning of a movement to establish additional missions in towns. The more far seeing amongst the Catholic body were beginning to realise that if the Catholic Church was to have any future in England, the missions in country seats, which had done such important work in the days of persecution under the penal laws, must be supplanted by chapels in the actual centres of population. Now that the penal laws were abolished the Catholics could not be expected to continue to go out into the country to hear Mass. It was time to bring their religion out into the light of day, and to live down prejudice by actual contact with Protestants.

The Relief Act is unclear on the provision for legalising Catholic schools. On the one hand Clause XII enacts that no Catholic who has not taken the oath shall henceforth be prosecuted "for teaching and instructing youth as a Tutor or Schoolmaster", with a restriction specified in Clause XIV that he must not "receive into his school for education the child of any Protestant father". The next clause requires that the head master or mistress of any such school must be registered at the quarter sessions by the Clerk of the Peace. Despite this, however, the following clause enacts, "that nothing in this Act contained shall make it lawful to found, endow or establish any religious order or society of persons bound by monastic or religious vows, or to found, endow or establish any school, academy, or college by persons professing the Roman Catholic Religion".

The new Act renewed all former laws as to the disposal of money for what was considered "superstitious purposes", so that it continued to be fraught with grave risk to leave legacies for any Catholic charities, and in some cases these were positively illegal. Catholics therefore continued for long after this to, leave such moneys to personal friends whom they would privately instruct as to their application. The levying of the double land tax was not affected, for this formed part of the ordinary Land Tax Act, and could only be remitted by omitting the clause in future.

In the case of the professional classes, the advantages gained were very real. This was especially the case with those in the legal profession, who were henceforth allowed to practice as "Counsellor-at-law, Barrister, Attorney, Solicitor, Clerk or Notary". Previously Catholic lawyers had exclusively practised as conveyancers. In general, however, Catholics were very sparsely represented. Even in professions to which their religion was not an absolute obstacle, it was always so serious a drawback to success that few of these were inclined to take the risk. There were a few Catholic doctors, who obtained their medical degrees abroad, but their number was always exceedingly small.

The Relief Act was far from the Catholic Emancipation Act which took a further thirty eight years to achieve. It remained unlawful for a Catholic peer to take his seat in the House of Lords, or for a commonor to sit in the House of Commons, to which indeed he was never likely to be elected, for Catholics were not even allowed to vote at a Parliamentary election. No Catholic could be a judge, or a king's counsel, nor hold any office of trust under the Crown. Catholics could not hold commissions in his Majesty's army or navy, those who wished for a military life were accustomed to seek it by going abroad and joining the Austrian army. All marriages between Catholics had to be celebrated in a Protestant church. This had been the case ever since the Marriage Act of 1753, which had been passed without any references to Catholics, with a view to preventing runaway marriages. In order to conform to it, Catholics would first go through the ceremony in their own chapel, which would be valid according to their consciences and would confer the sacrament. They would then go to the Protestant church merely as a civil act, to render their marriage legal. Milner never ceased to complain of the numerous irregularities to which this gave rise, for partly through ignorance and partly through timidity, Catholics often went to the Protestant church first, and sometimes even omitted the Catholic marriage altogether. Indeed, if the proper order were adhered to, the priest who performed the ceremony incurred some risk, being legally liable to severe penalties, though there is no record of these having ever been enforced. The practice at funerals was much the same, the Catholic service being usually read by the priest at the house of the deceased. A special clause in the new Act forbade a priest to officiate in any cemetery, and the Protestant service would be read there by a clergyman of the Established Church.

So long as these disabilities remained, the Catholic question could not be considered as solved, but for the moment the surviving disabilities were forgotten in the satisfaction of the substantial relief afforded by the new Act.

Extracts from: *The Dawn of the Catholic Revival in England* by Rev Bernard Ward later first Bishop of Brentwood, published by Longman & Co. London
Bibliographical Dictionary of the English Catholics by Joseph Gillow
Published by Burns & Oates, London

Chapter Eight

Towards Emancipation

ENGLISH Catholics became pre-occupied about new and unexpected events in the latter part of 1792, which had a permanent and far reaching influence on the future of the Catholic Church in England. This was the arrival of the French refugee priests, most of them in a state of poverty and destitution, which produced one of the greatest acts of charity in our nation's history. The English people had always been regarded as the hereditary enemies of the French. They differed from them in race, sympathy and religion. Yet as soon as they understood the true meaning of the events which were happening on the other side of the Channel, and recognised that the refugees who arrived in such vast numbers were in truth the victims of religious persecution, they rose as one man, irrespective of religion or party, and joined together in making a supreme effort to help the exiles. Hundreds and thousands of English people, Protestants as well as Catholics, helped the French refugee clergy by their gifts of money and personal effort. In 1789 and 1790 a considerable number, both laity and clergy had come to England. These were the *emigres* properly so-called, supporters of the *Ancien Regime,* who went into voluntary exile on account of the Revolution, and whose property in France was confiscated. In May 1791, Edmund Burke, speaking in the House of Commons on the Quebec Government Bill, took occasion to express his warm sympathy with the clergy and others who were suffering in France for their religion, and his remarks were received with cheering in the House.

The events which led up to this situation may be said to have begun when the law of the Civil Constitution of the clergy was passed, on 12 July 1790. By this law the priests of France were called upon to take the so called "Civil Oath", by which they professed themselves servants of the State. The oath was cleverly drawn up, and at the outset not every one realised that it was definitely schismatical. The great majority of the clergy indeed refused to take it, but a certain number thought that it might be taken without open rupture with the Church. In two briefs, dated 10 March and 13 April 1791 respectively, Pope Pius VI decided definitely against the lawfulness of the oath, and from that time forward, no Catholic was able to take it in good faith. In the event, in Paris out of about 800 priests, some 200 took the oath, and in the provinces about 10,000 out of 60,000. Many of these however

161

afterwards retracted and went into exile. Out of all the French episcopate only four took the oath. As a result of a further law passed on 27 November 1791 the clergy who had not taken the oath were deprived of their office and benefice, under threat of persecution as a disturber of the public peace. It became manifestly impossible to fill the vacant posts with "Constitutional Priests" as they became called, leaving no alternative but to suppress a large number of parishes and some of the episcopal Sees.

Among the first to leave, was Monseigneur de la Marche, Bishop of St. Pol de Leon, a small town in Brittany near St. Malo. He was smuggled out of France by English smugglers and after an arduous voyage arrived in London, resting for a while at Wardour and afterwards at Lulworth. Priests were already arriving in large numbers and the first English priest to devote his time and work to their assistance was Rev. Thomas Meynell the ex-Jesuit.

Events in France took on a more frightful development. On 10 August 1792, the great attack on the Tuilleries Palace took place, with its attendant massacres. The King was now a prisoner. Priests were also rounded up and imprisoned. The National Assembly was now supreme, and on 26 August they passed a law by which all priests who had not taken the oath were ordered to leave their residences within eight days, and to quit the country within a fortnight. In default of which they were to be deported to French Guiana, in South America. Every priest was free to select the country of his exile, he was provided with a passport and an allowance of three francs a day for travelling.

Many of the priests who set out never reached the frontier. The early days of September were marked by the horrible massacres which began in Paris, and were taken up throughout the country. On the evening of 2 September, nearly all the 180 priests who were imprisoned at the *Carmes,* including the venerable Archbishop of Arles, and three other bishops, the General of the Benedictines, several Jesuits and Capuchins, were murdered in cold blood. The Abbe Pannonie, who escaped in an almost miraculous manner, had been close to the archbishop at the moment of his martyrdom. When he arrived in London he was able to provide a full account of the horrible scene.

Similar massacres followed in the provincial towns of France, marked with equal cruelty and violence. Under these circumstances many of the clergy considered that by applying for passports they would become marked men, with little chance of escape. Some spoke openly of the passports as "death warrants", and most priests preferred to take the risk of travelling without them. The clergy naturally made their way to the frontier which was nearest to the place where they lived. Those in the south of France went to Spain or Italy. In the Papal States alone there were over 12,000 refugee priests. The priests who came to England were for the most part from Brittany, Normandy, Picardy or Paris itself.

In England the number of priests who arrived in the first stream of exiles was estimated at about 3000, including sixteen bishops. The population of London at that time was less than a million, so the arrival of many hundreds of exiles could be clearly seen. Writing on 15 September 1792, Sir Samuel Romilly says that "It is impossible to walk a hundred yards in any public street or thoroughfare here without meeting two or three French priests", and he wonders at "the phenomenon that priests should be thus walking unmolested in London twelve years after the Gordon Riots". The Catholic clergy in London at first showed some inclination to be less sympathetic with the exiles than the rest of the people. It appears that the newcomers used to present themselves at the churches in large numbers in order to say Mass, and they would sometimes be rather exacting in their requirements. It was not customary in those days for priests to say Mass daily. In the London churches there were no side altars, and the accommodation was hopelessly inadequate to the ever-increasing crowd of priests awaiting their turns to celebrate. Some arguments took place, and this led to a coldness between the resident clergy and the newcomers. Bishop Douglass wrote a pastoral letter dated 8 October 1792 exhorting both clergy and laity to continue to help the refugees.

A committee was formed to help the refugees instigated by the Marquis of Buckingham and Mr. John Wilmot. Thirty one persons attended, most of them men of standing and influence. They included William Pitt, the Prime Minister, Edmund Burke, Sir Philip Metcalfe MP, Mr. William Wiberforce MP, three other members of the House of Commons, three Protestant clergymen and two Catholic laymen. The committee proceeded to work immediately in close liaison with the Bishop of St. Pol de Leon. The initial appeal to the English nation resulted within a few weeks to a subscription which amounted to £33,775. The amount subscribed was enough for the immediate needs of the exiles. At the commencement, each priest received £2 each month. The bishops received £10 each month.

Most of the refugee clergy and lay people, found accommodation throughout the southern counties of England. Winchester was a centre for over 600 clergy who had accommodation at the King's House until 1796. They were then moved in smaller groups to other establishments, as the Government required the King's House as barracks for the troops to guard against possible invasion by the French. The *emigre* priests followed the ordinary way of life of a seminary. In addition, under the patronage of the Marchioness of Buckingham, a carpet and tapestry manufacturing unit was established, the profits of which went to the benefit of the exiles. The religious exercises in the King's House were kept up with regularity and fervour.

The Blessed Sacrament was exposed during the entire day - a form of devotion at that time hardly known in England. Continual prayers were offered from the midst of Protestant England for the welfare of Catholic France. No charge was made by the Government for the use of the King's House, but the cost of living there was defrayed out of the subscription fund. This fund, large as it was, only lasted six months. The King himself took an active interest, and issued a formal letter dated 17 April 1793. This letter was sent to the two archbishops, of Canterbury and York, and by them forwarded to the other bishops of the establishment. It was read in all the Protestant churches in the kingdom, and was followed by a house-to-house collection. The amount raised was £41,304 and this was almost equalled by a number of private donations. These voluntary subscriptions, however successfully raised could not be more than a temporary expedient. By August 1793, the fund was reduced to £21,000. The committee turned to the Government and they proved receptive. Pitt proposed to the House of Commons that the refugees should be assisted out of the national exchequer and not one dissentient voice was raised. Parliament voted public money for the relief of the refugees at the rate of £200,000 annually.

Towards the end of 1793, another milestone was reached. Monsignor Erskine arrived in London on 12 November as a special envoy from Rome to the government of St. James. Erskine was a Scotsman by descent on his fathers side, his mother was Italian. While quite young, he lost his father, and was adopted by the cardinal Duke of York, who sent him to the Scots' College in Rome. He left after five years and embraced the legal profession, where he attained some eminence. In 1782 he planned to marry, he was then forty-three years old, however the post of *Promoter Fidei* or Devil's Advocate as it is popularly called, became vacant. The Pope unexpectedly offered it to Erskine and this opened up the prospect of a new career. He immediately broke off his intended marriage, became a subdeacon and accepted a canonry of St. Peter's. He never proceeded beyond subdiaconate, but devoted himself to a public career in Rome, his office being a well known step to the cardinalate.

There had already been some informed discussions between the English royal family and the Pope. The Duke of Sussex, one of the King's sons had married in Rome, he was a frequent visitor to the Vatican and was on personal friendly terms with the Pope. This paved the way towards a more formal kind of relationship between the two courts and resulted in the declaration by the English Government of their intention of protecting the Papal States from the attacks of the French. However, Erskine was disappointed at not being welcomed formally, his position was never officially acknowledged. He always wore lay clothes - always wearing black and carried a sword. He met the King following an introduction by his cousin Lord Kellie, and afterwards went to court several times. Erskine did not succeed in bringing the re-opening of diplomatic relations between England and the Holy See any nearer, however he continued to reside in England until 1802.

Out of the calamity of religious persecution on the Continent, the Catholic Church in England was blessed, not only with the great influx of refugee French priest and religious but also with the dissolution of the English colleges and convents on the Continent, refugees now included English clergy and religious. This could have been a problem, as there was a special proviso in the Act of 1791 forbidding the foundation of colleges or convents in England. In the event of a popular outcry, this clause might easily have been put into force. Fortunately, however, the French Revolution allowed no other choice in the matter and the religious communities were received into England with every sympathy. No objections were raised to their permanently settling in this country and the establishment of colleges and religious houses in their midst gave new life and vigour to the Catholics of England.

The schools and colleges of education suffered the loss of all their possessions and funds. The English College at Douay came to an end when the students and professors were imprisoned on 16 October 1793. This was not entirely unexpected, England and France had been at war more than six months. As soon as news of the closure reached Bishop Douglass he realised the pressing need to make provision for the education of the clergy without delay. He naturally turned towards his own school at Old Hall Green, and he conceived the idea of making it develop into a new Douay. He consulted Dr. Milner, and largely followed Milner's advice on the matter. Bishop Douglass recorded in his diary: "1793. On the 12th November I took Messrs. William Beauchamp and John Law to Old Hall, and on the 16th, the feast of St.Edmund, Archbishop of Canterbury, we commenced studies, or established the new college there, a substitute for Douay. Mr. Thomas Cook, who had been at Old Hall Green half a year, employed in teaching the children, and Mr. John Devereux joined the other two. These four communicated at my hands. I said Mass, and after Mass exposed the Blessed Sacrament, and these four, with Mr. Potier, sang the *O Salutaris, Pange Lingua, and Laudate Dominum omnes gentes ad finem.* Thus was the new college instituted, under the patronage of St. Edmund, Archbishop of Canterbury, the afore-mentioned students recommencing their studies in Divinity. *Felx, faustumque sit!*". Within a few weeks the total number of students numbered between fifty and sixty.

Bishop Douglass considered it desirable to have only one general college for all England and naturally thought Old Hall would be satisfactory after some enlargement of the buildings. Bishop Gibson argued for an establishment in the north and looked to an existing school at Tudhoe, a little village not far from Durham. The school, which was a property of Sir John Lawson, was kept by Rev. Arthur Storey. Influential members of the laity backed Bishop Gibson's plan, including Mr. Weld, Lord Arundell and Lord Clifford. Mr. Weld had already indicated his willingness to offer the property at Stonyhurst as an alternative. A printed appeal was issued by the three vicars apostolic, dated 20 June 1794. The Church students at Old Hall were ordered to be ready to move to the north. On 16 August Mr. Storey wrote that Bishop Gibson had found a more suitable house a short distance from Tudhoe, and would be ready to receive new-comers immediately.

At the last moment the whole scheme collapsed. Two reasons were the cause of this. One was that the Cisalpines and Bishop Talbot came to an agreement for conducting Oscott as a joint school. According to the agreement, there was to be a board of Governers, who were to make themselves financially responsible for the conduct of the school. They were to have a right to veto the appointment of the president, who was however to be nominated by the bishop.

The other reason for abandoning the scheme had a more important bearing on Catholic education in England. Because of the war raging on the Continent and the French invasion of the Netherlands, the ex-Jesuits were forced to quit Liege, in a body, crossed to England and decided to accept Mr. Weld's offer and establish themselves at Stonyhurst. This was not altogether a simple matter. At Liege they had been living practically as Jesuits, but on their return to England they came under the jurisdiction of the bishops, as though they were ordinary secular priests. They were willing enough to show proper subordination to the bishop, but they wished to keep the election of their president or rector in their own hands. Bishop Gibson at first showed some opposition to them which was only gradually overcome. However, in the spring of 1796 they received a special brief from Rome dated 14 February, giving them similar rights with respect to the establishment of the college to those they enjoyed at Liege.

This caused the supporters of the Jesuits to remove their patronage from the proposed foundation at Tudhoe, and the project of a college there was abandoned. Bishop Gibson found a more suitable house for his own purpose at Crook Hall, near Durham. The president of Crook Hall was the Rev. Thomas Eyre, who had been a fellow student of Bishop Gibson at Douay. They were both deeply attached to their *Alma Mater,* and their natural ambition was to reproduce Douay life and customs at Crook Hall so far as the changed circumstances would permit. Dr. Lingard, then only in deacon's orders, became vice-president. He was ordained priest the following year. Both he and Mr. Eyre continued all the time the college was at Crook Hall, and both were still in office at the move to Ushaw fourteen years later. The original six students at Crook Hall soon increased to three or four times that number, and later on some sixty or seventy students were housed there.

Early in 1795 the collegians of Douay and St. Omer were set at liberty and arrived in England, they landed at Dover on 2 March. The Benedictines found their way to Acton Burnell, in Shropshire, the seat of Sir Edward Smythe, one of their former pupils. He received them warmly, and for a time the community resided there. The Benedictines from Dieulourd, in Lorraine, were likewise there for a time. They were there before the arrival of the Douay community, but when it became evident that one or other must go elsewhere, they gave way and eventually settled at Ampleforth in Yorkshire in the year 1803. The St. Gregory's community remained at Acton Burrell until their removal to Downside in 1814.

The north versus the south dispute raged as before. The northerners, however, based their contention not on any claim in consequence of the Catholics being more numerous and influential in that part of the country, but solely on the grounds that the cost of property, provisions and coal was cheaper in the north. It was agreed that both Crook Hall in the north and Old Hall Green in the south should give way, provided that a suitable house could be obtained. A large house at Thorpe Arch near Wetherby, in York-shire was chosen and negotiations for its purchase were already in progress. However, Mr. Pitt strongly urged that no new foundation should be made, in case public opinion should be aroused. Pitt suggested that if the new col-lege was built, people would only regard it as an expansion of the existing establishment. Mgr. Erskine was in favour of the Prime Minister's sugges-tion, and proposed that Rev. John Daniel, the last president of Douay should go there to resume his office. Bishop Gibson and John Daniel ar-rived at Crook Hall on 23 June, the intention was to install him as president. Dr. Stapleton, president of Crook Hall arrived on the following day and after lengthy conversations persuaded Daniel not to take the presidency of Crook Hall.

The future of Old Hall was confirmed by a gift of £10,000 by Mr. Sore a rich miller from Bedhampton, near Havant. Building work was commenced without delay. Every effort was made to persuade Daniel to become presi-dent, but he remained loyal to Bishop Gibson. On 19 August the foundation stone of the new college was laid at Old Hall, and Dr. Stapleton was installed as president.

In late August an important meeting of the Lancashire clergy was held at Preston, they passed a resolution in favour of establishing a general college in the north. Bishop Gibson intended to continue with Crook Hall if at all possible. In the event all three establishments continued - Oscott, Old Hall and Crook Hall, the precursor of Ushaw.

Meanwhile, French troops had invaded Italy. By February 1798 General Bertheir took possession of the Castle of St. Angelo, with part of the French army in Rome. The Pope's soldiers were disbanded, although the Pope and most of the cardinals remained in the city. General Bertheir read a declaration making Rome his own independent republic and the arms of the Pope are to be stripped from buildings everywhere. All distinctions are abolished, no more princes, cardinals, prelates, all are equal citizens.

Thousands were fleeing Rome, thousands more were dying of starvation and disease. The English and Scots' College were sequestered in the name of the French Republic. The students were given passports and were allowed to leave for England, the rector remained in charge of the building. The property was looted regularly and eventually the desecration was complete.

The Pope was eventually removed from Rome under an escort of one hundred French troops to Siena, where he was confined in the Augustinian monastery, then moved again to a Carthusian monastery outside Florence where he remained for nine months. Early in 1799 the French determined to remove the Pope to France, a long and arduous journey through the Alps. By August His Holiness was at Valence on the Rhone where he was taken ill. On the 29 August Pope Pius VI died.

Pius VII was elected on 14 March 1800, as Cardinal Chiaramonti, he was a Benedictine. Since the death of his predecessor, there were changes to the political scene. Chief among them, and most closely affecting the pontiff, was the condition of affairs at Rome. Nine months after the French had entered the city, Lord Nelson had appeared off Leghorn with one frigate and four ships of the line, on board were 3000 Neapolitan troops. The French withdrew and Rome was surrendered on 30 September to Captain Trowbridge, Commander of His Majesty's ship *Culloden*, then laying off Civita Vecchia. The Neapolitan troops entered Rome in triumph, however Mr. Smelt writing to Bishop Douglass on 3 January 1800 says: " Great misery still prevails there, some days there is no bread to be had. One of my correspondents says the rich are become poor, and the poor miserable. It is dangerous to go out after dark, the town swarming with thieves, the number of whom is considerably increased by the Neapolitan soldiers, the greatest rogues in the universe. No fewer than 18,000 of these raggomuffins are maintained there, which contributes much to increase the scarcity of provisions. The Romans hate the Neapolitans, some even prefer the French to them"

As soon as the Neopolitans had occupied the city, Sir William Hamilton, the minister at the court of the King of Naples, took steps to secure all British property. Mr. Fagan was commissioned to take possession. Fagan was the son of a baker in Long Acre, London, he was educated by the Jesuits at Liege, and later came to Rome as an artist. He was successful in reclaiming a fair amount of British property, although with respect to the English College there was a conflict of jurisdiction. The Cardinal Protector considering that he was the proper person to reclaim the building, Fagan however, succeeded in pacifying Cardinal Dandini. The building was in a state of dilapidation, the French had sold everything they could lay their hands on, not only furniture and books, but even the locks off the doors. When Mr. Smelt saw it a year later, he describes it as entirely un-inhabital, with scarcely a single pane of glass remaining, adding that "it looks like some houses in London destroyed by the Gordon mob in 1780".

Among the turmoil, in July 1800 two priests, Revv. John Nassau and Gregory Stapleton, came to Rome on a secret mission, that of submitting the question of the marriage of Mrs. Fitzherbert and the Prince of Wales to the judgement of the Holy See. The facts are briefly these. After the secret marriage which took place before a clergyman of the Church of England in Mrs Fitzherbert's house in 1785, for some years the two had remained on good terms. In June 1794 however, they separated, and the following April a public marriage was celebrated between the Prince of Wales and Princess Caroline of Brunswick. This marriage from the first was an unhappy one, and a separation took place at the end of a year. The Prince then turned his thoughts once more towards Mrs Fitzherbert. For a long time she refused to encourage him. In 1799 she consented to renew relations, provided that the question of the validity of her marriage could be referred to the Holy See, and only on condition that the decision was favourable.

It would seem at first sight that such a decision was no more necessary now than before. If the marriage was invalid now, it must have been so throughout, whereas, if it was valid in the first instance, the subsequent marriage of the Prince of Wales to Caroline of Brunswick, however publicly celebrated would not vitiate the former one in the eyes of the Church. In theory this argument is correct, but in practice, considering the publicity of the official marriage of the Prince in 1795, we cannot wonder that Mrs Fitzherbert should have been unwilling to ignore it, and to resume relations as though it had not been, without an authoritative decision on her side. She therefore deputed her confessor Rev. John Nassau, of Warwick Street chapel, to undertake the mission accompanied by Dr. Stapleton.

Considerable delay occurred before the deputation started. During the whole of the year 1799 it was known that there were no cardinals in Rome, and the Sacred Congregations were disperesed. During the Conclave, and for some time after the election of Pius VII had taken place, great uncertainty prevailed as to the future. As the spring wore on, it became known that the Pope would return to Rome. The cardinals were re-assembling, and the ordinary work of the Church was being resumed. It was therefore time for the deputation to set out. Bishop Douglass recorded in his diary: "1800. May 22. On this day, sacred to the Ascension of Our Lord, after Vespers, all matters being at length arranged, Messrs. Stapleton and Nassau set off to Italy, to His Holiness Pope Pius VII, on the business of etc. Mr. John Nassau takes from me a letter of introduction to His Holiness, also letters from me to the Cardinals Gerdil, Antonelli and Borgia, also one to Mr. Smelt our agent. The object of their mission has been covered by the following plea *viz.* That they are going to His Holiness on the business of our college at Rome".

The secret of the cause was well kept. Milner wrote that he was conviced that they had gone at the instigation of the Ministry, on some diplomatic errand. Mgr. Erskine was so angry at not being taken into confidence that he flatly refused to give them a single introduction to anyone in Rome, which was surprising as he had been endeavouring to procure Dr. Stapleton's nomination as the rector of the English College there. Bishop Douglass alone knew what they had gone for, and he eventually notified in his diary the Pope's decision, but realised that this was unwise, he so completely erased the entry that to this day it remains un-decipherable.

Dr. Stapleton and Rev. Nassau reached Rome on 4 July, the day after the solemn entry of the Pope into the city. The question was quickly decided and we know now that it was in favour of the validity of the marriage, as to which indeed there would seem to us today little reason for doubt.

An indirect consequence of Dr. Stapleton's visit to Rome was that he was appointed vicar apostolic of the Midland District. It appears that Propaganda, acting on the advice of the other vicars apostolic, had decided upon recommending Milner for the post, and according to Mr. Smelt his briefs were being actually drawn out when, by the wish of the Pope, a change was made. The reason given was connected with Milner's controversy with Dr. Sturges. Milner's style was characteristic of himself, plain spoken and blunt, and he wrote without thought of any offence he might give to others. Moreover, he viewed everything from the Catholic standpoint, making no allowance for the different outlook which a non-Catholic would necessarily have. Thus his work could hardly fail to give offence to Protestants. Milner had written in his *History of Winchester* of Dr. Hoadly, Bishop of Winchester that "both living and dead he undermind the Church of which he was a prelate". This brought a reply from Dr. Sturges, Chancellor and Prebendary of Winchester. It consisted of seven letters on Popery and was characteristic of the attitude towards Catholics of the Protestants of that period.

Representations were made to the Holy Father that the appointment of Milner at that particular time would not be acceptable to the English Government, and remembering all that the papacy had owed to England during the late wars, he consented to be guided by this consideration.

In the meantime important events were taking place in France. The ruling Directory had been overthrown the previous autumn in favour of a Consulate, Bonaparte being 'First Consul'. Soon after this it became known that he was willing to treat with the Pope for the restoration of Catholic worship, and after some hesitation negotiations were opened by Archbihop Spina of

Corinth. The negotiations lasted many months. Napoleon proposed that the Church should agree to the spoliation of all her lands and property, and that all the bishops should be called upon to resign their Sees, so that he could redistribute the dioceses and nominate a completely new episcopate. In return for these concessions, the Catholic religion was to be re-established, and supported by an annual payment, but in future, the nomination of all the bishops was to be in the hands of the state, subject of course to confirmation by the Pope. After long discussions, the Concordat was ultimately signed by Napoleon on 15 July 1801, and it was subsequently ratified by Pius VII in Rome on 15 August.

The French priests in England had already begun to return to France, in the autumn of 1800 they were leaving in hundreds. In the early part of the year there were over 5,600 receiving aid from the Relief committee, by the end of November 560 of these had already left. The committee advanced them their allowances as an incentive to return home. The cost of travelling to France was estimated at six guineas, and most of the exiles had long distances to travel after landing. In the course of 1801 about 2000 priests went back. The general exodus to France was still in progress when the Peace of Amiens was signed on 27 March 1802, and a fortnight later, the Concordat was officially published. By the end of the year there were only 900 French priests left in England. The number of lay exiles diminished at the same time, by the close of 1802 the total number receiving relief, including both clergy and laity, was only 850, and many of these were English nuns, who of course remained in England for good. The aid from the Treasury grants continued to be paid to the survivors for more than fifteen years after this.

Some clergy remained having become attached to their pastoral work, some were strong royalists, and considered that the Concordat was at best only temporary, they looked forward to the restoration of the Bourbons as the only really secure hope for religion. The French influence remained strong for long afterwards in the Catholic congregations of the south and especially in London. This was visible in the material decoration of the churches, the pattern of vestments and the like for more than half a century afterwards. The French had a more salutary effect on the daily lives of English Catholics, the *emigres* who had always been accustomed to the open profession of their religion in France helped their English brethren to come out of their seclusion now that the penal laws were abolished. They introduced many Catholic customs and practices to which under stress of persecution, the English had been strangers. It took time however to acclimatise, no image of Our Lady was to be seen in churches for a quarter of a century after this, side altars were very exceptional. Processions of all kinds even inside the churches, were still unknown and there was a tendency to consider many of the acts of devotion freely practised in Catholic countries, as an abuse excusable perhaps abroad, but to be avoided in England. The tradition of Sunday Vespers and Benediction were among the good influences due to the refugees from France, in which country there has always been the custom of chanting the vesper psalms on the part of the laity. The English Committee for the relief of the emigrants dissolved in 1806.

In January 1803 Mgr. Erskine was raised to the cardinalate at a Consistory held in the Quirinal. Propaganda consulted with him as to who in England was the most suitable candidate for the episcopate, Cardinal Erskine spoke strongly in favour of Milner. This was remarkable from a man who during his stay in England had endured much hostility from Milner. In his usual uncompromising language he never hesitated to criticise the abuses which he considered still existed in the Roman Curia, and in the management of ecclesiastical affairs. Despite this, Ersking could not fail to see that Milner was by far the strongest man the Catholic Church in England had at that time.

In the event, Rome appointed Milner, Bishop of Castabala in Mesopotamia, vicar apostolic of the Midland District, in a brief dated 1 March 1803. He was consecrated at St. Peter's chapel Winchester on 22 May 1803, by Bishop Douglass, assisted by Bishops Gibson and Sharrock.

John Milner, whose real name was Miller, was born in London on 14 October 1752, the son of Joseph Miller, and his wife Helen Marshland both parents came from Lancashire. His father established himself in London as a tailor. Later he became deranged and remained so until his death. John Milner's first school was at the Franciscan school at Edgbaston and later he went to Sedgley Park school in April 1765. He was entered on the books as John Milner which name he retained. The following year he left Sedgley Park and on the recommendation of Bishop Challoner, was sent to Douay, where he remained for the next eleven years. He was ordained in 1777, for the London Mission and resided in Gray's Inn, but in 1779 he was moved to Winchester. He took the place of Rev. James Nolan, who had died of fever which had broken out among the French prisoners confined in the King's House in Winchester. Although he was considered too young by many Bishop Challoner approved his appointment and on the 15 October accompanied him to Winchester to formally induct him into the mission. After his arrival at Winchester he very soon became very popular. Following the death of Bishop Challoner, Milner gave a funeral oration on the deceased prelate, the first of his published works.

Milner took a leading part in the politics of the period and he was a strong force against the Catholic Committee in defence of the vicars apostolic. He wrote many controverial articles and pamphlets in defence of the Catholic faith and was eventually admitted a Fellow of the Society of Antiquaries. He had twice previously been named before Propaganda for a vicariate and passed over by the Congregation, but the influence of the Irish bishops induced Cardinal Borgia to select Milner. Because of the animosity felt towards him following his battles with the Catholic Committee, he was reluctant to accept the episcopate but he was persuaded by Rev. James Sharrock, brother of the bishop.

Much of his work was political and this period was eventful for the Church. Milner enjoyed the full confidence of the Irish bishops and acted as their agent in negotiations with the British Government. In 1806 it was proposed to Propaganda that Bishop Poynter the coadjutor in the London District, should exchange with Milner, in order that the latter could reside in London to fulfil his political services. This suggestion, probably made at the instigation of the Irish bishops was flatly refused by both Bishops Douglass and Poynter. Subsequently, the Pope gave Milner a dispensation dated 11 April 1808 which enabled him to reside outside of his District and to live in London.

In May 1808, the Catholic Board was formed in England. The issue of a royal veto was being debated and Milner was a fearless opponent. This caused some misunderstandings between himself and Bishops Poynter and Collingridge which led to his expulsion from the Catholic Board and to his exclusion from a meeting of vicars apostolic held in Durham in October 1813.

Catholics were divided into two separate parties, for or against in favour of obtaining Catholic emancipation on the terms of giving the British Government control over the Catholic clergy by means of a veto. This would apply in the selection of bishops and other matters. There were many nobles as well as Bishop Poynter and some of the clergy in favour of an arrangement with the Government. Bishop Milner and most of the Irish bishops were utterly opposed to any arrangement based upon a veto, which would have destroyed the independence of the Catholic Church.

In 1813, Grattan brought in his Bill for a settlement of the question of Catholic Emancipation, containing clauses introduced by Lords Canning and Castlereagh. Sir John Cox Hippesley, a Protestant had served Catholic interests well with the Government and this was duly acknowledged by Pius VI when Sir John was in Rome in April 1795, was in favour of the Bill. However Milner denounced the plans of Sir John Cox Hippesley as if they had been framed for the subjugation of the Catholic Church to the temporal power of a Protestant government.

The following year while in Rome, Milner gave a written account to Cardinal Litta the prefect of Propaganda, of the controversies he had in England with Bishop Poynter and the Catholic Board. He offered to resign his vicariate if he was thought unworthy by the Holy See. This offer was not accepted and it was indicated to Milner that his conduct was in the main approved of by the Pope and cardinals. At the same time it was recommended to him to be more cautious and moderate, and to refrain from the use of irritating language towards adversaries. In 1816, in a report concerning the Midland District, Milner is described as disliked by the other vicars apostolic and by the British Government. He was described as learned and zealous, but of small prudence, impulsive, variable and quick to give hard words and an adversary of Bishop Poynter.

Milner gave offence to some bishops in his articles which appeared in the *Orthodox Journal*. The Prefect of Propaganda wrote to Milner in a letter dated 29 April 1820, instructing him to discontinue his articles. Milner obeyed the injunction but continued to defend in various books and pamphlets the principles which he believed to be essential to the welfare of the Church.

The health of Bishop Milner began to break down. In 1824 he suffered slight attacks of paralysis. In 1825 he received a coadjutor, Dr. Thomas Walsh president of Oscott, who was consecrated at Wolverhampton on 1 May by Milner. There were eight bishops present together and Bishop Poynter stood next to Milner throughout the ceremony, anxiously watching to prevent the aged bishop from omitting anything. It is pleasing to note that Bishop Milner was thoroughly reconciled with his former controversial opponents, Bishops Poynter and Collingridge.

On 25 March, Milner took to his bed, from which he never arose. When those around him addressed him as usual, as 'My Lord', he said: "Don't call me so any more, I am nothing now but plain John Milner, a poor sinner". He blessed each of the priests kneeling at his bedside and passed away on the feast of St. Elphege, the martyr-bishop of Canterbury, 19 April 1826.

The following year Bishop Poynter vicar apostolic of the London District died aged sixty-five. William Poynter was born on 20 May 1762 in Petersfield, Hampshire. In 1775 Bishop Challoner sent him to Douay where he was ordained priest in 1786. He suffered imprisonment during the worst period of the French Revolution, but in 1795 he arrived in England. He was appointed vice-president at Old Hall Green and president in 1801. Following the death of Bishop Stapleton, Poynter was appointed coadjuter with right of succession to Bishop Douglass. Bishop Poynter disagreed with Bishop Milner, and in 1810 he signed a resolution prepared by the Catholic Board with a view to pledging assent to State control by means of the veto. In 1813 he was persuaded to become president of the Catholic Bible Society instituted by the Catholic Committee and later in 1816, condemned by Rome. In 1823 he obtained from the Holy See the appointment of Dr. Bramston as his coadjutor.

A new phase in the struggle for full emancipation opened with the Act of Union with Ireland in 1800. Henry Grattan, one of the leaders of the former Irish Parliament was elected to Westminster in 1805 and he concentrated all his energies on the problem of emancipation. Year after year he introduced resolutions in favour of further legislation, without success, but with slowly increasing support. He died in 1820 without seeing the fruits of his labour. Grattan was succeeded by William Plunkett, member of Parliament for Dublin University, and a future Lord Chancellor of Ireland. He brought in an Emancipation Bill in 1821 which passed the Commons by a narrow majority but was thrown out by the Lords.

Political events in Ireland brought in a new protagonist. David O'Connell who organised a remarkably successful Catholic Association in Ireland which ultimately fought for a repeal of the Union, but as a first step, campaigned for complete emancipation from the penal laws. A similar Association was set up in England, but lacked the overwhelming popular support to the one in Ireland. Another Emancipation Bill introduced in 1825 failed to secure a majority. The crisis came when O'Connell was elected to Westminster for Clare in 1828. As a Catholic he could not take his seat. The wide spread agitation that followed convinced the Prime Minister, the Duke of Wellington, that there was need for action, otherwise there would be even more serious trouble in Ireland. The Prime Minister persuaded George IV with some difficulty, to agree to a further measure of emancipation.

Sir Robert Peel introduced the Bill to the Commons on 5 March 1829, it had its third reading three weeks later with a majority of 178, it passed the Lords on the 10 April with a majority of 109, and received the Royal Assent on 13 April. The incredible speed with which it passed through Parliament was clearly an act of expediency, certainly without the Irish crisis it would have taken years before a purely English Act could have been gained.

The Act gave the elective franchise to all Catholics including the right of election to Parliament, they could now hold civil and military offices and belong to any corporation. The Government did not claim any say in the appointment of bishops nor to have the right to scrutinise papal correspondence. There were a few remaining restrictions. Catholics could not present to Anglican livings of which they owned the advowsons. They could not hold the offices of Regent, Lord Chancellor of Great Britain, Lord Chancellor of Ireland, or Lord Lieutenant of Ireland. It is sometimes argued that according to the Emancipation Act, a Catholic cannot be Prime Minister. This is not correct. When the Act was passed the designation Prime Minister had no statutory authority. It was a kind of courtesy title, used since the days of Robert Walpole, it did not obtain official recognition until about 1905. So in 1829, in the eyes of constitutional law there was no such person as 'Prime Minister'. As soon as the Act came into force the Catholic peers at once took their seats in the House of Lords, and at the General Election in 1830 five Catholics entered the House of Commons.

Immediately on the passing of Wellington's Catholic Emancipation Act in April 1829, the picture which a previous generation of Catholics had known changed. Pope Leo XII had died in February, when Peel and Wellington were still engaged in their last efforts to overcome the resistance of the King. On 31 March, Pius VIII was elected, in June 1830 George IV had died. A new era, in which so many old landmarks were to vanish, had already dawned. The Reform Bill of 1832 was to introduce a new chapter in English history, which before long had broken down the old monopoly of political power held by the landed aristocracy. But among the English Catholics the feudal tradition of aristocratic leadership endured long after the Reform Bill. The peculiar circumstances of the English Catholics, a very small and scattered remnant among a great Protestant population, gave to the gentry a special claim upon the allegiance of the poorer Catholics. Through the centuries of Catholic persecution in England, it was the gentry who alone succeeded in keeping the faith alive.

Not until the English Catholic Relief Act of 1791 was it made legal for Catholic churches to be built. The result was to some extent to lessen the former direct dependence of the Catholics generally upon the great houses. It is to the credit of the Catholic landowners, who were chiefly responsible for the Bill, that they appreciated this effect on their own work, and welcomed it. Lord Petre, for instance, who was the most conspicuous example of those Catholic aristocrats who considered that the laity ought to have a deciding voice in various ecclesiastical matters, was among the first subscribers to the building of a chapel in Monmouth, and wrote to the coadjutor of Bishop Walmesley who had been one of his chief opponents, that "the collecting of the Catholics into towns in places of straggling missions has always been a measure much recommended by me. On these, now legal, establishments, the Catholic religion must ultimately depend. The middling classes will find themselves more independent . . .I, therefore, willingly subscribe".

Long after Lord Petre's death, great changes had taken place. It was almost forty years between the writing of that letter and the passing of the Emancipation Act in 1829. The industrial revolution had caused a steadily increasing drift of the people into new factory towns. The population had multiplied rapidly, and was further augmented by a gradual infiltration of poor labourers from Ireland. New groups of Catholics were forming in the new cities of England, who were as yet unorganised and desperately poor, and who most often had no priests to minister to them. Throughout the rest of England the conditions were still practically the same as before. The gentry still provided their own chaplains to conduct the work of missions among scattered Catholics throughout large districts. Catholics everywhere around them recognised their own dependence upon the fidelity and generosity of the great houses for the very existence of the Church in most parts of England. As yet, there was no question of Catholic affairs being directed, or even influenced, by anyone other than the small group of Catholic landowners who had constituted the self-appointed Catholic Committee and had conducted all the negotiations with successive Governments. It was only natural, when such conditions had continued for centuries that the Catholic gentry should regard their position as a heritage that would never be challenged. It was scarcely surprising that they had refused to allow the clergy even to be members of the original Catholic Committee, and that they had adopted an attitude of aggrieved resentment when the vicars apostolic denounced the Oaths of Allegiance and other concessions which they had themselves agreed upon in negotiations with Ministers.

No clearer picture of the condition of the English Catholics in the early part of the nineteenth century could be given than is contained in a passage in Newman's famous sermon on the 'Second Spring', preached after the restoration of the hierarchy in 1850. Looking back to the days before his own conversion to Catholicism, he recalled how "You have seen it on one side, and some of us on another, but one and all of us can bear witness to the fact of the utter contempt into which Catholicism had fallen by the time we were born . . . No longer the Catholic Church in the country, nay, no longer, I may say, a Catholic community, but a few adherents of the Old Religion, moving silently and sorrowfully about, as memorials of what had been. 'The Roman Catholics' not a sect, not even an interest, as men conceived of it, not a body, however small, representative of the great communion abroad, but a mere handful of individuals, who might be counted, like the pebbles and *detritus* of the great deluge, and who forsooth, merely happened to retain a creed which in its day, indeed, was the profession of a Church. Here a set of poor Irishmen, coming and going at harvest time, or a colony of them lodged in a miserable quarter of the vast metropolis. There, perhaps an elderly person, seen walking in the streets, grave and solitary and stranger, though noble in bearing, and said to be of good family, and a 'Roman Catholic'. An old fashioned house of gloomy appearance, closed in with high walls, with an iron gate, and yews, and the report attaching to it that 'Roman Catholics' lived there, but who they were, or what they did, or what was meant by calling them Roman Catholics, no one could tell, though it had an unpleasant sound, and told of form and superstition. And then, perhaps, as we went to and fro, looking with a boy's curious eyes through the great city, we might come today upon some Moravian chapel, or Quaker's meeting-house, and tomorrow on a chapel of the Roman Catholics, but nothing was to be gathered from it, except that there were lights burning there, and some boys in white, swinging censers, and what it all meant could only be learned from books, from Protestant histories and sermons, and they did not report well of the Roman Catholics, but, so the country deposed, that they had once had power and had abused it. And then again, we might, on one occasion, have it pointedly put out by some literary man, as the result of his careful investigation, and as a recondite point information, which few knew, that there was this difference between the Roman Catholics of England and the Roman Catholics of Ireland, that the latter had bishops, and the former were governed by four officials, called vicars apostolic.

"Such was the sort of knowledge possessed of Christianity by the heathen of old time, who persecuted its adherents from the face of the earth, and then called them a *gens lucifuga,* a people who shunned the light of day. Such were Catholics in England, found in corners, and alleys, and cellars, and the housetops, or in the recesses of the country, cut off from the populous world around them, and dimly seen, as if through a mist or in twilight, as ghosts flitting to and fro, by the Protestants, the lords of the earth. At length, so feeble did they become, so utterly contemptible, that contempt gave birth to pity, and the more generous .of their tyrants actually began to wish to bestow on them some favour, under the notion that their opinions were simply too absurd even to spread again, and that they themselves, were they but raised in civil importance, would soon unlearn and be ashamed of them. And thus, out of mere kindness to us, they began to vilify our doctrines to the Protestant world, that so our very idiotcy or our secret unbelief might be our plea for mercy".

To the non-Catholic the remoteness and isolation of the English Catholic was constantly apparent. They were still almost conspicuous by their absence from the public life of the country, before they gradually began to assume the active and distinguished part to which their social influence and their political integrity amply entitled them. But even the mere thought of Catholics entering public life, once the Catholic Emancipation Act had been passed, already aroused fear in the more strict among the clergy. Their views were expressed with an emphasis which seems startling in our present time, by Bishop Bramston, the vicar apostolic of the London District. His pastoral letter issued for the New year of 1830, was nothing less than a solemn warning to English Catholics to avoid the dangers to their faith which might be involved in close association with the public life of a Protestant country. "The present era", he wrote, "is new and most important to the Catholics of this island. Whilst they are by the wisdom and bounty of the legislature placed civilly and politically on a level with their fellow subjects, they may be liable to be thrown into situations where, rather than before, the maxims of the world may endanger the steady practice of their holy religion. Hence it would seem that they ought to be exhorted to have a truly religious guard, that the temporal advantages which they now enjoy do not lead to a forgetfulness of their eternal interests, and that in the present circumstances, more than ever heretofore, they should continually put to themselves the Divine interrogation, *'What will it avail a man to gain the whole world and lose his own soul?'* Those in the higher sphere of life will naturally wish to avail themselves of their freedom from past disabilities by the employment of the talents they may possess for the benefit of their country. Hence, places and offices of high trust and important dignity may be looked for by them, and justly and religiously, too, if the service of their country be, indeed, their principle object. But it is far otherwise if the passion of ambition or the thirst of worldly lucre be their leading motive . . . But, while you may with all virtuous propriety accept of any office, place, trust or dignity to which your talents may deem to entitle you, you are earnestly exhorted to remember ever, and now more than ever, that it is your greatest glory and highest interest to be members of the one fold of the one shepherd".

It was not only to the "higher orders of your communion" to whom the pastoral was apparently addressed in the first instance, that this stern moralist addressed his urgent episcopal warnings. "The disabilities from which you have been relieved", he insisted, "reach to others professing the Roman Catholic religion in the inferior walks of life. To these will be opened various situations where many and very dangerous temptations may assail them. In such situations they may be exposed to be corrupted by bribery, and by taking or allowing others to take false, unlawful and unnecessary oaths, and prompted to all this by avaricious feelings and the plea of custom. But be it known to them that no custom can be pleaded against faith and justice. Those principles are eternal and must be observed by all who look forward to the glory of heaven". The time was to come, within half a century, when no bishop in England would have ever dreamt of issuing such an amazing document, addressed directly to the English landowners and referring to the "inferior orders" as though the bishop and the gentry were discussing them as a class apart. But this pastoral, written by an intensely devout bishop of very simple views, who was anxious to restrain the alleged ambition of the aristocracy as to warn the "inferior orders" of their temptations to sell their religious convictions for bribes, is extraordinarily illuminating as evidence of the prevailing atmosphere at the time.

"You of every rank", he continued, "are to be warned, moreover, that you may probably be thrown into a different order of intercourse and association from that to which you have hitherto been accustomed, and on this account you may be forced to mix with persons unhappily impressed with the false philosophy, or rather irreligion and infidelity, with which the world is in these days so lamentably infected. You are not called upon to be preachers or fiery disputants, but you are called upon and warmly exhorted to express sentiments and to exhibit practices in entire opposition to the evil spirit which is abroad. Heretofore, living in comparative separation and exclusion

179

from the pomps and vanities of the world, you may now be cast more immediately within the vortex of that unhappy world. What, then should you do? Allow your hearts and minds to be purged by bad example to yield to the destructive maxims of this world, and so relax by fatal degrees in the virtuous and pius practices of your religion? Or, to stem the torrent of delusion and corruption, ought you not to increase your attention and the regularity of your observance to the duties of prayer, pious reading, and serious reflection on saving truths and holy maxims of the Gospel? Ought you not to be more diligent and devout frequenters of the Holy Sacrament of Penance and the Eucharist? And bearing in mind the Divine admonition that evil communications are the corrupters of virtue, ought you not to observe a more steady watchfulness over all your thoughts, words, actions and impressions?

"What could possibly be more gratifying", asked the good bishop in conclusion, "than the conviction that your talents, your learning, your integrity and exertions cause you not only to be eligible, but to be elected to places of trust, emoluments, honour and dignity, and that in all the various situations and offices to which you may be chosen you may prove to your fellow citizens that you were worthy of their choice, and that a rightly-believing and practising Catholic is of all men most trustworthy. May the bounty and goodness of Almighty God pour down upon you every temporal blessing, and may every temporal blessing by your virtue and piety, be the means tending to your bliss and glory for all eternity".

Reading that pastoral in the light of after events, it becomes less difficult to understand the continual conflict which persisted between the more active leaders of the Catholic Committee and the vicars apostolic, who were more concerned to preserve the devout traditions of an oppressed Catholic minority than to join with them in asserting their civil rights as loyal subjects. There was a definite antipathy between the two points of view. While the bishops generally were most anxious to secure freedom of religious worship, the right to build churches and conduct schools, and to receive endowments that would ensure their continuance and development, the leaders of the laity were much more immediately concerned with the removal of political and civil disabilities.

A generation had passed since the very acute conflict, before the Relief Bill of 1791, between the bishops and the Catholic Committee. But the traditions of the laity were still strong and in the controversy over Grattan's abortive Relief Bill in 1813 the conflict had broken out again over a similar question of principle. The divergence of view was rooted in the political and social history of the eighteenth century. The founders of the first Catholic Committee represented a generation which had completely outgrown all sympathy with the Stuart cause and was desperately anxious to vindicate the loyalty of English Catholics to the House of Hanover. Looking back, they had come to feel that the distrust of Catholics in England need never have continued for so long if the Holy See, and the bishops of England, had not persisted in the hope of a restoration of the Stuarts, and in giving active support to their discredited cause. They had come to regard the Church itself as being largely the cause, through its misguided interference in politics, of the humiliation and persecution that Catholics still endured. Towards the end of the eighteenth century the more active leaders of the Catholic laity, who actually possessed a wholly abnormal influence over all ecclesiastical affairs through the fact that they appointed and maintained almost all the clergy, had definitely made up their minds to dissociate themselves clearly from the suspicion of being subservient in political matters to Rome.

The tradition of timidity and self-consciousness was still a considerable factor for many years. There is, indeed, a remarkable contrast between this timorous and apprehensive outlook of Bishop Bramston upon the new era, which the Act of 1829 had opened after so many years of effort, and the joint pastoral issued a month later by the Irish hierarchy. To them, as to all Irish Catholics, the Emancipation Act was the triumph of a cause in which many noble spirits had been broken, and many more had suffered persecution and imprisonment. They made no secret of their own deeply affectionate gratitude to Daniel O'Connell as the chief organiser and author of emancipation. To the Irish Catholics, the Act of 1829 had been the opening of the Promised land. To Bishop Bramston in the London District it was the beginning of new fears. He was old in years, though he had only recently succeeded to the position of vicar apostolic, and within eight years he was in his grave. But his views were all the more remarkable, as those of a convert to Catholicism educated outside the narrow atmosphere of the old Catholic families of England. He was a graduate of Cambridge, less inclined than they, by his past training to adopt a timid view of the results of participation in the national life.

James Yorke Bramston was born in 1753. He was originally a Protestant and a lawyer. After his conversion to Catholicism he went to the English College at Lisbon, where he remained for eight years and was ordained priest. He returned to England and was appointed to a mission in the Midland District, later he joined the London Distict, and in 1802 was one of the priests in St. George-in-the-Fields, Surrey.

He became Bishop Poynter's vicar general and later coadjutor and succeeded to the London vicariate at the age of eighy-four. He applied for a coadjutor and was granted the following year Dr. Gradwell who was then rector of the English College, Rome. However Dr. Gradwell died in 1833 and Dr Griffiths was appointed in his place. Bishop Bramston died in July

1836 at Golden Square, London and was buried in the clergy vault in Moorfield church.

Bishop Griffiths was to be the last vicar apostolic of the London District. Thomas Griffiths was born in London in 1792. Under the influence of his father, who was a Protestant, he was as a youth brought up in that religion. His mother was a devout Catholic and under her influence he converted to Catholicism, much against the wishes of his father. As a boy he was an altar server in the chapel of St. George-in-the-Fields, which later became the cathedral at Southwark.

In January 1805 he was admitted to St. Edmund's College at Old Hall Green Ware. He became a classical scholar, an expert mathematician, and a profound theologian. In 1814 he was ordained priest and during the following four years he served the local population of Old Hall Green. In 1818 he moved with the students from Old Hall to the new college and was appointed president in succession to Dr. Bew.

For fifteen years he governed St. Edmund's with great skill and care. He succeeded Bishop Bramston in 1836. In the following year in his report he recorded that the Catholics in London numbered 146,068 and in the rural parts of his District 11,246 making a total of 157,314 Catholics for the entire vicariate. The population of London at this time was 1,500,000.

In 1846 Pope Gregory XVI increased the number of vicariates in England and Bishop Griffiths was appointed to the new London District. His health rapidly declined and he became almost blind. He died at his residence in Golden Square, London on 12 August 1847 aged 56 and was buried in the clergy vault at Moorfields.

A new generation was gradually arising which, in the years after the Reform Bill, was to confront a very much altered situation with a more virile point of view. The admission to Catholics to Parliament had for the time being made very little difference, beyond satisfying the claims to social and political equality which had for so many years weighed upon the minds of the Catholic aristocracy. The Duke of Norfolk and a handful of other Catholic peers had gained the right to sit in the House of Lords, his son, together with eight or nine other Catholic gentlemen, had obtained seats in the House of Commons, either by straightforward election or by the fact that their families still controlled the representation of certain pocket boroughs. These few Catholic legislators were all Whigs by tradition, and the Catholic members of Parliament remained Whig for long afterwards. In public life they did little more, in fact, than demonstrate how baseless had been the old fears of what would result from admitting Catholics to Parliament. They were so determined to prove their own loyalty and respectability, and their desire to uphold the existing constitution, that there was no possibility of their undertaking any active organisation or movement as a separate

Catholic group. Such an attitude on their part was inevitable, in view of their traditions and of the conflict which had preceded the vindication of their rights.

It was not the newly emancipated laity, but a great ecclesiastic, whose name was still unknown in England, who was to lead the Catholic Church forward in England in a grand and spectacular advance. It was not the old Catholics, but the new converts, who did not yet dream that they would have become Catholics within a few years, who were to galvanise Catholicism in England into a vital and expanding force. In Rome, two famous ecclesiastics had already made their mark. Bishop Weld, who was before very long to be made the first English cardinal for several centuries, and Mgr. Acton, who was to attain the same dignity after Cardinal Weld's death. But much greater than they, and still only a young man in his twenty-eighth year when Catholic emancipation was enacted, Dr. Wiseman had already succeeded to the rectorship of the English College in Rome. He had not long carried his new dignity when he was called upon as rector of the English College to be the messenger who had to convey the great news of Catholic emancipation to the newly elected Pope.

Extracts from: *The Dawn of the Catholic Revival in England* by Rev Bernard Ward later first Bishop of Brentwood, published by Longman & Co. London.
Bibliographical Dictionary of the English Catholics by Joseph Gillow published by Burns & Oates, London

Chapter Nine

Cardinal Nicholas Wiseman

IT was paradoxical that Nicholas Wiseman should have become the head of the English College in Rome, and his peculiar training and antecedents were to have a profound effect in later years upon the development of the Catholic body in England. Wiseman, though he always regarded himself as an Englishman, was the son of Irish parents. His grandfather had been a Catholic tradesman in Waterford in the years when the penal laws produced a wholly unexpected result in the rise of a new class of prosperous Catholic merchants. Their activities could not be controlled or restricted even by the elaborate and carefully planned contrivance of the penal code. They gradually built up a flourishing direct trade between Ireland and the Catholic countries on the Continent. It was this new merchant class who, almost alone, had the courage to join the early pioneers in organising the first Irish Catholic Associations, and who provided the money with exemplary generosity for the propaganda and the litigation which, in the beginning, were all that the oppressed Irish Catholics could attempt. But James Wiseman, like many other of the merchant class had left Ireland to find more tolerable and civilised conditions of life in Spain, and he conducted his trade in Irish produce from there. His son, James, became a Spanish merchant in Seville. From his second marriage, with a daughter of the Strange family of Aylwardstown Castle, County Kilkenney, there was born in 1802, the future Archbishop of Westminster. The younger James Wiseman died three years later, and the future archbishop was brought back to Ireland as a child by his mother, and received his early schooling at a boarding school in Waterford, where he first learned to speak English as fluently as Spanish.

At the age of eight he was sent to Ushaw College, where he acquired the traditions of one of the most honourable of the old English Catholic Schools. He was sixteen and still a schoolboy there when the Pope decided to act upon Cardinal Consalvi's recommendation and attempt to revive the English College in Rome, which had been closed since the invasion by the French in 1798. Young Nicholas Wiseman was selected as one of the group of candidates for the priesthood who were sent from Ushaw and other colleges to be pupils at the re-opened college in Rome. For six years he studied there, until his ordination in 1825. Two years later he was nominated as its vice-rector, and in the following year he succeeded to the rectorship, on the appointment of Dr. Gradwell to a bishopric.

184

William Pitt addressing the House of Commons
by Karl Anton Hickel (1745-1798)
reproduced by courtesy of the National Portrait Gallery, London

Rt Rev John Douglass
Bishop of Centuria
Vicar Apostolic of the London District 1790-1812
From a painting at St. Edmund's College, Ware, Herts.
reproduced by kind permission of the Trustees of St. Edmund's College

NICOLAUS CARDINAL WISEMAN
ARCHIEP. WESTMONAST.
1850 — 1865.

Cardinal Nicholas Wiseman
Bishop of Melipoyamus
First Archbishop of Westminster 1850-65
from a painting at St. Edmund's College, Ware, Herts.
reproduced by kind permission of the Trustees of St Edmund's College

Cardinal Henry Edward Manning
Second Archbishop of Westminster
1865-1892
from paintings at Archbishop's House Westminster
reproduced with permission of
Westminster Roman Catholic Diocesan Trustees

Top right: as Archbishop
Top left: in his early years as Cardinal
Left: towards the end of his life

Cardinal John Henry Newman 1801-1890
by Sir John Millais at Arundel Castle
reproduced by courtesy of the National Portrait Gallery

William Bernard Ullathorne OSB
First Bishop of Birmingham 1850-1888
from a painting at Oscott College, Sutton Coldfield
reproduced by kind permission of the Trustees of Oscott College

Cardinal Herbert Vaughan
Third Archbishop of Westminster 1892-1903
from a painting at St. Edmund's College, Ware, Herts.
reproduced by kind permission of the Trustees, St. Edmund's College

Cardinal Francis Bourne
Fourth Archbishop of Westminster 1903-1935
from a painting at Archbishop's House, Westminster

During his long residence in Rome, he was personally acquainted with the leaders of the contemporary religious revival throughout Europe. He was already inspired and dominated by the ideals that animated the leaders of the Catholic revival in France and Germany when he returned to England for a protracted visit in 1835. His impressions of the English Catholics, as he found them during his stay in England for more than a year, convey vivid glimpses of the conditions which still prevailed. He set out deliberately to ascertain all that he could of Catholic life in the country. Travelling from house to house, inquiring with diligent sympathy in a determination to understand the whole mentality and tradition of the English Catholic body, whose sons were committed to his own care in Rome. Wiseman learned many stories at first hand of the persecutions and penalties which had been borne by men with whom he talked, or who could convey the picture to him from incidents within the living memory of their own families.

During this year of travelling through England, Wiseman with his cosmopolitan training and his Roman enthusiasm, was brought into direct contact with the old English Catholics, it gave him for the first time a sudden realisation of the great religious upheaval that was already taking place in England. As the friend of Lacordaire and Ozanam, he had dreamed of a Catholic revival, though there seemed to be no apparent means by which it should arise. In England he now met men who actually talked as confidently of the imminent conversion of England to Catholicism. Everywhere he found a profound dissatisfaction with the Established Protestant Church, and a widespread conviction that it had so disintergrated that it could scarcely survive at all through another generation. He was so encouraged that he undertook to give a series of public lectures in London, addressed to Protestants as well as Catholics, on the revival of Catholicism in Europe. Their success was immediate, and he repeated it several times with other lectures, which drew always larger audiences and attracted an astonishing amount of attention. He not only discovered possibilities, but had convinced himself beyond all doubt that a new generation had arisen which was genuinely anxious to learn about the teaching and the activities of the Catholic Church. With his immense vista of his own life's work opening before him, he was brought in contact for the first time at close quarters with the extraordinary and incalculable reaction towards the traditions of Catholicism which was already becoming feverishly active in Oxford under the guidance of John Henry Newman. Wiseman, with all the impulsive energy of his generous temperament, threw himself heart and soul into encouraging the Oxford Movement, little knowing how immense would be the consequences of the movement itself in shaking the foundations of English Protestantism. He had no perception of the extent to which the influx of so many brilliant converts from the Oxford Movement would challenge, and eventually destroy, the traditional supremacy of the old aristocratic families in the affairs and in the outlook of the English Catholics.

The Oxford Movement, and the revival of Catholicism in England to which it contributed so largely, was but a symptom of the sweeping reaction against eighteenth century agnosticism, and the revolutionary upheaval which it had produced in France and throughout Europe. A new generation, utterly disillusioned with the catchwords of Liberty, Equality, Fraternity, and exasperated by the intellectual anarchy which the scepticism of Voltaire and others had created, now turned in a revulsion from agnosticism towards tradition and religious belief. But great changes had come about during the Revolution and the subsequent Napoleonic wars. The old ideas and beliefs now made their appeal under very different conditions, to a generation which accepted democracy as an accomplished fact, and was concerned chiefly to organise it upon new lines which would give free play to the vital principles of the older traditions. O'Connell, in Ireland, Montalembert and Lacordaire, in France, Schlegel and Mohler, in Germany, were all engaged in a very similar movement which aimed broadly at Christianising the new conditions which had arisen from the years of upheaval. In Rome itself, Wiseman, whose intellectual activity and enthusiasm had brought him into personal contact with all the leaders of the Catholic revival in Europe, was at the very centre of the great transformation which was taking place.

Most English Catholics believed the Tractarians were attempting to keep their privileged position and to safeguard their livings in the Established Church, while pretending that the Anglican communion was fundamentally Catholic, even though this was denied by most Anglicans. Wiseman's openly sympathetic attitude was deplored as an encouragement of hipocrisy and self-deceit, and it was only excused by his critics as evidence of his ignorance of English conditions. Ambrose Phillips supported Wiseman and he was also deeply engaged in organising George Spencer's Crusade of Prayer for the conversion of England, he was also making efforts to establish personal relations with the writers of the Tracts at Oxford. He had compiled arrangements for the Rosminian, Fr. Gentili to come to Leicestershire as his chaplain, since Bishop Baines had removed Gentili from Prior Park. Bishop Walsh was giving him every encouragement, and Phillipps had been delighted by the success of Wiseman's latest visit to England. George Spencer even decided to go boldly to Oxford in January 1840, to meet Newman and his friends in person and ask them to join in prayers for unity. He came just when Newman had published in the *British Critic* his latest attempt to clear the air, since the confusion which had been aroused by Wiseman's essay on the Donatists. Newman entitled his article *The Catholicity of the Anglican Church* and he explained afterwards in the *Apologia* that at this time his "main argument for Anglican claims lay in the positive and special changes which I could bring against Rome". His confidence had been shaken badly, and he was in no mood to meet Catholics who desired to fraternise.

On 8 January, Newman received a visit from George Spencer, the youngest son of Earl Spencer, who had converted to Roman Catholicism several years before and was now a priest teaching at the seminary at Oscott. Newman had been invited to meet him at dinner the previous evening but had refused on the ground that Spencer, who had been in Anglican Orders, was an apostate saying: "That if Roman Catholics and Anglican Catholics meet togther, it should be in sackcloth, rather than at a pleasant party". They talked together for an hour. Afterwards Newman wrote to Bowden: "I wish these Roman Catholic priests had not so smooth a manner, it puts me out. He was very mild, very gentlemanlike, not a controvertialist, and came to insist only on one point, that we should take steps to get Anglo Catholics to pray for the Roman Catholics. He said he was sure that if we felt the desirableness of unity, and if we prayed for each other, where there was a will there would be a way. He said that he had been instrumental in beginning the practice in France, that it had spread all over that country, and was now being taken up in Germany. Thursday being the day fixed on. It is certainly, a most dreadful thing that we should be separated from them, but your account of the Southern Churches makes one almost feel as if a formal union would do no good. If we could make strong terms with them so as to act upon them, that would be the thing".

Newman wondered if the priest's "sadly smooth" manner was the result of the Roman clergy's habit of internal discipline, the necessity of confession etc. Later he was to note: "Demureness is the Roman manner, as pompousness is the Church of England's". But he was taken with the idea of a fixed day for mutual ecumenical prayer. Too many people reviled Roman Catholics, instead of praying for them.

George Spencer was the son of Lord Spencer who had been a Minister under Pitt and whose brother, Lord Althorp, had been Chancellor of the Exchequer. From this family descended the tragic Diana, Princes of Wales of our present time. As a younger son, George Spencer had taken Holy Orders in 1823 and was given a comfortable living on the family estate. He had developed ascetic ways of life and devoted himself entirely to work among his poor parishioners. In 1830 he made the acquaintance of Ambrose de Lisle Phillipps, whose father had for years been MP for the county and was the owner of important estates. Phillipps had dismayed his family by insisting that he must be received into the Catholic Church. Phillips and Spencer became friends, they discussed together their religious beliefs and eventually Spencer was completely won over, resigned his living and became a Catholic at once. Bishop Walsh persuaded Spencer to go to the English College in

Rome for a time, to study under Mgr. Wiseman, and to test his vocation to the priesthood.

George Spencer was three years older than Wiseman, and it was not easy to fit him into the College routine, with students who were much his junior. He was assigned as an interpreter for the Italian Passionist, Fr. Dominic Barberi, who was appointed to instruct him in ceremonial. They became great friends and along with other English converts, spent days together in Rome planning the future conversion of England.

In 1838, Fr. George Ignatius Spencer devised a plan for a movement of prayer for Christian unity. This was the first such movement of any significance in the English speaking world. In 1844 he took his crusade of prayer for unity to the Continent, where he spent three months travelling about telling people about the religious situation in England. He dedicated his life to this work for unity among Christians through prayer and mutual co-operation.

During his stay in Paris, he urged the French clergy to offer a Mass every Thursday for the conversion of England. The centre of this devotion was at Notre Dame des Victoires, which eventually became a place of pilgrimage to those who prayed for the conversion of England. A marble plaque is inscribed to the memory of Fr. Spencer: "Hon. and Rev. George Spencer who began prayers at Notre Dame des Victoires in October 1837 for the conversion of England and died on 1 October 1864".

Rome increased the number of English bishops and the young Wiseman was appointed coadjutor to Bishop Walsh in the Midlands. There he would have more practical scope, in association with Lord Shrewsbury and other leaders of the revival, than in any other part of England. Moreover, he would be within easy reach of Oxford, and he could be relied upon to keep Rome fully informed of the extremely interesting developments in progress there. His position was further strengthened by appointing him president of Oscott, which had recently been re-built and enlarged and had every prospect of important expansion.

Wiseman arrived in England before the other new bishops were consecrated, and on 16 September 1840, he was given a triumphal welcome to Oscott. He was still editor of the *Dublin Review* besides being President of Oscott and coadjutor to Bishop Walsh. His recent essays in the *Dublin Review* had effected the Tractarians very notably, and he had real hopes of establishing direct relations between Oscott and Oxford. At Oscott he found his former pupil George Spencer in residence as Spiritual Director, and the convert Logan, whom he had sent to Prior Park from the English College some ten years before, now teaching at Oscott. Pugin, also came there frequently and was constantly busy with plans for the new churches being built around the country. Pugin, Ambrose Phillips and Lord Shrewsbury had relied upon Wiseman as an ally for their campaign to restore Gothic art, medieval vestments and plain chant. Wiseman was sympathetic, but he preferred Roman to Gothic art. Pugin regarded a rood screen as being indispensable to any church, however small, because they symbolised the separation of the congregation from the mysteries of the altar. Wiseman was inclined to share Lingard's view that such separation was not only unorthodox but had been one of the causes of religious indifference before the Reformation, when screens had been widely introduced for the convenience of monastic choirs.

Rood screens and medieval vestments were not the only matters over which conflict arose with Wiseman, when Pugin and Phillipps had counted upon his fullest sympathy. Pugin was uncompromising in all things, he wrote frantically to Ambrose Phillips: "Yesterday, I was informed the screen was not to be allowed, but what a miserable state of things, the grand division between sacrifice and the worshippers, between priest and people, to be attempted to be abolished by those who should be foremost in their restoration. My dear Phillipps, we nearly stand alone, if we except the Oxford men, for among them I find full sympathy of feeling. But the real truth is the churches I build do little or no good for want of men who know how to use them". In the same letter he asserted with tragic emphasis that "till the old Gregorian music is restored nothing can be done". His views on the prevalent Church music were almost inexpressible. "St. Anne's in Keighley was opened the other day with a most horrible scene. Not only was all decorum violated but a regular row took place between the musicians, who quarrelled about their parts in the church . . . The present state of things is quite lamentable and were it not for the Oxford men I should quite despair".

Peace was eventually restored, though Pugin's explosive protests continued on many other occasions. But Wiseman was almost alone in sharing the enthusiasm of both Pugin and Phillipps for the Oxford men, and they both succeeded in establishing contacts which were not possible for Wiseman. He believed earnestly that Oscott, "this noble college in the very heart of England" was intended to be something far more than a school or seminary in those years of critical transition.

In February 1841, Newman published his famous Tract XC, the last of the long series which had begun in the autumn of 1833. Newman's influence had grown immensely during those years, and he dominated the intellectual life of the university. As Rector of St. Mary's, and as an otherwise unimportant Don at Oriel College, he had attracted a following of all ages. During the past year he had been trying to consolidate his position, in defence of the Established Church as being at once fully Catholic and also reformed. Wiseman's essays had compelled him to go deeper in his contention that the Anglican Church had not excluded itself from Catholic unity. Tract XC was intended to remove all doubts on this point among his followers, by demonstrating more definitely than ever before, that even the Thirty-nine Articles of the Church of England could only be interpreted "according to the sense of the Catholic Church".

Obviously, the old-fashioned Protestants would resent this assertion vigorously, but Newman believed that he had established his case beyond dispute. His disciple W. G. Ward hated Protestantism and loved keen controversy, and he tested the reaction to Newman's Tract at once by bringing it to Tait in Balliol, who was then a tutor and afterwards became Archbishop of Canterbury. Tait read it through without any protest until he reached one passage which he brought to Ward immediately, demanding a statement of how Ward interpreted it. Ward agreed with Tait's interpretation and then Tait proceeded to rouse the other tutors against it. A few day later, he and three other tutors lodged a formal protest. One bishop after another repudiated publicly any association with the Tractarian leaders, and in deference to urgent representations from the Bishop of Oxford, Newman agreed to discontinue all further publications of the Tracts.

Ever since their first meeting in Rome in 1833, Wiseman had watched the development of Newman's religious views with affectinate interest. Now, at last, his full acceptance of Catholicism seemed to have been brought definitely in sight. But this new phase had none the less surely destroyed most of the dream which had filled Wiseman's mind for so long. He had hoped that, through Newman's influence, the Church of England would become more and more definitely Catholic, until the time arrived when the conversion of the Tractarian leaders would bring the majority of Anglicans as a body into the Catholic Church. But Tract XC, while it revealed the progress of Newman's views to a more decisive stage, had wrecked his influence within the Church of England. Newman withdrew to the seclusion of Littlemore. Over the next few years Newman struggled with his dilema, he saw a number of his friends going over to Rome, he had to contemplate the destruction of all that he had striven to accomplish within the Church of England. By 1845, Wiseman had for some months previously heard that Newman's mind was a last made up, and the news of his final surrender was expected from day to day.

For several years Newman had scarcely stirred from his hermitage, where he lived among the few friends - Dalgairns, Edward Stanton, Bowles and Ambrose St. John - who occupied the converted farm buildings with him. They had adopted a monastic routine of life, restricting themselves to one meal a day, spending half the day in strictest silence, and reading, writing or praying all the time except during their daily walk. Newman himself was completely engaged in writing his *Essay on Development*, and he wrote standing erect at a high desk for almost incredible periods of uninterrupted work. All this ascetic routine had developed in the interval since Bernard Smith had shaken them all, by his surrender to Wiseman nearly three years earlier. Now Wiseman deputed Smith to go to Oxford and make direct investigations on Newman's progress. Smith was appalled now to see what ravages had been wrought in Newman's fragile frame and sensitive face by the mental strain which he had undergone. Newman who had regarded him with such affection of old, greeted him with an austere frigidity, and he was left alone with the others, to answer their many questions as to how he had adapted himself to his new surroundings. So the afternoon passed, and at dinner time Newman himself reappeared. He was more reserved and reticent than ever, but as soon as he entered the room, Smith realised that he wished to convey an unmistakable message. To his amazement, Smith saw that Newman had put on a pair of grey trousers. For his former curate, the action was more eloquent than speech. It was like the hoisting of a white flag, and it meant that Smith was to inform Oscott that his old master no longer regarded himself as being in Holy Orders.

Bernard Smith, who was familiar with Newman's fastidious, secretive ways and his strange manner of conveying great decisions by unobtrusive signs, returned to Oscott triumphant. But it required all Wiseman's sanguine faith to accept Smith's statement that the end was now at hand. Again the weeks passed, but by the end of July, Lord Shrewsbury conveyed to Wiseman definite word that W. G.Ward was about to convert. By September, news arrived that Newman's closest disciples at Littlemore could wait no longer. Dalgairns and Ambrose St. John departed from Littlemore together. At Aston in Staffordshire, Dalgairns made his submission to the Italian Fr. Dominic Barberi, and at Prior Park where Bishop Baggs was now in charge, since the death of Bishop Baines, St. John was received as a Catholic. Stanton had decided that he must do the same, and in October he wrote to Newman that he intended to be received by the Jesuits at Stonyhurst.

The end had come at last. Left alone with Bowles at Littlemore, Newman could hold out no longer. He replied to Stanton at once, begging him to come back, and announcing that Fr. Dominic Barberi was coming to receive him into the Church. But even Fr. Dominic had not been told what was the purpose for which he had been summoned. Not until he stepped out of his coach at Oxford, soaked through already by the torrents of rain that had poured all day, did he receive any positive intimation that Newman wished to be received into the Church. They had met only for a few minutes some months before when he had come one afternoon to visit Dalgairns at Littlemore. Newman knew of him only as a humble missionary priest who had dreamed from his boyhood that somehow he would play a part in the conversion of England, who had written a long and sympathetic reply to a letter from one of the Tractarians which had appeared in the *Universe*, and who

191

had through the years kept up an earnest intermittent correspondence with Dalgairns. Reports of Fr. Dominic's activities among the poor Catholics in the factory towns of the Potteries had reached Newman. He had heard of the indomitable courage and simple faith of this Italian priest, born of the humblest stock, who had been labouring through fierce opposition, against outbursts of violence and daily demonstrations of hostility, in his self-imposed attempt to bring the Catholic faith to the English cities.

Four years before, Newman had written, almost scornfully to Ambrose Phillipps, to complain that the Church of Rome gave no evidence of sanctity, and to say "if they want to convert England, let them go barefooted into the manufacturing towns, let them preach to the people like St. Francis Xavier, let them be pelted and trampled on, and I will own that they can do what we cannot". Perhaps these words of reproach still haunted him? It was no mere coincidence, but the direct result of Fr. Dominic's persistent friendship, that Dalgairns had gone to Fr. Dominic in Aston, and now came back to Littlemore as a Catholic. To Dalgairns Newman murmured almost in a whisper, as Ambrose St. John set out to meet the coach in Oxford on that drenching afternoon, "When you see your friend, will you tell him that I wish him to receive me into the Church of Christ?". Stanton had arrived by the same coach, and they were all united again at Littlemore. That evening, Fr. Dominic entered the building and sat down to dry his sodden clothes before the fire, when the door opened Newman threw himself at his feet, and begged him to hear his confession and receive him into the Church. Early on the following morning the ceremony took place and Newman, Bowles and Stanton were all received at the same time, while St. John and Dalgairns, already Catholics, assisted in the little oratory.

The first meeting between Newman and Wiseman after these long years in which they had contended as the leaders of opposing forces, was an ordeal for both men. Even the presence of George Spencer and Bernard Smith could not mitigate the tension of the moment. Newman's shy and fastidious reserve left him all but dumb. He and Wiseman sat together almost in silence, having exchaged scarcely a word beyond a few remarks about the journey. On 1 November, next day, the confirmation took place. Wiseman offered his new converts the old buildings at Oscott to provide a home which should take the place of Littlemore. Newman accepted it gratefully, and renamed it Maryvale. To Wiseman, the incidents connected with Newman's confirmation had seemed an omen of great promise. "We had ten quondam Anglican clergymen in the chapel", he wrote to Dr. Russell of Maynooth. "Has this ever happened since the Reformation?"

Wiseman and Newman soon established relations of mutual confidence, and he was entirely satisfied that "the Church has not received at any time, a convert who has joined her in more docility and simplicity of faith than

Newman". Wiseman was increasingly conscious of the hostility that would arise among the old Catholics, who still regarded Newman with distrust as well as a certain natural jealousy. But he proceeded deliberately to plan for the fulfilment of his earlier prediction, that if the Tractarian leaders could be won over, he and the other recognised leaders of the English Catholics must be prepared to stand down and give full scope to their superior abilities and religious fervour.

Without Wiseman's instigation and sympathetic encouragement the path of the Tractarians towards Rome would have been much more laborious. But it was in helping them after their conversion, that he contributed most to the infusion of new blood and the creation of new energies in the Catholic Church in England. Newman in his submission was followed by an influx which gathered momentum as the years passed. Faber had been among the first to feel the consequences of their giving way, he too decided that his position as a clergyman in the Church of England had become untenable. Before long Wiseman was faced with the urgent, and apparantly insoluble, problem of making provision for the temporal needs of those who became popularly known as "Mr. Newman's victims". There were many sad instances where converts had lost their livings, support of families and who faced great hardship. Faber had already arranged to form a small community of converts in Birmingham. Even W.G. Ward, when he presented himself to Bishop Griffiths in London, was coldly informed "that while they were delighted to welcome him, there was of course, no work they could offer him".

Wiseman had felt isolated in his support of the converts and he turned to Rome in his loneliness and despondency, when insomnia was already increasing the ill-health from which he had begun to suffer seriously. In 1846, when he had arranged for Newman and Dalgairns to go to Rome with others to complete their theological training, Pope Gregory XVI, who had been his personal friend for twenty years, died. Problems which then developed in the Papal States made it impossible for the new Pope, Pius IX, to do more than express his paternal blessings upon Wiseman's work, his first idea, that Newman and his friends should be trained to become teachers in the Catholic seminaries, had become plainly impossible in view of the distrust with which they were still regarded. However, Newman accepted the suggestion of forming a community of converts into an Oratory on the model od St.Philip Neri's work in Rome. Gradually the plan took shape, on the basis that they should make the experiment in Birmingham where they would be in direct dependence upon the cathedral, and at the same time close to Oscott. It was Wiseman who had suggested the idea, and had recommended Newman to cultivate a special devotion to St. Philip Neri, and in all the after years Newman's gratitude to Wiseman on that account was unceasing.

Developments had been taking place so rapidly since Newman's departure to Rome, that the time was plainly approaching when the number and power of the bishops would have to be increased. The influx of converts continued, and the situation required a more authoritative and organised direction than the vicars apostolic could provide. But a much greater factor than the influx of converts had unexpectedly arisen.

The momentous year 1845 had brought a failure of the potato crop in Ireland, and by the winter starvation had already overtaken many thousands of Irish labourers and tenant farmers. Swarms of them began to emigrate with their families into the north of England, where the growth of industry in the mining and manufacturing districts offered the prospect of employment. The summer of 1846 failed to bring relief, on all sides blight spread and rotted the crop that was the only food for millions of poor people. A tragic exodus of starving refugees from Ireland to America and to England began on an unprecedented scale. Liverpool was both the port of departure for America and the gateway to the industrial area of England. As the third year of famine, 1847, wore on, with the blight still prevalent all over the country, the immigration grew always larger. Multitudes of starving Irish Catholics swarmed over the north and midlands of England and into South Wales, carrying famine-fever with them as they came. The calamity reached such proportions that it affected large parts of England. The vicars apostolic were faced with the necessity of providing not only material relief but churches and schools for an immigrant Catholic population which far surpassed any expansion such as Wiseman had anticipated.

Father Dominic Barberi was now largely occupied with the Irish immigrants in the Potteries. He was now assisted by Fr. George Spencer, who had joined his community of Passionists. The Rosninian Fr. Gentili was wholly employed as an itinerant missionary, labouring with his colleagues among crowded congregations of Irish refugees in the new industrial cities. In Liverpool and elsewhere, scores of devoted priests died of the famine fever in working among the destitute Irish immigrants. The need for the restoration of the English hierarchy had suddelnly become a matter of the greatest urgency. Wiseman was deputed by the bishops to conduct the necessary negotiations in Rome. In July 1847, he set out upon his mission, after the bishops had considered the whole question at their meeting in the spring.

Great political changes had taken place in Italy in the seven years since he had left Rome to become president of Oscott. The movement for a united Italy had been gathering strength on all sides, and the former policy of repression had produced dangerous explosives. Pius IX, when he became Pope in 1846, had been hailed with enthusiasm as 'the reforming Pope', and many nationalists looked to him as the future head of a Federation of Italian States. Early in July 1847, when Wiseman arrived in Rome, expectations of an imminent war with Austria had created a fever of excitement. It was not a convenient moment for approaching the Holy See with complicated negotiations. But the essentials of the case were simple enough, and its urgency was undisputed. For nearly a hundred years, since the time when there had been barely 100,000 Catholics scattered in small groups throughout the country, the Church in England had been governed by the constitution established by Pope Benedict XIV in 1753. Part even of this had been repealed by the late Pope, and the Catholic population now was ten times as numerous. It was composed chiefly of unassimilated Irish elements, while the converts were rapidly becoming a considerable body as well. The eight vicars apostolic had to cope with this chaotic situation while their authority was virtually undefined. Only two alternatives were possible, either the establishment of a new and highly complicated constitution with vicars apostolic, or else as Wiseman stated in his later *Appeal to the English People* "the real and complete code of the Church must be at once extended to the Catholic Church in England, so far as compatible with its social position".

To achieve that objective, Wiseman argued, "the Catholics must have a hierarchy". Canon Law is inapplicable under vicars apostolic, and there could be no episcopal synod to adjust minor difficulties. But there were many obstacles to overcome. Not least among them was the opposition of Cardinal Acton, the Pope's adviser in Rome on English affairs. He believed that the English vicars apostolic lacked apotolic spirit and were distrustful of the Holy See. Before Wiseman could make headway with the negotiations, he became involved in sudden international complications which resulted in his being sent back at once to England by the Pope. He was to discuss with the Foreign Office, on the Pope's behalf, how far England would support him in his reforming and liberal policy in case of pressure being applied against him by Austria. Early in September Wiseman was in London again and was requested to draft a full memorandum on the subject for Lord Palmerston. It was immediately effective, and Lord Palmerston despatched Lord Minto at once as Minister Plenipotentiary for a special mission.

For Wiseman himself the journey to Rome had momentous consequences. Dr. Griffiths, the vicar apostolic of the London District, had died suddenly while he was in Rome, and the Holy See desired that Wiseman should succeed him. However, Bishop Griffiths had distrusted Wiseman, and most of the London clergy were equally distrustful of his Roman training and particularly of his encouragement of the converts. Rome solved the problem by appointing him temporarily as pro-vicar apostolic in London while the hierarchy negotiations were proceeding. His lucid statement of the case had won over the authorities in Rome, and Cardinal Acton's sudden death about the same time removed the chief objector to the proposals. Early in 1848 Bishop Ullathorne who had been appointed vicar apostolic of the Western District, went to Rome to resume negotiations and found that the cause had already been won. But he too arrived when Rome was in a state of ferment.

The liberal movement which had at first commanded the sympathies of the Pope, had gathered a momentum which could no longer be controlled. Within a few months Ullathorne was able to accomplish his mission, but in the first days of his journey homewards, revolution suddenly broke out. The Pope's Prime Minister, Count Rossi, was assassinated and Monsignor Palma, who played a decisive part in Ullathorne's successful negotiations, was shot. The Pope had to escape secretly by night from Rome, and took refuge under the King of Naples at Gaeta. Not until the spring of 1849 was Pius IX able to return to Rome. By then, the Powers had met in conference, and France undertook to guarantee his safety by sending a garrison of French troops to the Papal States. In the interval old Bishop Walsh had been transferred from the Midland District to become vicar apostolic of the London District, with Wiseman as his coadjutor. Bishop Walsh died soon afterwards, and in February 1849, Wiseman succeeded him as vicar apostolic.

He immediately proceeded to give wider scope to the converts. They had been completing their Catholic education under his direction and hoping forlornly to find employment. He had invited both Newman and Faber to give missions in London in 1848, when Newman had completed the term of his noviciate in Italy, and had established his oratory in Birmingham. To the consternation of the old Catholics and against all the reproachful admonitions of his old friend Dr. Errington, Wiseman appointed W. G. Ward, who was not only a recent convert but a married man, to the profersorship of Dogmatic Theology at St. Edmund's seminary. The flow of new converts still continued, and now Wiseman found means of providing scope for many of them by inviting more religious congregations to England, which they joined.

In July 1848, as acting vicar apostolic, he had the joy of assisting among fourteen bishops from all over England and from the Continent, at the opening of St. George's church at Southwark, which had been the scene of the Gordon Riots seventy years before. It was one of the most ambitious churches that Pugin had yet designed, and its size, its noble design and its internal decorations marked the growing strength of Catholicism in London. St. George's, Southwark, was the largest as well as the most ambitious Catholic church built in England since the penal laws. In addition to a hectic round of attending public dinners, meetings, sermons, openings etc., he had to cope with special difficultes among his clergy. His zealous championing of the converts had aroused a definite antagonism before he came to London from Birmingham. Now his Roman ideas also were to create more opposition, among those who still adhered to the traditions of English isolation. For years there had been a strong undercurrent of opinion among the clergy and the more influential laity demanding a direct voice in the selection of the English bishops. Despite their opinions, Wiseman had been appointed by Rome as successor to Bishop Griffiths without any consultation with the London clergy. They were now subjected to Wiseman's strongly Romanising tendencies, and many of them resented his encouragement of continental devotions and religious communities from abroad. For years Wiseman was confronted with deliberate and organised resitence of many of his clergy, who considered that his innovations would outrage English opinions, and were alien to the English character.

The constant stream of conversions, more than anything else, sustained his spirits. One convert who became a Catholic as a university student in the first half of 1850, has left a clear description of him at this time. He had grown much heavier and the signs of diabetes, which made him so corpulent later, were beginning to show. Fr. Purbrick S.J., who afterwards became Provincial of the Jesuits, contributed for Wilfrid Ward's biography, an account of his first meeting with Wiseman shortly after his conversion, at one of Wiseman's weekly evening gatherings at his episcopal residence in Golden Square. "On entering", writes Fr. Purbrick, "he was standing between Monsignor Searle and Father Lythgoe, and they formed a trio somewhat formidable for a timid stranger to encounter. I thought, is this then, the effect of prayer and fasting? Three such mountains of flesh I had never before seen. Dr. Wiseman's aspect was at first sight forbidding, his shaggy eyebrows, and wide, thick lipped mouth, being neither handsome nor attractive. But the reception he gave us was warm and hearty in the extreme, and his inquiries about the prevailing tone of young men at Oxford showed at once his keen interest in the Oxford Movement and the sympathetic attitude of his mind. I soon found that any reserve or shyness produced in him similar effects, but however young one might be, frankness even to familiarity, instead of meeting with the rebuff it might seem to deserve, only placed him completely at his ease, and was responded to with unaffected expansiveness. It was also very noticeable that he was very fond of children and that they were equally fond and fearless of him".

The time was aproaching when his greatest hopes were to be fulfilled. Early in 1850 a new crises had arisen in the Church of England. A judgement by the Privy Council rejected the claim of the Anglican Bishop of Exeter to refuse employment to Mr. Gorham, a clergyman who repudiated belief in the doctrine of regeneration by baptism. Since Newman's conversion, those who had declined to follow his example had gradually regained confidence and tranquility of mind. They had found a new leader in Archdeacon Manning of Chichester, whose close friendship with Gladstone gave him a wide influence among the laity. They felt now that the Tractarian Movement could be regrded as an episode, and that its collapse need not effect their programme of beliefs. But now another unexpected crises had arisen. The Protestant forces had rallied in support of Mr. Gorham when he insisted on accepting the parish which had been offered to him, though the Bishop of Exeter refused to induct him.

In March 1850, the surviving leaders of the Tractarian party found it necessary to issue a joint letter of protest against the decision of the Privy Council. They had claimed that the Church did in practice exercise an absolute control, without interference by the State, over all questions involving religious belief. But that claim was now shown to be untenable as the Privy Council could overide the Bishop of Exeter. It revived all the old doubts and anxieties in a more mencing form than ever. Wiseman seized upon his opportunity at once. In a sermon at St.Georges's church he challenged all those Anglicans who were outraged by the Gorham judgement to reconsider their position. It looked as though this new development might precipitate a crisis which would repeat the effects of Newman's surrender five years before.

Wiseman received a sudden summons to return to Rome. A letter from Cardinal Antonelli, the papal Secretary of State, announced that the Pope had decided to appoint him a cardinal, and that he was to leave England for Rome within a month. He was forty-eight, and his ten years in England had been marked by great achievements. That he should be made a cardinal was the highest tribute that could be paid to the work he had already accomplished. But it apparently could only mean that he was to return forthwith to Rome and reside there for the remainder of his life, as the Pope's special counsellor on English affairs in succession to Cardinal Acton. He would be cut off from any possibility of continuing the work to which he had consecrated his life, at the moment when greater achievements seemed to be plainly imminent.

Although the restoration of the hierarchy was regarded among Catholics as being almost decided, Wiseman did not realise that his own appointment as a cardinal might be the first step in that great decision. He had bade farewell to his closest associates with sincere grief. He had impressed upon Faber and Newman and the converts who were most dear to him, his sense of the absolute necessity of obedience, endeavouring to set an example to them of fortitude in the frustration of his hopes. He reached Rome in the first week of September, and on the 13th, he had his formal interview with Pius IX. Only then did he know that the historic step was about to be taken. The Pope had decided to send Wiseman back to England as the head of a new hierarchy.

On the last day of September his nomination as cardinal was duly made. He then drafted his first pastoral letter as Archbishop of Westminster, with 7 October as its date, to announce the great news to the Catholics of England. His pastoral had been sent on ahead, and he proceeded in slow stages on his journey, receiving with dignity the demonstrations of enthusiasm that his appointment had aroused in the Catholic countries through which he had to pass. It was in Vienna, after he had been honoured by the Emperor, that he first learned with dismay how the news had been received in England. *The Times* had devoted its chief article to his appointment, and he read the article while he drove through the streets of Vienna in his state carriage. "That Dr. Wiseman should have been raised to the purple was no surprise", *The Times* declared, in view of his distinction "as one of the most learned and able members of the Roman Catholic priesthood in this country. It is no concern of ours, whether Dr. Wiseman chooses in Rome to be ranked with the Monsignori of the capital. He is simply at Rome in the position of an English subject who has thought fit to enter the services of a foreign power and accept its spurious dignities. But this nomination has been accompanied by one other circumstance which has a very different and very peculiar character. We are informed by the *Official Gazette* of Rome that the Pope having recently been pleased to erect the City of Westminster into an archbishopric, and to appoint Dr. Wiseman to that See, it is on this newfangled Archbishop of Westminster, so appointed, that the rank of Cardinal is so conferred".

What *The Times* asked, was this new dignity and appointment intended to convey? Did it mean "no more than if the Pope had been pleased to confer on the editor of *The Tablet* the rank and title of the Duke of Smithfield?" If so, it might be dismissed as a "clumsy joke". But if not, then "we confess that we can only regard it as one of the grossest acts of folly and impertinence which the Court of Rome has ventured to commit since the Crown and people of England threw off its yoke". *The Times* would not believe that "this ridiculous and offensive step" was intended as a retaliation on the British Government for the hostility which had been imputed to it. The suggestion could not account for "one of the most daring assumptions of power it has put forward in this country for three centuries". Its verdict was that the Pope had completely mistaken the attitude of the English people, believing their tolerance to imply indifference, and the "renovated zeal" of the Church of England to betoken "a return towards Romish bondage". It was "not sorry" that his indiscretion and that of his advisors had "led them to show the power which Rome would exercise if she could, by an act which the laws of this country will never recognise and which the public opinion of this country will deride and disavow, when ever His Grace the titular Archbishop of Westminster thinks fit to enter his diocese".

Wiseman might well have qualms at the thoughts of the pastoral letter which he had already despatched to London. It would have been published all over England before he could consult with his friends. If the mere announcement that he was to be Cardinal Archbishop of Westminster aroused such fury, what sort of reception would await the enthusiastic pastoral in which he had conveyed the official decision? That evening he wrote a personal letter to Lord John Russell the Prime Minister, to clear up misunderstandings which were almost certain to arise.

"I spoke to your Lordship", Wiseman wrote "as I was about to leave England without intention of returning, and it may possible be insinuated now that such was not the case. I beg, therefore, to assure your Lordship that I was most sincere when I spoke of my departure as final, with no idea that I should return. I am anxious that no impression should remain on your Lordship's mind that I had the slightest intention to deceive you". He reminded him that the new hierarchy had been agreed upon three years before, "and a copy of it was shown to Lord Minto by the Pope on the occasion of an audience given to his Lordship by His Holiness. "Its scope", Wiseman now formally pointed out, "was purely ecclesiastical", without any "secular or temporal delegation". His own duties would still be, as before, "to promote the morality of those committed to my charge, especially the masses of the poor, and to keep up those feelings of goodwill and friendly intercommunication between Catholics and their fellow countrymen which I flatter myself I have been the means of somewhat improving".

Long before this letter had reached Lord John Russell, the Protestant fury in England had been inflamed. Wiseman had been too severely shaken to enjoy any further the greetings which he encountered while he now hurried home. At Cologne he could only visit the Cathedral for early Mass, and in the morning have a cordial meeting with the Archbishop, Cardinal Geissel, who stayed with him until his train left the station. At Bruges he at last received letters from his friends in England. They increased his distress, and he decided to complete his journey immediately. Before his return his pastoral had been published all over England.

Indignation that the English bishops were to have territorial titles was already rising in intensity. A few days after publishing the first article which Wiseman read when he was in Vienna, *The Times* of 19 October 1850, had demanded "is it, then, here in Westminster, among ourselves and by the English throne, that an Italian priest is to parcel out the spititual dominion of this country - to employ the renegades of our national Church to restore a foreign usurpation over the conscience of men, and to sow division in our political society by an undisguised and systematic hostility to the institutions most identified with our national freedom and our national faith? Such an intention must either be ludicrous or intolerable - either a delusion of some fanatical brain or treason to the Constitution".

Wiseman's pastoral, written under the stress of great emotion in Rome, and expressing the consummation of his hopes for many years, was so provocatively jubilant that it could not fail to intensify the public anger. His effect was even more inflammatory than Dr. Whitty, his vicar general, had feared. Public demonstrations assumed such a violent form all over the country, and particularly in London, that Wiseman's friends considered that he should be prevented from landing in England. Only a few were in favour of his coming. They feared for his personal safety, and they feared that he would make some new *faux pas* when, he had expected a triumpal return. By 27 October, the pastoral had been read publicly in all the churches in the London District.

It began with the challenging announcement that it was issued "from out the Flaminian Gate of Rome". After describing in highly coloured language the historical importance of the new hierarchy, and the vast possibilities it brought for the future, he announced his own appointment as Archbishop in the following terms: "By a Brief dated the same day, his Holiness was further pleased to appoint us at the same time the administration of the Episcopal See of Southwark. So that at present, and till such time as the Holy See shall think fit otherwise to provide, we govern and shall continue to govern, the counties of Middlesex, Hertford and Essex, as Ordinary thereof, and those of Surrey, Sussex, Kent, Berkshire and Hampshire, with the islands annexed, as Administrator with Ordinary jurisdiction".

The pastoral had been composed in Rome, in a mood of spiritual exultation, and amidst congratulations on all sides. In its concluding passages he gave expresson to ideas which went far beyond even the attitude of many devout English Catholics. Its language was certain to inflame that irritation which had been growing among the Protestants of England, since the Tractarian leaders had first challenged their conception of the Anglican Church. "The great work, then, is complete", he wrote, "what you have long desired and prayed for is granted. Your beloved country has received a place among the fair Churches, which normally constituted, form the splendid aggregate of the Catholic Communion, Catholic England has been restored to its orbit in the ecclesiastical firmament, from which its light had long vanished, and begins now under its course of regularly adjusted action round the centre of unity, the source of jurisdiction, of light, and vigour. Then truly is this to us a day of joy and exaltation of spirit", the pastoral went on, "the crowning day of long hopes, and the opening day of bright prospects. How must the saints of our country whether Roman or British, Saxon or Norman, look down from their seats of bliss with beaming glances upon this new evidence of the Faith and Church which led them to glory, sympathising with those who have faithfully adhered to them through centuries of ill-repute for the truth's sake, and now reap the fruit of their patience and long suffering! And all those blessed martyrs of these later ages, who have fought the battles of the faith under such discouragement, who mourned, more than over their own fetters or their own pain, over the desolate ways of their own Sion and the departure of England's religious glory, oh! how must they bless God, who hath again visited His people".

Such language stung the traditional Protestants of England to fury, and Wiseman's critics among the English Catholics were aghast at his lack of comprehension. Even his friends were over-whelmed by his indiscretion. *The Times* had become the most important organ of conservative opinion, and it had modified its former habit of vituperation, which had been so outrageous in its attacks upon O'Connell only a few years before. But it rose to lurid flights in commenting upon the new Cardinal's announcement of the Pope's decree. Wiseman had given it a new weapon with which to attack the Whig Government. *The Times* had discovered in a French Catholic paper what purported to be an account of Pius IX's own words in regard to the appointment. The Pope, it appeared, had discussed the matter with Lord Minto, and *The Times* now protested that although the plan had apparently been commuincated to Lord Minto at that time, "yet the British Government has seen no reason to offer any adverse expression of opinion to it, so that while one of the effects of Lord Minto's unfortunate journey was to promote the revolution in Italy, the other is to promote the re-establishment of the Roman Hierarchy in England. For a Scottish nobleman who is neither a Jacobin nor a bigot, it must be confessed that these results are strange instances of diplomatic ability, and Lord Minto will be consigned to the judgement of posterity between Cicervacchio and the Archbishop of Westminster".

Disraeli was not slow, like many other politicians to join in the public protest against the "Papal Aggression". Lord John Russell had already written his famous reply to the Bishop of Durham, in answer to his demand for an official protest against what the Bishop termed the "insolent and insidious" assumption of authority by the Pope. Lord John Russell replied at once expressing his agreement with these denunciations. "I therefore feel as indignant as you can do upon the subject", he wrote. To forestall such attacks as Disraeli was quick to deliver, he had explained at once that "I not only promoted to the utmost of my power the claim of the Roman Catholics to all civil rights, but I thought it right, and even desirable that the ecclesiastical system of the Roman Catholics should be the means of giving instruction to the numerous Irish immigrants in London and elsewhere, who without such help would have been left in heathen ignorance. This might have been done, however, without any such innovation as that which we thus have now seen. There is an assumption of power in all the documents which have come from Rome", his letter confirmed, "a pretension to supremacy over the realm of England, and a claim to sole and undivided sway, which is inconsistent with the Queen's supremacy, with the rights of our bishops and clergy, and with the spiritual independence of the nation, as asserted even in Roman

Catholic times". Nevertheless he confessed that his own feelings were of indignation rather than alarm. He had already received, though he made no mention of it, the reassuring letter which Wiseman had sent to him from Vienna immediately after seeing the first outbursts of fury in *The Times*.

"Even if it shall appear", wrote Lord John Russell. "that the ministers and servants of the Pope in this country have not transgressed the law, I feel persuaded that we are strong enough to repel any outward attacks. The liberty of Protestantism has been enjoyed too long in England to allow of any successful attempt to impose a foreign yoke upon our minds and conscience. No foreign prince or potentate will be permitted to fasten his fetters upon a nation which has so long and so nobly vindicated its right to freedom of opinion, civil, political and religious". Knowing well how unfounded was all the outcry against the Catholic hierarchy, he sought to sidetrack the agitation into an outburst against the Catholicising movement within the Church of England. That, he declared, was "a danger which alarms me much more than any aggression of a foreign sovereign", the action of clergymen of their own Church "who have been most forward in leading their flocks step by step, to the very verge of the precipice. The honour paid to saints, the claim of infallibility for the Church", he went on, "the superstitious use of the sign of the cross, the muttering of the liturgy so as to disguise the language in which it is written, the recommendation of auricular confession and the administration of penance and absolution, all these things are pointed at by clergymen of the Church of England as worthy of adoption, and are now openly reprehended by the Bishop of London to the clergy of his diocese. What then, is the danger to be apprehended from a foreign prince of no great power, compared to the danger within the gates from the unworthy sons of the Church of England?"

It was the signal for a general outburst of execration against the Tractarians, which was to have the effect soon afterwards of driving the most influential Anglican leader since Newman into surrender to Rome. But Lord John Russell was incapable of understanding the wider issues that he had raised. Meanwhile, he reassured the Bishop of Durham by declaring that he himself "would not bate a jot of heart or hope so long as the glorious principles and the immortal martyrs of the Reformation shall be held in reverence by the great mass of a nation which looks with contempt on the mummeries of superstition, and with scorn at the laborious endeavours which are now making to confine the intellect and ensnare the soul". Lord John Russell's abusive language, however, was mild in comparison with that of *The Times*. It denounced the "impudence and absurdity of one of the strangest pieces of mummery we ever remember to have witnessed" which it "could only receive as an audacious and conspicuous display of pretentions to resume the absolute spiritual domination of this island which Rome has never

203

abandoned, but which by the blessing of Providence and the will of the English people, she shall never accomplish".It concluded by asserting that "the creation of a hierarchy assuming the names and cities and provinces and distributing counties amongst their Sees is a step which the Pope could not have taken in any other civilised country in Europe, and it is hardly less preposterous than the Bull of one of his predecessors in the fifteenth century which assigned to the crown of Portugal the undiscovered limits of the New World".

Such outbursts had helped to produce the atmosphere of angry excitement, upon which Lord John Russell's letter to the Bishop of Durham had fallen opportunely on the eve of Guy Fawkes' day. The firework displays and bonfires which resulted were without precedent for generations. The Prime Minister's letter had been an open provocation to demonstrations against the Tractarians and their disciples. Crowds assembled everywhere in the streets, and violent expression was given in all the districts around London to the hatred of the new hierarchy and of the Tractarians alike. The contemporary newspapers contain lively descriptions of how Cardinal Wiseman's effigy appeared in every procession, and was burned amid howls of jubilation. At Ware the Pope was burned in effigy on a height overlooking the town, "dressed in full pontificals, with the triple crown on his head, and the addition of a large pair of ram's horns, while in the wagon was a donkey, to represent his Excellency the Cardinal Archbishop of Westminster, suspended by the neck on a gallows over a huge pile of faggot-wood and tar-barrels". It was burned amid shouts of joy after a solemn procession round the town. Similar scenes were enacted throughout the country.

Meanwhile Wiseman was still hurrying homewards, and he did not arrive in London until 11 November. The campaign against him had developed considerably further. The Bishop of London had denounced the whole Catholic clergy as "emissaries of darkness", the Bishop of Manchester had proclaimed that "Rome clings to her abominations". These were only the first samples of a series of episcopal attacks upon the Catholic Church during the closing weeks of November. The Bishop of Bangor referred to "a foreign prince insolent in his degredation", and even the Bishop of Oxford described Catholicism as "subtle and unclean". In December the Bishop of Hereford spoke more picturesquely of "the sorcerer's cup" and the "crafts of Satan", while the Bishop of Carlisle boldly declared, just before the end of the year, that her claims were "profane, blasphemous and anti-Christian". By that time the excitement was beginning to subside. But it had reached its climax on the day before Wiseman arrived in London, when the newspapers contained reports of the Lord Chancellor's speech at the Mansion House dinner, in which he had boasted, amid great applause, the lines: "Under our feet we'll stamp the Cardinal's hat, in spite of Pope or dignities of Church".

When threats to his personal safety had been issued by leading newspapers, and when the Lord Chancellor had just delivered almost a direct incitement to violence against him, Wiseman returned home. His friends were intimidated, and they feared that he might make some new effort to retrieve his first error of judgement, which would only make matters worse. He arrived very early in the morning of 11 November at Mr. Bagshawe's house in Fitzroy Square, as his own was in the hands of decorators. He sent at once for his vicar general and for Sir George Bowyer, as one of the leading laymen in the new archdiocese, and commissioned him to go immediately to interview some members of the Government to counteract the misrepresentation of what had occurred. Bowyer obtained an interview with Lord Lansdowne, who was Lord President of the Council, and he learned that the Prime Minister had published his letter to the Bishop of Durham without any previous consultation with his colleagues. Lansdowne himself declared that he deeply regretted the letter, and after several more interviews, expressed his own view that there had been an "enormous misunderstanding".

At his first meeting with Dr. Whitty, Wiseman showed him the page of foolscap upon which he had already begun to write the first paragraph of an "appeal to the English people". Whitty was sceptical, Wiseman's style was always flamboyant, and his first pastoral had provided evidence of his inability to appreciate the extent of Protestant prejudice in England. That he was likely to mend matters by issuing a second public proclamation might well be doubted. But Wiseman's mind was made up, and amid all the feverish interruptions, he was continuing rapidly the preparation of the manifesto in which he intended to appeal for fair play to the people of England. It ran to enormous length, but it was written with scarcely an erasure or an altered word. Dr. Whitty could only conclude that the idea had turned in his mind when he had received the first shock in Vienna, and that he had been thinking out his pamphlet closely during the journey home. Before the end of the week he had sent it to the printers, and on 20 November, five morning newspapers in London published it in full. Within another week some 30,000 copies had been sold in pamphlet form as well. He had hoped particularly that *The Times* should publish it in full, and when Mr. Bagshawe's son persuaded four of the other dailies to publish it, *The Times* could not refuse to do the same. It occupied six and a half columns of small close type.

Both as a reply to his critics, and as a vindication of the decision to create a Catholic hierarchy in England, it was a really impressive combination of straight forward argument and eloquence. He was convinced that the people of England would never fail to respond to a direct appeal for fair play, and that they would appreciate the courage of any man who faced opposition squarely. Reviewing the course of events since the hierarchy had been announced, he protested that the storm had burst with such "absolute fury" that "the energies of all seemed concentrated upon one single point, that of crushing if possible, or denouncing at least to public execration, the new form of ecclesiastical government which Catholics regarded as a blessing and an honour. For this purpose nothing was refused, however unfounded, however personal, even by papers whose ordinary tune is courteous, or at least well-bred. Anecdotes without a particle of truth, or what is worse, with some particles of distorted truth in them, have been copied from one into another, and most widely circulated. Sarcasm, ridicule, satire of the broadest character, theological and legal reasonings of the most refined nature, bold and reckless declamation, earnest and artful argument - nothing seemed to come amiss, and every invocable agency from the Attorney General to Guy Fawkes, from *praemunire* to a hustling, was summoned forth to aid the cry, and administer to the vengence of those who raised it".

In the general hue and cry, the young Cardinal argued that the Prime Minister, who could have mitigated the storm by a few words, in view of his own knowledge of the facts, had joined shamelessly as a leader. Wiseman contrasted his attitude vigorously with that of Peel when a similar outcry had arisen over the increased grant to Maynooth College. Peel, he recalled, had "nobly stemmed the tide, carried his measure with calm dignity through the legislature, and yielded nought to public outcry". In the present crisis, on the other hand, when Catholics of England had neither expected nor asked for any co-operation from Government but "had the right of every citizen to impartiality", the Prime Minister had not only failed to remain neutral but had "astonished not this country alone, but all Europe, by a letter which leaves us but little hope that any appeal to the highest authority which rules over the empire would be received, to say the least, with favour". Against the disgraceful outburst by the Lord Chancellor he protested in the same dignified and vigorous strain, before declaring his own intention to appeal, in the last resort, to the one tribunal in England before which he was confident that justice would never be disowned.

"While thus the avenues to public justice seemed closed against us", he went on, "while the press has condemned us and raised our death-whoop, in spite of proffered explanations, deaf to every call for a fair hearing, while we may consider that the door of the Treasury may be barred against us, if we knock to ask, not for pension or funds, but for reasonable hearing, when the very highest judicial authority has prejudged and cut off appeal from us, what resources have we left? What hope of justice? One which, after God's unfailing providence, we place unbounded confidence. There still remain the manly sense and honest heart of a generous people, that love of honourable dealing and fair play which, in joke or in earnest, is equally the instinct of an Englishmen, that hatred of all mean advantage taken, of all base tricks and paltry clap-trap and party cries employed to hunt down even a rival or a foe.

To this open-fronted and warm-hearted tribunal I make my appeal, and claim, on behalf of myself and my fellow Catholics, a fair, free and impartial hearing. Fellow subjects, Englishmen, be you at least just and equitable. You have been deceived, you have been misled, both as to facts and as to intentions".

Having replied in detail to the accusation that the Pope's establishment of a Hierarchy infringed the prerogatives of the Crown, he argued with quotations from the highest legal authorities that it was no crime for a Catholic to maintain and defend the supremacy of the Pope, that the Dissenters were no less opposed to the authority of the Crown in religious matters, and that the whole question of religious toleration in England was involved in controversy. "Believe me", he wrote, "at this moment the danger to the religious and civil liberties of Englishmen is not from any infringement of them by the Pope, in granting to English Catholics what I hope to show you they had full right to obtain from him, but from those who are taking advantage of the occurrence to go back a step, if they can, in the legislation of tolerance, and take away from a large body of Englishmen what at present is lawful to them in regard to the free exercise of their religion". Again and again he quoted from judgements delivered by Lord Chancellor Lyndhurst to show that the Catholics were absolutely entitled to exercise their religion which was essentially episcopal in character.

The recent outcry had been based upon a misrepresentation, alleging that the Catholic bishops contemplated some sort of tangible authority within the territory allotted to them. He insisted that "the new bishops will not have occasion to cross the path of the prelates of the Anglican Establishment in their sphere of duty, they will find plenty to do besides their official duties, in attending to the wants of their poor spiritual children, especially the multitudes of poor Irish, whose peaceful and truly Catholic conduct, under the whirlwind of contumely which has just assailed them, proved that they have not forgotten the teaching of their Church, not to revile when reviled, and when they suffer, not to threaten". From Lord John Russell's own speeches in Parliament he showed the gross absurdity of suggesting that the Pope had claimed territorial sovereignty over any part of England. From the records of previous Governments he showed that precedents for the restoration of the English hierarchy had already been established in Australia and in Ireland without any objection being raised. In the final passages he dislayed his unsuspected power of commanding popular synpathy. The Chapter of Westminster Abbey had issued an hysterical protest "as though some practical attempt at jurisdiction within the Abbey was intended".

"Then let me give assurance on that point", he wrote, "and let us come to a fair division and good understanding. The diocese, indeed, of Westminster embraces a large district, but Westminster proper consists of two very different parts. One comprises the stately Abbey, with its adjacent palaces, and its royal parks. To this portion the duties of occupation of the Dean and Chapter are mainly confined, and they shall range there undisturbed. To the venerable old church I may repair, as I have been wont to do. But perhaps the Dean and Chapter are not aware that, were I disposed to claim more than the right to tread the Catholic pavement of that noble building and breathe its air of ancient consecration, another might step in with a prior claim. For successive generations there has existed ever, in the Benedictine Order, an Abbott of Westminster, the representative in religious dignity, of those who erected, and beautified, and governed that church and cloister. Have they ever been disturbed by this 'titular'? Have they ever heard of any claim or protest on his part, touching their temporalities? Then let them fear no greater aggressions now. Like him, I may visit, as I have said, the old Abbey, and say my prayer by the shrine of good St. Edward, and meditate on the olden times, when the church was filled without a coronation, and multitudes hourly worshiped without a service. But their temporal rights, or their quiet possession of any dignity or title, they will not suffer. Whenever I go in, I will pay my entrance fee like other liege subjects, and resign myself meekly to the guidance of the beadle, and listen without rebuke, when he points out to my admiration detestable monuments or shows me a hole in the wall for a confessional.

"Yet this splendid monument, its treasures of art, and its fitting endowments" he went on, "form not the part of Westminster which will concern us. For there is another part which stands in frightful contrast, though in immediate contact, with this magnificence. In ancient times, the existence of an abbey on any spot, with large staff of clergy and ample revenues, would have sufficed to create around it a little paradise of comfort, cheerfulness and ease. This, however, is not now the case. Close under the Abbey of Westminster there lie concealed labyrinths of lanes and courts, and alleys and slums, nests of ignorance, vice, depravity, and crime, as well as of squalor, wretchedness and disease, whose atmosphere is typhus, whose ventilation is cholera, in which swarms a huge and almost countless population, in great measure, nominally at least, Catholic, haunts of filth, which no sewage committee can reach, dark corners, which no lighting board can brighten. This is the part of Westminster which alone I covet, and which I shall be glad to claim and to visit, as a blessed pasture in which sheep of Holy Church are to be tended, in which a bishop's Godly work has to be done, of consoling, converting and preserving. And if, as I humbly trust in God, it shall be seen that this special culture, arising from the estblishment of our hierarchy, bears fruit of order, peacefulness, decency, religion and virtue, it may be that the Holy See shall not be thought to have acted unwisely, when it bound up the very soul and salvation of a chief pastor with those of a city, where of the name, indeed, is glorious, but the purlieus infamous, in which the very gran-deur of its public edifices is a shadow to screen from the public eye sin and misery the most appalling. If the wealth of the Abbey be stagnant and not diffusive, if it in no way rescues the neighbouring population from the depths in which it is sunk, let there be no jealousy of anyone, who, by what-ever name, is ready tio make the latter his care, without interfering with the former".

The effect of his Appeal to the English people was immediate. Almost the entire press now acknowledged the power and force of his pamphlet. They generally adopted the same attitude as did the *London News*, in explaining that the misunderstanding had been the fault of "the blatant indiscretion of the many over sanguine priests of the Roman persuasion, who have tortured what, if we are to believe Cardinal Wiseman, was a harmless domestic ar-rangement among the Roman Catholics themselves, into an aggression".*The Times* sheltered itself behind a similar complaint that "if we have pro-nounced an opinion against the Pope and the cardinal unheard, it has not been from any wish to deny them fair play, but because they did not conde-scend to give us any more tangible explanation of their acts than was to be gathered from empty gasconades and pompous manifestoes, the very sweep-ings of a literary wardrobe now nearly worn out, and never very tastefully selected. We congratulate Dr. Wiseman on his recovery of the use of the English language", it declared sarcastically. "If the popular demonstrations with which the arrival of the new cardinal who has come with a commission from Rome to govern half a dozen of the dioceses of our Church, and some two of the kingdoms of the Saxon Heptarchy, have not been all that was agreeable in other respects, they have, at any rate, as the Scottish say, brought him to his English". But *The Times* abated none of its hostility to-wards the Catholic Church. "In her authorised documents, whatever is not within herself is treated as non-existent, her language, her logic, are all founded on this principle. Whatever is not her own she absolutely ignores. The Pope employs the same old style in constituting an Archbishop of Westminster as in appointing a prelate of some petty town in Latium. The existence of the crown, of the prelates, of the mighty people of England, he cannot acknowledge, all he sees is the land, a few Roman Catholics scattered up and down it, and those bishops among whom he divides it, the rest to him is nothing".

Wiseman threw all his energies into the contest. His indiscretion had aroused a wider interest in the Catholic Church in England than could have been expected, moreover, he had galvanised the Catholic body into new life. The hysterical outbursts of the Prime Minister and the Lord Chancellor af-fected the High Church party as directly as it affronted Catholics. Gladstone and other influential politicians with strong Tractarian sympathies were driven to taking up the defence of their friends. The Liberal veteran, J.A. Roebuck, entered the fray soon after Wiseman's *Appeal* had been published, with an open letter to Lord John Russell which denounced, in scathing terms his incitement to religious persecution and his abandonment of the principles which the Whigs had for so long held sacred. "The same sort of feeling as that which, in 1780, roused the mobs of London against Sir George Saville", he wrote, "and made that madman Lord George Gordon a hero, the idol and leader of the people, is now exercising a fatal influence upon the good sense of the English people. This feeling you have most unfortunately countenanced, you have given dignity and importance to an antipathy which you ought certainly to have allayed, and by your ill-timed support, have done your utmost to keep alive for years a detestable intolerance, of which in your heart I believe you to be thoroughly ashamed. To you my Lord, posterity will refer as a man who, just when the real difficulties were conquered, when, by the united and continuous labours of our greatest statesmen, the law had become just, and peace and goodwill were about to be established, took advantage of your great position to rouse up the spirit of strife and hate among us, to quicken into active life the demon of persecution, and to render assunder a great empire which, but for your fatal interference, would soon have become firmly united, peaceful and prosperous. A melancholy distinction this my Lord, for one who all his life has styled himself the friend of religious as well as civil freedom. Your common sense must long since have shocked at the wretched fanaticism which you have evoked, and which unfortunately, you will find a spirit beyond your power to lay".

Wiseman carried his own campaign a stage further by preparing a series of addresses which he delivered in St. George's Church at Southwark, and these attracted large and respectful audiences. His unexpected success in mastering the situation gave new heart to the Catholic body, and they acclaimed him as the first leader of genius and of national stature who had arisen among them since Bishop Milner's death. At the outset there had been several deplorable instances of cowardice in face of intimidation. Even on the day that Wiseman's *Appeal* was published, Lord Beaumont saw fit to write a letter to the Earl of Zetland, in which he stated publicly that "the late bold and clearly expressed edict of the court of Rome cannot be received or accepted by English Roman Catholics without a violation of their duties as citizens". He even announced that Lord John Russell's conduct towards the establishment of the new hierarchy was "that of a true friend of the British Constitution". Still more deplorable was the action of the Duke of Norfolk. On 28 November, he wrote formally to Lord Beaumont to express entire agreement with his protests against the new Hierarchy, and announced that "I should think that many must feel, as we do, that ultramontane opinions are totally incompatible with allegiance to our Sovereign and with our Constitution".

To give confirmation to his protest, the Duke publicly accepted the sacrament of the Church of England, and ceased thereafter to be a Catholic until near the end of his life.

The Duke of Norfolk's apostacy had been the worst public scandal in the Catholic body for many years. But the old preponderant influence of the Catholic nobility and county families had diminished rapidly in recent years. The immense increase of the Catholic population, the arrival of many more clergy from Ireland and from the Continent, the growth of a new prosperous Catholic middle class and the accession of many converts, had all combined to change the character of the Catholic community. Already even *The Guardian* noted that "the strength of Romanism in this country, even as a political power, is no longer confined to noblemen's castles". It had become "something rougher, more energetic, more aggressive, less English in its attachments and sympathies and less amenable to influences which may not uncharitably be supposed to have some weight with the Premier Duke, Earl Marshal, and hereditary Marshal of England".

Wiseman's impressions of the campaign were reported to Rome in a series of letters to the convert Monsignor Talbot. "The first great effort of the excitement", he wrote from London early in December, "through the Press, was to keep me out of the country by frightening me. Many timid Catholics were going to write to me, for god's sake not to come over, as my life was not safe". He requested Talbot to impress upon the Pope that he had travelled "as quick as I possibly could", but he admitted that it had been just as well that he was not in England for Guy Fawkes day. "I believe that had I been here that day, something very disagreeable might have occurred, for the people were fearfully urged on. The Protestant Association at Exeter Hall contributed, it is said, £1,400 towards that day, Hoare's house gave £100, and so on. For several days or evenings, groups of people, evidently sent, were about Golden Square". But he was quite satisfied that "my arrival in London, my going at once to St. George's and doing everything calmly and without showing either fear or forwardness, had a most beneficial effect. The next trial was my publicly officiating. While at St. George's I said Mass every morning at eight in the Madonna Chapel, so there was no concealment. But many people feared a row on our first function. I did not, because independently of higher reasons, I had seen how orderly everything had been at all our churches. On Friday it was thought better to admit by ticket, and though no pains were taken to make the thing public we had a full church and about one hundred and fifty priests. I preached and assisted at Mass. Nothing could exceed the decorum and respect shown by all. On Sunday the church was open, and you may judge of the crowds when I tell you that the take was £94. I had received continual warnings that I should be shot or attacked that day, but of course, I despised all that. I sang High Mass and preached as usual to an immense congregation. In the evening the church was crammed, and I gave my first of three lectures on the hierarchy. Everyone seemed completely absorbed on the subject. Through the whole day there was not a disagreeable occurrence, crowd, pressure or trouble at all. You may now therefore consider all danger of tumult or commotion at an end. As for myself, I have not experienced the slightest approach to an insult, or any other behaviour than the most respectful".

One surprising consequence, Wiseman found that there had been a remarkable increase in the number of conversions. He was able to convey to the Pope through Mgr. Talbot direct evidence of this unexpected result. At the Oratory, Newman reported that there had never been so many applications from intending converts. There were many similar symptoms in unlikely places. "In the little dead city of Canterbury", Wiseman wrote, "under the very nose of John Bird Cantuar, twelve persons have at one time put themselves under instruction, including a niece of Sir Walter Scott (Miss Peat) and Miss Stephanoff, daughter of the artist. Archdeacon Manning and Dodsworth are considered certain, and most probably Bennett and Archdeacon Wilberforce. In a few days we shall hear of Lord Dunraven and Mr. Monsell MP, Lord Norreys I consider very hopeful. I saw him in Belgium and he sees Lord Arundel and Surrey almost daily, Lord Nelson likewise, and others. Mr. Rogers, Dr. Hook's curate, has been received by Oakeley. A declaration has been signed by at least twelve clergymen that the Church of England must ask for reconciliation with the Holy See, 1,800 have signed the declaration against the Royal Supremacy. The sale of Catholic books is unprecedented!" He wrote confidently to Talbot: "I do not see anything ought to have been done otherwise than it has been. Without any personal feeling on the subject, I believe that, if I had not been sent back, there would have been serious difficulties in establishing the hierarchy. I have borne the entire brunt of the excitement, the other bishops have escaped almost unnoticed, and as I have broad shoulders and some public estimation and good friendship among the aristocracy, I could stand a great deal".

Meanwhile the interest in the hierarchy seemed to increase. Wiseman's lectures at St. George's had been more crowded than ever, and inside a week the whole edition of 30,000 copies of his third lecture had been entirely sold out. Converts had continued to pour in, Manning's conversion was now imminent, and with Manning there was a hope that Gladstone would also come. "I now begin to expect Gladstone to follow him, especially if James Hope does, which seems certain", he was able to write enthusiastically to Rome. "Assure the Holy Father", he told Talbot, "that every day convinces not only me, but all Catholics, more and more that religion has been pushed on inestimably by all that has happened".

Cardinal Nicholas Wiseman

In spite of Wiseman's optimistic enthusiasm, the popular discontent against the establishment of the hierarchy which the Prime Minister and Lord Chancellor had helped to inflame, created a storm which had risen so fast that the Government found it necessary to introduce some measure to appease public opinion. In February 1851 the Ecclesiastical Titles Bill was introduced in Parliament. Cardinal Wiseman attended the debate. A majority of three to one carried it quickly through all its stages, in spite of resistance by Gladstone and others. But the Act, which imposed a fine of £100 upon any Catholic bishop who assumed the title of his See, was a dead letter from the first, and after twenty years Gladstone carried its repeal.

Extracts from: *Cardinal Wisemen* by Denis Gwynn
published by Browne & Nolan, Dublin

Chapter Ten

Cardinal Henry Edward Manning

HENRY Edward Manning was born on 15 July 1808, his father William Manning was a banker and Governor of the Bank of England and he could trace his family back to Norman times. Early schoolboy years were spent at Harrow competent in his studies and excelling at cricket, and later at Oxford where he became friends with Gladstone. When he reached the age of 21 his father gave him £700 in Consols saying with regret that he could do no more, having previously become bankcrupt. After leaving Oxford he struggled with financial depression, but had leanings towards politics. Friends from Oxford found him a Government job and for a short spell he was a clerk in the Colonial Office.

At this time he had little faith, despite the exhalted company he kept at Oxford, he heard Newman, rubbed shoulders with Pusey, but politics filled his mind.

He would often visit his friend Robert Bevan, the family were deeply evangelical, Miss Bevan was talented and pius and she was determined to save the soul of Manning. She was successful, she wrote on 24 November 1831, "H.M. is in the hands of One Who can guide by His cousel and fit for His own work by His Spirit. Who knows but that after being tempest-tossed for a season he may seek the services of his master?"

Manning informed his father on 31 January 1832 that he was to enter the Church. He wrote to his brother Fredrick on 3 February: "I have ever felt, when opposing your wishes on this subject, that you were urging me to a better, while I was perservering in the pursuit of a worse object. You were aware that my reasons for not entering the Church were scruples, I say not whether erroneous or correct. I could not consent to regard so sacred a profession solely as a means of procurring an income, and I also felt that the absence of a positive wish to undertake its duties constituted a sufficient disqualification in my own case". He was ordained a priest by Bishop Maltby of Chichester in Lincoln's Inn on 9 June 1833.

Manning became curate at Lavington in Sussex. He served under the Rector, John Sargent. On 7 November 1833 he married his Rector's daughter Caroline and for seventeen years he worked in an unspoilt Sussex. At that time there was no railway, no intrusion on a calm rustic countryside. His flock were mole-catchers, copse-cutters, poachers and shepherds, all patient country folk in embroidered smocks. He introduced a daily service, tolling the bell and reading the psalms himself. He showed himself paternal, instead of patronising, to ordinary people, who came to love and trust him as their father and protector. His parishioners were the hardworking peasantry who helped to pay off the debts of the Napoleonic Wars.

Manning's social conscience was honed by the laws that pressed down upon the country poor, Sussex tithemen marked "hay in cock and wheat in shock" and carried away a tenth. Manning denounced "the sin of exacting the largest rent and doing least repairs". His parishioners loved him and he became legendery as the tall lonely man wearing a threadbear cloak over his white surplice, who passed them twice daily on the road.

His married state lasted only four years, Caroline like her sisters sank into consumption. Years later he wrote: "Knowing nothing of the Catholic life, or instincts, or perfection, in November 1833, I married, and in July 1837, found myself again in the state in which I have been for more than forty years".

He grieved for his beloved Caroline, her living room was kept, museum like, with work box and thimble in place. Caroline died a month after Victoria came to the throne. On the day that Disraeli was returned to Parliament, Manning wrote to his close friend Gladstone, 27 July 1837: "God has been graciously pleased to lead me into a way that is desert, and to bid me serve Him with entire surrender of myself. On Monday last at ten minutes to five in the evening my beloved wife was taken out of this evil, changeful world. I bless God for the tender, pitiful hand with which He dealt out both her sufferings and my sorrows. I know you will both feel and pray for me. As indeed I do for you in your very different and perhaps severer trial - for I have ever found the time of our tribulation safer than the time of your wealth. I give you joy in your success, and may God be with you always".

July, he wrote, was "Like a church yard path to him". He kept the Octave of St. James as a "holy week", and offered the Holy Sacrifice "for my beloved wife". As he drew nearer to the Catholic Church he came to think of her as a Guardian Angel. He wrote to Mary Wilberforce: "How often I have said, what would she have thought of what I am doing and feeling and believing? If it is a delusion, perhaps she could have saved me". In a letter to Gladstone, 22 May 1838 he wrote: "The Reformation has brought on a most perplexing problem, how we are to deal with persons having the Christian theology without participating in the continuity of the Christian Church". It was the problem which was to drive Manning into the grip of Rome.

Manning was neither High nor Low Church, but of what he called "old Church Englandism". To the men of the Oxford Movement he was "morbidly moderate". A religious change came during an illness. He noted the milestones: "My admission to Lavington, 1833. My bereavement, 1837. The hearing of Confessions, 1844. The growing up of hope, 1845. My Illness, 1847. These are, I think, the chief agents under God in my conversion".

In a letter to Miss Maurice, 5 August 1850 he wrote: "I always felt that the Low Church had no objective truths, the High Church little subjective religion. Now I see that in the Catholic system the objective and subjective are the concave and convex. I do not say that the body and the soul, because these are two, and the objective and subjective become one. God and man are one by Incarnation. A Theology of 300 years is in conflict with a faith of 1800 years. I was born in the 300. My mature thoughts transplant me into the 1800. This is the real balance, but people will not so look at it. I believe a man might hold what he likes in the English Church if he would be quiet and uphold the Church. The dishonesty is to be honest".

The Privy Council's intervention in the Gorham Judgement had polarised many in the Church of England. The revelation of where the ultimate authority in the Church of England really lay, had left many Anglicans in a state of suspense. Their teaching concerning the supremacy of the Church in religious matters had been repudiated and disproved by the decision of the Privy Council, and the controversy which it provoked had intensified still further the Protestant reaction against the Tractarian movement. Following the restoration of the Catholic hierarchy which aroused such a revival of Protestant principles in the Church of England, they found themselves isolated. Since Newman's surrender in 1845, most of the Tractarians who had declined to follow him in submission to Rome had relied upon Archdeacon Manning of Chichester as their leader. Aloof from the general movement in Oxford, and devoting himself primarily to his work in Sussex, he had withstood the storm.

Then suddenly there had come the mad popular outcry against the "Papal Aggression". Manning was bombarded, like most of the senior Anglican clergy, with requests to convene a meeting of protest against what the Pope had done. To comply in the existing circumstances, could only mean a deliberate repudiation of the concept of a Universal Church towards which he had been drawn with overpowering conviction. To refuse meant much more than a conflict with his clergy and with the Anglican bishops. It would raise the whole question of whether an archdeacon, holding views so strongly opposed to the episcopate of the Church of England, could honestly continue in his position of authority. Through a week of painful suspense, Manning faced the necessity for a decision. Within a few days after Wiseman's return to England, he had felt it his duty to explain formally to his bishop that he believed the royal supremacy to be contrary to Christ's law, that it had severed the Church of England from the Universal Church, that the Pope's action in constituting a rival hierarchy had been inevitable and justified, and that he personally could not oppose the Pope. Manning met with his clergy to explain to them his position and informed them that he would never appear with them again, and with tears in their eyes they parted for ever. His resignation spread consternation and provoked entreaties from his many friends, from bishops, from Gladstone and others who had shared his anxiety over the Gorham Judgement. Before the end of January 1851, he had decided to go over to Rome, but the "bonds of duty" caused delay. Not until March did he legally resign his position as archdeacon. Soon after, going in company with Gladstone to the little chapel off the Buckingham Palace Road, he decided during the service that he could stay no longer. Laying his hands on Gladstone's shoulder, he said simply: "Come", and as Gladstone stayed, he went out into the wilderness alone.

On 6 April 1851, the former archdeacon, together with James Hope Q.C., was received into the Catholic Church at Farm Street, and on the following Sunday was confirmed by Cardinal Wiseman. By Wiseman's express wish, he received the tonsure immediately on the same day. The few weeks between Palm Sunday and Whitsuntide were regarded by the Cardinal, in the excitement of the moment, as sufficient time to prepare him for the priesthood. It was a precedent which outraged the older Catholics and provoked letters of remonstrance. But Wiseman's position was now incomparably stronger than when he had silenced his critics by receiving the submission of Newman and his disciples. Wiseman never doubted, since the success of his own *Appeal* that the hierarchy had given a new impetus to the Catholic revival. While cautious men were dismayed by the favour he had shown to Manning, he had no misgivings. "I knew how much Manning would feel the *ignominia saecularis habitus,* after seventeen years of a devout ministry with a most clerical appearance and leading a most strict life", he wrote to Mgr. Talbot in April. "No conversion yet has produced the effect of his", he wrote with absolute confidence, "nor caused such deep regret through all the 'Divided House' as I call the Anglican Establishment".

Within five years following the conversion of Manning, the Pope, who shared Wiseman's desire to encourage the new converts had appointed Manning as Provost of the Chapter. Manning now combined that position of great influence with absolute control over his new congregation of Oblates of St. Charles. Their ordinary purpose was to serve the Cardinal's plans, but they were responsible directly to Manning. This caused deep mistrust among Dr. Errington, Bishop Grant of Southwark, the Cardinal's secretary Mgr. Searle and his vicar general Dr. Maguire. Every rumour or cause of complaint against the cardinal and his convert provost was now immediately reported to Errington and to Bishop Grant. However, Wiseman was determined to encourage Manning in the execution of plans which he had himself cherished for years. Wiseman gave Manning guarantees and facilities which the Chapter resented as an encroachment upon the rights of the clergy. At

St. Edmund's, where Errington as much as Wiseman had for long wished to raise the standard of teaching and of discipline, there was a rooted traditional antipathy towards Roman or Continental ways. The problem soon became more complicated when several of the most proficient of the staff, including the young vice-president, Fr. Herbert Vaughan, enrolled as Oblates under Manning's jurisdiction.

A crisis had been precipitated, and the Chapter now met to confront Manning with the Canon Law, alleging that his rules infringed it. The Cardinal became directly involved, when the Chapter were able to produce rules which he had drawn up for them and had since forgotten. A sense of persecution and of being surrounded by enemies on all sides grew upon him, causing him great pain and depression of spirits. He was thrown more and more into close association with Manning and the other converts, who shared his views. The Chapter felt that they must assert their rights once and for all, or else allow the creation of disastrous precedents. They pressed the matter vigorously against Manning with a view to breaking his alliance with the Cardinal, until Wiseman at last took the law into his own hands and simply annulled their proceedings. The result was to mobilise Archbishop Errington on their side in open revolt against Wiseman. A clear case for dispute in Canon Law had arisen over the control of St. Edmund's and Errington now came forward as the champion of the chapter in their appeal to Rome against the Cardinal.

Only extreme provocation, and a conviction that great issues were at stake, could have led the whole Chapter to support Errington, or have led Errington himself to oppose his oldest friend in this almost unprecedented way. Wiseman was thrown completely off his balance, and distraught by the loneliness of his position. He asserted himself with lamentable lack of judgement by dismissing his vicar general, Dr. Maguire, and replacing him with a plainly incompetent successor. Not only Errington, but Searle, his secretary, who had also been his close friend since their student days in Rome and again at Oscott, now sided openly with the Chapter in their revolt. Manning's diplomacy failed to convince Rome that the Chapter must be overridden. The question was referred back to England and every effort was made to produce a peaceful settlement. Wiseman had obviously committed grave blunders and mismanaged a difficult situation, but Errington's position had become impossible. Twice within ten years of the restoration of the hierarchy, English bishops had now appealed to Rome, in personal quarrels with the Cardinal who was not only their chief, but the founder of the hierarchy. Rome might well deplore the uncompromising quarrels of these English bishops, to whom such relatively small matters seemed to raise enormously important issues. The intervention of Manning had made Errington regard himself as the champion of English traditions against the innovations of an ambitious convert, who was notoriously out of sympathy with the traditions of the old English Catholics. Errington had come to believe that a special duty was laid upon him of saving the Church in England from the tendencies which Manning personified.

It was Wiseman's misfortune to have brought together as his principle assistants two men who each represented the opposing forces which he had desired to amalgamate, Both were inflexible and uncompromising in insistence upon their own views. Wiseman at no time had been gifted with the capacity for firm decisions in settling disputes, and for several years his old vitality had gone. In body he had grown enormously corpulent and lethargic, and at some periods diabetes gave him an insatiable craving for food and drink which was pitiful in a man who had been abstemious in his tastes. Frequent heart attacks added to his infirmity, and there were occasions when his life seemed to hang by a thread. "I dare say that often I am found irritable and worried", he wrote in confidence to Manning. "I ought to check it, and with God's help I often do, with great effort and after pain. When some eight or nine years ago I was the first to tell Mr. Hawkins that I feared diabetes had come upon me, he had no idea of it, and asked by what symptoms I judged. After mentioning others, as thirst, I added that what convinced me most was irritability of temper. For though when young, I was very hot, and perhaps passionate, my years of quiet study, and higher means, had brought me into a state of habitual peace, which had not been broken ever by much to plague and provoke me. Yet suddenly there had come upon me a fretfulness about trifles which perhaps even showed itself in my manner, which I knew from observation in others was a symptom of that complaint (dependent mainly on overwork of brain) as much as gentleness and softness is in consumption. I trust, therefore, that at least before God this may form some excuse for what man may not have so easily overlooked".

Lonely and isolated, surrounded by constant warfare in his own house, he relied more and more upon the austere, ascetic Provost whose energy sustained his flagging vitality, and whose efforts were directed towards the purposes that had inspired his whole life in England. Complaints became more and more general that he now governed the diocese through Manning and saw everything through his eyes. The conflict arose, not from personal jealousy, but from opposing principles, and Manning, with a conviction that Wiseman's whole life's work was at stake, prepared grimly to fight to the last ditch. "All my affairs are of little importance to me compared to the trial in which your Eminence stands for a moment", he had written to the cardinal at the end of 1858, when the storm over the Oblates was raging. "I say for a moment, because I believe it to be a crisis permitted to put an end for ever to an unsound state, full of future dangers of a graver kind. I am as calmly and firmly convinced that all this is for the solid good of the diocese and of the seminary, for the final rooting of the Congregation, and the ascendancy of a Roman over every other kind of spirit, as I can be of anything which rests on the acts of men. I go to this Chapter with a light heart and with a feeling that nothing can give me pain, for I have felt that all the pain has come upon your Eminence. I wish I knew how I could lighten it. I can only renew what I have said. Your judgement and will shall guide us in everything. The work is yours. We will do all the labour with our whole heart and strength, and you shall direct. And it shall be seen who has at heart the *jura episcopi*. Our very existence, our charter of privileges, are all the grant of the Bishop for his own service and we wish to be in your hands".

Manning, with his bolder conceptions of the new tasks that lay ahead of the English clergy, had gained the confidence and support not only of Monsignor Talbot in Rome but also of the Pope. "It seems to me" he wrote to Talbot in Rome in June 1859, "that the work of the Church in England has so rapidly become both so much larger and so much more exacting, that men are needed now who, twenty or even ten years ago, were comparatively not required. The first thing I see is that the Church has begun to touch upon the English people at every point, and that entirely new demands are made upon it. Before emancipation, and even until the hierarchy, the work of the Church consisted (1) In ministering to the old Catholic households and missions on family estates, and (2) In ministering to the Irish settlers driven over by poverty, or drawn by industry, into our large towns. Now, for these two works the English priests were eminently fit, from their great goodness, devotion and detachment from the world. But since the Church has re-entered into the public and private life and order of the English people, entirely new kinds of work are demanded. (1) First the contact, and sometimes conflict with English society in all its classes, from the lowest to the highest - the most educated, intellectual, and cultivated - requires a new race of men as teachers, directors, and companions. (2) Next, the whole work of the Church in relation to the Government, in all the public services, civil and military, at home and in the colonies, needs a class of men of whom we possess very few. (3) Thirdly, the Catholic laity, including Catholics by birth, are beginning to be dissatisfied with the standard of education both in themselves and in their priests. The close contact with the educated classes of English society forces this on them. (4) Again, a large number of our laity, chiefly converts, are highly educated, and our priests are, except individuals, not a match for them. (5) This touches on a larger subject which I can only put in a few words. The educated laymen, in London at least, are passing out of the spiritual direction of the secular clergy of the diocese. They find their spiritual and intellectual wants sufficiently met and they go to their religious bodies. I think this a very serious matter for the diocese and for all its active works, and I see no hope of redressing it, unless Spanish Place, Chelsea, and

Warwick Street can be made vigorously efficient, both spiritually and intellectually, before five years are out". In the same letter to Talbot he explained that he could see no hope of remedying the existing state except by "raising the standard of the future secular clergy, the first step to which is Council of Trent seminaries, of which we have not as yet got one. And I do not believe that seminaries will ever be what they ought to be in England unless they are directed by secular priests who have learned to live by rule and who can act with unity of mind and purpose".

With much of this Errington also would have fully agreed. But it was the autocratic methods, the provocative insinuations and the special proposals of Manning that aroused hostility. Even at this stage Errington might have been willing to relinquish his self imposed task of wrecking Manning's influence, which he sincerely regarded as the bane of the Cardinal's rule. But Monsignor Talbot spurred him to a last stand by accusing him of disloyalty to the Holy See. Errington, declining to answer Talbot's letters, replied with dignity to Cardinal Barnabo that he had done all in his power to refuse the position in which he had been placed. "But now", he wrote, "as I have been accused by Monsignor Talbot, and others, of anti-Romanism, Anglo-Gallicanism, and other failings which, if they really existed, would be incompatible with the faithful fullfilment of the episcopal duties, and as these accusations are given as reasons why I should not remain here, it does not seem to me that I can of myself take any step for my own removal, since such a step would bring much damage not only on myself and my future work, but also on the credit of those (not a few) who are said expressly, or supposed by the same accuser, to think as I think, instead of viewing our affairs with the same eyes with which Monsignor Talbot and others see them".

Talbot, he complained, had in Cardinal Barnabo's name threatened him openly that if he did not resign, he must expect to be deprived of his position. He appealed, therefore, for the right to defend himself. Talbot's injudicious accusations had indeed made it all but impossible for him to resign. Again the Archbishopric of Trinidad had become vacant, and was now offered to him, but he refused to take any step which might seem to imply that he admitted the charges with which he had been accused. In the last resort Pius IX appealed to him personally to resign. At the heated interview Errington told the Pope to his face, even taking down a verbatim report of the words in the Pope's presence, that he would not resign unless by the Pope's express command. The command was eventually given, after a committee of three cardinals had reported against him, and Errington retired for ever from the scene, to the end of his life as a simple parish priest in the Isle of Man. He refrained thereafter, with the self-sacrificing devotion to duty which he had always shown, from any word or action that might tend to revive old quarrels.

So the long feud was closed, and Manning now reigned with greater authority over a hostile Chapter. They would not forgive him for the humiliation and sacrifice that he had brought upon Errington, whom everybody loved for his fearlessness and integrity. Wiseman's policy had triumphed with Errington's removal, but the victory had been fraught with much bitterness. At one stage of the proceedings in Rome Wiseman had a heart seizure, and it looked for a time as though he would not live. The reversion of the See would then have gone automatically to Errington, against whom the only formal complaint considered by the Holy See was his incompatibility with Wiseman. The Cardinal's health declined continually while he struggled on, lonely and disconsolate, in his conviction that the future of the Church in England required the new blood and the new methods which, twenty years earlier, he had proclaimed to be indispensable. But the interval had brought many new causes of division. The dismissal of Errington made the other bishops more determined than ever to resist any infringement upon their individual or collective jurisdictions. Their hostility made Wiseman more high-handed and more suspicious of opposition for any cause.

Not the least tragedy of the years that followed was the conflict of views between Manning and Newman, who had become deeply attached to Bishop Ullathorne in Birmingham. In the years since his conversion he had acquired more sympathy with the traditions of the Church in England. No less than Wiseman and Manning, Newman wished to improve the standard of education among the Catholic laity, and he had given active encouragement to several literary reviews which were founded for the discussion of Catholic affairs. Sir John Acton had returned from Germany where he had been a disciple of Wiseman's old friend, Dollinger, and gave promise of his future eminence as a historian. He was soon closely connected with the *Rambler* which Newman had welcomed and helped considerably. But the *Rambler's* criticisms of the bishops and its speculative excursions in theology provoked Manning's stern disapproval. The old distrust of Rome began to find expression in print with an appearance of academic authority. Talbot, Manning and Cardinal Wiseman himself as their principal patron, became the target for many attacks or insinnuations. Capes, the editor of the *Rambler,* had a tendency to bishop-baiting which even W. G. Ward in his Anglican days scarcely surpassed. His publication of highly provocative articles, raising doubts as to the soundness of various beliefs which were generally regarded as matters of faith, soon led to such a crisis that its suppression was inevitable. Wiseman as usual tried to avoid any open conflict, and he appealed urgently to Newman to undertake the editorship of the *Rambler,* in order to save it from condemnation. Newman complied with great reluctance, and within a few months he had incurred serious suspicions of unorthodoxy in consequence.

Troubles continued to multiply while Wiseman's health and courage steadily declined. Bishop Ullathorne had shared with Newman the desire to found at Oxford a college of some kind where Catholic laymen could obtain a University education. At Ullathorne's request Newman had actually bought land in Oxford with the object of founding a branch of the Oratory there. Manning heard of this with alarm, and immediately set to work to arouse Wiseman's opposition. The controversy inflamed all the suspicious side of Manning's nature, and before long Newman, like Errington, was being accused in Rome of Gallicanism and anti-Romanism. He was even accused of unorthodoxy in some of his recent writings, and formally delated to Rome.

Manning's persistent denunciations gained such influence upon Wiseman that the other bishops began to take counsel among themselves without reference to the Cardinal. This new development caused Wiseman acute distress, and he never considered, while he was subject to Manning's dominating influence, that his own attitude might be at fault. He was so isolated that he received no confidences from those who differed from him, and ill-health made him a tragic figure. "I pass nights awake and my old worst symptoms are hovering about my chest", he told Manning in February 1862. In the long sleepless nights he was driven to composing light Latin verses, which he would send to Manning, for lack of any more appreciative friend. "Let Herbert (Vaughan) give me a few lines occasionally" he wrote pathetically. "You know how little sympathy I find about me, and I really want a little". Wiseman learned with dismay that the bishops had been holding private meetings of their own without including him. "The policy is now evidently to carry by *majorities*, not by weight of arguments", he wrote plaintively to Manning. "It was not so at Synod (1859), it was so last summer, and so it is again. Eight against one or two, such is to be our mode of carrying on affairs. In reality it is two or three against two or three, the rest being dead weight thrown into the scale".

While Wiseman thus refused to accept decisions by majorities, the other bishops preferred to discuss things among themselves in his absence, knowing that they would be expected to bow to his decision if he were present. In March, 1862, he wrote of Ullathorne to Manning that "I fancy the episcopate is roused to exhibition of its true colours. They have hauled down the Tiara and keys and displayed their 'confederate' flag, the Gallic cock that crowed against St. Peter. However I have given up troubling myself much on the matter but calmly await the decision of the Holy See". But Wiseman's expressions were only a feeble echo of what was said by Manning and Herbert Vaughan, who were now almost alone in sharing his confidence. Ullathorne became known among them as "Monsignor Ego Solus", and Herbert Vaughan was writing of him to Manning as having "come out in his true colours, Anglican and Gallican in the strongest way".

223

Misunderstandings only deepened as Wiseman felt it his duty to assert himself. When the annual Low Week meeting of the hierarchy was due to be held that year, most of the bishops on one pretext or another begged to be excused from accepting his invitation. Their attitude drove him to further assertions of his authority. "I think it is not too much to consider these two letters as conspired and deliberate insults to the head of the hierarchy", he told Manning in his Easter letter to him, "and you had better put the matter as another phase before Cardinal Barnabo. Circumstances, of course, may be created, but if such an excuse be admitted, every one may stay away when he likes from anything. It is indecorous in the last degree, and surely will not be tolerated". The situation was fast becoming intolerable. It was not made easier by the fact that Pius IX was on Wiseman's side. To Cardinal Barnabo, as Prefect of Propaganda, the bishops turned for protection of their rights, and his influence gradually averted what to Roman eyes looked like the possibility of an open schism.

The main trouble had been Wiseman's inability to allow for English ways and prejudices. The procedure of Rome, in delaying a decision indefinitely upon each appeal, only aggravated their discontent and their sense of being unfairly treated. At least the climax was reached when almost all the English bishops assembled in Rome on the occasion of the canonisation of the Japanese martyrs. Pius IX took the opportunity to speak plainly to them all in Wiseman's presence. Talking to them as though they were schoolboys, while they stood around him, the Pope said that he was not surprised that differences should have arisen, as they had arisen even between St. Peter and St. Paul. But he told them that he wished to hear no more of their continued disputes and that they must henceforward find means of agreeing among themselves. Not a word was spoken at the audience except by Wiseman and the Pope, and the bishops all filed out, as Wiseman recorded at the interview "blank and speechless. In the ante-room, where many bishops had come, I hunted each one out, asked him if he was going next day, and shook hands, wishing a pleasant journey. Not a hand was kindly held out. I had almost to lift some up dead from the side. They went into St. Peter's where a person who saw them wondered what had come over them. Talbot called on them at dinner and found them very low and prostrate". Wiseman concluded, "Such is the grand total of this unhappy attempt to make void the hierarchy and return to vicarial regimen" he wrote in a later letter, "So I trust is ended the great campaign of 1861-2, God grant that it may never have to be renewed". Rome had asserted the authority of the Cardinal, but it had also imposed clear restrictions upon the supremacy which in the first stage of the new hierarchy, Wiseman had assumed to be is right.

A series of disappointments and personal conflicts, with those upon whom he had counted for unqualified support in his programme of reviving

Catholicism in England, had cast a deepening gloom over Wiseman's last years. The sufferings of his acutely sensitive temperament undoubtedly hastened his death in 1865. The achievements of his twenty years activity in England were prodigious. The hierarchy had been not only restored, but securely and successfully established.

In January 1865, a sudden illness made it necessary for him to receive the Last Sacraments. For a month more his life dragged on. In the days of waiting for the end, fragments of conversations revealed the trend of his thoughts. "I have never cared for anything but the Church", he said one day. "My sole delight has been in everything connected with her. As people in the world go to a ball for their recreation, so I have enjoyed a great function". His own funeral, as the first Cardinal Archbishop to be buried in England since Wolsley, was to be the most impressive and magnificent function of all. On 2 February he insisted upon having his bed carried downstairs to the drawing room. Manning arrived on the 12th, but he could scarcely recognise him, he could only whisper "I thank him, I thank him", when Manning told him that the Pope had sent his special blessing. As he lay on his death-bed, one of the last things Cardinal Wiseman said was "I think a good many will be sorry for me - Protestants, I mean. I don't think they will always think me such a monster". While he lay dying, many, including Gladstone, had come to pay homage at his house. He died quietly and peacefully on 15 February. As the body lay in state after his death, such crowds had come that only personal friends could be admitted. Immense crowds lined the streets to watch the funeral procession, everywhere the cortege was received with marks of profound respect at least three out of four shops along the route were closed.

Changed indeed were the days since *The Times* had led the reckless campaign which threatened public violence against the Cardinal, when the Pope had restored the English hierarchy fifteen years before. "Altogether the feeling among the public seemed deeper than one of mere curiosity - a wish perhaps, to forget old differences with the Cardinal and render respect to his memory as an eminent Englishman, and one of the most learned men of his time". Scarcely less significant than this changed attitude of *The Times* was the fact that among the distinguished congregation which filled the pro-Cathedral to overflowing, was Lord Campbell, whose father had, as Lord Chancellor, declared at the Mansion House that England would "trample underfoot the Cardinal's hat".

Wiseman had done more than any Catholic for centuries to capture the affections and the real respect of the English people for a cause which he represented. The tributes paid by many newspapers to his abilities and his virtues after his death are extraordinary to read.

The work which he had commenced was, in fact, to be carried on as he had himself forseen, by the converts for whom he had said, years before, that the old Catholics like himself must be ready to make way. Manning the most recent of them, was to be his own succesor as Archbishop of Westminster. For a generation the two names of Newman and Manning were to dominate the history of the Catholic revival.

Before his death, despite the frequent urging of Manning, Wiseman had decided against any further intervention in regard to his own succession, and he told the Chapter to choose for themselves "that name that you consider most fit and worthy to fill this high office". The Chapter felt that they should choose Errington to vindicate his honour and impugned character. They sent a list of three names, Errington, Bishop Clifford and Bishop Grant. Manning was obliged as provost to send the list to Rome, although he himself urged upon Talbot the name of Bishop Ullathorne. Newman's name was proposed among others in Rome, but Manning's name was never suggested from any other source than Talbot. The list came to the Pope as a deliberate affront. "He rose from his chair", wrote Bishop Neve, "said it would be an insult to him, said then *so faccio Pio Nono,* and that he would disregard the paper". The Pope was so much disturbed that Cardinal Barnabo, the Secretary of State, had to call in the assistance of other cardinals to mollify him. The chapter had completely stultified their own wishes. Whoever was to succeed Cardinal Wiseman, none of the names they had suggested now stood the remotest chance.

For weeks the expectancy became more intense, while it was known that the Pope had decided to reserve the nomination entirely to his own judgement, and he spent days in prayer. Errington's candidature was completely ruled out, there was no personal ill-feeling or resentment against Errington, but the Pope had pronounced that he was unfit for Westminster, and he was not prepared to reconsider his decision. Finally the staggering news arrived that the Pope had appointed Manning. No one was more overwhelmed by the news than Manning himself. But he faced his invidious position without a moments hesitation, and the old Catholics bowed in submission with an unqualified loyalty to the Pope's decision. "The old Catholics of England", wrote Manning to Mary Wilberforce, "have shown me a charity which shows how little *The Times* knows", for *The Times* had spoken of him slightingly as "an aspiring refugee". He set himself immediately to win the confidence of the Chapter who had previously fought with him so bitterly. One after another they gave expression as time passed, to their profound appreciation of his integrity and his real charity. Although it was thought more tactful not to invite Errington to the celebrations, the other two defeated candidates assisted Bishop Ullathorne in consecrating the new Archbishop in June at the pro-Cathedral in Moorfields.

The question of building a great church arose almost immediately after his consecration, when a committee of prominent Catholics was formed to decide upon the most suitable memorial to Cardinal Wiseman. Opinion was strongly in favour of building a cathedral in Westminster, and Manning was expected to give his name to the project at once. But he would only consent to purchase the site, and he told the meeting in a long speech, that he regarded the school-less children as the first charge on his resources. "I hope I have kept my word", he wrote in his journal long afterwards, "for I bought the land which the builders never thought of, and some thousands are given and others left for the building. But could I leave 20,000 children without education and drain my friends and my flock to pile up stones and bricks? The work of the poor children may be said to be done. We have nearly doubled the number in schools, and there is school room for all, and about 8000 have been saved from apostasy and from the streets. My successor may begin to build the cathedral. I have often said the Cardinal's death bought the land, perhaps mine will begin the building". A year after his consecration, Manning summoned the first Catholic meeting to form the Westminster Diocesan Fund for poor children's schools.

The next great object to be undertaken was the provision of a seminary for the archdiocese, and in 1869 he transformed the Benedictine convent at Hammersmith into a seminary for his ecclesiastical students. Twenty years afterwards he wrote in retrospect: "When I began to work as a priest, the first work was the congregation of the Oblates, and of this the first result was St. Charles's College. The congregation has about twelve schools with about 1,300 children and two colleges, a lesser, St. Michael's, and a greater, St. Charles's. Then as soon as I had my present office the Westminster Diocesan Fund was formed with its annual meeting, and the work of the poor children, 14,200 have passed through our hands, 3,000 are always in education in our twenty two diocesan schools and orphanages. Then, finally, came St. Thomas's Seminary - I hope I have not withdrwan my hands from the plough".

He had already been foiled during Wiseman's lifetime in his efforts to reorganise St. Edmund's College at Ware, where he had introduced his Oblates. His action had aroused Errington's fierce distrust. Now, ten years later, he undertook the reorganisation of the English College at Rome. His opinion of the average of the English clergy was still low, and he was determined, notwithstanding their natural resentment towards his interference as a convert, to improve the standard. "I can't tell you the dearth of men above the average", he wrote to Monsignor Talbot, " or out of the line of routine in the diocese, indeed in England generally. Good, zealous, faithful, unwordly as our priests are, their formation has not lifted them above the old level. We are rapidly coming in contact with public opinion and with society in such a way as to make a new race of men absolutely necessary". Talbot at first proposed handing the college over to Jesuit direction, not knowing Manning's increasing dislike of the Society of Jesus. Manning parried the suggestion and Talbot was able to secure, without informing the Archbishop beforehand, the appointment of one of Manning's Oblates, Father O'Callaghan, as Rector on the resignation of Dr. Neve. The appointment of an Oblate, who was also an Irishman, was far from being welcome by the English bishops, and before long murmurs were heard on all sides. Manning found it necessary to write urgently to Talbot to obtain a formal statement from Rome as to the reasons for change. Manning had been working unceasingly to heal old sores and to establish cordial relations with the other bishops. The affair of the English College in Rome now brought to a crisis the undercurrent of discontent which had been gradually gathering force. "The amount of murmuring here is endless", Manning wrote to Talbot, "not on this subject only, but on everything. I add, in strict confidence, that the centre of it is at Birmingham. Everything runs to this point - the Oxford question, Newman, Ward, the Dublin Review, English College, you, me, everything. The restless nature of that mind is reproducing what harassed the last years of the Cardinal".

The 'restless mind' was that of Bishop Ullathorne, whom Manning had recommended so strongly for the archbishopric which he now held for himself. There was a profound antipathy between these two stong minded prelates, whose natural inclinations were yet so similar. Ullathorne in his earlier days had taken an active part in public affairs, which from its results were even more important than Manning's own intervention in the London docker's strike of 1887.

William Ullathorne was born in Pocklington in Yorkshire on 7 May 1806. He was the eldst of ten children. His father was a grocer, draper and spirit merchant. He supplied the town with coal before it had a canal and in the absence of a bank he discounted bills. His father was descended from gentle family of landed estate in the West Riding. The estate came through his marriage with Miss Binks, her mother was a lineal descendant of Sir Thomas More. The estate was forfeited through the Stuart insurrection of 1745. Ullathorne's mother was a native of Spilsby in Lincolnshire where her father was chief constable. His father and mother met in London where they were both engaged in Townsend's great drapery business in Holborn. Shortly after they married they commenced their own business in Pocklington. There was a little chapel at Pocklington with only two windows and a small presbytery. The priest was the Abbe Fidele, a venerable French emigrant who was noted for his piety, simplicity and charity. He used to kneel before the little altar in a Welsh or worsted wig, saying his prayers, until Miss Constable, the patroness of the mission, arrived in the vestry, which was also his dining room and parlour. He would then rise and in sight of his little flock he pulled off his wig, powdered his head and vested for Mass. As a young boy William could remember a number of French emigrant priests occasionally visiting his house.

When he was about ten years old, his father transferred his business to Scarborough. Here he saw the sea for the first time and was inspired after reading 'Robinson Crusoe' to go to sea. Young William attended a protestant school which was situated in the transept of the old church of St. Mary's, and formerly had belonged to an Augustinian monastery. Although Scarborough had a good chapel and presbytery, there was no resident priest. One priest, Fr. Haydock came once every three months and another priest Fr. Woodcock also came every three months. They were both Douay priests and on their visits they dined at the Ullathorne home. William was fascinated by the college stories. On the five Sundays between the visits of the priests, the parishioners attended the chapel morning and afternoon as usual. His father and a Mr. Pexton, who had been a student at Ushaw but had given up his studies for the priesthood, were appointed to act as readers. First the usual prayers in English were said aloud, then all the congregation read in silence the prayers for Mass in Challoner's *Garden of the Soul*, making a sort of spiritual communion.

At the age of twelve, his father put him into his business. He learned all about accounts and figures and writing up account books. In the evening he was allowed to indulge his passion for reading, making full use of the circulating library that visited the town. His reading filled him with a strong desire to see the world and he set his mind on going to sea. A friend of his father was about to launch a new ship and the master was a Captain Wroughton. He was by nature a gentleman and always sailed with his wife. The crew were all Scarborogh people and of good character which persuaded his father to allow him to go to sea. Fr. Haydock, however did not like the idea and tried to dissuade the young Ullathorne. When he saw that the boy was determined he told him to prepare to receive the Sacraments. The strong will of youth resisted the priest's interference and William went to sea without receiving the Sacraments. He spent five years at sea, full of adventure and wonder, all the time reading as much as he could.

He suffered severe burns to his right foot and developed gangrene his foot was saved by the good care he received. When the ship eventually reached London William wrote to his parents and told them he wished to leave the sea and return home. He was again employed in his father's business. He resumed his reading and received lessons in French in the evening. One day a linen manufacturer from Knaresborough was visiting his parents. He had a son studying for the priesthood at the Benedictine Priory at Downside. He tried to persuade William's brother James who had a fine voice, to go to

Downside as a Church student. James was not interested in the proposition but William asked his father if he could join the Benedictines.

William arrived at St. Gregory's Priory, Downside in February 1823. He had never been present at Benediction before or heard the Litany sung. The prefect at that time was Fr. Polding, later to become the first Archbishop of Sydney. It was to him that William made his first confession. It was not until Christmas later that year that he received his first Communion. He began formal studies in Latin grammar and soon found a natural ability to learn other languages. His progress was such that in twelve months he had passed through all the classes and stood alongside students who had spent six or seven years in study. On 12 March 1824 he received the religious habit and made his profession on Easter Tuesday 9 April 1825.

His change of clothing from old brown or blue lay clothes to clerical clothing consisted of a black-tailed coat, shorts with gaiters and a white limp cravat. In the monastery he wore a soutane, a college gown and acap. He read everthing the library could produce. He had a lisp as a youth and worked on perfecting his pronunciation. Sundays and feast days or festivals as they were called, were days of Holy Communion and were devoted exclusively to spiritual studies and Scripture. In 1828 he began his course of Theology, and on October of that year he received the Sacrament of Confirmation from Bishop (afterwards) Cardinal Weld. On the same day he also received Minor Orders. His superiors wished him to be ordained to the priesthood before he had completed his course in theology. A petition was sent to Rome through Cardinal Weld, the Protector of the English Benedictines. His Eminence replied that it belonged not to the dignity of a cardinal to act as agent as well as protector. Instead William was sent to assist the new prior in restoring the Monastery and College of Ampleforth. He was ordained to the priesthood in September 1831 by Bishop Penswick at Ushaw. Soon after his ordination he was sent to the small missions of Craik and Easingwold celebrating Mass at each on alternate Sundays. It was here that he preached his first sermon and where he developed that style of public speaking that made him afterwards such a master of oratory.

Father Ullathorne returned to Downside in 1831. He had scarcely settled in, when Dr. Morris a member of the Downside community who had for many years been the only member of any regular Order employed on the London Mission, was appointed as apostolic visitor to the Mauritius. Dr. Morris asked Ullathorne if he would accompany him, but the ever positive Ullathorne said that he would much prefer to go to Australia.

Thus young Ullathorne went out as a young missionary to Australia, and was soon compelled to undertake, almost single-handed, the religious care of the convicts. He found they were practically employed as slaves by the planters, and that their punitive treatment and moral degradation were indescribably shameful. Ullathorne had found the proportion of Catholics among the convict population extremely large. The inhuman treatment, and the savage system under which they were forced to live, had converted the great majority of the convicts into a drunken and barbarously immoral population. Ullathorne was one of the first to plead for a reform of their conditions, and he incurred the fierce hostility of the planters and traders who depended upon convict labour. His published accounts of the conditions which he spent his life in trying to mitigate by religious ministrations created such scandal in England that he was brought home to give evidence before a Parliamentary inquiry. As a young priest he had to bear single-handed almost the entire brunt of an agitation which aroused passionate feelings on both sides. But his pleading was so forceful that he carried his point, and the abolition of the convict settlements in Australia was directly due to him.

He travelled from Australia with Bishop Polding calling at New Zealand, South America and Ireland seeking recruits for the Mission in Australia. When he arrived in England he resigned from his Colonial responsibilities and returned to Downside. After a short spell teaching, he was sent to the mission of Coventry. Bishop Polding, now Archbishop of Sydney wrote to him with the news that Ullathorne had been appointed to the See of Adelaide. Ullathorne was adamant that he would not accept the episcopate, and later went to Rome to plead his case. Cardinal Franzoni, the Prefect of Propaganda freed his from the appointment to Adelaide. Before he left Rome he had an audience with Pope Gregory XVI. The Pope told him how much the Archbishop of Sydney regretted that he could not be one of his suffragans and gave Ullathorne a special blessing to his mission in England.

Bishop Baines, of the Western District of England died suddenly in July 1843. Cardinal Acton's secretary Dr. Grant informed Ullathorne that Propaganda proposed to Pope Gregory XVI that Bishop Brown of the Welsh District should be transferred to the Western District, and Ullathorne be appointed to succeed Bishop Brown in Wales. In the evnt Dr. Baggs Rector of the English College was appointed to the Western District. Bishop Baggs died in October 1845 and in May 1846 Cardinal Acton wrote to Ullathorne that he had been appointed to the Western District. He was consecrated Bishop of Hetalona and vicar apostolic to the Western District on Sunday 21 June 1846 by Bishop Briggs. Bishop Wiseman preached and all the Bishops of England were present as was Bishop Brady of Perth in Australia. Also present was Newman and his companions. It was the same day on which Pope Pius IX was crowned. When the Hierarchy was established in 1850 he became Bishop of Birmingham.

As Bishop of Birmigham Ullathorne had Newman's Oratory immediately under his supervision, and an intimate friendship developed between him and Newman. His own temperament was extremely pugnacious, and Man-

231

ning constantly irritated him. This personal irritation towards Manning contributed considerably to his taking Newman's side in the antagonism which had been steadily growing between the two great convert clergymen, and by 1867 various causes had accentuated it still further. The articles which appeared in the Jesuit *Month* and the *Tablet,* re-acted so strongly to W. G. Ward's extreme views about the temporal power of the Pope, and still more about papal infallibility conveyed the arguements of the old Catholics to be used with rather more emphasis than they might have otherwise used. Newman who disliked Manning's high-handed methods and regarded his views about the papacy as being wildly extravagant, felt a growing sympathy with the Liberals such as Lord Acton. The *Tablet* did not long continue to disturb Manning's peace. Its financial difficulties necessitated its sale, and in 1868 Manning acquired it and so became the owner of two Catholic reviews to conduct his propaganda.

When the First Vatican Council was called, there was political turmoil in Europe. The temporal power of the Pope was challenged over the Papal States by the growth of nationalism in Italy, and the prospect of war loomed over Europe. The rumours about a Council began to increase as did the question of a proclamation of papal infallibility. In 1867 bishops had assembled in Rome from all over the world, and on 26 June, Pius IX announced his intention. The Bull of Invitation *Aeterni Patris* was issued to all the bishops assembled in the Vatican Basilica on 8 December.

In February 1869, the intention of establishing the Syllabus of Errors in a dogmatic form and to include as dogma the infallibility of the Pope was leaked in the *Civilta Catholica.* The other proclamations to be confirmed by the Council Fathers was the dogma of the Assumption into heaven of the Blessed Virgin. The source of the leak was a memo that the Paris nuncio had sent to Cardinal Antonelli, the papal secretary of state. Although the conservative or ultramontane view was the prevailing mood in the face of growing liberalism throughout Europe, there was a sizeable minority who believed it was inopportune and were absolutely opposed to this policy.

In Europe it came mainly from German bishops, the most famous advocate was however Fr. Ignaz von Dollinger. In France Archbishop Darboys and Bishop Dupanloup and in England, Newman and especially Sir John Acton were equally opposed to the views being expressed in Rome. Acton wrote: "The attempt to establish the infallibility of the Pope by decree of a General Council is a phase of controversy which the internal disputes of the Church of Rome have made almost inevitable. The Catholic opposition in its several forms, national in Italy, scientific in Germany, liberal in France, has uniformly been directed against one or other of the papal claims".

The bishops acquiesced with the Pope in proclaiming a new dogma in 1854, pronounced in favour of the temporal power of the Pope in 1862, and accepted the Syllabus of Errors in 1864. It was considered by the liberals including Acton that in the previling mood of the majority of bishops, the new proclamation and dogmas will be accepted. Archbishop Darboys and Bishop Dupanloup of France led the minority opposition to infallibility supported by Bishops Hefele and Kettler from Germany, Cardinal Schwarzenberg of Checkoslovakia and Bishop Strossmayer of Croatia. Fourteen of the twenty-two bishops of the German hierarchy wrote collectively to the Pope expressing their fears of the results of the definition of papal infallibility.

Gladstone offered a peerage to Acton in November 1869, he believed Acton would have more influence at Rome as a British peer. Most of the European bishops came from noble families and Acton's family connections in Europe were considerable. The Council was seen as the culmination of the struggle between authority and liberty in the Church. The Church created in her organisation an increasingly authoritarian trend. Pius IX changed from his liberal, idealist views after numerous clashes with revolutionary elements which brought about his conservative reaction. His defence of the Papal States and of his temporal powers clouded the spiritual claims of infallibility as dogma.

The issue of papal infallibility on questions of faith and morals had been accepted since the 16th Century. The view of the liberal minority was that papal infallibility promulgated as dogma would operate retrospectively and would include papal responsibility for discredited acts of the past. The secular view, especially Acton's was that infallibility would be a cause for concern by non-Catholic countries like Britain, which only in the recent past had experienced an outcry against papal aggression. Cardinal Manning loyally supported the Pope and disliked Newman's articles and Acton's influence on Gladstone. However public opinion in Britain was firmly anti-Catholic and little interest was shown in the Council. The English and Welsh bishops were divided on the issue and only Bishop Cornthwaite fully supported Manning. Bishop William Clifford had said the danger in England was that Anglicans would see the Roman Church as a despotic institution.

The first decree *Dei Filius* (against rationalism) was passed after a stormy debate which dealt chiefly with the relationship between faith and reason. When the vote was taken in the Council on the 13 July on the whole constitution *Pastor Aeternus* concerning infallibility, there were of the 601 bishops who voted, 451 accepted, 88 rejected and 62 in favour of modification of the definitions. Finally on the 18 July the constitution was voted on again, in public session, the result was 533 accepted and only two against, an Italian and the American Bishop Edward Fitzgerald. The other eighty-eight bishops of the opposition had either left or stayed away from St. Peter's to avoid any form of scandal.

The Empire of France fell and the Franco-Prussian War broke out on 19 July 1870, which brought the Council to an abrupt end, most of the bishops left Rome immediately. The Council was adjourned for a few months but soon after Rome was occupied by the Piedmontese troops and on 10 October Pius IX prorogued the Council indefinetly, with only a small fraction of its programme completed. Formal closure would not take place until 1962. Archbishop Georges Darboy of Paris, one of the chief opponents of papal infallibility was arrested by the Communades on the 4 April 1871 and held as a hostage. The interrogation of Archbishop Darboy by a Blanquist police chief was widely reported: "What is your occupation?" "Servant of God" "Where does your master live?" "Everywhere" "Clerk, write that the prisoner claims to be the domestic of someone named God, of no fixed abode". On 24 May the Archbishop was shot, after blessing his executioners, along with twenty-three other clergy who were either shot or lynched. The anti-clerical, radical reaction reached an appalling climax in the same month when the Paris Commune condemned by conservatives and liberals, produced a tumult of violence and crime. It led to the most savage purge of the century, at least 10000 people were killed in Paris between 21-28 May, a massacre unparalleld in nineteenth-century Europe, and some 40000 were arrested.

The earlier revolutions in France, which Tocqueville had described as political revolutions that operated in the manner of religious revolutions, were essentially anti-Catholic by nature of the Enlightenment ideology that the Revolution espoused. It was precisely this unique character of modern political culture spreading throughout Europe that brought about the reactionary theology of Pius IX. His *Syllabus of Errors* condemned eighty modern errors, including religious toleration, the secular State and "progress, liberalism and the modern world".

Archbishop Darboy had written to the Pope to declare his acceptance of the decrees of 18 July 1870. When the Pope heard of the death of the most determined opponent of the definition of papal infallibility, he exclaimed: "He has washed away his defects in his own blood, and put on the martyr's robe".

In the feverish weeks during which Vatican I lasted, Manning played a decisive part and its result might even have been prevented if it had not been for his tireless and determined energy. It was his personal intervention with Odo Russell, the British diplomatic agent in Rome, that frustrated the attempt which Dr. Dollinger had made, through the influence of the King of Bavaria to form a political alliance between the States which opposed the decree. Manning's intellectual powers, scarcely less than his energy, became a decisive factor in Rome during the Council. By his close alliance with Odo Russell and his personal relations with the Pope he was able to exert a diplomatic influence perhaps even greater than that of any other member of the Council.

In Germany, the controversies of the Council created the Old Catholic movement which developed rapidly into a schismatical Church and rejected Catholic dogmas of the Immaculate Conception, Transubstatiation, and the rule of celibacy. Dollinger distanced himself from the schismatical direction the movement was taking, but even so he was excommunicated in 1871. He said his last Mass the day before his excommunication after being a priest for fifty years. He abided by the penalty and remained to the end a Catholic priest at heart.

In England Newman submitted without hesitation and accepted the new dogma. Newman's view on the "sovereignty of conscience, the voice of God" guided him through the turmoil. He was ahead of his time and his influence on Vatican II a century later, when both he and Acton were vindicated, was clear. The Second Vatican Council restored the collegiate relationship of bishops and Pope and adopted Newman's ideas 'on consulting the faithful in matters of doctrine'. This was the title of a controversial essay written by Newman and first published by Acton in the *Rambler* and was delated to Rome by an English bishop. Newman distanced himself from Dollinger and the German Catholic scholars who had left the Church, but he remained supportive to Acton. In a letter to Newman, Acton wrote: "You know, and I need not tell you, what the value of your sympathy has ever been to me, when I could think that I obtained it, and it would never be so valuable as now". He went on to explain his position, that the Vatican decrees were not his problem, but that if he were asked whether to accept them "with definite understanding and inward conviction of their truth, I can't say yes or no. But this is the question which the Archbishop, taking his letter and pastoral together, wants me to answer to. I certainly cannot satisfy him. I hope you will understand that, in falling under his censures, I act from no spirit of revolt, from no indifference, and from no false shame. But I cannot accept his tests and canons of dogmatic development and interpretation and must decline to give him the only answer that will content him, as it would, in my lips, be a lie". Acton was asked by Manning in the letter, had he any heretical intent, and did he accept the Vatican decrees? In the letters that followed between them, Acton was evasive and obscure. He was sure that he would be ecommunicated. He had told Lady Blennerhassett that he would rather die than having to live without the sacraments and to leave the Church.

Manning's uncompromising attitude in forbidding Catholics to attend the older universities caused friction. Newman particularly had always been in favour of establishing some sort of Catholic centre at Oxford, while encouraging Catholics to enter the university. With customary foresight Newman had bought land in Oxford for such a centre. However, Manning was determined at all costs to prevent any possibility of Newman himself being associated with any such venture at Oxford. Because of the objections, Newman resolved to have no personal connection with any Catholic college at Oxford, but on the main question he was most strongly in favour of Catholics going to Oxford. Manning remained obdurate on the question until his own death, he was convinced that the anti-Catholic atmosphere of Oxford and Cambridge would undermine the faith and loyalty of the Catholic gentry.

Manning regarded the agitation in favour of university education as being insincere for the most part, except for the small proportion of "intellectuals" whom he described as the "literary vanities". "In truth, nobody cared for higher studies", he wrote, with bitterness and with exaggeration, in a note among his papers many years later. "Certain Catholic parents wished to get their sons into English society, and to have latch keys to Grosvenor Square. Nevertheless, a great noise was made about the need for higher studies". Eventually he overcame his personal distrust of Newman and invited him to resume in England the work he had attempted in Dublin. There can be little doubt that a Catholic university could have been founded with every prospect of success, but its staff would have naturally been recruited largely from the Jesuits, as the ablest and most highly trained body of teachers in England at that time. The fact was that Manning was even more antagonistic to the Jesuits than he was to Newman. The result of his prejudices was the most complete failure of his career. When he established a Catholic university college at Kensington he deliberately excluded Newman and the Jesuits. So strong was his aversion to the Jesuits that he would not even allow Jesuit students to attend its lectures.

In contrast Manning's great work was for the poor and the working class. He was by instinct a strong democrat, in spite of his own upbringings as the son of the Governor of the Bank of England. In 1872 he made his first incursion into politics as archbishop, when he appeared at the Exeter Hall to support the agricultural labourers. Soon afterwards he wrote to Gladstone "My beliefs that the laws (of landed property) must be greatly relaxed. The Poor Law has saved them for a century, but the Poor Law has broken down. Why cannot you do these things for the labourer? Prohibit the labour of children under a certain age. Compel payment of wages in money. Regulate the number of dwellings according to the population of parishes. Establish tribunals of arbitration in counties for questions between labour and land. If our unions were like the guilds which created the City of London, I should not fear them. But the *Soul* is not there". His democratic sympathies had been apparent even in his Anglican days, and at Westminster he became a close friend of many radical reformers.

Cardinal Henry Edward Manning

To Manning, the recognition of the rights of labour was the supreme challenge of public life. When his old friend Pius IX died, and a new Pope was elected, he found in Leo XIII a pontiff who faced the modern world with a sympathy which was remarkablley similar to his own. The Pope relied on Manning's advice on a number of important encyclicals, from slavery to social justice in Ireland and the rights of the working class. The great encyclical *Rerum Novarum* which has ever since inspired Catholic social thinking is accepted by most historians to be the result of Manning's influence. In the English translation which was undertaken by the Bishop of Newport, Manning personally revised the draft and insisted on using the word 'strike' rather than any other vaguer term. Manning was on friendly terms with the labour leaders, and although no believer in Socialism in any form he recognised the crying needs of the workers. Following the rioting and bloodshed in Trafalgar Square in 1887, he wrote: "The combination of Socialists and the outcast population which is our rebuke, sin, shame, scandal will be our scourge and is a misrepresentation of law, liberty and justice. The appeal to physical force is criminal and immoral - venial in men maddened by suffering, but inexcusable in others".

He was prejudiced against the employers when he entered the controversy over the dock strike of 1889. To the labour leaders the intervention by the old Cardinal Archbishop, already in his eighty-second year, brought encouragement for which they dare not hope. Manning drove in his carriage to the City, he tried unsuccessfully to find both the Lord Mayor and the Home Secretary, but they were both away on their summer holidays. He had no alternative but to go directly to the dock owners. The only pretext he could use for the right to interfere was that his brother had formerly been chairman of the docks. Within a few weeks, with the assistance of the Lord Mayor and the Bishop of London, a committee of conciliation was formed. Manning spent day after day from ten in the morning until seven or eight at night, interviewing, discussing, negotiating, sometimes waiting hour after hour patiently at the Mansion House. The strikers had issued a manifesto repudiating all they had agreed to through Burns and Tillett. The Directors and Bishop Temple withdrew in disgust, leaving the cardinal alone. On 10 September Manning drove down alone to Poplar. He met with the dockers for three hours in the Wall Street School, but nothing could persuade the men to accept an agreement to start work on 4 November. Manning persisted and eventually won over the Irish dockers and eventually he carried the argument. The men voted 28 to 15 to return to work on the 4 November. It was a personal triumph for the cardinal and although there was a public celebration on 4 November, the old Cardinal declined to attend. Instead he celebrated the day, the feast of St. Charles Borromeo, in the quiet of the

Oblates' house where his own first ministrations as a Catholic priest in London had been centred.

Manning's life came to a close on 14 January 1892. He was eighty four and he predeceased Newman by seventeen months. He did not wish to die, he believed that his work was as yet unfinished. He had been taken ill with bronchitis. On 9 January Vaughan arrived and ordered the old Cardinal to bed. In the evening he refused a stimullent emphatically, he had received the Last Sacraments and the papal blessing and said that he had no desire to add a minute to his life by such means. During the night Vaughan and Dr. Gasquet watched by the bedside. In the morning while Herbert Vaughan said Mass, Cardinal Manning died peacefully. Dr. Johnson gave him absolution and Dr. Gasquet closed his eyes.

Cardinal Manning lay in state in the Brompton Oratory. Bishop Clifford, the last of Wiseman's hierarchy, sang the Requiem Mass, and Bishop Hedley preached the sermon. After the service his body was carried through the fog to Kensal Green, where it remained until it could be translated a decade later with the body of Wiseman to Westminster Cathedral.

Manning's life was long and eventful. Shane Leslie descibed him thus: "He was at a Georgian Harrow and a pre-Victorian Oxford. He was a High Churchman outside the Oxford Movement and a Sussex parson before railways. His wife died the same year Queen Victoria came to the throne, and he himself became a Catholic in the year of Lingard's death. He wore the prelatical purple in the last days of papal Rome. He won his mitre in time to take a leading part at the Vatican Council and his red hat in time to share in the Conclave which elected Leo XIII. In many ways he was a link with the past and a prophet of the future. He was a cricketer before round arm bowling, a Free Trader before Cobden, a Home Ruler before Gladstone, an imperialist before Chamberlain, and a Christian Democrat before Leo XIII".

A week after Manning's death Herbert Vaughan said to Baron Friedrich von Hugel, who recorded the words, 22 January 1892: "I was by his bedside, he looked around to see that we were alone, he fumbled under his pillow for something, he drew out a battered little pocket book full of a woman's fine handwriting. He said: 'For years you have been as a son to me, Herbert, I know not whom else to leave this - I leave it to you. Into this little book my dearest wife wrote her prayers and meditations. Not a day has passed, since her death, on which I have not prayed and meditated from this book. All the good I may have done, all the good I may have been, I owe to her. Take precious care of it'. Soon afterwards unconciousness came on him". It is thought that Herbert Vaughan placed the book in the Cardinal's coffin.

Extracts from: *Cardinal Wiseman* by Denis Gwynn
published by Browne & Nolan, Dublin

Cardinal Henry Edward Manning

Henry Edward Manning by Shane Leslie
published by Burns Oates & Washbourne, London
A Hundred Years of Catholic Emancipation by Denis Gwynn
published by Longman Green & Co., London
The Autobiography of Archbishop Ullathorne
 published by Burns & Oates, London
Lord Acton by Roland Hill
published by Yale University Press
with permission from the publisher

Chapter Eleven

Cardinal Herbert Vaughan

HERBERT Alfred Vaughan was the oldest child of John and Louisa Elizabeth Vaughan, and was born on 15 April 1832. It was assumed by John Vaughan That his eldest son Herbert would succeed him and become squire at Courtfield, and after he left Stonyhurst he thought his son would pursue an army career. His mother however had dedicated all her children at birth to the service of God and His Church and her example and influence on her children was immense.

The Vaughan's who were themselves one of the most famous Catholic families in the country, were interelated by marriage with almost all the other leading Catholic families. No other family had given such an extraordinary number of its members to the priesthood in modern times, and their zeal and energy had brought them all to high positions in the Church. One brother became Archbishop of Sydney, another was Bishop of Plymouth, a third became the most popular preacher of his time as a Jesuit at Farm Street.

When Herbert was sixteen he decided that he would become a priest and devote himself to the Welsh Mission. An ancester Thomas Vaughan was ordained priest in 1627 and worked in South Wales. Herbert went to Downside in 1850 although he did not become a Benedictine, but studied theology. A year later on 15 October 1851 he left to begin his studies for the secular priesthood in Rome.

He travelled by horse-drawn coach through Paris, Avignon, Marseilles, Genoa, Pisa, Florence and Siena. On 15 November, he arrived in Rome and attended the Roman College. When he travelled to Rome for his second year his travelling companions were Henry Manning, Robert Whitty (who became Wiseman's vicar-general) and William Lockhart. Vaughan was impatient with Manning on the journey, he said to Whitty "I can stand this old parson no longer. Let us go straight on and leave him to follow as long after as he liked". In Rome, however, he became friends with "the grave and solomn parson" which lasted throughout Manning's life.

His student days in Rome were full of problems, he had difficulties with the self discipline required, and his health often suffered as a consequence of his periodic heart disease which troubled him throughout life. His mother died in 1853 and this caused him great distress. Elizabeth Vaughan was forty-two and died in childbirth, she had delivered her forteenth child, John, in January 1853. Herbert's periodic illness was of such concern that Mgr. Talbot petitioned the Vatican for a special dispensation that would allow Herbert to receive Holy Orders earlier than laid down in Church Law. He was ordained on 18 October 1854 by Archbishop Givilio Arrignoni of Lucca. His first post at the age of twenty-three was the vice-presidency of St. Edmund's College, Old Hall. It was a priority of Cardinal Wiseman, following the restoration of the hierarchy in England to improve the quality of training for students to the priesthood at St. Edmund's.

Wiseman was determined to introduce Roman methods to the English Church, despite the antipathy of old Catholics who disliked the Italianate enthusiasm of new missionary orders such as the Passionists, Redemptorists and the Rosminians. Generally the old Catholic priests dressed plainly, lived simply and exercised the liturgy with the minimum of ceremony.

W.G. Ward was appointed to the staff at St. Edmund's. He was a married man, a convert, and although one of the leading theological experts of his day, there was much opposition to him. Vaughan himself intended to remove him, but after hearing his first lecture, realised the true qualities of Ward, and became his chief supporter.

Wiseman wanted to form a band of priests, although secular, would work in an almost regular state, and be at the direct service of the diocese. Manning gathered a number of priests around him to serve Wiseman and among them was Herbert Vaughan. The congregation was called the Oblates of St. Charles. Manning's rule approved by Pius IX, was based on the 16th Century Oblates founded by St. Charles Borromeo in Milan. On 1 June 1857 Manning, Vaughan, four priests and two clerics held their first General Chapter at 12 Sutherland Place, Bayswater. This little group were dedicated to perform tasks which the secular priests of the diocese could not perform due to their parish responsibilities. Vaughan's enthusiasm for missionary work remained with him throughout his life. He believed in two missionary activities, those priests and religious who worked for the conversion of England, and those who were sent overseas to convert heathen populations to Christianity. One of his many achievements was the founding of the St. Joseph's Society for the Foreign Missions, based in the north west of London at Mill Hill, his foundation was the first foreign mission to be established in the Catholic Church in England.

His lifelong desire to work in the foreign missions took a practical turn when he obtained permission to go on a begging tour of the Americas to raise funds for missionary work. When he returned to England he had collected an amazing total of £11,000. With the help of Mrs Frances Ward he found Holcombe House in Mill Hill. The sale was completed on 17 March 1866 and on Monday 19 March, the feast of St. Joseph, Mass was celebrated in the presence of Archbishop Manning. The college was named St. Joseph's College of the Sacred Heart.

In the autumn of 1872 Vaughan was appointed Bishop of Salford and for the following twenty years he dedicated his energies to the diocese. However the Pope had allowed him to become superior general of his missionaries and he continued to influence missionary work in America, India and Afghanistan.

A major concern at Salford was the growing influx of Irish imigrants and the provision of schools for Catholic children. Vaugan founded the Catholic Children's Rescue Society in 1886, during the first year, he devoted one night each week to host a dinner for people who might assist him with advice or more material help. He toured, with the help of the police, the worst and most disreputable areas of the city. This disturbing experience he could never forget. When he left Salford in 1892 as a direct consequence of his organisational abilities over two thousand people were helping in the work of the Rescue Society.

Herbert Vaughan's background was not the ideal preparation for the work he had to confront while at Salford. His personal prefernce for a missionary life in Wales could not be realised, but he did at least play a crucial role in the founding of a major missionary society. The plight of orphaned and deprived children was in stark contrast to his privliged upbringing. Nevertheless he applied himself with charactereristic determination and flamboyance. His conservative roots and country gentleman's sympathies created some difficulties during the political turmoil on the question of Irish Home Rule, which he opposed. Politically the quadmire of Home Rule and the question of Catholic voluntary schools created complications. Vaughan continued to work for equal treatment on behalf of voluntary schools during his years at Westminster concluding in the successful passage of the Education Act of 1902. But he carried to his death the unpopularity aroused by his opposition to Home Rule for Ireland.

Manning's death marked the end of a long epoch in which the two great converts had towered above the rest of Catholics in England. His own tenure of office as Archbishop had lasted for nearly twenty seven years. He had outlived Newman, whose personality had dominated Catholic thinking in England, just as his own had dominated Catholic affairs. As cardinals they met on a footing of equality. A new generation had grown up in the meantime, to whom even the Oxford Movement was little more than a legend. Ullathorne, the most able and most commanding figure among the old Catholics, who had been personally responsible for completing the negotiations which Wiseman began for the restoration of the hierarchy, had died in 1889. The generation which had produced the Victorian giants had all but disappeared. The Catholic body had changed during the long period of

Manning's rule at Westminster. Irish immigration had been preponderant for many years, and this influx had greatly increased the Catholic population. This was in complete contrast to the one section that was responsible for maintaining the Catholic faith over centuries of persecution. The old Catholic aristocracy preserved to a great extent their traditional exclusiveness and coherence as a distinct group within the Catholic body. Among the hierarchy they were still very strongly represented. They had in fact during the later years of Manning's life supplied at last, from among their own body, by far the most vigorous and attractive figure in the hierarchy. The abilities and the outstanding personality of Herbert Vaughan was so generally recognised that there was little doubt as to who would succeed Manning.

He was almost sixty years old and was not in good health, when he learned that the Chapter had nominated him to Rome. He wrote to Pope Leo XIII begging his holiness to choose someone else for Westminster. On 29 March Herbert Vaughan was appointed Archbishop of Westminster and was enthroned at the pro-Cathedral of Our Lady of Victories in Kensington on Sunday 8 May 1892.

He had resolved to make the most out of the ceremony in which an archbishop is officially installed by Rome. He was to receive the pallium from Pope Leo XIII. He could have gone to Rome for the ceremony, but asked that the pallium be sent to London "to provide an ecclesiastical pageant which would serve as an object lesson reminding the English people of certain vital truths in the story of their own past". The last archbishop to receive the pallium in London was Cardinal Pole on 25 March 1556. The ceremony was to set the scene of his ten years at Westminster.

At this time the estimated Catholic population of England and Wales was 1,500,000. In Scotland there were 365,000 and in Ireland 3,500,000. In the diocese of Westminster there were 253 secular priests and 103 regular priests. Over the whole diocese there were 129 public churches.

In January 1893 Vaughan was raised to the rank of cardinal at a consistory in Rome. Cardinal Vaughan arrived back in England in March 1893. At Westminster his aristocratic bearing and imposing figure dressed in cardinal's robes brought great dignity to the Church in England.

In addition to his continuing work and interest in foreign missions there were three major issues which marked his final decade. One which many thought uneccessary and damaging was the issue on Anglican Orders which culminated in the Papal Bull *Apostolicae Curae* of Pope Leo XIII on 13 September 1896. Charles Lindley Wood, second Viscont Halifax was the leading Anglican layman and president of the Anglo-Catholic English Church Union. He was born into the old whig aristocracy of wealth and privilege. Through the influence of the Tractarian movement at Oxford he became Anglo-Catholic and all through his life he dedicated himself to God. He was

243

deeply religious and had great humility, he attended daily Mass and had unshakable belief in the reality of Anglican sacraments. Halifax in conjunction with the French Catholic Abbe Portal chose to discuss the validity of the Orders of the Anglican priesthood. Their objective was a hoped for rapprochement between the two Churches. Rome examined the proposition that Anglican Orders were valid to the Roman Church.

Cardinal Vaughan was the head of a commission set up in 1895 which included Canon James Moyes, Dom Adrian Gasquet and David Fleming a Franciscan. They concluded that Anglican Orders are null, and convert Anglican clergy must always be ordained again absolutely and not conditionally. Their report was published in 1896.

Vaughan held the belief, like Wiseman before him, that the Catholic Church, in time, would become the established Church once again in Eng land. He considered that the ever increasing number of converts would continue into a swell with irresistable certainty. Vaughan disliked the idea of Halifax's movement towards corporate reunion.

In March 1896 Pope Leo XIII appointed an international commission to meet in Rome to look into the question. Cardinal Mazzella was the president and Merry del Val was the secretary. Other members were Gasquet, de Augustinis, Duchesne, Gasparri, Fleming and Moyes. Two Anglicans, Lacy and Puller advised, and later Fr. T. Scannell and Jose Calasanzio de Llevaneras joined the commission. They met on twelve occassions between 24 March and 5 May 1896. They finally voted on the issue on 7 May, Duchesne and the Jesuit Augustinis voted for recognition of Anglican Orders. Gasparri and one other member advised that the Orders were doubtful, the Vaughan group voted against it. The commission could not reach a conclusion and its documents were handed to the Dominican Raffaele Pietti, he was requested by the Pope to sum up the findings and present his report to the Holy Office. On 16 July, the Holy Office met with the Pope and voted unanimously that Anglican Orders were not valid.

Leo XIII's letter *Apostolicae Curae* of 13 September 1896 dismissing Anglican Orders as "absolutely null and utterly void", on the grounds that the Edwardine and Elizabethan ordinals lacked the "form" and "intention" of ordaining a sacrificing priesthood. The Anglican Archbishops of Canterbury and York replied in *Saepius Officio* that in the Preface to its Ordinal, the Church of England had expressed its intention to retain the orders of bishop, priest and deacon as of Apostolic origin, but that the Roman definition of priesthood in terms of offering the Eucharistic sacrifice was neither Scriptural nor patristic nor in accordance with Eastern Orthodoxy. Perhaps the greater significance of the controversy was for the Church of England, in inducing an anxiety about the validity of Anglican orders, which made relations with the other Protestant Churches difficult, and led to the participation in the consecration of Anglican bishops by 'Old Catholic' bishops ultimately deriving their orders from the eighteenth-century Dutch Catholic schism of Utrecht, whose orders were valid even in Roman terms. Cardinal Vaughan feared that any admission of the validity of Anglican orders would discourage Anglican conversions to Rome; indeed he and his theologians thought that *Apostolicae Curae* would encourage them. The Converts' Aid Society, founded in 1896, sought to aid former Anglican clergy with practical assistance towards their new Catholic life.

For many years the Church had forbidden Catholics to enrol at Oxford and Cambridge. Manning during his years of authority was inflexible on the matter. Vaughan had supported Manning and so it was thought the prohibition would continue. In June 1894 the Duke of Norfolk presided over a meeting of lay people. It was decided to send a petition to Rome. Four hundred and forty eight signatures were collected, headed by most of the prominent Catholic families. The Duke of Norfolk contacted Vaughan to discuss the issue. There were about fifty Catholic undergraduates at Oxford and Cambridge and Vaughan knew that he could not justify continuance of the prohibition of Propaganda Fide.

The greatest achievment that most Catholics associate with Cardinal Vaughan is the building of Westminster Cathedral. Cardinal Wiseman had considered building a cathedral. Manning purchased the land and had intended building a cathedral as a memorial to Wiseman. Vaughan often described his vision of a cathedral that would be the head heart and spirit of the Church in England and a "splendid and fitting shrine for the Sacred Liturgy".

To reduce costs Vaughan proposed to build a shell of the cathedral big enough for all practical purposes, and adopted the style of an ancient basilica, using Constantine's church of St.Peter in Rome as the model. John Francis Bentley was chosen as the architect. Vaughan committed himself to raise the funds. The foundation stone was laid in 1895 and was built in eight years.

Vaughan's dream of Westminster Cathedral as a centre of the Sacred Liturgy was frustrated by his inability to attract the Benedictines to have monks based at Westminster. He finally decided to have the secular clergy sing. On 7 May 1902, the Divine Office was sung by the new cathedral choir for the first time, bringing to fruition the dream of Herbert Vaughan.

Vaughan had suffered all his life with heart problems, and his last years saw more frequent attacks. On 19 March 1903, St. Joseph's feast day, his condition became critical and he received the Last Sacraments. He was taken to St. Joseph's Missionary College at Mill Hill. On the 19 June, the feast of the Sacred Heart, a great calm came over the cardinal. He was certain that he was to die before the feast of the Sacred Heart was over. He insisted throughout the afternoon that he should not be given more drugs or sleeping draughts. "Don't let my thoughts get entangled tonight by stimulants and drugs. I want to be with Jesus and the Holy Family".

When the summer evening was ending, he was with the nurse and asked him to say the rosary. He had been growing weaker during the day and was having difficulty breathing as he remained seated in an armchair. Later he asked that the nurse, Mr. Christie Young, who had cared for him for four months, excuse him for the trouble he had given. "You must try to bear with an impatient and irritable old man". The nurse left about 11pm and the night nurse, Mr. Keating, came on duty.

At about 11.30pm the Cardinal grew worse and Young was called back, he found Vaughan conscious but rapidly sinking. The Cardinal whispered "I have had a bad attack, the worst I have had. A short time later he was calm again in his chair praying "Jesus, Mary and Joseph". Minutes went by, and then the words came more slowly and faintly, until an ashen veil seemed to close over his face. Fr. Henry was called and he noted the time as he ran to the Cardinal's room, it was ten minutes before midnight. By the time he and another priest reached the sickroom Herbert Vaughan had died quietly.

The Requiem Mass for Cardinal Vaughan was held in Westminster Cathedral. There was a choir of fifty priests in addition to the Cathedral Boy's Choir. The coffin was covered with a black velvet pall with gold edgings, while his cardinal's hat rested at the foot. There was more than five hundred secular and religious clergy seated on each side of the coffin. As the Mass was about to begin the bishops took there place in the sanctuary, at their head was Cardinal Logue, Primate of Ireland. Among the lay mourners who filled the cathedral was the Duke of Norfolk, the American Ambassador, representatives from the Spanish, Portugues, French, Chilean and Austro-Hungarian embassies. Finally after the ceremony, mourners passed by the catafalque until late afternoon. Religious Sisters kept watch over the coffin until Friday morning when it was removed to St. Joseph's College at Mill Hill for burial.

In Cardinal Vaughan's final instructions to his executors a note read "I beg pardon for all the scandal and bad example and for much neglect of God. But I die in peace in the arms of the Blessed Virgin Mary, my mother, professing all that the Church professes and teaches".

Extracts from: *Cardinal Herbert Vaughan* by Robert O'Neil
published by Burns & Oates, London.
From Without the Flaminian Gate edited by V. Alan McClelland and Michael Hodgetts,
published and copyright 1999 by Darton, Longman and Todd Ltd
used by the permission of the publishers.
A Hundred Years of Catholic Emancpation by Denis Gwynn published by
Longman Green & Co., London

Chapter Twelve

Cardinal Francis Bourne

POPE Leo XIII died a month after Cardinal Vaughan, and one of the first acts of his successor, the saintly Pius X, was the translation of Francis Bourne, Bishop of Southwark, to the See of Westminster in August 1903 at the age of forty-two.

Francis Bourne was born at Clapham in 1861 of an English father who was a Civil Servant and an Irish mother. From childhood he was closely attached to London and as a man was profoundly English. At the age of eight he was sent to Ushaw, which in those days was a hard school for young boys. Eight years later he went to St. Edmund's College, and at the end of his philosophical studies, for a short interlude, he tried his vocation with the Dominicans at Woodchester. In 1880 he proceeded to the college at Hammersmith and in the following year went to St. Sulphice in Paris. He always regarded his two years there as one of the greatest gifts he received. The Sulpician recollection and devotion remained with him always and he developed a sympathetic understanding of French Catholicism. He completed his studies at Louvain and in June 1884 was ordained priest at Clapham.

After some parochial experience at Blackheath, Sheerness and Mortlake, he was sent in 1889 to Henfield and West Grinstead, where he began the foundation of the Southwark Diocesan Seminary which in the following year was moved to Wonersh. In 1896 he was consecrated Bishop of Epiphania and coadjutor to Dr.Butt, Bishop of Southwark. Although he was a young man when he translated to Westminster, Bishop Bourne had already gained much experience in all spheres of priestly work.

He was of average height and had white hair, he had a dignity of bearing which never left him and, like Cardinal Vaughan, he was perhaps seen at his best in some of those great ceremonies in the magnificent setting of Westminster Cathedral which he carried through so perfectly.

He was heavily engaged in the question of education. There had been much dissatisfaction among the general public with the Education Act of 1902 and which gained a catch phrase among many 'Rome on the Rates'. The Catholics of England had to face the effects of proposed education legislation on their own schools for which they had striven so hard and at such sacrifice. Bourne was unremitting in his efforts to secure equitable treatment by the State. The Education Act of 1902 had provided for the maintenance

247

of the voluntary schools and when the Liberals came into office in 1906 it was with the understanding among their Nonconformist supporters that neither Catholic nor Anglican schools should remain 'on the rates'. By the Bill of 1906, accordingly, voluntary schools, unless entirely self-supporting, were to be transferred to the local education authorities and only 'undenominational' religious teaching would be permitted. Before the Bill was published, but while its trend was a matter of common knowledge, Bourne began to mobilise Catholic opinion. His Lenten Pastoral plainly set out the issues and declared that, if necessary, "we shall be prepared, to continue the struggle of the past rather than sacrifice our children". A demonstration was organised in the Albert Hall by the archbishop and supported by the Duke of Norfolk and other leading laymen. This rallied Catholics of every political persuasion to the defence of the schools. As *The Times* noted, "This remarkable protest could not be ignored". The Irish members in the Commons gave their support but this would not have been enough if the Anglicans had not been fighting for the same principle. The Bill did not become law, nor did three later attempts of the Liberals to solve the religion-in-schools problem. This fight for the right of Catholic parents to send their children to Catholic schools and the rights of the Church to maintain her responsibility was a continuing campaign during his reign of office.

Archbishop Bourne was however primarily concerned with the education of future priests. Almost immediately he reversed Vaughan's central seminary policy and the Westminster theological students returned to St. Edmund's College, where he also developed the secondary school. Since the closing of Hammersmith they had been sent for their theological studies chiefly to Oscott or Valladolid. Bourne wished the students to have their basic formation in England and then go abroad for higher studies. He did not favour their having their whole training at, for instance, the English College in Rome. One of his objectives was a Catholic theological faculty at one of the older universities, he never achieved this but he did send Ronald Knox to the Oxford chaplaincy.

The Archbishop set to work at once on enlarging St. Edmund's and in 1904 the new divines wing of the College, eventually called Allen Hall after the founder of Douay, was opened. A shrine chapel was also built to house the relic of St. Edmund of Canterbury. There were now twenty-five divines and nearly two hundred lay boys at the College. Ten years later Allen Hall was burnt down but it was soon rebuilt on a grander scale by the ever enthusiastic Cardinal. The gradual improvement of St. Edmund's was his life long preoccupation. Before the First World War he built new dormitories and classrooms for the lay boys, as well as an airy and handsome refectory for the philosophers and theologians of the divines side. Ultimately as an offering of thanksgiving for the protection of his diocese during the First World

War, he built the Galilee Chapel. He also made what he called a return to old English ideals by recreating the school department of the college on the house system, reserving the old central college building for the residence of the Church boys, and setting up houses for the lay boys under house masters.

Bourne again clashed with the Government in connection with the Eucharistic Congress of 1908. For the first time for three centuries a papal legate was to come to England. This in itself made the event a landmark in the history of the Church in England, but the presence of seven cardinals and over a hundred archbishops, bishops and abbots added to the significance of the occasion. It had been planned that, on the last Sunday of the Congress, a procession of the Blessed Sacrament should pass along streets near the cathedral, The Archbishop, with his usual thoroughness, had made careful preparations and had sought and obtained the approval of the police authorities. This proposal roused the antagonism of some fanatical Protestants and threats were made that the procession would be attacked, but the police were confident they could deal with any trouble. A few days before the procession, the Archbishop received indirectly a message from the Home Secretary, H.H. Asquith, suggesting that the plan should be abandoned as "provocative to Protestant sentiment". The Archbishop wrote to the Prime Minister saying that he would of course obey an official order but not a private communication "and I shall give the matter the fullest publicity in order that my action may be amply vindicated". After some shuffling Asquith gave the official order and the procession was cancelled, but the Government suffered a bad press. Following this and for the rest of his life Bourne developed a singularly harmonious relationship with the Government. The "silent cardinal" was always dignified, never irresponsible. He could speak when need be, never without necessity, and this was increasingly appreciated and stood the Catholic Church in England in good stead. He had happy relations with Lord Baden-powell and his encouragement of scouting for Catholics reflects his realisation of civic values and ideals of service in the Commonwealth of nations.

During Bourne's early years at Westminster, the so called modernists continued to give grave concern to the Church. Among the English writers was the Jesuit priest George Tyrrell, He was anxious, as other thinkers were, that the Church should face up to the progress in knowledge of the times and restate its theology in terms of the day. This particularly affected the official attitude towards Biblical criticism. The leader in France was Alfred Loisy who tried to bring Catholic teaching in line with what was sound in Biblical studies. One of his close supporters was Baron Friedrich von Hugel who was also a friend of Tyrrell. The Jesuits expelled Tyrrell from the Society in 1906 and he was later excommunicated. Bourne had no part in this as it was a Jesuit concern, but it was through his influence that there was no condemnation of von Hugel, nor of Wilfrid Ward who had been appointed editor of *The Dublin Review* by Bourne in 1906, a post he held with great distinction until 1916. Ward was not an extremist, he was not out to shock the hierarchy, he could see that the 'modernists' were troubled with serious problems which could best be dealt with by equally serious dicussion.

The modernists were condemned in 1907 by Pius X in a decree *Lamentabile* and in the encyclical *Pascendi*. Further measures taken were the setting up of vigilance committees in all dioceses to report suspects, in addition an anti-modernist oath was exacted from all priests. Moreover Pius X saw that the membership of the Biblical Commission set up by Leo XIII in 1902 was restricted to the most conservative theologians. These draconian measures set back the Church intellectually for a generation and it ceased to play a meaningful part in the study of the Scriptures and in theological inquiry. It was not until the issue of Pius XII's encyclical *Divino afflanti spiritu* in 1943 that the strait-jacket was loosened.

In 1908 Catholic affairs in Britain ceased to be under the direction of the Congregation of Propaganda and eventually the hierarchy in England and Wales was given the powers that are normal in a Catholic country. On 28 October 1911, the Apostolic Constitution *Si qua est,* rearranged England ecclesiastically into three provinces, making Liverpool and Birmingham metropolitan in addition to Westminster. The last named retained Northampton, Nottingham, Portsmouth and Southwark as suffragan Sees. Brentwood was added in 1917 on its creation with Mgr. Bernard Ward of St. Edmund's as its first bishop. In 1924 the diocese of Lancaster was formed. (Ed.Wales became a separate province in 1916 with an archbishop at Cardiff and Menevia as a suffragan See).

These changes were necessitated by the increase in the Catholic population. When Cardinal Bourne died in 1935, the Catholic population was estimated at 2,350,000 out of a total population of forty millions. In 1850 the number of Catholics had been about 68,000 out of a population of eighteen millions, and the number of priests was less than 800. By 1935 their number had increased to 4,500. In 1875 there were about a thousand Catholic churches, in 1935 the number was 2,400. There was much bickering within the English hierarchy and as a result, the papal decree *Si qua est* decreed that the Archbishops of Westminster were to be permanent president, but not primate, at the meeting of the bishops of England and Wales, (Ed. now called Bishops' Conference), that he should take rank above the other two archbishops, that he should enjoy the privilege of wearing the pallium, of occupying the throne and of having his cross carried before him throughout the two countries, and that in all dealings with the supreme civil authority, he should in person represent the entire episcopate of England and Wales.

Great progress had been made since 1850. As Archbishop Bourne himself pointed out: "The two new provinces each possess more churches and larger bodies of clergy than were contained in the whole country in 1850, while the third and smallest province falls but very little short of the same degree of expansion". In Westminster alone the number of priests had been multiplied by five, the number of churches by four, and the Catholic population had been increased by one hundred and fifty thousand.

In November 1911, Archbishop Bourne was raised to the Sacred College of Cardinals with the title of St. Pudenziana which had been Wiseman's. He was to take his place in two Conclaves, that which elected Benedict XV in the year of the outbreak of The First World War, and that which chose Pius XI in 1922. The cardinalate gave him a new and recognised ascendancy in his own country and enabled him to emerge as a great spiritual leader during the First World War. His love for France also stood him in good stead. The establishment of the Legation to the Vatican in 1915 and the whole course of the relations between England and Rome was partly his work. A round of visits began not only to camps in the homeland but across the Channell to the troops at the front. After Jutland, he was for some days the guest of Admiral Jellicoe. In 1918, before the end of the war, he wrote his pastoral on the new order enunciating the principles of the Encyclicals and the conditions for a just and lasting peace. "Peace without justice", he said, "is not worth having, human nature is still the same, the old passions and sins may easily revive and may work among conquerors and conquered the old prolific evils which ultimately give rise to civil contest and war of nations. The world is not at rest. Even within our own borders, there are potents of danger".

Cardinal Bourne has sometimes been regarded as unsympathetic in relation to Ireland. This is based on three main charges: that he did not share the enthusiasm of the Bishop of Southwark for the cause of Terence MacSwiney, that he remained aloof in the affair of Archbishop Mannix, and that he allowed and participated in the Requiem at Westminster Cathedral for the English Catholic victims of "the Dublin murders".

The hunger-strike of the Lord Mayor of Cork, imprisoned on a political charge at Brixton, raised a doubtful moral point. Was he committing suicide or sacrificing his life for a glorious ideal? The Cardinal did not see the answer as clearly as Dr. Amigo, but anyhow, it had not happened in his diocese. Archbishop Mannix was prevented by the English Government from visiting Ireland after journeying all the way from Australia. The Cardinal stood aloof in this matter also and avoided a meeting which would have been perhaps embarrassing to both parties. When he was accused of conspiring with the Government against the Archbishop, he issued a statement in which he said: "I desire it to be known that neither directly nor indirectly was I consulted in any way on this matter". With regard to the

251

was I consulted in any way on this matter". With regard to the Requiem he said: "To have allowed the Catholic Three to be trundled off to suburban cemeteries, unwept, unhonoured and unsung, while their comrades-in-arms, the Protestant Nine, were being wept, honoured and sung in the Abbey would have been 'taking a side' indeed".

The Cardinal was a Home Ruler in the modified sense. He always wanted the widest possible self-government for Ireland compatible with the maintenance of the link with the Crown and the safeguarding of the essential defences of the Empire. He certainly had all the moral teaching of the Church behind him in the condemnation of secret organisations and the excesses on both sides. He also spared no pains in doing all he could to obtain a just and peaceful settlement to the troubles in Ireland. There is no doubt, however, that his attitude was always coloured by his belief in the Empire: "The protection of the Empire", he said, "is as important for Ireland as for us, and it is important for civilisation, I think, as for us both. Given that, I am for Irish self-government as far as the Irish people themselves desire it. I want England to trust Ireland and Ireland to trust England, for I love them both as I love justice and peace". He was present at the Eucharistic Congress in Dublin in 1932. He received a great reception, for after all he was a Prince of the Church and the son of an Irish mother.

Between 1921 and 1925 The Malines Conversations took place between Cardinal Mercier of Brussels and Lord Halifax. A quarter of a century earlier Lord Halifax was involved with Abbe Portal in the abortive talks which ended when the Vatican ruled against the validity of Anglican Orders. Cardinal Bourne was annoyed with his eminent brother in Brussels for arranging talks with Anglican representatives without consulting the English bishops. Incredibly Cardinal Mercier had sent the Archbishop of Canterbury confidential reports of the talks while ignoring the Archbishop of Westminster. Cardinal Bourne did not make any immediate or direct protest but Father Woodlock, the well known Jesuit, in the name of English Catholics voiced a protest at what he called the mystery of Malines. The pius Lord Halifax on his return from Malines had declared that "Reconciliation with Rome does not involve any denial of the historic claims of Canterbury" in other words the faith and orders of Anglican archbishops are precisely the same as those of St. Augustine the first Archbishop of Canterbury.

There was a minor furore between Cardinal Mercier and Father Woodlock. The Jesuit had written to Cardinal Mercier but had received no reply. He then wrote to the *Tablet*. He asked if the teaching of the Catholic Church was really different in Brussels and Westminster. Cardinal Mercier replied at once with an abusive letter about Woodlock. Ernest Oldmeadow the editor of the *Tablet* refused to publish the letter and sought advice from Cardinal Bourne. The Cardinal promised to write to Brussels himself:

"Your Eminence had kept honourably the silence imposed upon or accepted by you. But it is manifest that the same discretion is not being observed by Anglicans, and they openly declare that the views on the Holy See held at Malines are not the same as those taught by us in England. The Abbe Portal is allowed to speak in Belgium, and we are not allowed even to have an accurate account of what he actually said. The Anglicans are treated as friends, we the Catholics of England, apparently untrustworthy.

"I am powerless to intervene, for Your Eminence has thought well to leave me – who after all am the pricipal Catholic prelate in this country and your colleague in the Sacred College – absolutely in the dark. It would have surely been but right and seemly that Your Emminence should have stipulated from the outset that there should be no secrets from me. Yet, with the exception of Your Eminence's communication at the end of 1923, I have been treated as if I did not exist. The Archbishop of Canterbury has been given the fullest information of the proceedings at Malines – I have been excluded from all such knowledge and thereby a grave wrong has been done both to me and to the Catholic Church in England. Out of respect and affection for Your Emminence I have been patient and have kept silence, with the result that I am quite unable either to correct or to control free-lances like Father Woodlock who has many sympathizers in Rome.

"Had I in a matter affecting Belgium, acted towards Your Eminence and the Belgium bishops as Belgium has now acted towards us in a matter most profoundly affecting the Catholic Church in England, there would have been just cause for complaint". In the wider field there was much for which to be thankful. Apart from its obvious defects which a man of Cardinal Bourne's perspicacity could not fail to recognise, the League of Nations was at work. The number of conversions to Catholicism had greatly increased in the war period and in 1922 G.K. Chesterton was received into the Church. The Cardinal himself gave thanks for the Silver Jubilee of his episcopal consecration in 1921, and the Society of St. Augustine was founded to assist with the maintenance of Archbishop's House. The building of churches and some schools went apace throughout his reign. The Cardinal Vaughan School had been started. The number of clergy had increased also. In his book *Ecclesistical Training,* Cardinal Bourne left them a legacy, as his predecessors had done, on his own ideals of the priesthood. Apart from *Occasional Sermons,* it was his only publication. Sulpician in its inspiration, it reflected the mature conclusions of a spacious mind which had rated priestly formation before other episcopal work.

In 1926, from the pulpit of Westminster Cathedral, he condemned in no uncertain terms the General Strike for which, he contended, there was no moral justification. Speaking on 9 May at High Mass he said: "The time through which we are passing is of exceptional character, and the present strike is of a nature quite unlike the many others which have preceded it. It is necessary that Catholics should have clearly before their minds the moral principles which are involved:

"1. There is no moral justification for a general strike of this character. It is a direct challenge to a lawfully constituted authority and inflicts, without adequate reason, immense discomfort and injury on millions of our fellow countrymen. It is therefore a sin against the obedience which we owe to God, who is the source of that authority, and against the charity and brotherly love whih are due to our brethren.

"2. All are bound to uphold and assist the Government, which is the lawfully constituted authority of the country, and represents, therefore, in its own appointed sphere, the authority of God Himself.

"3. As God alone can guide both rulers and ruled to a wise and successful understanding, it is the duty of all to pray earnestly and constantly for His guidance, that the day may be hastened when these unhappy conflicts shall terminate in a just and lasting pece" He was an authoritarian in the right sense, and his action won admiration from many quarters.

The Cardinal had an acute sense of responsibility with regard to the many overseas journeys he took. In 1918-19, he made an extensive tour of the Near East. He said of the journey: "The purpose of the journey was two fold, official so far as the visit to the Catholics in the Navy were concerned, quite unofficial, but perhaps no less useful on that account, to Church and State in all other aspects. It was felt by the competent authorities, at home and abroad, that the presence and passage of a British subject holding high ecclesiastical rank through countries in which the problems of the future were likely to be specially acute would make clear the relations between the British Government and the Catholic Church at the prent day, would allay groundless fears, and might gather at first hand information more readily given, perhaps to one coming in this two-fold character, for both Church and State". The national and international importance of the Archbishop of Westminster was never more fully recognised by a British Government than on this occasion. Doubtless the recognition was opportunist. There was great fear on the French side that British post-war policy in the Near East would seek to bolster up the advance of Protestantism at the expense of Catholicism and Orthodoxy. The cardinal's official tour, accompanied with full honours, was meant to allay this fear. Perhaps he allowed himself to be too closely associated with the mind of the Government in all this. There is no doubt however that he was absolutely convinced of the Government's complete integrity. Speaking in French at Cairo, he said: "There is one word in your address of welcome which is not acceptable. You have spoken of my country as a Protestant State, I would rather say that our Government is a Christian Government. From my own experience I can declare that there is nothing to fear. One may openly be a Catholic, a practising and even a militant Catholic".

In 1927, he visited Poland, in 1929 he was present at the Orleans celebration of St. Joan of Arc and in1931 he was Papal Legate at the St. Joan celebrations in Paris. In 1932 he attended the Eucharistic Congress in Dublin. Perhaps the apogee of his career was reached at the magnificent celebrations held to commemorate the centenary of Catholic emancipation in 1929.

Ill health made itself apparent in 1933 and the Cardinal had to curtail his engagements. In 1934, however, he was able to celebrate the Golden Jubilee of his priesthood and opened the new Chapter House at Westminster. The new pulpit in the cathedral also commemorates this occasion. His last great act as spiritual leader of the Catholics of England and Wales was to be present at Walsingham on 19 August 1934, when the shrine of Our Lady was set up once more in the Slipper Chapel. It was an occasion which rejoiced his heart and a fitting conclusion to a great episcopal reign. His love for Our Lady of Walsingham and the English Martyrs is indicative of his essential patriotism. He died peacefully in the early hours of New Year's day 1935. The memorable Requiem was held in the cathedral and burial took place in the Galilee Chapel at St. Edmund's College, where his cardinal's hat now hangs.

At his memorial Viscount Fitzalan of Derwent spoke of him: "To understand the Cardinal, one had to be on intimate terms with him. He had a reserve which sometimes gave an impression almost of coldness, but to an individual in a time of trial or sorrow he would unbend with an overwhelming rush of sympathy. His rather cold and calm reserve concealed a profound spirituality which was known to very few and meant that this close communion with his God was the chief feature of his life". In official circles he was appreciated for his frank sincerity. "You always knew where you are with Bourne" was an expression often heard.

During Cardinal Bourne's tenure at Westminster, the life of another famous bishop came to a close. John Cuthbert Hedley was one of a long line of Benedictines who had governed in Wales both as vicar apostolic and bishops in ordinary. John Hedley was born at Morpeth in 1837, and in 1848 he was sent to the Benedictine school at Ampleforth. At the end of his studies he offered himself as a postulant and he was professed a monk, taking the name Cuthbert, in 1855 he was ordained priest. He later was appointed to teach in the newly established general house of studies at Belmont Priory near Hereford. The church of this priory was the pro-cathedral of the diocese of Newport and Menevia, and from its monks the cathedral Chapter of the See was formed. Dom Cuthbert would spend the rest of his life in Wales.

At Belmont he was to teach the young monks the theory and the art of preaching, and then philosophy and theology. He set very high standards and like Ullathorne and his other Benedictine brother, Thomas Joseph Brown, first Bishop of Newport and Menevia, Hedley became a great reader of the Fathers. It was now that he began to write and to be published.

Dom Cuthbert Hedley was just under the age of thirty-six and canon Theologian of the Chapter when, in 1873, at the petition of Bishop Brown now in his 75th year, he was named auxiliary bishop. Some years later the old bishop died, and after an interval of almost a year in 1881, the bishop-auxiliary was appointed in his place. Three years before, in 1878, he had accepted the editorship of the *Dublin Review,* in succession to W. G. Ward and he retained it for a further three years. At about this time Hedley made his first declaration in favour of the ban being lifted that kept Catholics from the universities of Oxford and Cambridge.

Bishop Hedley had a fine mind, cultivated and developed through a lifetime's study, and ceaselessly exercised upon all the thoughts of the day, secular and religious, theology, philosophy, history and natural sciences. His biographer wrote: "He could give an appreciation of Professor Zahm, he could advise Baron von Hugel or correct Professor Mivart, he could offer criticism of Herbert Spencer, he could appraise the work of Darwin and Huxley and assess its influence on current thought". Hedley the scholar who was so gifted was at heart an artist and musician. He was austere in appearance, sturdy in feature, yet he had an excellent sense of humour, which was not diminished by his forty-two years of Episcopal duties. He had seven books published along with scores of pastoral letters and countless sermons and speeches.

His diocese was one of the smallest in England and Wales and as a consequence he had to turn his hand to every variety of tasks, the diocese of Newport and Menevia had no staff of canonists, financiers and secretaries to take the burden of administrative work. When he commenced his work in the diocese there were only thirteen secular priests, eight of them loaned by other bishops, working in forty-seven churches and chapels. When Bishop Hedley died there were fifty-four secular clergy and the churches and chapels had risen to eighty. This achievement made all the more impressive when the diocese was split in 1881 with the loss of the South Wales counties. He had had forty-thousand Catholics to care for when he succeeded to the See, and this number had doubled by the time of his death. When he died in November 1915 the *Tablet* said: "This day a prince has fallen in Israel". Cardinal Bourne said of him: "He was the leader of the bench of bishops". The Catholics of Wales remembered him as the great English monk who so glorified the hierarchy of this country.

Extracts from: *Bishops of the Century* by Philip Hughes published in
The English Catholics 1850-1950 edited by Rt. Rev. George Andrew Beck
Published by Burns Oates, London

Chapter Thirteen

Cardinal Arthur Hinsley

THERE was no obvious successor to Cardinal Bourne in 1935. The appointment of Archbishop Hinsley came as a total surprise. He was in his seventieth year and relatively unknown in his own country. Yet the events of the next few years were to show that no more distinctively English a character could have been chosen.

Arthur Hinsley was born in 1865. He came from Irish stock, his mother, Bridget Ryan before her marriage, was a saintly woman and had a profound influence on the young Arthur. His father, Thomas, had been a carpenter in Carlton, Yorkshire. Arthur was educated first at the little private school in Carlton, later at the age of eleven he went to Ushaw where he studied for fourteen years until 1890. At the English College in Rome, in addition to taking a doctorate in theology, he studied for a further degree in the Academy of St. Thomas, lately formed by Pope Leo XIII to give impetus to the reawakened interest in Thomism. He returned later to the former as a professor and to the latter as rector from 1917-30. He was for a time curate at St. Anne's Keighley in the West Riding of Yorkshire. He founded, and was headmaster of St. Bede's School at Bradford. After a quarrel with Bishop Gordon of Leeds, he spent twelve years in the Southwark diocese at Amberley, Sutton Place and Sydenham.

In 1917 he was appointed rector at the English College in Rome. As rector of the Venerabile, he both imbibed and infused the Roman Spirit – personal loyalty to the Pope and a devotion to the Church which is neither national nor parochial. The finances of the Venerabile were chaotic, the building dirty and inadequate. War had reduced the number of students to about a dozen. The first impression the students received was of a kindly but strong man with smiling eyes and strong jaw. He was often impulsive, he rarely collaborated with anyone and he was always busy. He had a comsuming impatience to learn more, to learn it quickly and to inspire others with an equally intense love of learning.

He resigned from the Venerabile in obedience to Pope Pius XI to become first visitor and then apostolic delegate in Africa, and consecrated bishop in 1926, and four years later he was raised to the rank of a titular archbishop. The period he spent in Africa was he said the most soul-satisfying of his life. He was at his best when giving encouragement to men and women persevering in desparately difficult tasks. He was not afraid to show them how their apostolate could be made more fruitful. On one occasion, a Sister Superior, of acknowledged virtue and good sense, approached Monsignor Hinsley with an unheard-of request. She asked permission to have some of her nuns trained as midwives. The conditions under which the native women gave birth were often appalling beyond description. It had always been considered improper for Religious, even nursing sisters, to attend confinements. Hinsley's reputation for plain common sense had encouraged the Sister Superior to ask the impossible. Hinsley of course, was in hearty agreement with the nun's sentiments but sadly he shook his head. There are limits to the powers and discretion even of apostolic delegates. He had no authority to give permission for a departure so completely revolutionary. He explained all this to the disappointed missionary and then consoled her with these words: "Reverend Mother," he said, "I cannot countenance any breach of your Holy Rule. You must observe it in the letter but, above all in the spirit. Now if in the future some poor woman is in great distress, remember the rule of charity. That rule is greater even than your Holy Rule. Now go away, get the Sisters to say their prayers and remember that charity covers a multitude of sins". There was a notable decline in infant and maternal mortality during the next few months. Today, as is well known, many nursing sisters are trained in midwifery. To the great benefit of African motherhood.

On his return from Africa, he was made a canon of St. Peter's and everyone thought that his career had terminated. It had yet to reach its zenith. He was appointed archbishop and succeeded Cardinal Bourne at Westminster in 1935. His tenure of office was divided into two clearly distinct phases. From the time of his enthronment until the outbreak of war he was almost entirely engaged in the administrtion of Westminster Archdiocese. From September 1939, until the day of his death he was engrossed, not to say overwhelmed, by affairs of national and international matters. From the first weeks of the war he was widely acclaimed as an egregious spiritual leader whose sympathy and appeal were restricted neither to his co-religionists nor his own countrymen. The war forced him, not altogether unwillingly, to direct more and more of his attention to issues only remotely connected with his responsibility as Ordinary of Westminster Archdiocese. The routine work of the diocese was increasingly deputed to his auxiliry bishops and vicars-general. In December 1937, when he had been Archbishop of Westminster for just over two years, Pope Pius XI raised him to the Sacred College of Cardinals with the title of St. Susanna.

The *Daily Telegraph* stated in 1943: "It should not be invidious to say that no English cardinal since Cardinal Manning has made a deeper impression on his own community and on the national life". What was the secret of Cardinal Hinsley's emergence as the greatest of all religious leaders in Britain in so short a span? It must be put down first and foremost to his distinctly English character. He had all the warmth of northern origins, the downrightness and brogue of a Yorkshire man, a native simplicity and straightforwardness, a deep faith, an overwhelming humility coupled with a high sense of duty. He was the blunt Englishman possessed of a great innate dignity divorced from all attachment to pomp or ceremony. His sincerity was unquestionable. He believed in the justice of all British administration. He was the perfect Christian patriot. He had in addition absorbed a wealth of experience of all kinds, in the purely pastoral sphere of parochial administration, in secular and ecclesiastical education, above all, perhaps, in Africa. He was gregarious and loved the companionship of the young. He was impulsive and sometimes unguarded in his pronouncements, but these human frailties only served to endear him still more to his fellow countrymen, they could see the real person of Arthur Hinsley. Above all he had a deep-rooted devotion to the Person of Christ and the English Martyrs from whom he drew his inspiration.

Secondly, the circumstances of his reign as archbishop afforded full scope to the play of his qualities. War intensified and clarified all his predilections and called him out of a circumscribed field to be a great spiritual leader for the whole land. The *Daily Mail* said of him in 1943: "He was probably the best loved cardinal England has ever had". He cared nothing for all this except in so far as it might mean a new advance for Christian and Catholic principles.

For the first four years at Westminster, Archbishop Hinsley concentrated on the administration of his diocese. He had come at a disadvantage compared with all his predecessors. He knew little of ecclesiastical affairs in England, apart from his contacts with the English hierarchy at the Venerabile. He knew none of his clergy. To remedy this, he at once set out to visit them in their own homes and to establish personal contacts. It was not easy for a man of his age and his memory for faces was not all that it had once been. They liked his informality and approachability but they could never feel that he had his finger on the pulse of their activities. The long and fatherly reign of Cardinal Bourne had made it difficult for anyone to take his place in their particular sphere. Atrchbishop Hinsley ordered a General Mission throughout the diocese in which he participated to the full. He sought advice in everything and from many quarters. There was no autocracy. Perhaps he did not always sufficiently realise that bureaucracy has its dangers too. In addition to the Diocesan Council, which advises on clerical appointments and general affairs, he inaugurated a Schools Commission and a Finance Board. He also set up a considerable number of minor Boards to advise and guide him. Moral welfare, youth, Catholic action, art, music, every aspect of diocesan activity, in fact, provided a sufficient reason for forming a committee usually composed both of priests and laymen. From the autumn of 1939, when the Cardinal became more and more occupied with national and international affairs, the routine work of the diocese was increasingly delegted to the auxiliary bishops and the vicars general.

The question of education was to the fore again. The fate of Catholic schools remained the Cardinal's chief preoccupation to the end of his days. It could be said that his fear of impending injustice in the proposed new Education Act may have hastened his end. Even so, he was convinced that Catholics would receive fair treatment if only their fellow Englishmen could be made to understand the true issues. He seized upon every opportunity in letters to *The Times* and pronouncements on other occasions to state in reasonable terms the Catholic claims. He fought for the most part a lonely battle. The Anglicans were giving up more and more of their own denominational schools. The Nonconformists had few strong feelings in the matter. Rising costs after the First World War had made it increasingly difficult for Catholics to build new schools or improve existing ones. The school leaving age was being raised and standards of building were becoming increasingly exacting. The Act of 1936 met these difficulties to some extent by giving power to local authorities to pay up to 75 per cent of the cost of new schools and improvements to existing ones. Many Catholics felt that even this should be opposed as an inadequate half measure. But three quarters of a loaf is better than no bread and the Act was welcomed as a precedent in the right direction. Unfortunately its effects were nullified by the Second World War and in 1944 the whole educational system in this country was to be revolutionised by an Act which repealed that of 1936. Cardinal Hinsley saw this coming and was horrified by the vision of a completely State controlled system which seemed in so many ways to embrace the very principles which we were fighting against in the war with nazi Germany. He was afraid that the craze for monotype education, made popular by the misleading slogan 'equality and opportunity' would produce an unspiritual and highly undesirable youth.

If the British public showed little understanding of the education question, they were on the other hand deeply interested in Cardinal Hinsley's exposition of Christian social doctrine. For them, he appeared in the role of another Manning. That he was a friend of the people was manifested by his pronouncements at the time of the Gollden Jubilee celebrations of *Rerum Novarum* and by his ardour for the lay apostolate expressed in the joint pastoral of the hierarchy in 1936. His elucidation of the concepts of Christian justice increased in crescendo when he saw their revocation in totalitarian countries, and his vigorous broadcasts were regarded as great patriotic contributions to a conflict which the western democracies were about to embark. It was this above all which won him 'the primacy of England'. It was

the Manning touch complimented with an endearing capacity rarely surpassed. His love of Poland and all the victim nations, his impatience with
pacificism, his approval of the United Nations, his hatred of tyranny, his
admiration for Malta, his pride in the heroism of his people, made him one
with them in the widest of all fields. Like Cardinal Bourne, he personally
visited Army camps, R.A.F. stations and Naval units.

Perhaps his greatest achievement in the eyes of his non-Catholic contemporaries was the inauguration of the *Sword of the Spirit,* on 1 August 1940.
The movement came about through a radio broadcast by Cardinal Hinsley
of the same name. A group of influential lay people, including the historian
Christopher Dawson and the writer Barbara Ward (who became adviser to
two Presidents of the United States), visited the Cardinal and suggested
starting a movement open to all regardless of denomination. One of its first
fruits was the initial proclamation signed by Dr. Lang, the Archbishop of
Canterbury, Cardinal Hinsley, Dr. Temple and the Archbishop of York, and
published in *The Times* on 21 December. It was the explicit acceptance of
the Five Peace points of Pope Pius XII. The original idea of the *Sword of
the Spirit* was the unification on an international scale of all Christian effort
for justice in peace and war in a campaign of prayer, study and action. Many
ways were devised, such as lunch time sermons, addresses to gatherings of
members, retreats, study circles and public meetings. At one notable three
day conference in May 1941, at the time of the London blitz, the Stoll Theatre was packed to overflowing to hear the Catholic and Anglican archbishops
and other leaders. Similar meetings were held all over the country. The sense
of fellowship among Christians was notably strengthened. With her many
exiles and refugees, London had become more international and Catholic
than ever before. The Cardinal wanted to unite these elements with his fellow countrymen in an organisation which would aim at the restoration in
Europe of a Christian basis for both public and private life, by a return to
the principles of international order and Christian freedom. Clearly, he had
the vision of what became the European Economic Community. The campaign of the *Sword of the Spirit* swept the country in an extraordinary manner and gained support on all sides. It caused disappointments and misunderstandings as well. Hinsley was reprimanded by Rome for publicly saying
the Lord's Prayer with the Anglican Bishop Bell of Chichester, he cautiously
gave instructions that at joint meetings, if prayers were led by a non-
Catholic, Catholics present could join in with the *Our Father,* but should
remain silent during any other prayer. Archbishop Downey banned the
movement in his diocese and some of the other bishops were not prepared
to pray with non-Catholics consequently the 'Sword' had little influence in
Northern England. The Cardinal had to make it clear that co-operation with
members of various religious bodies did not involve any revision or com-

promise of Catholic doctrine. Full membership was for Catholics only. The *Church Times* and other publications expressed disappointment, but through the good offices and understanding of people like Dr. Bell of Chichester, charity was maintained and the good work continued.

Cardinal Hinsley was ever hopeful of the results of Christian co-operation. He worked for it with intense charity but always under the guidance of faith. Faith forbade compromise. Charity led him to encourage the approach of all men of good will. But faith and charity, as well as providing inspiration, often produced a dilemma. Hinsley did not regard himself as having a common faith with non-Catholics. With them he was united – in the words of Pius XII in his first Encyclical – by "all those links which bind them to us, our common love of Christ's person, our common belief in God". The Cardinal could not bring himself to use expressions suggestive of common faith which, in fact, merely disguised fundamental divergence. The current phrase 'the Churches' was never heard fall from his lips. His unwillingness to co-operate by using agreed theological formulae was dictated not by lack of charity but motives of deep sincerity. "Our hearts are united," he once wrote to a canon of St. Paul's, "in the earnest desire to eliminate the present confusion among Christians in face of the common danger. I feel keenly this lack of harmony, as I am sure you know, and would go to the utmost limits consistent with the integrity of Christ's revelation. If only we could be of one mind and soul. But can we reconcile these two principles: Unlimited private judgement and the authority of a teaching Church, or the Magisterium, that is the *living voice,* with the Bible only?"

During the Cardinal's lifetime some suspected that he would have been willing to travel much further along the road of religious co-operation, that is to the point of agreement on some statement of minimum belief, had he not been brow-beaten by theologians and curbed by his brother bishops. He was of course faithful to the celebrated Encyclical of Pope Pius XI *Mortalium Animos* 'True Religious Unity'. This was a strong pontifical condemnation of anything remotely resembling a confederation of Christians united on specifically religious issues. It is clear however, that Cardinal Hinsley's leadership on the subject of religious co-operation was directed not towards dogmatic unification but towards the improvement of the whole social order. With hindsight, we can see Cardinal Hinsley's efforts as foreshadowing the ecumenical movement that we now associate with Pope John XXIII and the Second Vatican Council

Cardinal Hinsley's reign also saw the establishment in 1938 of an apostolic delegation in London for Great Britain. This at first caused some alarm and questions were asked in the House. However the appointment is not a diplomatic one, the delegate represents the Holy Father to the clergy and laity. It was welcomed by Cardinal Hinsley, and the apostolic delegate,

Cardinal Arthur Hinsley

Archbishop Godfrey, had succeeded Hinsley as rector of the English College. The delegation is an established factor in the Catholic life of England and marks an important advance, perhaps the most important since the restoration of the hierarchy, in ecclesiastical organisation.

His physical decline started, or became more obvious with the fall of France, which he felt acutely. Angina, aggravated more and more by arteriosclerosis, caused periods of acute suffering, attacks which slowly increased in frequency and duration. He began by losing weight very considerably, then the angina attacks began to come on also during the night so that he lost sleep and dreaded going to bed. Often during the last year he spent the greater part of the night in an armchair.

Cardinal Hinsley died on 17 March 1943, at Hare Street, the country house bequeathed by Mgr R. H. Benson to the Archbishops of Westminster. He had the distinction of being condemned by Nazis and Facists for being the friend of Communism and by Communists because they regarded him as their implacable enemy. The Requiem in Westminster Cathedral was a spontaneous reflection of a nation's grief. Here there was no question of mere official representation. The Government was present almost *en masse* to pay tribute to a great Father of the people, and the Archbishop of Canterbury broke with precedent and attended the funeral, as did the Anglican bishops of Chichester and Gloucester, the Greek Archbishop Germanos. Also attending was General de Gaulle representing France and General Sikorsky representing Poland. The body was interred in the Cathedral in the Chapel of St. Joseph and the Scarlet Hat, like a gigantic pendulum whose motion has ceased, hangs over a simple marble slab. He was Archbishop of Westminster for only eight years, yet in that time he had become a much respected national figure. *The Times,* in a leading article, stated that "He leaves a happier relation between his communion and the national Church than has been known since the Reformation". It could have added with equal truth, a happier relation with all the Churches and with the people at large.

Extracts from: *Cardinal Hinsley* by John C. Heenan, later Cardinal
published by Burns Oates & Washbourne, London

Chapter Fourteen

Cardinal Bernard Griffin

CARDINAL Hinsley's death had come at a crucial stage of the war. The allied armies were beginning to take the initiative and a new confidence was emerging. Post war plans for re-building Europe were being planned by the Western democracies. The Vatican, too was trying to re-build the lines of communicatons with the different parts of the Catholic Church. In England the Church had in 1943, suffered the loss of two bishops and the See of Westminster and also the See of Nottingham were vacant. It was thought that months would pass before the Pope chose a successor to Cardinal Hinsley. However, in November of that year, Rome appointed the young forty-four year old auxiliary Bishop of Birmingham to be Archbishop of Westminster.

Bernard William Griffin was born on 21 February, 1899, in Birmingham. With him was born a twin brother, Walter. His father was a manager in a factory manufacturing bicycles. Both boys from a very early age had decided to become priests, Bernard going to Oscott and Walter to Douay having joined the Benedictines. After completing his course of philosophy where he was judged to be an outstanding student, he was sent to the English College in Rome where he took his Gregorian Doctorate of Theology, and later at the Beda he took his Appolinare Doctorate of Canon Law. He was ordained priest on 1 November 1924. The young Dr Griffin returned to his native Birmingham, but instead of going to a parish as he had hoped, he was given the job of secretary to Archbishop McIntyre, now in his 70's. Five years later in 1929 when Archbishop Williams succeeded to the See he was again asked to serve as secretary. In addition to his duties as Archbishop's secretary, he also undertook the posts of diocesan chancellor, vicar-general, administrator of Fr. Hudson's Homes, chairman of the diocesan Youth Council, member of the Warwickshire Educational and the B.B.C. Religious Advisory Committees, director of the Catholic Evidence Guild.

In 1937 he was appointed parish priest to Coleshill and the following year he was consecrated auxiliary bishop to Dr. Williams. His energy and dedication, despite other priorities of wartime, were channelled into the social welfare of the whole district and also the re-building of his church, which in 1942 was opened and dedicated to St. Teresa of the Child Jesus. The effort he spent in these early years may have been the cause of his poor health in later years. Perhaps his herculian energy was the main reason why Pope Pius

XII chose this provincial auxiliary bishop, in the flower of health and energy, to fill the vacant See of Westminster. Of course the Pope would have known that he was equipped through brilliant studies in England and Rome, with the perfect understanding of Catholic doctrine, history and law, someone who was quite outstanding for his age for the breadth and depth of his experience in every department of ecclesiatical administration.

The Bull of appointment for the new Archbishop was dated 18 December 1943. He travelled from Birmingham to London by car in a pea-soup fog. He saw clearly however, what God was asking him to do. The people of London welcomed him with sincere warmth attracted to their youthful looking prelate. In the New Year he was enthroned and during his address he said: "Had I been a native of this great city of London, I could not have received a more generous welcome". In his first public address he referred to the social conditions of the time: "One of the most pressing needs of the Church and nation in this fair land of ours is a revival of Christian family life, which has suffered through the enforced absence of the father, through the removal of the children from the influence of their parents, and through the absence of the mother from her home during long periods of the day when she is in outside employment. A nation depends for its well-being on sound family life, therefore we should endeavour to remove all those obstacles that exist to the restoration of Christian family life".

Within the first months of becoming Archbishop he was visiting troops abroad, in one of his talks he said: "The day after war was declared, I was passing through the streets of Birmingham just as the factories were emptying, and I watched the young men and women, boys and girls, as they passed by. Many of them looked physically underdeveloped, round shouldered and lacking that sense of *joie de vivre* which one naturally associates with youth". At the end of the war he would contrast this view with the troops "Fine, strong, healthy men, clean living and filled with magnificent Christian spirit". It was this description that he wanted applied to the family in the post war nation. In speech after speech he applied Christian doctrine always expressed in clear, simple language of common sense. He was always ready to appear everywhere and teach his people.

He was equally at work behind the scenes or at great receptions and banquets speaking with ministers and officials. The first official challenge which met the new Archbishop was the Educational Bill of 1944. He said: "Catholic parents throughout this land have publicly insisted on their rights to have their children educated in schools which will not offend their consciences. Whilst others are satisfied with the proposals of the Bill, we Catholics are not satisfied. As loyal members of the state, and as tax payers equally with others, our parents claim that they should not be allowed to suffer because of their consciences, but should be granted equal facilities with other members of the community". There were many long and heated discussions about the role of the Catholic schools in the State system that Butler was proposing. Griffin shared Cardinal Hinsley's concerns about the proposals that were offered to Catholics. He argued without success, that major reforms such as this Bill should not be introduced in wartime with a coalition Government and no electorate input. He called Butler's legislation "a hotch potch sort of an Act". Eventually he had to agree to the compromise whereby Catholic schools had all their day-to-day running costs met by the Government, but had to pay 50 per cent of all capital costs in return for control of what was taught in the classroom.

In July 1945, Father Derek Worlock then aged twenty-five joined the new Archbishop's staff as under-secretary which was the beginning of a nineteen year period as secretary to three cardinals.

In December 1946 he was elevated to the Sacred College of Cardinals. He received his Red Hat on his forty-eighth birthday, 21 February 1947. Pius XII embraced him with the words "My beloved Benjamin". The Pope had specially encouraged him to think in terms of the universal mission of the Church, and ever after, he did his utmost when travelling the world to help forge Catholic international understanding and practical co-operation.

He was constantly travelling, across liberated Europe, and to America. He did much work to relieve the plight of refugees stranded throughout the Continent, Yugoslavs, Croats, Slovenes and many others who were affected by the Iron Curtain.

At home Bevan's new National Health Service, in Griffin's view posed a threat to the Catholic hospitals which had such an enviable reputation and Bevan was keen for them to be absorbed into the new system. Griffin did his best to resist, trying to preserve the Catholic ethos of these hospitals. He said: "It will be a sad day for England when charity becomes the affair of the State". The Cardinal was able to influence Bevan, with whom he had a good working relationship, by threatening to influence the Irish nurses, who were recruited in large numbers for hospitals in England. He suggested that such recruitment might well be jeopardised if there was an open fight on this question between the Catholic community and the Government. Bevan agreed and the seventy or so Catholic hospitals were listed as disclaimed hospitals, and were enabled to opt out of the National Health Service.

Similarly, with the National Insurance Act, complex questions were raised about the position of priests and nuns within the system. The Cardinal was able to negotiate a satisfactory solution to all concerned. He was very concerned that Catholics should play a full part in public life, in politics and within the trade unions. No doubt thinking about his own father who had been a member of the Birmingham City Council, he said in a speech on an official visit to Finchley: "I am a firm believer in local government because it seems to me that in it we have a true expression of democracy and liberty. The bond between those who are governing and those who are governed is much more intimate, and local needs will be better understood and more easily dealt with by local authorities than by direction from Whitehall".

In February 1949, a protest meeting was held at the Albert Hall. Cardinal Griffin was to chair the meeting protesting at the arrest of Cardinal Joseph Mindszenty. The Cardinal was missing and Archbishop Downey of Liverpool had to take the chair. Earlier Cardinal Griffin was taken ill suffering from exhaustion. He had in fact been anointed for the first time in this first phase of his illness and he spent his fiftieth birthday in the care of the nuns of the Hospital of St. John and St. Elizabeth. He recovered slowly and his optimistic hope that he would return to work within a few weeks was frustrated by his high blood pressure. It was not until December 1949 that he had virtually returned to a normal work load.

The following year the Catholic Church in England would celebrate the centenary of the establishment of the hierarchy in 1850. This was a joyful and unique event and would mark the health of the Church in the postwar years. This event would demand much of the Cardinal not only for the preparation and planning, but for his personal appearance especially as he had been appointed the Pope's legate for the great occasion.

The Cardinal became very seriously ill again in July, only two months before the great day when the Centenary Congress would draw 100,000 Catholics to Wembly Stadium. The condition of the Cardinal was such that those close to him thought it impossible for him to be present. Cardinal Griffin however, was determined to appear. His fear was that the Congress itself would have to be postponed if the papal legate was unable to attend. He did recover in time for him to be solemnly received as papal legate in Westminster Cathedral, he preached at the Mass for the clergy in the ruins of Southwark Cathedral. Preaching in the cathedral he said: "From the small beginnings of 1850 so much as come that we clearly see the hand of God in the increase that he has granted. As we look around us at this congregation of clergy, can we not marvel at seeing in this very church more priests present than there were in the whole of England and Wales one hundred years ago. The development for which Cardinal Wiseman and his faithful flock hoped and prayed has been made. We have more churches, more monasteries, more convents, and more schools. Here are the fruits of the labours of those who have gone before. Full of confidence, therefore, as they were in 1850, let us go forward, resolving anew to cooperate with the graces made available to us by Almighty God, that we may not prove unworthy in the tasks that lie ahead". He attended the Wembley Rally and was the chief guest at the banquet at Grosvener House given by the laity in honour of the hierarchy. His appearance at Wembly showed the effort he made for the occasion.

He entered the stadium, a sick man, leaning on the arm of an attendant as he slowly limped across to his throne. The crowd of 90,000 people cheered and applauded the Cardinal Legate showing their appreciation for his immense courage.

Shortly afterwards he went to Rome with Archbishop Masterson where the Pope was to define the Dogma of the Assumption. The Cardinal was concerned about his ability to carry on because of his illness and during a meeting with Pius XII the Pope agreed that Bishop Myers would be promoted to archbishop and made Cardinal Griffin's coadjutor. He was also greatly assisted by his devoted secretary Monsignor Derek Worlock. However at the end of January 1951, the Cardinal suffered a severe attack of coronary thrombosis and was anointed for the second time. He was forced into a long period of rest and convalescence. Gradually he recovered, not to full health, his voice was weaker and he walked with a slight limp, but sufficiently to once again take control.

In the early 1950's we saw the attack on the Church both in Eastern Europe and in Asia, by atheistic Communist regimes. In this country there were the beginnings of the indifference to spiritual and moral principles with worship and Christian upbringing in family and school decreasing. Cardinal Griffin saw this deterioration as an opportunity for the Catholic Church to become more aware of its faith and strength. The Catholic body in this country was awakened to be fully conscious of itself and its total and complete emergence from the ghetto mentality, that state of siege which prevailed within the Church for so long. Cardinal Griffin saw the need for a lay apostolate to play a full part in the life of the Church. In his Lenten pastoral of 1952 he wrote: "Today, we cannot over-emphasise the importance of Christians living a full Christian life, a life that is in accordance with the teaching of Him who is the way, the truth and the life. At no time in the past has it been more important that the laity should be conscious of their role and adequately trained for their task. Their apostolate is to be fulfilled as ever under the direction of those who have received their authority from the Church founded by Christ. It is for the laity to share in the apostolate of the hierarchy and, if their role is dependent on the hierarchy of the Church, this in no way diminishes the importance of their task or the very real responsibility which is theirs. There is grave danger that this field of the lay apostolate may be thought to be closed to all save specialists and experts. The lay apostolate is open to all. It is the duty of all, irrespective of class or background, to play their part within the life of the Church. Each apostle must be trained and prepared for carrying his Christian principles into the very sphere in which he has is being. This is as true of intellectuals and students as it is of professional men and women and working youth. The university professor has a part to play in the life of the Church as much as has the member of a trade union".

The Cardinal also spoke of the apostolate within the family and within the boundaries of local communities "Some will be called to more extensive activities by membership of Catholic societies and organisations, in which they will be able both to work for their personal sanctification and also to bring the charity of Christ to their non-Catholic brethren". He also spoke about the need for men and women to work in the field of politics and in international affairs.

Despite his re-occuring illness he was determined to be among the people. In 1952 he visited over sixteen dioceses in the country and made a number of visits abroad, including spiritual refreshment at Lisieux. He made every effort to work at the pace he once did in his younger days.

In 1953 he received the title of domestic prelate. Derek Worlock took over more and more the running of the archdiocese. He was obsessively loyal to the Cardinal and over protective which caused some problems among some of the clergy of Westminster. The following year Gordon Wheeler became adminstrator of the cathedral at the request of Cardinal Griffin. Wheeler had left the Anglican Church and had been appointed chaplain to the University, after a spell as a curate in a north London parish. He had trained for ordination as a Catholic priest at the Beda College in Rome. He was editor of the Westminster Cathedral Chronicle and became a close friend of Derek Worlock. Both were destined to become bishops. Before he died Cardinal Griffin gave his ring to Gordon Wheeler and his pectoral cross to Derek Worlock, predicting to them both that one day they would need them.

Changes were already being introduced into the liturgy with the dialogue Mass and the advent of evening Masses, whilst the Friday abstinence laws were also revised. Following the Coronation of Queen Elizabeth in June 1953, Catholics prayed for her and Masses were offered for her in every Catholic church in the land. The Catholic bishops were given permission to go into Westminster Abbey during their annual gathering at Westminster on 13 October to pray at the shrine of St. Edmund on his feast day, although the visit took place after dark when the Abbey was officially closed.

Cardinal Griffin was thought by many to be too ill to continue and that he should retire. Derek Worlock had become indispensable to the Cardinal. He was his eyes and ears, he also produced much of the correspondence and speech writing. Griffin trusted him completely and consequently it was possible for the Cardinal to remain in office. Bishop Myers, one of the titular auxiliary bishops of the archdiocese was made titular archbishop with the right of succession.

Cardinal Griffin presided at the Low Week meeting after Easter 1956 and led the National Pilgrimage to Lourdes in May. He also attended a ceremony in Rouen in honour of St. Joan of Arc. One of his last visits to Westminster Cathedral was on 28 June to mark the bravery of Catholic holders of the Victoria Cross. During the ceremony he had a heart attack, but incredibly he remained in control. He collapsed later in his house. The doctors advised a complete rest and on 7 August, Derek Worlock along with Father Bernard Fisher took the Cardinal to a holiday house at Polzeath near St. Minver Highlands overlooking the sea to Pentine Point. The Cardinal seemed a little better, and he retired for the night on 19 August. In the early hours of the morning he suffered a fatal heart attack. It was the feast of his patron, St. Bernard.

Extracts from: *Cardinal Bernard Griffin* by Michael de la Bedoyere published by Rockcliffe Corporation, London

Chapter Fifteen

Cardinal William Godfrey

WILLIAM Godfrey was the obvious choice as Cardinal Griffin's successor. He succeeded to the See of Westminster at the age of 67 when many thought a younger man was needed. He was the last of the old guard who were entrenched in the past traditions of the Church. He was not interested in ecumenical work and at times criticised his future successor Heenan for his close contacts with Anglicans.

A Liverpool man, from the Kirkdale area of the city he was a distinguished pupil of the English College in Rome. He had been professor of theology at Ushaw and then rector of the English College in Rome. He was appointed apostolic delegate to the British colonies in Africa by Pope Pius XI following the request from the British Minister in Rome, D'Arcy Osborne. In 1938 he was then sent as apostolic visitor to the seminaries of England, Scotland and Malta. Later the same year he was appointed apostolic delegate to Great Britain.

He became Archbishop of Liverpool, destined to stay in that post for only three years after which he was translated to Westminster. William Godfrey had great regard for his predecessor and maintained some of the key policies. He also retained Derek Worlock as his private secretary. However, the first instruction Worlock received from the new Archbishop of Westminster was to cancel all the evening Masses which Griffin had introduced.

Unlike his predessor, Godfrey was still full of vigour and he immediately embarked on a series of parish visitations throughout the archdiocese. In addition he travelled extensively abroad. Including trips to Rome for the funeral of Pope Pius XII and the Coronation of Pope John XXIII. One of the most memorable trips was the visit to Rome for the Consistory of 17 December 1958, at which Cardinal Godfrey received the red hat from the newly elected Pope John XXIII. Godfrey was held in very high esteem in Rome. At this time the liturgical ceremonies in the Vatican expressed an unashamed sense of triumpalism reflecting the confidence that the Church felt about its own position in the world.

On 25 January 1959, the feast of the Conversion of St. Paul, Pope John speaking to seventeen cardinals at the Basilica of St. Paul-Outside-the-Walls in Rome, made the historic announcement of his intention to hold Vatican II. He announced, in fact, that he intended to take three extraordinary actions. He had observed, he said, the need to provide an updating of Church practice and language to more adequately address the modern world. He announced, therefore, his intentions; (1) to hold a synod for the Diocese of Rome, of which the Pope is the local bishop, (2) to hold an ecumenical council of the Church, and (3) to update the code of canon law. The Synod in the Diocese of Rome was held on 24 to 31 January 1960. In order to keep this synod focused on his own desired objectives, Pope John decided to do the speaking at the synod himself. He gave several talks which dealt with a wide range of issues, including: Belief in God as a Trinity of love. Redemption from sin by the earthly sufferings and death of Jesus Christ. The Resurection and the hope of seeing God face to face. The pitfalls and dangers of modern life that may lead to damnation.

Pope John insisted on the *via positiva:* modern men and women putting their shoulder to the wheel of life, he argued, can achieve decency, stability, security, and a touch of holiness, no matter what the living conditions in which they find themselves. One of the synodal statutes also provides for a more compassionate treatment of priests who have left the Church or the priesthood than was prevalent in the recent past. Many of the notions he articulated at this synod were later reflected in the opening sections of the Constitutions on the Church, one of the key documemts eventually emerging from Vatican II.

Once the Roman Synod was completed and its statutes promulgated, preparation for Vatican II could get under way. The first step, was to declare Vatican I officially closed. It had been adjourned because of the Franco-Prussian War in 1870 and the siege of Rome by Italian nationalists, but it had never been officially closed.

The formal preparation for Vatican II began with a worldwide consultation with some 2,500 residential bishops, heads of male religious orders, and faculties of Catholic universities. The consultation got under way through an invitation sent the previous year by Cardinal Tardini, Pope John's Secretary of State. The invitation asked the bishops of the world to express their desires for the council.

More than 2000 bishops responded. Cardinal Godfrey and his secretary Derek Worlock spent the summer of 1959 preparing their response. All the letters received in Rome were photocopied and filed. The photocopies were cut into pieces so the various subjects could be grouped into categories. The work was detailed and painstaking. Most of the responses were submitted in Latin and the effort to study them, determine their subject area, and file them appropriately was done by only five priests, working with Archbishop Felici. All the material was eventually collated by nation and printed in book form. The books were then passed along to a group of preparatory commissions which were instituted by Pope John at a solemn Vespers on Pentecost Sunday, 5 June 1960.

Archbishop Heenan was appointed to the Secretariat for the Promotion of Christian Unity. The Archbishops of Canterbury and York appointed representatives to the Vatican. This confirmed the idea in the British media that the purpose of this Ecumenical Council was to improve relationships between Christian Churches.

Cardinal Godfrey was appointed to the Central Preparatory Commission. It was intended to be an objective filtering system for all the ideas and views sent in from the bishops around the world, which would make up the Council's agenda.

In the late summer of 1961, the Cardinal again became ill and was admitted into St. John and St. Elizabeth Hospital in London. Godfrey's only concern was to be well enough to attend the Vatican Council. Despite his illness Cardinal Godfrey was a master of detail and he took great care to come to grips with the complexities of the preparatory papers for the Central Commission. He was competent in several languages and expert in Latin and took a lead in dealing with the vast documentation, all in Latin sent from Rome. Much of the routine work of the archdiocese at this period was handled with great skill by his ever faithful secretary Derek Worlock.

Despite his frequent spells in hospital and operations for cancer in the groin, Godfrey was determined to play a major part in the Council's business. At the first meeting of the Central Commission in November 1961, fundamental divisions appeared between the cardinals. This formed two groups, 'progressives' and 'conservatives'. Godfrey's natural inclinations were with the conservatives. However the majority of the Northern European bishops were in the progressive camp and they revolted against the influence of the Curia and the attempt by Cardinal Ottaviani to dictate policy. This first clash on the authority of the Holy Office set the scene for further confrontations and the eventual victory of the progressives.

On Thursday 11 October 1962 the momentous opening ceremony took place, almost three thousand bishops assembled. The procession to St. Peter's was led by the College of Cardinals at a very slow pace. Cardinal Godfrey who was recovering from a recent cancer operation was in agony as he reached his designated seat. The great bsilica of St. Peter's had become the Council's debating chamber. There were long benches for bishops, eight tiers of them reaching right up on high and above these, tribunes for *periti* and observers. The cardinals were seated all in one section of the benches immediately opposite the famous statue of St. Peter. The breathtaking view of all the assembled dignitaries of the Church led by the Pope was a scene that became so familiar to the world at large.

Pope John XXIII in his opening speech said:

" The entire Church rejoices today because that longed-for moment has finally arrived when, under the watchful eye of the Virgin Mother of God, the Second Vatican Ecumenical Council is opened, here beside the tomb of St. Peter. The previous ecumenical councils of the Church, some twenty in number, plus many other regional ones, all prove clearly the vigour of the Catholic Church and are recorded as shining lights in the Church's history.

"In calling this particular council, I assert once again the Church's enduring authority to teach the faith, and I hope that in these times, filled with needs and opportunities as well as errors, the Church's teaching will be presented exceptionally well to all people. It is natural for us to look back into our history today and listen again to the voices of Church leadership, both in the East and the West, where, beginning in the fourth century, councils like this have gathered. But despite the joys of these previous councils, there has also been a trail of sorrow and trial, just as Simeon foretold to Mary that Jesus would be the source of both the fall and the rise of many.

"What confronts the Church today, therefore, is not new. Those who are in Christ enjoy light, goodness, order and peace. Those who oppose Christ sink into confusion, bitter human relations, and the constant danger of war. Ecumenical councils like this, whenever they gather, are an occasion for the celebration once again of the unity between Christ and the Church. They lead to a clear announcement of the truth, to guidance for people in everyday life, and to the strengthening of spiritual energy for goodness's sake.

"We now stand in the wake of twenty centuries of such history as we begin. For the sake of the historical record, let me mention the first moment when the idea of calling such a council came to me. I first uttered the words on 25 January 1959, on the feast of the Conversion of St.Paul, in the church dedicated to him in Rome. It was completely unexpected, like a flash of heavenly light, and it gave rise to three years of tremendous activity throughout the world in preparation for this day. These years alone have been an initial gift of grace. I confidently trust that under the light of this council the Church will become richer in spiritual matters and, with this new energy, will look to the future without fear. In fact, by bringing itself up-to-date where needed, the Church will make people, families, and whole nations really turn their minds toward divine things. Therefore, we are all very grateful for this moment. Moreover, I also want to mention before you now my own assessment of the happy circumstances under which this council begins its work.

"As I go about my daily work as Pope, I sometimes have to listen, with much regret, to voices of persons who, though burning with zeal, are not endowed with too much sense of direction or measure. These people can see nothing but a decline of truth and the ruin of the Church in these modern times. They say that our era, in comparison with past ones, is getting worse, and they behave as though they had learned nothing from history, which is, nonetheless, the teacher of life. They behave as though at the time of former councils, everything was a full triumph for the Christian idea and religious liberty. I feel I must disagree with these prophets of gloom who are always forecasting disaster as though the end of the world was at hand.

"In fact, at the present time Divine Providence is leading us to a new order of human relations which, by the very effort of the people of this time, is directed toward the fulfilment of God's great plans for us. Everything, even human differences, leads to a greater good for the Church. It's easy to see this if you look even casually through history. Most of the councils called in the past were forced to address serious challenges to the Church brought about by civil authorities, even when they thought they were helping the Church.

"Most of the world today does not live under such civil tyranny, and this is a great thing. I am saddened, of course, by those places where such oppression still exists, and indeed, some bishops are noticeable here today mainly by their absence where they are imprisoned for their faith. And even though modern life brings with it great stress and pressure from economic and political sides, nonetheless, it at least has the advatage of having freed the Church from obstacles to its freedom in most parts of the world.

"The greatest concern of this council is this: that the sacred and central truths of our Christian faith hould be guarded and taught more effectively. These central truths embrace the whole human person, composed as we are of body and soul, and since we are pilgrims on earth, they lead us always toward heaven. This puts into perspective that we are to use earthly things only to attain a divine good. According to the sixth chapter of the Gospel of Matthew, Jesus himself called on us to seek first the Reign of God, addressing our energy to that. But Jesus also completed that thought by saying that, if we did seek that first, all worldly things would be given to us as well.

"Both sides of this equation are presnt in the Church today, as they have always been, and we take this into account as we begin. In this effort, we will not depart from the truth as it is passed on to us by the early Fathers and Mothers of the Church. But we will also be attentive to these times, to the new conditions and new forms of life present in the modern world which have opened arenas of work for Catholics. So while the Church is mindful of marvellous human progress, it is also eager to remind people that God is the true source of wisdom and beauty.

"Having said this, it is clear that much is expected of us here regarding the passing on of the doctrines of the Church, as we have done without fail for twenty centuries, despite occasional difficulties in that regard. The important point of this council is not, therefore, a discussion of one article or another of the fundamental teachings of the Church, a council would not be needed for such work. Instead, the work of this council is to better articulate the doctrine of the Church for this age. This doctrine should be studied and expounded through the methods of research and literary forms of modern thought.

"Here is a key distinction on which our work is based: The substance of our central beliefs is one thing, and the way in which it is presented is another. It is this latter presentation of the faith with which we are concerned here, and our approach to this will be a thoroughly pastoral one. As we open this council we see, as always, that the truth of Jesus is permanent. Often, as one age succeeds another, the opinions of people follow one another and exclude each other. Errors creep in, but vanish like fog before the sun. In the past we have opposed these errors and often condemned them. But today we prefer to make use of the medicine of mercy rather than that of severity. We meet the needs of the present day by demonstrating the validity of our teachings rather than by condemning others. In fact, error today is so obvious when it emerges that people themselves reject it. People are ever-more convinced of the high dignity of the human person, the evil of violence, and the dead end of arms and political domination.

"That being so, the Catholic Church in this council desires to show herself as the loving mother of all: benign, patient, full of mercy and goodness towards all who are separated from her. The Church does not offer riches that will pass away to the people of today. Like Peter when he was asked for alms, we say that we have a certain power in Jesus Christ to offer the world: a way to walk in truth. We distribute the goods of divine grace to all people, and this raises the children of God to great dignity. We open here the fountain of our life-giving doctrines which allow all people to understand their real dignity and purpose. Finally, through our members, we spread Christian charity, the most powerful tool in eliminating the seeds of discord and in establishing harmony, peace and unity.

"True peace and salvation are associated with having a complete grasp of revealed truth. The truth is passed on through the doctrines of the Church, and the Church wishes very much to promote and defend this truth so that everone can have access to it with a unity of understanding. Unfortunately, the whole Christian family does not have this unity of mind. The Catholic Church considers it a duty to work actively to bring about that unity, which Jesus himself called for in his final prayers. It is a triple sort of unity which we seek. First, a unity among Catholics themselves which we want to keep firm and strong. Second, a unity of prayer and desire among those other Christians now separated fom Rome. And third, a unity in esteem and repect for those who follow non-Christian religions.

"It is the clear aim of this council to bring together the Church's best energies and to strive to have people welcome more favourably the good tidings of salvation. This council will prepare and consolidate the path towards that unity of humankind which is required as a necessary foundation in order that the earthly may be brought to resemble the heavenly one where truth reigns, charity is the law, and eternity the timetable.

"In conclusion, I direct my voice to you, my venerable fellow bishops of the Church. We are gathered here today in this great Vatican basilica upon which the history of the Church is hinged, where heaven and earth are closely joined, near the tomb of Peter and so many others who have gone before us in faith. The council now beginning rises in the Church like daybreak, a forerunner of most splendid light. It is now only dawn, and already, at this first announcement of the rising day, how much sweetness fills our heart! Everything here breathes sanctity and arouses great joy. The Church is now in your hands, gathered as you are here from all the continents of the world. We might say that heaven and earth are united in the holding of this council, the saints of heaven to protect us, and the people on earth looking for inspiration and guidance.

" Indeed, our work is expected to correspond to the modern needs of the various peoples of the world. This requires of you serenity of mind brotherly concord, moderation in proposals, dignity in discussion and wisdom in deliberation. God grant that your labours and work towards which the eyes of all people and desires of the entire world are turned, may generously fulfil the hopes of all. Almighty God! In you we place all our confidence, not trusting in our own strength. Look down kindly on these pastors of your Church. May the light of your grace help us in making decisions and making laws. Graciously hear the prayers which we offer you with unanimity of faith, voice, and mind. O Mary, help of Christians, help of bishops, arrange all things for a happy and helpful outcome. With your spouse, St. Joseph, the holy apostles, Peter and Paul, St. John the Baptist, and St. John the Evangelist intercede to God for us. Jesus Christ, our loving redeemer, immortal ruler of people and the ages, be love, be power, and be glory for ever and ever. Amen".

Among the various schemata considered, one of the most important was the schema (draft document) on Liturgy. This represented the Council's intention of the internal renewal of the Church. It was passed with only forty-six negative votes. This was a major victory for the progressives, and a clear sign that this Council was indeed undertaking real reform. On 7 December the Council approved the first chapter of the document of the Liturgy with 2,102 yes votes to 11 no votes and 5 invalidated ballots. The chapter allows certain changes with which to update the Mass, including the use of the vernacular languages and a more participatory rite. The chapter contains the fundamental principles which the following chapters will implement. The Church's sacramental and prayer life is moved to centre stage. The following day the first session of the Second Vatican Council was formarlly adjourned for nine months.

Cardinal Godfrey, accompanied by Derek Worlock returned to England after the First Session of the Council on 10 December 1962. Five days later the Cardinal was in hospital for his fourth operation for cancer. He had a difficult Christmas and on the 19 January 1963 he suffered a mild coronary. Bishop Cashman his auxiliary bishop came to anoint him. He died at 5 pm in the evening of 22 January 1963. Archbishop Michael Ramsey arrived at the door of Archbishop's House, he was too late to see the Cardinal before he died. On 3 June Pope XXIII died and three weeks later Paul VI was elected.

Extracts from: *Not the Whole Truth* Archbishop John C.Heenan
pulished by Burns Oates & Washbourne, London
Vatican Council in Plain English by Bill Huebsch
published by Thomas More Publishers, Allen, Texas, USA

Chapter Sixteen

Cardinal John Carmel Heenan

JOHN Carmel Heenan was born in Ilford on 26 January 1905. His parents were from Ireland, in fact they lived next door to each other in Clareen and they both attended the same school. His mother Annie Pilkington, was the eldest of seven children and at the age of ten, her mother died and she was left to bring up five young children. Ten years later her father also died and she now had the further responsibility of looking after the farm.

In 1896 his father James, who was now working in England, went home to Ireland for a holiday. He met up with Frank Pilkington who had emigrated to Chicago and was also home for a holiday. He confided to Frank while cycling along one day that he would like to ask Nan his sister to marry him but was afraid that because of all her responsibilities that she would never intend to get married. Frank interceded and Nan agreed. They had to wait until Easter 1898, when they were married in the old church of St. Kieran in Clareen.

They settled down in Fulham for the first four years of their married life. Their first born were twins, George and James. George died shortly after birth. Eventually came brother Frank and sister Mary, John was the youngest. Their neighbourhood was very respectable and Ripley Road where they lived later produced a cardinal, a bishop (Bishop Foley of Lancaster) and two priests, including his brother Frank. When John was nine years old the First World War broke out. His father worked as a Civil servant in the Patents Office in Chancery Lane. When his own office hours were over he would go to work in Whitehall to work on civil liabilities which dealt with compensation for civilians who had suffered loss through enemy action.

By the age of seven John had decided to become a priest, he shared this secret desire only with his mother. To achieve his objective he had to win a scholarship which in those days were not readily available. The only scholarship at his school had been won by his friend Ted Harding, but by some act of providence, his parents later withdrew him from the Jesuit school and sent him away to boarding school. John was able to take his place and transferred from Sts. Peter and Paul parochial school to St. Ignatius' Grammar School in April 1918. He remained there until he was seventeen, when he was sent to Ushaw College in Durham. At Ushaw he received something of a culture shock, it was his first contact with northerners. Most of the students came from Lancashire, Yorkshire and Northumberland. The régime and diet in those days were spartan, there were virtually no vegetables except potatoes, and supper was usually just bread and butter.

The young John Heenan considered his two years at Ushaw boring and wasteful. Latin nearly all day long, he said, is not enough to satisfy the inquisitive mind of youth. On the other hand he realised that this kind of boredom was a great test of his vocation. He experienced the exercise of meditation for the first time. He thought it extraordinary to have to rise at half-past six to kneel for half an hour before Mass, no one told him how to occupy his time. Spiritual exercises, like everything else at Ushaw was the fruit of tradition. The College was immensely proud of being descended from the English College in Douay. Tradition was so highly regarded that the only truly genuine Ushaw man – called 'cat and pod man' – is one who had started in the junior house –'sem' – and ended as one of the fourth year divines –'Divs' the name for theological students. Cat is the Ushaw game, not unlike baseball. Balls and sticks were made by the boys. The balls were as hard as concrete and quite lethal. Pod is the Ushaw pudding, a species of suet pudding, but on special occasions when full of fruit it tasted like Christmas pudding. To play cat and eat pod were marks of a true Ushaw man.

During his time at Ushaw he contracted scarlet fever, he was isolated and during his recovery he spent his time playing golf and walking round the Durham countryside. After a few weeks he was allowed to go away to convalesce. One of the students arranged for him to stay with his family in Newcastle-on-Tyne. He was free of domestic authority for the first time in his life and he relished the feeling.

Returning to Ushaw he felt miserable. For several weeks he had been pampered and now school life seemed unbearably hard. He had also met a charming girl of his own age and thinking about her constantly made the seminary seem like prison. He felt unable to endure the separation. He spoke to nobody about his anguish and could find no comfort in prayer. The Mass which had been the chief source of his strength and comfort now became a penance. He had to make a decision whether or not he had a vocation for the priesthood. He spent the next day in the school chapel, for hours he wrestled with his problem. By the early evening he became increasingly convinced that he had no vocation. He knelt before the shrine of Our Lady to say a prayer of thanksgiving that his mind was made up. Then all at once his doubts once more returned. As he knelt before the altar he read the words embroidered on the altar cloth, *Monstra te esse matrem* – show yourself a mother. With blinding clarity he saw his problem in simple terms. He realised that he had no problem, there was no real doubt in his mind about

Rt Rev John Cuthbert Hedley OSB
Bishop Auxiliary of Cardiff 1873-1881
trans to Newport and Menevia 1881
died 1915

Bishop Hedley in old age

Most Rev Francis Mostyn
Consecrated as Vicar Apostolic of Wales
trans to Menevia 1898
trans to Cardiff as
Archbishop and Metropolitan 1921
died 1939

Cardinal Arthur Hinsley
Fifth Archbishop of Westminster
1935-1943
from a painting by Simon Elwes
at Archbishop's House, Westminster
reproduced with permission of
Westminster Roman Catholic Diosesan Trustees

Left: as a curate in Keighley c.1912

Cardinal Bernard Griffin
Sixth Archbishop of Westminster 1943-1956
from a painting at Archbishop's House, Westminster
reproduced with permission of Westminster Roman Catholic Diosesan Trustees

Cardinal Willam Godfrey
Seventh Archbishop of Westminster 1956-1963
Photograph: Westminster Archives

Cardinal John Carmel Heenan
Eighth Archbishop of Westminster 1963-1975
Photograph: Westminster Archives

Cardinal Basil Hume OSB
Ninth Archbishop of Westminster 1976-1999
Photograph: Catholic Media Office

Cardinal Cormac Murphy-O'Connor
Tenth Archbishop of Westminster
Photograph reproduced with the permission of the Cardinal's Private Secretary

His Eminence Cardinal Godfried Danneels, the Pope's Special Envoy with
His Excellency Archbishop Pablo Puente, Papal Nuncio to Great Britain
and members of the Hierarchy of England and Wales,
at St George's Cathedral, Southwark. May 2000, to mark the
150th anniversary of the restoration of the Hierarchy in England and Wales

his vocation. God was calling him to become one of his priests but he was shrinking from accepting the invitation. He was not prepared to give up comfort and the delights of human love to follow God. Self questioning began again, was he putting good food before the priesthood? Was the friendship of the girl he had met more valuable than the sharing of the priesthood of Christ? He realised that his real trouble was nostalgia, he was hungry and homesick, he needed his mother. That afternoon he found her, never again in the long years of preparation was he to be troubled by doubts about his vocation.

At Ushaw he learned the meaning of self discipline. Unlike his days at the Jesuit Grammar school where the rules had no spiritual significance, he began to realise that seminary rules form an important part of training for the priesthood. His short time at Ushaw was full of interest and joy and he came to appreciate the qualities of the rough spoken northerner. He left Ushaw at the age of nineteen, for two years he had withstood the burden of a school curriculum devoid of variety. He had forced himself to keep the rules. Above all he had begun to learn how to pray and his enthusiasm for the priesthood had increased enormously.

Towards the end of October 1924 he left England for the English College in Rome. He was overawed by the sheer size and beauty of St. Peter's. Inside he was equally bewildered by the crowds and overwhelmed by the singing of the Sistine Choir. High Mass was in progress and the celebrant was Cardinal Merry del Val. After Mass he went outside with his companions who were dressed in cassocks and black beaver sombrero. He was still dressed in his lay clothes. They stood watching the colourful procession of prelates when Cardinal Merry del Val halted it and came over to the group of students. He asked the young Heenan if he were a new man and to which school had he been. When he was told Ushaw, he was delighted. "I am also an Ushaw man" he said, "and I am going to give you some good advice. Do not work too hard in your first year, it will take time for you to become acclimatised to the air in Rome after the cold air of the North". He was thrilled by this meeting and assumed that students and cardinals would often rub shoulders in Rome. In fact it was several years before he spoke to another cardinal.

The rector at the English College was Monsignor Hinsley. He told Heenan that the English College was not a seminary but a half way house to the mission. Hinsley, who was referred to as the Boss, wanted the students to think of themselves as men and he treated them as men. At the same time he maintained firm discipline. He was a man of moods and often deep depression. Because he was the most humane of disciplinarians the students loved him and made allowances for occasional moodiness. Hinsley led by example and the high ideals which he set himself. He would start the day with private prayer in chapel. To miss or be late for morning prayer was the only student failing to which the rector was never indulgent. It was his conviction that men who could not rise promptly to give the best hour of the day to God while in training were not likely to become holy and zealous priests.

Towards the end of his sixth year in Rome he was busy making preparations for ordination. Some bishops called their students home for ordination but most men were ordained in Rome. He had always wanted to be ordained, like his brother Frank, in the parish church in Ilford where he had been baptised and received his first Holy Communion. Through the intervention of Cardinal Merry del Val he received a dispensation that allowed him to be ordained in England.

At the end of June 1930 Heenan left Rome for England. He made a week's retreat at the Jesuit house in Roehampton. On 6 July he was ordained in the parish church at Ilford by Dr. Doubleday, Bishop of Brentwood. He then returned to Rome in October, for a year to complete his studies for his doctorate. After a holiday in the United States, paid for by his cousin Anne Blyth, he took up his first appointment as curate in the parish of St. Ethelburga in Barking, Essex.

Barking was an ideal place for a young priest's apprenticeship. There were two Catholic schools, a hospital and a number of old and sick parishioners. Most of the parishioners in those days were poor, In 1932 the country was still suffering from the effect of the great depression. The Welfare State had not yet emerged. It was still the era of the means test. For the new curate Barking was an almost perfect parish. There were virtually no social distractions. Long before his ordination he had resolved never to dine in the homes of parishioners. Poor people cannot invite their priests to dinner, it would therefore be too easy to belong to the better-off section of the parish by indulging in social visits.

In his early years as a curate he was completely immersed in the day to day matters of parish life. He also began to take an interest in writing. His first book published by Sheed & Ward in 1936 was *Priest and Penitent.*

Cardinal Bourne died after a long illness on the last day of 1934. As a priest in the Brentwood diocese he would not usually have much contact with the Archbishop of Westminster. However Monsignor Hinsley's appointment greatly effected Father Heenan. Cardinal Bourne sent any student from within the Westminster diocese to either St. Sulpice in Paris or the Procure of St. Sulpice in Rome. There had not been a single Westminster student in The English College under Hinsley. Both Archbishop Hinsley and his secretary Val Elwes approached Heenan to ask for help in drafting speeches and articles for Archbishop Hinsley to whom much of the contemporary English scene was foreign. He had been out of touch with such matters as education for over twenty years. In the increasingly difficult political climate Hinsley became embroiled in controversy over his explanations about the Pope's inability to censure Mussolini when he attacked Abyssinia.

Archbishop Hinsley felt the need for advisors close enough to be able to keep him more in touch with public opinion. Heenan resisted the approach for him to become a second secretary to Hinsley, as he felt this would alienate the Westminster clergy. The compromise was that Heenan continued to draft speeches and provide memoranda on current affairs without moving from his parish in Barking.

Heenan underook a long journey to the Soviet Union under the guise of a simple tourist, keeping the fact that he was a Catholic priest secret from the authorities. He wanted to find out at first hand what conditions were like in Russia and the effect of Stalin's regime of terror on the Church. On his return he was able to speak at public meetings with some authority about Russia and communism. He also wrote articles for the *Catholic Times* under the anonymous title of 'Our Special Investigator'.

Cardinal Hinsley in 1937 found himself becoming more involved with domestic politics and again tried to secure the services of Heenan. This time he made approaches to Bishop Doubleday of Brentwood. The Bishop pointed out to the cardinal that as he was so short of priests Heenan was indispensable and perhaps to prove the point he appointed Heenan to be parish priest of Manor Park. Heenan was just thirty-two years of age.

He used his considerable energies to the full in parish work and during his spare time he continued to lecture and to write. He also became involved with the B.B.C., Kemsley Press, Reuters and the Ministry of Information in addition to his contributions to the Catholic press. He used his earnings to help pay for rebuilding his school which suffered a direct hit during the blitz. Through his writing he established a friendship with John McCormack who lived in Ireland in retirement. During the war John McCormack offered his services to sing in England for the soldiers, the sick and the old. Heenan persuaded John McCormack to sing during Benediction at St. Nicholas' church ar Manor Park. The church was filled to overflowing. John McCormack sang two hymns, 'Panis Angelicus' and 'Sweet Sacrament Divine'. Unspoiled by his success and wealth, John McCormack never lost his deep faith and his talent moved many to tears.

Bishop Doubleday censured Father Heenan on a number of occassions it was some years before Heenan realised that the bishop was suffering from increasing dementia. As soon as the war was over Heenan wanted to rebuild the bombed school. War damage funding would cover most of the cost. However he needed to borrow a few thousand pounds to keep the contractors happy. The Bishop refused to allow him to borrow the money. Heenan was now in a serious dilemma. He had never previously defied the Bishop despite all the trials, but now he could see no alternative. He took the

Bishop's letter forbidding him to borrow the money to the apostolic delegate, Mgr Godfrey, whom he had known both at Ushaw and in Rome. Godfrey unhesitating, told him to proceed without scruple. He also added that for some time he had been receiving reports of the bishop's increasing loss of contact with affairs.

He now had to find the money. The usual source of borrowing funds was through the Alliance Assurance Company, but they would only act through the bishops. The Archbishop of Westminster was now Bernard Griffin. He had been in his last year when Heenan arrived the English College in Rome. Some months after his arrival in Westminster Archbishop Griffin telephoned Heenan at Manor Park. He knew what Heenan had done for Cardinal Hinsley and asked why Heenan had not offered to help him. Heenan explained his reasons but Griffin insisted in a meeting to discuss the matter further. As a result Heenan continued to provide his services to the archbishop. At the same meeting, Heenan showed Griffin the letter he had received from Bishop Doubleday. The Archbishop immediately wrote a cheque for the required sum, as an interest free loan pending the Government grant for war damage.

In 1947 Heenan was asked to become Superior of the Catholic Missionary Society. This is a company of priests from various dioceses, not members of religious orders, founded by Cardinal Vaughan early in the century to preach the faith throughout England and Wales. Its chief function was to be the provision of lectures on Catholic theology for non-Catholic audiences. Each summer the C.M.S. priests organised what was called the motor mission. A mobile chapel was taken to villages and country towns where ignorance of the Catholic religion was hereditary. During the war the Catholic Missionary Society came to a halt. The whole project had again to start from scratch. A small band of four priests were gathered and eventually a house in Hampstead was acquired for their headquarters. They each took turns on the Catholic Evidence Guild platform at Speakers' Corner in Hyde Park, they also preached regularly at St. Edward the Confessor's, the parish church in Golders Green. They honed their skills taking notes of each others sermons and later in the evening they held an inquest. They began their regular mission work in February 1948.

While preaching a mission in Billingham, Co. Durham in 1951 he received a telephone call from Archbishop Godfrey, the apostolic delegate. Speaking in Latin he informed Heenan that the Holy Father wished him to accept the See of Leeds, which had been vacant for over a year since the death of Bishop Poskitt.

In the same year his brother died. The sadness of the loss of another member of his family, barely three years following the death of his mother, he bore with sorrow. He was equally sad at the realisation that his episcopal duties would mean the loss of the many pleasures he enjoyed as a priest - parish duties, visiting the homes of his parishioners, at the bedside of the sick, in the confessional. He realised that the greatest sacrifice a bishop has to make is to give up most of the direct and intimate cure of souls. He recalled an occasion during the war when he was summoned to Westminster. When he arrived he found Cardinal Hinsley in his room trying on a new mitre. Playfully the cardinal placed it on Heenan's head. Cardinal Hinsley said "One day you will wear a mitre of your own and you will find it a crown of thorns". Many of his friends and other well-wishers sent letters and telegrams of congratulations. One in particular, from Ronnie Knox, gave him great pleasure. Monsignor Knox expressed his satisfaction and went on "I don't suppose you will enjoy being a bishop but at least you can enjoy giving pleasure to your friends by becoming a bishop".

It was difficult for him to prepare for his consecration, which was scheduled for 12 March, the feast of St. Gregory the Great. His sister Mary was in a critical condition suffering from leukaemia. She had been treated in the London Hospital. Despite the skill of the physicians, her condition deteriorated gravely towards the close of the year 1950. She was so clearly beyond the help of doctors that her family decided after Christmas to remove her from the London Hospital to St. Andrew's Hospital which was in the care of the Blue Nuns. Her family decided that since she could not be cured it was kinder to let the Sisters prepare her for death.

His sister was a woman of extraordinary determination. She astonished the Sisters at St. Andrew's by announcing her intention of being present in Leeds Cathedral for her brother's consecration as bishop. The doctors told her that a four-hour train journey would kill her, so she persuaded her husband to hire a private plane. The weather intervened and the plane could not take off, so she decided to go by train afterall accompanied by a doctor and a nurse. She arrived in Leeds exhausted but in high spirit. The following day she had to be carried up the steps at the entrance to the cathedral by her husband, ample cushions were placed in her pew and she survived the long ceremony without disaster. The next day she received a blessing from the apostolic delegate who had been the chief celebrant at the consecration. He had been a student in Rome during the pontificate of Pope Pius X. He brought a relic of Pope Pius with which he blessed Mary Reynolds. From that day she began to improve. To the amazement of her doctors and the immense plesure of her family she eventually made such a remarkable recovery that in subsequent years she was present at the ordination of her youngest son Michael, was able to travel to America for the marriage of her eldest son Brian. She was also present in St. Peter's Rome, for the canonisation of St. Pius X.

After the death or translation of the bishop a diocese is in the care of a vicar capitular. Canon law decrees that nothing may be changed while the See is vacant. Monsignor Hawkswell the vicar capitular interpreted the rule literally. When Monsignor Hawkeswell showed Bishop Heenan the list of matters urgently awaiting decision, the new bishop invited him to be his vicar general He also asked the old monsignor to give him the history of the diocese as a prelude to advising him on policy. The vicar general was nearly blind but his mind and memory were clear. The new bishop listened patiently while the old monsignor told him the story of the last fifty years in Yorkshire.

He began with Bishop Gordon who became Bishop of Leeds in 1890 and died just before the first world war. William Gordon, he said, had been known to hit children with his crozier if they did not answer his questions at confirmation. Heenan remembered from his researches for his biography of Cardinal Hinsley that Bishop Gordon was an irascible man. Hinsley was the founder and first headmaster of St. Bede's grammar school in Bradford, he became so aggrieved by Bishop Gordon's treatment that he left not only the school but the diocese. He was accepted by the Bishop of Southwark and made parish priest of Sydenham. For the last six years of his life Bishop Gordon had been unable to administer the diocese and was given a Coadjutor. Joseph Cowgill was consecrated bishop in 1905 and lived until 1936. When he died at the age of seventy-six he had been in charge of the diocese for over thirty years.

Bishop Cowgill was known as the children's bishop. Before going on his daily walk he used to fill his pockets with sweets to distribute to his little friends. Naturally they adored him. He was even more beloved by those children to whom he gave not just sweets but a home. In the early years of this century poverty was regarded as culpable. When sickness, unemployment or death struck a family there was no social security payments except the humiliating help of the poor-law guardians. The Cowgill Home for orphans was the fruit of his solicitude. It was natural for the children's bishop to be father of the poor. The Bishop himself, Monsignor Hawkeswell said, was something of a child and he found it difficult to issue an order and quite impossible to give a reprimand. When a priest was guilty of a misdemeanour the Bishop would send for Monsignor Hawkswell. The priest in question would then be admonished by the vicar general in the presence of the silent Bishop. In Leeds the senior clergy took over the authority Bishop Cowgill was reluctant to exercise. They even went so far as to appoint or dismiss junior clergy without reference to the Bishop. Towards the end of Bishop Cowgill's life there was a breakdown of ecclesiastical authority which would have been disastrous but for the highly dependable character of the clergy who were either dogged Yorkshiremen or tough Irishmen. Between them they held the diocese together.

Before the First World War the diocese had been startled by a curates' strike. When Heenan arrived in Leeds the episode was remembered only as a prank but at the time it must have seemed like incipient anarchy. According to Monsignor Hawkswell, a small number of young priests met to discuss their financial misery. Their annual stipend of forty pounds was inadequate even when supplemented by the meagre offerings of parishioners on such occasions as weddings. Poverty was widespread in the industrial centres where most Catholics sought a livelihood. The young priests decided that on a certain Sunday they would refuse to make the outdoor collection. The token strike was crushed with such speed and severity. Each young priest was banished for several years to another diocese or even another country. At a subsequent diocesan synod legislation was introduced forbidding any meeting of curates to take place without leave. By 1951 those involved in the famous strike had all become venerable canons highly critical of undisciplined young curates.

Monsignor Hawkeswell like everyone who had known him recalled Bishop Cowgill with genuine love and affection. Through his priestly example and palpable love of his flock he achieved a success which might have eluded a mere administrator or strict disciplinarian. His successor, Bishop Poskitt, coming from the diocese of Middlesbrough, found Leeds in a healthy spiritual state. As a bishop he was little known and avoided social occasions. Even when visiting parishes to administer Confirmation he rarely stayed in the presbytery much longer than it took to drink a cup of tea. Although a reserved man he was much loved and respected. He was an excellent administrator and a shrewd judge of men. When Heenan took over he found the diocese in excellent order.

The new bishop found after several day reading reports and correspondence that a number of priests had been in conflict with authority, he also found that a large number of priests had been curates in the same parish for ten, sometimes fifteen years. It was clear to him that such curates would become better parish priests if they had been given experience of more than one parish. Heenan moved about fifty or more priests and in the period of disruption he received a number of requests from parish priests of long standing to be considered for a new post. It resembled a large movement of troops and became known as the autumn manoeuvres. Leeds became known as 'the cruel see', priests were alleged to have greeted each other not with "How are you?" but with "Where are you?".

Many years later Heenan himself admitted that he acted imprudently. He knew he was right to make the changes but most unwise to make them so soon after arriving in the diocese. Later experience taught him that little is lost by delay in dealing with human problems and the exercise of judgement requires reflection. The modern bishop is much nearer to his priests and people. The establishment of elected senates of priests and diocesan pastoral councils has made it easier for clergy and laity to make their views known.

Bishop Heenan was busy making his visitations throughout the Leeds diocese and administering Confirmation. However in 1952 he accepted an invitation to go to the Barcelona Eucharistic Congress and during his stay in Spain he met Cardinal Gilroy who persuaded him to speak at the Eucharistic Congree to be held in Sydney the following year. He also took on extensive travels visiting troops in Korea, Malaya and Japan.

Broadcasting and writing was an integral part of Bishop Heenans life. On more than one occasion he was embroiled in controversy. During one broadcast he was speaking about the loss of religious freedom in countries of Eastern Europe. During his broadcast he said: "You see, there are millions of Christians now suffering persecution who would have laughed at you if you had warned them a few years ago that night would fall. Bulgaria, Poland, Rumania, Chechoslovakia, Hungary, the Ukraine, the Baltic States, they all had their Christian schools and full freedom of worship the other day. But not now. We are so used to tolerance for minorities in Britain that we take it for granted. They don't everywhere – in Spain, for example, and in Northern Ireland" Telephone lines to the B.B.C. were choked with calls. An official complaint was lodged without delay. The Northern Ireland government sent a telegram of protest not only to the Director General of the B.B.C. but also to the British Prime Minister.

He was accused by a spokesman of the B.B.C. in Belfast of having altered the script prior to the broadcast when the producer's back was turned in order to launch an attack on the Northern Ireland government. It now seems incredible that such a furore was aroused by the short sentence "they do not take tolerance for granted in Northern Ireland" which today would be regarded as a serious understatement. While the controversy continued with customary ferocity in Northern Ireland Heenan tried to preserve a sense of proportion. It was of course impossible to let the matter rest. The B.B.C. by apologising for what he had said, created the impression that he had behaved in an underhand way. The accusation made by the B.B.C. spokesman in Belfast that when left alone in the studio he had made a surreptitious interpolation had been widely reported. The issue now was not whether tolerance is taken for granted in Northern Ireland but whether Heenan was lacking in integrity. Even if he had been willing to pursue it no further the question had now gone beyond the personal level. The Catholic community and, irrespective of their religious beliefs, Yorkshire people were angry with the B.B.C. Letters appeared in the national press and in great numbers in Yorkshire papers. It was felt that the B.B.C. had slandered the

Bishop to appease Lord Brooksborough, the prime minister of Northern Ireland. The B.B.C. was challenged to withdraw its apology.

Before correspondence began in the press he wrote to Francis House, head of the religious division of the B.B.C.

My dear Francis,

Needless to say, I am very sorry about the upset over Saturday's talk. The press reporters tell me that the B.B.C. intends to hold an enquiry. I imagine that this is unlikely but I thought you might want to know the facts.

Before giving them, however, I must express surprise that the B.B.C. made the regrettable apology after the one o'clock news. The apology, as reported, does me less than justice. But apart from that, the B.B.C. should not so quickly lay blame publicly on those who are serving them. Such a thing would not happen, for example, in the civil service. I must add that I do not imagine the Religious Division to be responsible for the apology. I am quite sure that you, personally, had nothing to do with it.

Her are the facts:

On Friday I was asked by the B.B.C. to reconsider the following passage: "Anyone who tells you that there is still religious freedom in those countries is either a knave or a fool. That is either he does not know the facts or he is a liar. The Church is enslaved wherever Communism is in control."

For the record it is important to say explicitly what objections were raised. (1) The B.B.C. felt that I should insert the word 'full' before 'religious' so that it would read: "Anyone who tells you that there is full religious freedom" (2) Knave, fool and liar were all felt by the B.B.C. to be rather too strong. (3) The B.B.C. objected to the sentence – "The Church is enslaved wherever Communism is in control" – on the ground that it was against B.B.C. policy to condemn Communism. It was explained that it is part of the general understanding between the B.B.C. and political parties that no attack on a Party will be allowed unless in a specifically Party broadcast.

I responded with the following:

(1) I rejected without hesitation, the suggestion to insert 'full' before the word 'religious'. I said that the only qualifying word I would use was 'real'. (2) I agreed to think about the offending epithets – knave, fool and liar. (3) It was the B.B.C.'s anxiety to be fair to the Communists that caused most trouble. I said on the phone that I would be willing to insert 'atheistic' before 'communism' since the political party does not call itself by that name. I said that I would think the whole thing over during the day.

Now comes the question of my personal integrity. The public has been told one story by the B.B.C. and another by me. The B.B.C. says that I made a last-minute interpolation. Belfast goes further and says that as soon as the producer left me alone I took out my pencil and stealthily changed the script. Let me assure you that mine was no last-minute interpolation. The B.B.C.'s anxiety to be fair to the Communist Party set up a train of thought in my mind. I do not, for a moment, accept that a broadcaster should tone down references to religious persecution for fear of wounding Commnists in England. But, at least, it is a point of view. So I began to question whether it was fair to talk of religious persecution in Communist controlled countries while making no reference to other kinds of intolerance elsewhere, Spain immediately came to mind. I know that there is no religious persecution there but there is intolerance of minorities. So I decided to mention Spain – a State associated in the public mind with Catholics. But if Spain – why not Northen Ireland where also there is intolerance? So, having had all day to think about it, on Friday night I deleted the paragraph to which objections had been taken and inserted the following:

"We are so used to tolerance for minorities in England that we take it for granted. They don't elsewhere – in Spain, for example, and Northern Ireland. But their intolerance is nothing compared with the savage treatment of believers where atheistic Communists are in control".

These are the facts. I expected that Falangists in Spain and Orangemen in Northern Ireland would resent reference to intolerance. But I must ask you to believe that when I broadcast on Saturday I did not think that there was any dispute about the *fact* of intolerance either in Spain or Northern Ireland. The only controversy, I imagined, concerned the causes and extent of intolerance.

I must say once more how sorry I am that you, personally and Father Agnellus have been involved in this unpleasantness. As I have said, it never occurred to me that my remark would cause offence to any but fanatics. Perhaps it didn't. However, this puts you in a difficult position regarding my own services to the B.B.C. I am due to record a programme on Thursday in the Leeds Studio. I shall also be ready to resign from the Central Religious Advisory Council, if you think that I would no longer command respect in that assembly. Please believe that I am ready to do whatever is best for the cause we both have at heart.

I am, Yours sincerely,
+ John C. Heenan, Bishop of Leeds

Francis House replied and expressed his regret that a misunderstanding over the details of the affair had caused so much trouble and distress. The storm rumbled on for eight or nine days.

Another historic event that year was the televised Pontifical High Mass from St. Anne's Cathedral, the first time Mass had been shown on television in this country. While Bishop Heenan was at Leeds he continued his writings and occasional broadcasts. At the local level he was also intrumental in working with a team of Catholic teachers on preparing new text books of

Christian doctrine for use in local schools. For nearly three years the teachers of Leeds diocese gave up their Saturdays and holidays to work on the old catechism and new textbooks. What had begun as a private initiative in Leeds soon attracted the attention and interest of the Catholic community in England. Heenan agreed to put the research at the disposal of the whole country and the hierarchy appointed Bishop Beck of Salford (and later Archbishop of Liverpool) and Bishop Rudderham of Clifton to join Heenan in this catechetical.

The original group had been formed to produce not a catechism but a set of books for the various age groups. Subsequently three books were published *My Faith* for infants, *My Lord and My God* for juniors and *Our Faith* for seniors. The bishops knew that this would take several years and they asked Heenan, as chairman of the committee, for an interim revision of the catechism which could be ready in two or three years. Consultations over the the comparatively minor task of revising the existing catechism were held with catechists in every diocese. The result was a mass of documents which eventually were handed to the national catechetical centre. The *Revised Catechism of Christian Doctrine* was published in the autumn of 1958.

In the summer of 1956 Bishop Heenan visited the West Indies. Cardinal Griffin had been in failing health for some years, he suffered his last and fatal heart attack on 20 Auguust. In December William Godfrey was translated from Liverpool to succeed Cardinal Griffin.In May 1957 Bishop Heenan was translated from Leeds to Liverpool.

The enthronment took place on the Feast of Our Lady of Mount Carmel, 16 July 1958. There was room for so few in the pro-cathedral that an open air service and rally was held on the following Sunday at Brownlow Hill on the site of the future metropolitan cathedral. A message from Pope Pius XII addressed to the new archbishop but intended for the priests and people of Liverpool was read at the rally by Monsignor Adamson, the vicar general:

"The Holy Father expresses the prayerful hope that your zealous apostolic activity will reap an even more abundant harvest of spiritual fruits among the flock now entrusted to your pastoral care. The reputation which the Catholics of the Metropolitan See of Liverpool have won for themselves gives every reason to hope that Your Grace's ministry among them will be fruitful. The people of Liverpool, and especially the workers, have always been noted for their living faith and unswerving loyalty to the Catholic Church. For this reason they have been particularly dear to the heart of the Vicar of Christ. The pontiff's purpose in relaxing the regulations for the Eucharistic fast and in giving permission for evening Masses was to enable workers to attend Mass regularly and receive Holy Communion more frequently. He feels confident that the working people of Liverpool will prove anew their loyalty to the Church by availing of these facilities and by renewing and intensifying their devotion to the Mass and the Blessed Sacrament".

In Liverpool the traditional division of the city's poor was Orange and Green. During the early years of this century their simmering bitterness used to burst into flame annually on 12 July, the day of the Orange parade. By the late 1950's the Orange parades had become no more than colourful processions of colourfully dressed children and adoring parents. Rivalry between Protestant and Catholic was fostered by segregation. Catholics avoided close contacts with Protestants through fear of mixed marriages. This was the common outlook of Catholics everywhere in Britain but in Liverpool abhorrence of mixed marriages was obsessive. Until the death of Archbishop Whiteside in 1921 it was virtually impossible for Catholics to obtain dispensations to marry Protestants. Later dispensations could be obtained but mixed marriages were still regarded in the words of the old catechism as 'unlawful and pernicious'. On the occasion of a mixed marriage some priests would keep the bridal couple waiting up to half an hour. The ceremony would be brief, brusque and cheerless. After the second world war it became easier for Liverpool Catholics to obtain a dispensation for a mixed marriage but there was little relaxation of the restrictions imposed on the ceremony itself. The marriage had to take place at a side altar, the organ was not played, no singing was permitted, the candles were not lit and the whole atmosphere was chilly.

Heenan felt very strongly that these rules should be relaxed. Liverpool was not the only diocese in the country which maintained these conditions, he had seen in his own parish the severity with which his parish priests had imposed the conditions on his parishioners who asked for dispensation for a mixed marriage. Sensitive to the devotion the priests had to the memory of Archbishop Whiteside, he did not set aside the old rules immediately on arrival in the diocese. Six months after his enthronement he addressed a letter to the clergy, the following is an extract:

"I am convinced that once a dispensation is granted the marriage should be performed in such a way that the couple and their families will not feel slighted. A bride, in particular, sets great store by all the details surrounding her wedding. She feels affronted if she has to be married at a small altar obscurely sited. The organ has an exaggerated importance in the estimation of the bridal couple, their family and friends. The fact is that to have been married at the side altar and to have been denied the organ can become an abiding source of contention after marriage. The Catholic sometimes becomes bitter and the non-Catholic hostile to the Church and disinclined to keep promises.

"Such unhappy results do not always follow as a result of a sombre ceremony at a mixed marriage but even practicing Catholics find a ceremony stripped of joy a source of resentment against the Church. Some priests whose opinions I value greatly may deplore any relaxation of the present regulations. While respecting their views I must act according to my conscience. I have therefore decided to allow mixed marriages to take place at the High Altar and the organ to be played before and after the ceremony. This ruling supersedes Appendix V of the last Synod. The Chapter knows that this is not a hasty decision. I raised the question with the canons in July and for six months I have given it prayerful consideration. Having hitherto refused to make exceptions I now find it impossible to continue to deny privileges which, despite the obvious risks, I believe to be for the greater good of souls".

Since the Vatican Council decrees on ecumenism and religious liberty many grievances of non-Catholics have been met. Even today it is impossible to find any perfectly satisfactory solution to the problems involved in mixed marriages but progress has been possible through the good will of both Catholic and non-Catholic authorities.

Pius XII died on 9 October 1958. Heenan had a great personal affection for him, and on the evening of the Pope's death he broadcast a tribute on radio newsreel. The following is an extract:

"To the world at large, the Pope stood as a figure apart, speaking words of peace, invoking blessings upon a stricken world. But to Catholics he was naturally much more. His wisdom brought the practice of their faith into line with the stress of modern life. One of the most far reaching of his reforms was his entirely new approach to the discipline of fasting before receiving Holy Communion.

"His was always an original approach, for example, he authorised bishops to arrange for the celebration of Mass in the evening as well as in the morning. Thousands of people who could never be at Mass except on Sundays are now able to enjoy the spiritual benefits of frequent Mass, and Holy Communion.

"He was not only original but courageous in his enterprise. To take one isolated example, he allowed a convert clergyman to be ordained priest, although a married man. Another example of his enterprise was his readiness to allow the age-old Latin texts to be translated in the administration of the Sacraments so that people might understand better. Catholics, at least, were anxious to know if the Pope's successor would allow experiments or return to conservative ways. One thing is certain that any modern Pope will follow the example of Pope Pius XII in thinking and speaking in a way which non-Catholics can appreciate. The affection and respect which the late Pope won from millions who did not share his faith was the greatest triumph of his pontificate".

Pius XII had also begun to reduce the domination of Italian cardinals, he could see the necessity for those prelates working in the Vatican, the centre of the Universal Church to be truly international in their representation. Paul VI, some years later put all the Sacred Congregations into the hands of foreigners.

The world was astounded when the Conclave elected Angelo Giuseppe Roncalli as Pope John XXIII. That he was an Italian was no surprise, but he was old and fat and everyone realised that he was a stop-gap. The last stop-gap had been Cardinal Pecci almost seventy years old at the time of his election. As Pope Leo XIII he became the greatest social reformer among modern Popes, he died in 1903 at the age of ninety-three.

Archbishop Heenan was very impressed when he met the new Pope. He said to Heenan that he was unfit to be Pope, that he was not a diplomat like Pius XII or a scholar like Pius XI. He kept asking Our Lord why He had put him in this position. He said that the only thing he had to offer was himself. He talked to Heenan about his desire to welcome all to their father's house, that there was no profit in controversy. The only way of winning people is by showing that you really love them. He talked about how the Church undervalues the Precious Blood of Jesus Christ. "The Protestants have something to teach us here" he said, " We have devotion to the Sacred Heart and the Blessed Sacrament but we rarely talk about the Precious Blood which is the price Jesus paid for our Redemption".

Pope John XXIII will always be associated with work for Christian Unity. Heenan was involved as a member and, later, vice-president of the Secretariat for Promoting Christian Unity under Cardinal Bea. In September 1959 the names of ten members to serve on the commission was announced. Although established at the same time as the various commissions to prepare for the Second Vatican Council to be opened in 1962, the Secretariat for Unity was expected to carry on its work independently of the Council and to remain a permanent department of the Holy See after the Council was disbanded.

Archbishop Heenan soon realised that he required the help of a second English bishop. He argued that the importance of the Anglican Church in the ecumenical context justified his request even though some countries had no representation at all. Pope John agreed and asked Heenan if he had a bishop in mind. Heenan told the Pope that he would prefer a bishop with wide experience of non-Catholics who was not a convert or of Irish stock. Heenan felt it would be tactless to offer Anglicans an ex-Anglican as a Catholic spokesman. He gave the name Thomas Holland who had recently been consecrated co-adjutor Bishop of Portsmouth.

Shortly afterwards on 31 October 1960 the momentous news of the visit of the Archbishop of Canterbury to Pope John was released. Heenan was full of admiration at the courage of Dr Fisher's gesture and imagination for him to visit the Vatican. He was not a notable ecumenical figure, he had an impatience amounting to contempt for 'papalistic Anglicans'. Heenan told the press: "Courtesy translated into the language of religion means charity. The primate's visit to the Pope is significant because it shows that differences of theology need not prevent mutual respect and love" The result of this visit was far greater and more lasting than Archbishop Fisher foresaw. By seeking an audience with Pope John he healed a breach extending over four centuries. He set the seal on the trust and affection with which Pope John had come to be universally regarded. Pope John himself was unaffectedly delighted to welcome the Archbishop of Canterbury but some of the Vatican prelates were less enchanted. They had no protocal to guide them. Catholic ecumenism being still embryonic there was no question of a joint service. It was not clear about the correct manner of receiving the head of another Church. Caution was the prevailing guide. Even photography was strictly and needlessly rationed. The Archbishop of Canterbury had as the main objective of his visit to reciprocate on behalf of Anglicans the goodwill so abundantly shown by Pope John.

Cardinal Bea, a German Jesuit, was the first president of the Secretariat for Christian Unity. He had been provincial superior of the German Jesuits and had experience of Lutherans and Calvinists. He was a close friend of Pope John who had complete trust in his judgement on ecumenical matters. He had also been close to Pius XII who gave the first impetus to Catholic ecumenism.

There was little enthusiasm for ecumenical enterprise among English Catholics before the Second Vatican Council and there could be few countries in which ecumenism presented more problems than in England. For the laity, the only opportunity for entering non-Catholic places of worship was at funerals and weddings. Priests of earlier generations had been trained during their long seminary course with the objective in mind of the conversion of England. It was theologically difficult and psychologically impossible to persuade such priests to approach Protestants without any intention of converting them. For Catholics the central problem of ecumenism is how to conduct honest discussions while insisting that the Catholic Church is the true Church of Christ. The purpose of ecumenism is the eventual reunion of all Christians in one Catholic Church. This seems at first sight to involve submission to the Church of Rome but ecumenists rightly claim that is only an assumption. By study and prayer true ecumenists try to find good in others and faults in themselves. What is true of individual Christians is true also of ecclesial communities. Through honest self-criticism both Catholic and Protestants learn that their religion does not require them to uphold rigidly all its traditional attitudes. Before the Second World War for example,

Catholics regarded it as sinful to take part in a non-Catholic religious service. The Catholic Church itself has made that rule of faith redundant. The Church has a completely changed outlook on sharing worship with non-Catholics.

Another example of the altered emphasis in Catholic teaching is to be found in the exercise of authority in the church. The First Vatican Council in 1870 was brought to an abrupt halt by the outbreak of the Franco-Prussian war. At that time the Council was half-way through its agenda and had dealt only with the question of papal authority. episcopal authority was still to be discussed. In the event, the infallibility and primacy of the Pope were promulgated without any complimentary statement regarding bishops. During the Second Vatican Council the doctrine of episcopal collegiality was developed. This put the authority of the Bishop of Rome in the context of the episcopal college of which he is head. This makes acceptance of the special position of the Pope as Chief Pastor of the Church and Patriarch of the West more easily acceptable to Protestants.

Papal infallibility is one of the most easily misunderstood dogmas of the Church of Rome. Theoretically the Pope could, of course, define a doctrine in an encyclical, sermon, or radio talk. In fact no Pope would attempt to define doctrine except after consultation with the bishops of the whole Church. The only example of a proclamation of dogma in modern times is the definition of the Assumption of the Blessed Virgin by Pope Pius XII. This particular definition was, in fact, superflous. No section of the Catholic Church, East or West, has ever denied the Assumption. Since Anglo-Saxon times it has been one of the major feasts of the year.

Heenan invited Cardinal Bea to come to England, as the greatest living authority on Catholic ecumenism, to be chief speaker at a conference of priests at Heythrop College. Every bishop and major religious superior was asked to send a priest as delegate. Nobody could doubt the humility and learning of the German Cardinal but not having lived in England he was obviously far from understanding the phenomenon of the Established Church. Like most foreigners he had a picture of the typical Anglican which applied only to high churchmen. He had yet to learn that the branches of the Church of England range from Anglo Catholics to Evangelical Protestants, with a wide and diverse spectrum and understanding of the nature of the Eucharist.

This visit of Cardinal Bea to England did not dispel the suspicions of some English bishops that he was responsible for the slow progress of the cause of canonisation of the Elizabethan martyrs. Cardinal Bea was thought to have been persuaded by the Archbishop of Canterbury to obstruct the cause in the interests of ecumenism.

The priests who assembled at Heythrop for the conference were not all enthusiastic ecumenists. They had been sent to Heythrop to make sure that in every diocese and religious community there would be priests with some knowledge of ecumenism. It was assumed that after a week in the company of Cardinal Bea they would learn Pope John's mind on Christian unity and be ready to follow it.

The papers of the Heythrop Ecumenical Conference were printed in a paperback *Christian Unity: a Catholic View* (Sheed & Ward, London 1962).

Shortly afterwards Heenan sparked a great controversy following a sermon he gave in Northern Ireland. He had gone to lay the foundation stone of a new Cistercian abbey at Portglenone. He preached at a Mass celebrated in the open air in order that friendly Protestant neighbours might attend as it was inconceivable for them to enter a Catholic place of worship. In the course of his sermon of which every word was meticulously chosen, he said that the friendship which had sprung up between the monks and the Protestant farmers did credit to them all: "You are all brothers in Christ", he said. "Remember that being a Christian is more important than being Catholic or Protestant". The sermon was widely reported in the press and Heenan was interviewed on Ulster Television. He received a huge amount of protest mail from clergy and laity. The context of his offending statement was clarified when a few months later he gave certain rules for ecumenical conduct in a pastoral letter. The last of the eight rules was: "While fostering Christian unity we must never forget our duty of bringing all men to a knowledge of the truth. Remember that the tragedy of England is not that many Christians are not Catholics but that so many citizens have no religion at all.

When Heenan became Archbishop of Liverpool one of the outstanding issues was the building of the new cathedral of Christ the King. Archbishop Keating translated from Northampton to the See of Liverpool in 1921 had resolved to erect a cathedral in memory of the much revered Archbishop Whiteside. By the time of his death Archbishop Keating had collected one hundred and twenty thousand pounds for the project. He had also begun to negotiate the purchase of the old wharehouse site on Brownlow Hill. His successor, Archbishop Downey, acquired the site a year later for the price of one hundred thousand pounds. He also appointed Sir Edwin Lutyens, the most famous architect of the day to design the new cathedral.

Work on the crypt of the metropolitan cathedral began in the 1930's. Despite the estimated cost of three million pounds and the prospect that the cathedral would not be completed before the middle of the twenty-first century the clergy and laity were enthusiastic. Dr Downey took the plans to Rome and Pope Pius XI gave them his approval. The Second World War held up the building. Sir Edwin Lutyens died and his plans were set aside. Dr Downey chose Adrian Scott, the brother of Giles Scott, architect of the Anglican cathedral. In 1953 after Dr Downey's death, Monsignor Godfrey was appointed to Liverpool and decided on grounds of cost to abandon the old design. Adrian Scott was instructed to draw plans for an entirely new building to be erected over the now half-completed crypt.

Archbishop Godfrey was only three years in Liverpool. This was not long enough for him to influence the development. He commissioned new drawings but never reached the stage of inviting contractors to submit tenders for the actual building. Within weeks of arriving in Liverpool Archbishop Heenan resolved to concentrate all effort on completing the crypt and putting it into daily use as a temporary cathedral. The opening of the crypt was made the occasion of a week of celebration. The highlight was the Pontifical High Mass sung by Archbishop Heenan and over four hundred priests from all parts of the archdiocese took part. This event brought fresh enthusiasm for a new cathedral. Some people thought that the crypt itself was sufficient, but Heenan realised that all the effort which had gone into raising funds over so many years must be honoured. However the costs of building a cathedral based either on the original or amended designs were now prohibitive. Heenan came up with the suggestion that a competition should be held inviting designs for a cathedral that could be built for £1m at 1959 prices. The building could then be embelished by future generations. The winner of the competition was Frederick Gibberd, he was later knighted on completion of the cathedral. It was left to Archbishop Beck, Heenan's successor to find the money to pay for its completion.

Angelo Joseph Roncalli was crowned Pope John XXIII on 4 November 1958. Three months later on 25 January 1959 he disclosed his intention of calling an ecumenical council. Pope John could not possibly have foreseen the result of his decision to hold a Council.

The two great events between sessions of the Council were the death of Pope John and the election of Pope Paul. There were few alternatives to Cardinal Montini who was known to have been a close friend of Pope John. He was also a close friend of Cardinal Bea and an enthusiastic supporter of ecumenical work. There was universal rejoicing when Pope Paul VI was elected, there was no hint of impending disintegration. Within a few short years neo-modernists and Catholic anarchists revolted against his leadership. The revolt began not as a personal attack on Pope Paul but in a rejection of prayer. The Religious Orders were the first to give up prayer. Inevitably this spread to the seminaries and last of all to the laity. Only stalwarts continued to make thanksgiving after Holy Communion and to keep hold of their prayer books and rosaries. The roots of the revolt lay in a loss of faith in everything supernatural. The attack on the priesthood was subtle and sustained. Catholic priests had hitherto been outwardly distinguished from others by celibacy and clerical dress. It was now argued – as the sixteenth-century reformers had argued – that celibacy is unnatural. Clerical dress was attacked on the grounds that it separated the priest from his people. Similar arguments were used against the religious habit which was said to alienate the nun from the children, the sick and the poor.

Catholics both lay and clerical reacted with dismay to Pope Paul's decision to leave unchanged the teaching of the Church on contraception. Theological revolutionaries, mainly in Europe, but also in North America, claimed that the Council was a failure because it had not really changed the Catholic religion. Selective theology under the name of pluralism became the fashion. Post-conciliar churches were built like Lutheran or Calvinistic chapels with no provision for adoration of the Blessed Sacrament. Mysteries, miracles and devotion to our Lady were discarded. Many lay theologians left the Church while new style priests and nuns began to practice the evangelical virtues unhampered by vows.

Cardinal Godfrey died at the age of seventy-three. He was a gentle prayerful man who made no great impact on the non-Catholic public. William Godfrey made little mark as a bishop largely because during his robust years he was in the diplomatic service of the Holy See. He was too old to establish himself as a national figure but he was very successful in the more important and much more difficult task of giving his priests and people an example of personal holiness. This was achieved not by what he said – he was a dull speaker- but by what he was.

There is always widespread speculation when the See of Westminster falls vacant. The reason is that although the strength of the Catholic Church is greatest in the north of England it is to Westminster that Catholics and the general public look for an official Catholic voice. Canonically there is no primatial See in the Catholic Church in England but the diocese of Westminster is so regarded. The apostolic delegate consults not only the bishops of the Westminster province but all the bishops of England and Wales. He also tries to ascertain the views of clergy and laity. The method of appointing bishops is not perfect but the alternative of a straight election would probably be much worse. Elections are satisfactory if the candidate is to hold office for a short period before being subject again to the judgement of the electorate. That is the basis of parliamentary democracy. A bishop is not part of a democratic machine nor does he receive power from his priests or people. He is appointed by the Pope acting in the name of the Church. The Holy See is aware that in the post-conciliar Church more consultation of priests and laity is desirable, but the ultimate choice will be left to the Holy See. The Church will never again leave the choice to the state. Although the Pope nominates every bishop it is obvious that he can know few candidates personally. He is advised by the Congregation of Bishops which meets in the Vatican six times a year to consider names proposed for the epicopate.

When a See falls vacant in England the archbishop or, if the metropolitan See itself is vacant, the senior bishop of the province presides at a meeting of the cathedral Chapter. At this meeting three names (the *terna*) are chosed by secret vote. These names are communicated to the bishops of the province who send them with their comments and, if they wish, with additional names to the apostolic delegate. It is his duty to obtain confidential views on each candidate from those in the best position to assess his qualifications and character.

Towards the end of August 1963, Archbishop Heenan was informed by telephone of Pope Paul's decision to send him to Westminster. He was greeted on arrival at Euston Station in London by a crowd of over ten thousand people. There was an equally large crowd when he arrived at Westminster.

His early years there were overshadowed by the Second Vatican Council, and later his energies were spent on the struggle to deal with its practical effects, and the expectations the Council created. Monsignor Derek Worlock, remained as private secretary to the new archbishop for six months, it was clear he was only to oversee the transition. There was some friction between the secretary and the archbishop. Worlock had established himself as a stong personality and an effective administrator. He had also gained a reputation beyond Westminster. He had made a considerable impact as the efficient behind the scenes co-ordinator. Despite Heenan's desire to make a fresh start, he required Worlock's unique experience about the Vatican Council's matters. Heenan was another incredibly hard working man he had a sense of purpose he had a zest for new ideas, was quick to take action, yet he was an intelligent and shrewed operator. He implemented the Council's decisions, introducing English in the liturgy, re-ordering churches, encouraging priests and laity against the criticisms from some charismatic theologians who were looking to diminish all authority in the Church.

The divisions caused by the encyclical *Humanae Vitae* in the Catholic Church when many English Catholics either left the Church or rejected the directive from Rome was particularly difficult for Heenan. He was particularly dismayed by the exodus of priests renouncing their vows. These disappointments led to increasingly poor health but despite the difficulties within the Church, Heenan worked well with Government. He had a particularly good relationship with Harold Wilson and strove to influence the Prime Minister in advance of the 1967 Abortion Act which legalised provision for women to end their pregnancies. However, despite his efforts the campaign against the Act was unsuccessful.

His final years were full of disappoinment and increasingly he suffered with poor health. Some say he died a broken man. He had seen through the dramatic changes in the liturgy and the life of the Church in general since the

Cardinal John Carmel Heenan

Second Vatican Council. He was the transitional figure between the old guard and the new, he passed over the leadership leaving the Church more intergrated into the mainstream of national life than it had ever known before.

Extracts from: *Not the Whole Truth* and *A Crown of Thorns* by Cardinal John C.Heenan published by Burns Oates & Washbourne, London

Chapter Seventeen

Cardinal Basil Hume

AT the end of Cardinal Heenan's prelacy, the image and character of the Catholic Church in England and Wales was set to change. Heenan's personality dominated the Catholic Church in this country but even he was swept along in the tide of change.

When Cardinal Heenan died, the apostolic delegate, Archbishop Bruno Heim, had, on the initiative of Cardinal Heenan, worked on the future needs of the Church in England and Wales. On the question of succession, he had collected a sizeable list of possible successors to Heenan. The choice of Archbishop Heim was Abbot Basil Hume. They both shared much of the same philosophy as Pope John XXIII.

In the 125 years since the restoration of the Catholic Hierarchy in 1850, the mission of the Catholic Church was to convert England back to ancient Catholicism. Unity was not on the agenda. The Second Vatican Council changed that view. Catholics in England and Wales realised that changes in direction were not only necessary but essential. It would require a very special kind of leadership to ensure that any change would not be too radical and yet be acceptable to both liberal and conservative minds.

On 25 March 1976, just two months into the final twenty-five years of the Millennium, Basil Hume, Abbot of Ampleforth was consecrated Archbishop in Westminster Cathedral at the age of 53. A few months later Pope Paul VI raised him to the cardinalate. This quite, unassuming monk had spent the past forty-three years at Ampleforth. From the age of ten at Gilling Castle, the prep school of Ampleforth College, then after two years he moved to the junior house. In September 1941 the young George Hume entered the monastery at Ampleforth as Brother Basil.

George Haliburton Hume, was born on 2 March 1923 the third child of William Errington Hume and his wife Marie Elizabeth. On his Protestant father's side were distinguished men from the medical profession and a number of Anglican divines. His father William became one of the most eminent physicians in the north of England. His French mother's family comprised high-ranking army officers, and industrial entrepreneurs, her father had been the French military attache in Madrid.

At the outbreak of war in 1914, William joined the Royal Army Medical Corps and was posted to France. Very soon he was appointed Consulting Physician to the entire 1st Army in France. He was billeted in Winiereux, and his landlady was teaching a pretty girl called Marie Elizabeth Tisieyre. William and Mimi, as she was called, fell in love and despite their difference in age, nationality, language and religion, they married in November 1918.

They returned to Newcastle and William resumed his rigorous life as a consulting physician, specialising in cardiology. Madeleine, Christine, George and Frances were all born in the space of five years. John arrived four years later. All the children grew up speaking French as naturally as English. The children had an extremely happy upbringing. George was a keen sportsman and football was a special favourite, along with his father they were passionate Newcastle United supporters. William Hume was a keen golfer, but later he took up fishing which George shared with equal enthusiasm.

George was a happy boy he had the talent to amuse and was always able to entertain the rest of the family and make them laugh. The children often performed plays, dressing up for variety shows and charades. At Christmas time they were taken to the Theatre Royal or the Empire Theatre to see a pantomime or shows like Peter Pan.

On Sundays the Humes occasionally attended the large Dominican church as a change from their own church St. Andrew's. George loved St. Dominic's with its beautiful liturgy and excellent choir. It was the Dominicans who influenced the young George and from those early years he was determined to become a priest.

There was no great show of religion in the Hume household. Mimi respected William's Protestant scruples, and would not exhibit pious objects, holy pictures, statues or holy water fonts. Grace was not said at meal times. William was not a church-goer, nor was he an agnostic. Mimi said that he knelt to say his prayers each night and later in life the vicar of Jesmond brought him Holy Communion from time to time. Mimi was however a devout Catholic and George was greatly influenced by her piety and devotion.

When George went to Ampleforth he became completely at home with the Benedictines and immersed himself in the religious practice of the College. Morning Mass at 7.15, on Sundays and Feast days High Mass sung in glorious Gregorian Chant. On Sunday evenings there was Benediction and Vespers. He was saturated with the liturgy. He was about average at his lessons, his contempories described him as 'a nice chap'. However he was conscientious and consistent.

He was very good at sports, especially running and he played in the College's First XV at the age of sixteen, and the following year he was made captain. He was a natural leader and very popular. His highly developed sense of fun remained with him, and he was an expert mimic. He loved the stage and performed in plays, he especially loved slapstick comedy and variety shows.

In his final years as a schoolboy, the Second World War started and he would read the list of casualties, many were serving officers from Ampleforth. He considered joining the army, or should he continue to develop his vocation to become a priest? These were agonising decisions for the young George. Despite his fellow students persuasive arguments to join the army and go to war, he firmly decided to enter the monastery and took the name Basil after St. Basil the Great who was the Bishop of Caesarea in Asia Minor (AD 330-380).

The Benedictine Order has been a central influence in the life of the Church in England since the time of Augustine who was sent by Pope Gregory to convert the Anglo-Saxons. The old Benedictine Abbey of Westminster has a direct link with Ampleforth. The monks who were sent by Pope Gregory the Great landed on the Isle of Thanet in 598. They built the great pre-Reformation Abbey of Westminster.

Following the suppression of Westminster Abbey in 1540, the English Benedictines were imprisoned or fled abroad. Towards the end of Elizabeth's reign, one of their members Dom Robert Sigebert Buckley, was frequently imprisoned, although Marian priests were usually treated less harshly than seminarian priests. There is a letter written by Dr. Christopher Bagshaw, a distinguished secular priest, who from 1593 was a fellow prisoner of Fr. Buckley in Wisbech prison. He wrote enthusiastically about Fr. Buckley describing him as "The last survivour of those monks who once lived in England and he is ready to meet death with Holy Simeon's joy because he has seen his Order rising once again, a thing which he earnestly prayed for with many sighs, as I myself know".

Pope Clement VIII signed the formal decree in 1602, which sanctioned the mission of the Cassinese and Spanish Congregations to return to England. The three considerations given were: (1) The need of more missioners in England. (2) The suitability for the mission of the English Benedictines as members of the same Order as England's first apostles. (3) The survival of Fr. Buckley, monk of Westminster, through whom the English Benedictines succession might be perpetuated.

When James I began his reign in 1603, he ordered a general release of incarcerated priests, among them Fr. Buckley. At the same time four Benedictines came to England, two from Spain and two from Italy. Among them was Fr. Anselm Beech. His record states "I entered England in the year 1603, landing at Yarmouth, where I remained throughout the winter, in the house of Mr Francis Woodhouse of Cisson, near Wendlam. I met with Fr. Sigbert Buckley, whom a few months previously King James had ordered to be released from the prison at Framlingham. Don Thomas and I took care of the old man until his death, which took place on 22 January 1610, in the ninety-third year of his age".

In 1606, Dom Augustine Baker, who was a trained lawyer, returned to England from Italy. He had been Recorder of Abergavenney, and had no difficulty in settling the question of procedure. He was also an historian and solved the congregational problem by producing a full record of the Acts of one of the pre-Reformation Benedictine Chapters.

There were two secular priests on the English mission who had long wished to be Benedictines. Frs. Robert Sadler and Edward Maihew. In the autumn of 1606, they were clothed as novices for the Cassinese Congregation. After their year's noviciate they went with the Cassinese Fathers to Fr. Buckley, and there on the 21 November 1607 they made their Benedictine profession as monks of the Cassinese Congregation. Then immediately afterwards they were handed over to Fr. Buckley and by him aggregated to his Abbey of Westminster and constituted successors and heirs of the old English Benedictines.

By virtue of Fr. Buckley's aggregation there was created a small body of Westminster monks who functioned and were recognised both among the English Benedictines and by Rome as the 'Congregation of the old English Benedictines'.

Because of an increase in their numbers, the English Benedictines eventually decided it would be advisable to establish monasteries of their own, nearer their mission than were the abbeys of Italy and Spain. Three monasteries were founded: St. Gregory's Priory, Douay 1606 (now Downside Abbey), St. Laurence's Priory, Dieulourd 1608 (now Ampleforth Abbey), and St. Edmund's Priory, Paris 1615 (now Douay Abbey).

The events following the French Revolution almost two-hundred years later resulted in the return of the Benedictine abbeys to England. The French Government abolished religious orders, confiscating their property and declaring their vows invalid. With the outbreak of war with England in February 1793 the situation became very serious, all protection for the English Benedictines had now gone. The Priory of St. Laurence at Dieulouard fell into the hands of the municiple guard. After 185 years the end of community life at Dieulouard had come.

The community returned to England, initially at the invitation of Sir. Edward Smythe, an old boy of St. Gregory's Douay, who owned Acton Burrell in Shropshire. He willingly put the house at the disposal of those Dielouard and Douay monks who had escaped from France. Two priors and two communities living under one roof was clearly impossible. The president of the Benedictines, Fr. Cowley had rented Vernon Hall in Lancashire and set up a new school. There he met with the two priors and it was decided that the monks from St. Gregory's would stay at Acton Burnell and those from St.Laurence's should move to Brindle near Preston.

President Cowley died in 1799 and was succeeded by Fr. Bede Brewer. He found a freehold property – Ampleforth Lodge where Fr. Anselm Bolton lived as chaplain to Lord Fairfax's daughter Anne, at Gilling Castle. Lord Fairfax had died in 1773 and Fr. Bolton became friend and protector to Anne Fairfax who was delicate and of a nervous disposition. In protecting the interests of Miss Fairfax, Fr. Bolton gained many enemies including the Pigott family who would inherit the estate on the death of Anne Fairfax. In 1783 he bought nine acres of land called Ager's Close including a house. In the next ten years, he gradually added about 32 acres of land, and re-built the house so that he and his successors could live there independently of the Gilling estate. In 1801 when President Brewer was looking for accommodation for the St. Laurence community, Fr. Bolton willingly made over Ampleforth Lodge.

Fr. Anselm Appleton was installed as prior and arrived at Ampleforth on 10 December 1802. The link between old Westminster Abbey and Westminster Cathedral was established. Ampleforth grew as a community. The school gained the reputation as one of the leading public schools in the country.

Into this heritage, Basil assumed a life of prayer, study and work – the Benedictine monastic way of searching for God, which fundamentally has remained unchanged for almost 1500 years. In September 1942 after one year's novitiate, he made his simple profession as a monk, and took solemn vows in 1945. He was sent to St. Benet's Hall, Oxford where he read history and gained second-class honours. The French Revolution was his main subject and he also held an enduring interest in history, especially medieval history and the ancient abbeys such as Selby, Durham, Rievaulx, Fountains and Westminster. After Oxford he was sent to study theology at the Catholic University of Fribourg in Switzerland. There he studied St. Thomas Aquinas and the *Summa Theologica* a rich source of spiritual fuel in his search for God.

On 23 July 1950, Brother Basil was ordained priest in the Abbey Church at Ampleforth. He was professor of Dogmatic Theology to the monks. In 1955 he became house-master of St. Bede's in the school. For a time Fr. Basil was also curate at Our Lady and St. Benedict in Ampleforth village.

In 1957, the Chapter of Ampleforth Abbey elected him as their delegate to the General Chapter of the English Benedictine Congregation. At that Chapter in August 1957, he was elected Magister Scholarum of the Congregation, and was re-elected to the post in the following Chapter of 1961.

In 1963 he was elected Abbot of Ampleforth, the year that the first Session of the Second Vatican Council ended, the year Pope John XXIII died and the election of Pope Paul VI.

It was the beginning of momentous changes in the Church. After the conclusion of the Vatican Council, which ushered in such renewal, he became chairman of the Benedictine Confederation's Commission on monastic renewal which meant considerable travel on the Continent. He was also deeply involved in ecumenism, both internationally and at the local 'grass roots' level. His experience of growing up as a child of a mixed marriage and the influence of his devout Catholic mother and her tact and sensitivity to her Protestant husband instilled in him an active interest in ecumenism.

Abbot Basil was actively engaged in work for Christian unity. For example, he arranged with the authorities of the Orthodox Churches – Greek, Serbian and Russian – for a dozen Orthodox boys to attend Ampleforth College and to reside in a special house under the care of an Orthodox priest. He was an active member of the local ecumenical Council of Churches in Rydale, the district in which the Abbey is situated. He became a personal friend of Dr. Donald Coggan, then Archbishop of York, and received a personal invitation to his enthronement when he became Archbishop of Canterbury in 1975.

The Confederation of Benedictines set up various commissions in the wake of the Second Vatican Council. Abbot Basil was the chairman of the Ecumenical Commission for four years and also served as chairman of the Commission *de re monastica* until his appointment as Archbishop of Westminster.

Abbot Basil grappled with all the complex challenges which shook the Church and the strain must at times have been almost unbearable as he saw members of the community at Ampleforth leave the religious life. His personal qualities impressed many, his simple sincerity, his directness and his clarity on the fundamental values of the Christian way of life helped to steer his Benedictine family through many a crisis.

He was serving his second term as Abbot of Ampleforth when Pope Paul VI appointed him to the vacant See of Westminster on 17 February 1976. He was installed as Archbishop in Westminster Cathedral on 25 March 1976 and created Cardinal at the Consistory of 24 May 1976. His titular Church in Rome was San Sivestro in Capite.

He immediately set to work in re-organising the diocese. When he arrived at Westminster there was a debt of six million pounds, through unavoidable capital spending on schools the debt had increased to twelve million pounds in 1985, at the time of his death the debt was almost completely eliminated.

He increased the number of auxiliary bishops in the diocese to five. His plan for cooperation and shared responsibility involved all the laity as well as bishops and priests. The work he initiated set in motion much that would enter the national stage in 1980 at the National Pastoral Congress in Liverpool, the brainchild of Archbishop of Liverpool Derek Worlock. This resulted in a renewal at parish level, with an increase in the understanding of and adoption of collaborative ministry, catechists, readers, eucheristic ministers and permanent deacons. In temporal matters the work in social caring and justice and peace also grew in importance in the life of the Church.

One of the many great qualities that Cardinal Hume possessed was his intimate knowledge of the culture of Continental Europe. The influence of his French mother, his studies at the German speaking university, his grasp of European languages, which he taught at Ampleforth, his links with Protestant and Orthodox Churches proves his qualifications. He greatly desired the coming together of East and West Europe. A revitalised and evangelised Europe, could thus play a key role in the responsibility of the affluent Western democracies towards the Third World, these views were also shared by Pope John Paul II. Cardinal Hume was a prime mover in the organisation of a conference in Rome organised by the Pope's old university of Lublin in Poland and the Lateran University in Rome, which crystalised the new priorities of Pope John Paul II.

A new political, cultural and spiritual unity across Europe, helped to sharpen Cardinal Hume's ecumenical vision. Eastern Europe, dominated as it is by the Orthodox Church, and Western Europe, largely Catholic required greater dialogue not only with the Protestant Churches, but also the Orthodox.

The Cardinal's commitment to ecumenism is well known and documented. When he was enthroned Archbishop in Westminster Cathedral, his first act after the proceedings were finished, was to embrace the Archbishop of York and other Church leaders. Then he immediately went with his Benedictine monks to Westminster Abbey to sing the old Latin vespers. It was the first time it had been sung in the Abbey since the Reformation, and Anglican Benedictines joined their Catholic Brethren.

He was inspired with the belief that Christian unity will be achieved by Churches praying together, the reliance on divine providence instead of a hasty thrust for organic unity. He spoke in Westminster Abbey to a congregation made up from all the Churches. He said "Wounds healed only with time and patience". In reference to Catholics and Anglicans he continued "Our two Churches give proof of this. Our wounds are ancient, the healing is slow. We have been, I think, like two sisters estranged, not on speaking terms, quarrelsome, misunderstanding each other".

The quest for unity is a frustrating tormenting, bedevilled by dogmatic stance and historic facts. Christians debate which kind of unity is attainable, organic unity or an alliance of Churches sharing communion but with legitamate variations in liturgy. In a sermon given in St. Paul's Cathedral during the week of prayer for Christian unity in 1983, the Cardinal said "We have now reached the stage in our journey together when we will have to face honestly and courageously the obstacles that lay ahead. There are many un-resolved questions before us all. We need more prayers, study and dialogue on the role of the Pope, on the role and mission of the bishops, and on the sacraments. As you well know, it is our Catholic belief that the authority of the Pope, has been divinely ordained as the way to preserve truth, charity and unity among Christians. Reconciliation of ministries cannot be cheaply bought, or sought for simple convenience. The progress of reconciling ministries will be long and arduous".

On the question of women clergy he answered a questioner on the BBC World Service phone-in "I accept the authority of my Church, which does not advocate the ordination of women to the priesthood. The answer given is that it is not part of our tradition, and that may be a good or bad argument. I personally, if the authorities of my Church agree the ordination of women, would have no problem about it. But I am a man under authority and I would not be in the Catholic Church if I did not accept that".

The aftermath of the Reformation, saw the Church of England developing between Catholic and Protestant concepts. As late as 1999 The Right Rev. Frank Weston, Anglican Bishop of Knaresborough told a gathering of Catholic ecumenists that the Church of England was "re-discovering its Catholic roots". Cardinal Hume said way back in 1977 "If the dialogue be-tween the two Churches was to make progress it must become tougher and more direct. We Roman Catholics must make our position absolutely clear. I also think the Anglican Church has to make up its mind what it really be-lieves because the spectrum is too wide". On the issue of the eucharist and specifically on inter-communion he said "We believe that this sharing pre-supposes not only the same belief in the reality of Christ's presence in the sacred species, but also a common faith in general". Clearly Cardinal Hume felt close to the Anglican Church through personal friendships and the simi-larity in ministry and liturgy. It was certainly through his influence and pres-tige that the Holy See and the Court of St. James re-established full diplo-matic relations in 1982.

The Cardinal was elected vice-president of the Catholic Bishops' Confer-ence of England and Wales in 1976, and later President in 1979. He held the office of president until his death. His leadership gave the Church a period of stability. He played a key role in the National Pastoral Congress and the official report published under the title of *The Easter People* was an attempt to promote the renewal of the Catholic Church in the light of the Congress and the Second Vatican Council.

The most controversial element from the report was on the subject of marriage, contraception and divorce. Only twelve years after Pope Paul VI's encyclical *Humane Vitae* had reaffirmed the traditional ban on contracep-tion, many conservative churchmen were against even allowing such discussions to take place. However Cardinal Hume and Archbishop Worlock allowed the debate. At the conclusion, 93% of delegates voted for the proposition "There is a widespread lack of understanding and widespread disagreement amongst Catholics about the present teaching on contraception". 81% of delegates voted for "The Church's teaching on marriage is at an impasse because of confusion, uncertainty, and disagreement over contraception, which affects the whole sacramental life of many Catholics". 87% of delegates voted for "The Church's teaching on marriage can only develop through a fundamental re-examination of the teaching on marriage, sexuality and on contraception". The proposition that "Non-contaceptive intercourse is the ideal for which everyone should strive" received only 52 votes, 17% of delegates.

The Congress dealt with many other matters on the life of the Church and was a notable milestone in the history of the Church in England and Wales. The laity had come of age. Gone were the passive, docile and obedient lambs. The bishops now encountered a liberated laity who were their fellow Christians in the vanguard of evangelisation. They recognised too that the modern Catholic could think and speak with more than enough knowledge of moral theology.

Following the Congress, the National Congress of Priests met to consider the publication *The Easter People* and passed a declaration welcoming the report. However, following the Synod of Bishops in Rome, the report of the NCP was suppressed by Cardinal Hume. The 1980 Synod of Bishops on the Family, which had met in Rome followed the conservative line. The Pope had spoken in praise of *Humane Vitae* and the stance taken by the Vatican over contraception became much tougher. The bishops of England and Wales had to reduce the expectations of the laity on these key issues of family life.

In a letter to Archbishop Worlock, Cardinal Hume wrote "I am in full agreement with what you say about the report concerning the NCP" The secretary of the NCP Mgr. David Norris reported how the cardinal had dealt with the priests' disappointment. "The Cardinal replied that he considered that conservatism was succeeding in many parts of the world and was also rising in Rome. We had to remember that Western Europe was now a minority in the Church and places like Africa and South America were very conservative. Our local Church has to find its way in the present circumstances and it is not always clear how it should proceed. The Cardinal was sure that it would not help to have public calls on our bishops to act by themselves. There were some conservatives in this country who were aleady attacking what had already been done by himself and Archbishop Worlock".

With Archbishop Derek Worlock of Liverpool, Cardinal Hume visited the Vatican in August 1980 to present Pope John Paul with copies of the documents of the National Pastoral Congress, and *The Easter People*. The Cardinal took this opportunity, in the name of the English and Welsh bishops, to invite Pope John Paul II to make a pastoral visit to England and Wales. The Pope immediately accepted the invitation.

Pope John Paul arrived in Britain on 28 May 1982 to begin a six-day pastoral visit of England, Scotland and Wales. This visit had been threatened by the outbreak of hostilities between Britain and Argentina in the Falkland Islands, but careful negotiation ensured that it took place. Prior to the visit on the 10 February the Cardinal said "Whether you take part in the celebrations in person, or follow them through the media, the few days of the Pope's visit are meant to deepen your understanding of the Gospel, to strengthen you in your faith and to arouse a spirit of prayer and Christian service".

Afterwards, the Pope himself described his visit as "A pilgrimage through the seven sacraments in which the life of the People of God is formed and developed".

One aspect of the papal visit which was of particular importance in Britain was its ecumenical content, symbolised by the visit to Canterbury Cathedral. The Cardinal said of it afterwards "Canterbury was a historic moment and a profoundly moving one. I believe that the relationship between the Churches can never be the same again after that ceremony in Canterbury Cathedral".

Cardinal Hume was also the first cardinal and second Roman Catholic bishop to address the Anglican Synod, which he did on 1 February 1978. His address was received with acclamation. He preached in several Anglican cathedrals, churches and chapels, including Westminster Abbey, St. Paul's Cathedral, and the Chapel of the House of Commons. By royal invitation he participated in the celebrations of Queen Elizabeth the Queen Mother's eightieth birthday in St. Paul's Cathedral, and also in the Royal Wedding of His Royal Highness the Prince of Wales and Lady Diana Spencer in July 1981. He was also present in Canterbury Cathedral when Archbishop Runcie was enthroned as Archbishop of Canterbury in 1980, and when Archbishop Carey was enthroned in 1991.

A new venture in 1983 of Christian Unity, which became known as the Inter-Church Process was supported by the Bishops' Conference. This led to the Swanick Conference in September 1987. The Cardinal made an historic speech to that Conference in which he committed the Catholic Church in England and Wales to playing a full part in the new structures for Christian unity in the future.

When the new ecumenical instruments were inaugurated in 1990, Cardinal Hume became president of both the Council of Churches in Britain and Ireland (CCBI) and Churches Together in England (CTE).

The Cardinal, as president of the Bishops' Conference, was responsible for presenting the bishops' response to the decision of the Church of England in November 1992 to ordain women to the Anglican priesthood. In his view, the decision by the Church of England to ordain women to the priesthood placed a grave obstacle on the road to further ecumenical progress. He was never in any doubt about the seriousness of this step and he warned of its consequences when he addressed the Anglican Synod in 1978. Before the Church of England took its decision, he wrote privately to the Archbishop of Canterbury to underline his anxiety. As a consequence of the decision by the Church of England, a large number of Anglican clergy and lay people were received into the Catholic Church. Cardinal Hume led a delegation to Rome from the Bishops' Conference to discuss the process of reception and the manner of ordination of those married former Anglican clergy who were seeking to become Catholic priests. In each case the final decision to permit ordination rested with the Pope, but the cardinal secured permission for preparatory work to be done locally, rather than having to refer each case to Rome immediately. He also secured the agreement of the Holy See to a form of wording in the ordination rite for former Anglican clergy, which gave explicit recognition to the fruitfulness of the ministry which they had previously exercised.

Many initiatives were taken by the Bishops' Conference during the cardinal's period as president in which the Cardinal himself played A significant role. These included: the bishops' response to the first report of the Anglican-Roman Catholic International Commission (ARCIC), which reviewed the stage of theological dialogue achieved at that time; the submission prior to the Extraordinary Synod of Bishops in 1985 which reviewed the life of the Catholic Church in England and Wales in the light of the teaching of the Second Vatican Council; the publication in 1996 of *The Common Good,* which presented and applied Catholic social teaching to contemporary society; and the teaching document *One Bread One Body,* a statement on the Eucharist issued jointly with the Scottish and Irish Bishops' Conferences in 1998.

From his time at Ampleforth, Basil Hume had sought to develop ecumenical links with the Orthodox Church. As president of the Council of European Bishops' Conference he worked closely with the future Russian Orthodox Patriarch Alexei. In April 1992, the Cardinal visited Russia for the first time. It was a private visit at the personal invitation of Catholic Archbishop Thaddeus Kondrusiewicz. During this visit, he renewed his friendship with Patriarch Alexei, and met other members of the hierarchy of the Russian Orhodox Church.

In May 1994, the cardinal returned to Moscow in the company of Cardinal Danneels of Mechlin-Brussels at the special invitation of Patriarch Alexei. As co-patrons of the St. Francis and St. Sergius Trust, which was founded with the intention of helping to improve relationships between the Catholic and Russian Orthodox Churches, they were able to travel to Moscow and to talk informally with Patriarch Alexei and other members of the Holy Synod. In January 1996, they revisited the Patriarch to discuss the growing tensions between the Catholic and Orthodox Churches. Both the Vatican and the local Catholic apostolic administrator, Archbishop Kondrusiewicz, were kept well informed of the content of these meetings. In a message to the Cardinal in May 1999, Patriarch Alexei expressed his affection and gratitude to him. He wrote of their encounters "These meetings were very memorable and significant. They contributed to the improvement in our inter-Church relationships on the way to Christian unity".

The Cardinal was a member of the Holy See's Secretariat for the Promotion of Christian Unity and between 1978 and 1987, as president of the Council of European Bishops' Conferences, he helped to organise and co-preside at major ecumenical conferences at Logumkloster in Denmark in 1981, and at Riva del Garda in Italy in 1984, in collaboration with the European Council of Churches.

Cardinal Hume also gave close attention to maintaining good relationships with the Jewish community. He was president of the Council of Christians and Jews for many years, and spoke regularly on Jewish-Christian relations. He delivered an address in November 1988 to a Jewish gathering on the fiftieth anniversary of *Kristallnacht,* the night when synagogues in Germany were firebombed. In December 1992, the Cardinal gave a major speech at the annual meeting of the Council of Christians and Jews.

In 1986, Cardinal Hume attended the meeting of world religious leaders hosted by the Pope at Assisi. In his later years, the Cardinal became increasingly convinced of the need to develop better inter-faith dialogue, which he valued as much as ecumenical relations. He encouraged the formation of the Three Faiths Forum in 1997, which brought together Muslims, Christians and Jews.

On the national stage, the Cardinal became concerned that there might have been a miscarriage of justice in the case of the Guildford Four and the Maguire family. He met Guiseppe Conlon, the father of Gerard Conlon, one of the Guildford Four, on a pastoral visit to Wormwood Scrubs prison in 1978. He then became convinced that there had been a possible miscarriage of justice in the Maguire case, and committed himself to finding out more about the case. Between 1978 and 1985 he wrote nineteen letters to three successive Home Secretaries. He also discussed his concerns with the Prime Minister, Margaret Thatcher, as well as the Home Secretaries. By 1985, concern amongst many people had also extended to the closely connected case of the Guildford Four.

By that time, Lord Devlin and Lord Scarman, and two former Home Secretaries, Roy Jenkins and Merlyn Rees, had also individually expressed their
concerns about the two cases. By late 1986, each of the four, of their own
volition and for their own reasons, came together with the cardinal to form
what came to be known as the Deputation. They all shared the conviction
that there had been a miscarriage of justice in both cases. They met frequently between October 1986 and October 1989, prepared many papers,
and made a presentation to the then Home Secretary, Douglas Hurd, in July
1987, to seek a referral of the Guildford Four and Maguire cases to the
Court of Appeal.

In September 1988, the Home Secretary visited the Cardinal to inform him
of his decision not to refer the case of the Guildford Four to the Court of
Appeal. Cardinal Hume refuted his reasons, and on behalf of the Deputation, subsequently wrote a powerful letter, an early paragraph of which reflected their determinaton to pursue the issue: "Unless a reference is made
now to the Court of Appeal, the country will have to face up to the fact that,
not only will the Deputation continue with what it regards s the puruit of
justice, but your successor, and probably mine, will be left to continue grap-
pling with the problem".

The Guildford Four case was finally heard by the Court of Appeal on 19
October 1989. Owing to the nature of some of the evidence, and the way in
which it had been handled, the Director of Public Prosecutions concluded,
"It would be wrong for the Crown to sustain the convictions". After two
hours, the Court gave judgement and the convictions were squashed.

This action by the Court of Appeal had an immense impact on the criminal justice system, and throughout the country. The Government consequently set up the May Inquiry to investigate the circumstances leading to
the arrest, trials and convictions of the Maguire Seven and the Guildford
Four. As a result of this, the convictions of the Maguire family were found
to be unsafe, and were subsequently quashed by the Court of Appeal in June
1991.

It was not long before the Birmigham Six convictions were also referred
back to the Court of Appeal for the second time. They were quashed by the
court of Appeal in 1991, and the Government set up a Royal Commission
on Criminal Justice. The Deputation gave substantial evidence to the Commission as it had done to the May Inquiry. The Commission led, amongst
other things, to the establishment of the Criminal Cases Review Commission
which was to take over the handling of possible miscarriages of justice from
the Home Office. The setting up of such a body had been advocated by the
Deputation from its early days in 1987. The work of the Deputation made
an important contribution towards the implementation of major reforms in
the British criminal justice system.

On foreign affairs the Cardinal was a consistent advocate of both Church and Government support for the plight of the poor overseas. He was also an enthusiastic supporter of the Catholic Fund for Overseas Development (CAFOD).

In November 1984, he paid a pastoral visit to the refugee camps in Ethiopia to see for himself the famine conditions, and the work of relief organisations. The visit to the camps made a profound and indelible impression on him, and on his return the Cardinal gave many interviews and talks. He visited the Prime Minister, Margaret Thatcher, to brief her on his trip. He was also highly critical of British Government policy, describing it as a "scandal". As he was also president of the Council of European Bishops' Conference at the time, he initiated a coordinated approach by the presidents of the other Bishops' Conferences to the European Economic Community to increase European aid to the starving.

In 1985, Cardinal Hume first took up the issue of international debt at a Fight Against World Poverty lobby at the Houses of Parliament. In the years that followed, he pursued the moral case in correspondence with Government ministers, and through speeches and articles in which he also consistently called for increases in the UK aid budget.

In June 1992, the Cardinal issued a statement to the Catholic community regarding the Earth Summit in Rio de Janeiro and wrote to the Prime Minister, John Major, wishing him well at the Summit, and urging him and his European Community colleagues to make a firm pledge to make the year 2000 the date by which 0.7 per cent of Gross national Product would be spent on overseas development assistance.

In December 1997, the Cardinal attended a meeting with the Chancellor of the Exchequer, Gordon Brown, lending his support to the new Government's efforts to achieve faster and more effective international action to tackle the problem of third world debt. He subsequently wrote articles published in *The Observer* and *The Times* on this issue.

In May 1998, Cardinal Hume wrote to the presidents of the Catholic Bishop's Conferences of Group of Seven countries in advance of the G7 Summit in Birmingham. As a result, a coordinated approach was made by all of them to their respective heads of Government before the summit, to urge them to promote the millennial goal of achieving the cancellation of the unpayable debts of the poorest countries.

The Cardinal was equally active behind the scenes of Government in the problems of Northern Ireland, the arms trade, disarmament both in the third world and of course on nuclear disarmament, on refugees and asylum seekers, and on homelessness.

On human rights the Cardinal showed unwavering concern and strongly supported work for racial justice in London, especially in the Notting Hill district. Together with the Bishops of England and Wales, he criticised the Labour Government's White Paper on the British Nationality Law in 1979. In 1981, he led protests about the new British nationality Bill introduced by the Conservative Government.

An important human rights issue arose on 1997 when the Government proposed legislation which would permit the police or security services to use bugging devices anywhere – including in a confessional. The Cardinal protested to the Home Secretary, Michael Howard, who visited Archbishop's House on 11 February 1997, and agreed to amend the proposals in the Police Bill to safeguard the confidentiality of the Sacrament of Reconciliation (confession).

The Cardinal also became directly involved in negotiations with the Home Secretary Jack Straw, in 1998 over the incorporation of the European Convention of Human Rights into UK law. Whilst the Cardinal strongly supported this move, serious questions had been raised in the House of Lords and elsewhere about the possible adverse impact on the Catholic Church, given the way the Human Rights Bill had been drafted. After the meeting with Mr. Straw at Archbishop' House in March 1998, the Home Office produced an amendment to the Bill to meet the concerns expressed by the Cardinal and others, the Government also agreed to the Cardinal's request to strengthen the provisions in education law to safeguard the right of Catholic schools to appoint Catholic teachers to senior posts.

As former teacher in a Catholic school, the Cardinal was both wholly committed to the principles of Catholic education, and determined to advocate more widely a vision of the purposes and scope of education which did justice to the moral and spiritual development of every person. In his public speeches to both Catholic and secular audiences, he probably spoke about education more often than any other subject.

The importance of the role of the Churches in education, which the cardinal had consistently upheld was recognised in the provisions of the 1998 Schools Standards and Framework Act, which strengthened and reinforced the position of Catholic voluntary aided schools within the State sector.

Cardinal Hume was equally vociferous on the issues of life and death, abortion, embryology and euthanasia. In 1980 the Catholic Archbishop's of Great Britain made a statement on *Abortion and the right to life*. It set out clearly the Church's teaching on abortion and the right to life, and at the same time placed it in the wider context of the Church's social teaching.

The publication of the Warnock report in 1984 advocating experiments on human embryos up to fourteen days old caused the Cardinal to react publicly and strongly. In a letter to *The Times* in 1985, supporting Enoch Powell's Unborn Children (Protection) Bill, the cardinal warned of the long term consequences: "The abandonment of objective moral principles and the dogmatism of permissiveness that have combined in our day to undermine society. This is a crisis".

He publicly attacked the legislation based on the Warnock report which came before Parliament in 1990, describing it as "fundamentally flawed". After the Act was passed, he said in an interview that he thought tht the country could no longer claim to be a Christian country.

During the 1990's the Cardinal spoke increasingly about the dangers of euthanasia, as the pro-euthanasia lobby gathered strength. He endorsed a joint submission made with the Anglican bishops to the House of Lords Select Committee, which reported in 1994. He subsequently wrote an article in November 1997 on euthanasia for *The Times,* warning of the dangers of legalising doctor-assisted suicide and highlighting the dangerous judicial precedent which had been set in the Bland case.

In a speech to the Life Conference in March 1999, the Cardinal warned the pro-life movement emerging life issues raised by the new genetics and the advent of cloning technologies.

A recurring theme of Cardinal Hume was the importance of marriage and the family. During the 1994 Internatinal Year of the Family, the Cardinal gave particular emphasis to families and family policy in his speeches and articles. He wrote for *The Universe,* as well as a long article in *The Tablet* entitled, 'The Christian Family: a pastor's reflections'. In January 1996, the Cardinal stepped into a heated parliamentary debate over the Government's proposals to reform the divorce law. Concerned that the Family Law Bill might further weaken marriage by sending a signal that divorce was 'no-fault', the Cardinal wrote an article for *The Tablet* in which he urged that the Bill be strengthened. The article was reproduced in *The Times* and widely quoted in the subsequent debates, and the Bill was strengthened.

In July 1993, the Cardinal drafted and published a document entitled 'Some Observations on the Catholic Church's teaching concerning homo-sexual people'. He expanded this document in 1995, and revised it in 1997. In February 1994, the Cardinal issued a statement on the age of consent concerning homosexual people. In July 1997, he wrote to the Prime Minis-ter, Tony Blair, to voice his anxiety over proposals to lower the age of con-sent for homosexual men to the age of sixteen.

Cardinal Hume was a member of the Pontifical Council for Promoting Christian Unity, the Congregation of Religious and Secular Institutes, the Pontifical Commission for the Revision of the *Code of Canon Law,* and the Joint Commission set up by the Holy See and the Orthodox Church in 1980 to promote theological dialogue between their Churches. The Cardinal held the unique distinction among English cardinals since the Restoration of the Hierachy in 1850 of having been twice involved in electing a Pope. He at-tended both conclaves in 1978, at which Pope John Paul I and Pope John

Paul II were elected. He also attended both special consistories of cardinals summoned by Pope John Paul II in 1979 and 1982.

The Cardinal was awarded many honours including Honorary Degrees of Doctor of Divinity from the English Universities of Newcastle-upon-Tyne, Cambridge, London, Oxford, York, Durham, Surrey, and an Honorary Doctrate of Law from the Univesity of Northumbria at Newcastle. He had a simarlar list of honours bestowed upon him from universities in America. In addition he received an Honorary Degree of Doctor of Divinity from the Benedictine International Athenaeum of St. Anselm in Rome.

His new style of episcopacy was apparent when in 1985 the bishops issued their considered response to the final report of the first Anglican, Roman Catholic International Commission. There was a warmth in attitude to many issues, especially on the vexed question of papal infallibility.

In the national arena, the humble and holy monk made his mark. He spoke with frank eloquence on a wide range of political matters. Equally on international affairs, his voice carried much weight overseas on famine and conflicts, nuclear disarmament, arms sales, and Third World debt reduction. Paradoxically the Cardinal does not enjoy controversy, and he has a restrained style of putting a point of view forward. This style has endeared him to the whole nation. His social background and political comments made him an ideal candidate for the British Establishment. His total lack of ambition however, his affinity with the meek and lowly, provided the perfect antidote to modern secular life. He strove to move the nation towards more spitritual matters, the average British family have turned away from religion and have rejected God. Basil Hume's image was of a man completely in love with God and through this he became a national figure, held in particularly high esteem by the nation as a whole.

In 1994, the Cardinal received the Duchess of Kent into the Catholic Church at a private service in his chapel at Westminster House. The following year, Westminster Cathedral celebrated its centenary. The Cardinal played a major part in launching the centenary and an appeal to support the choir, establish a new Centre for Spirituality and re-furbish part of the cathedral itself. Her Majesty Queen Elizabeth II attended a service of vespers in November, the Archbishop of Canterbury and the leaders of other Christian Churches were also present. In September 1997 on the eve of the state funeral of Diana, Princess of Wales, the Cardinal preached at a Requiem mass in Westminster Cathedral attended by over three thousand people. Just one week later he again preached at a Requiem Mass for Mother Teresa, attended by a similar number of people.

On 2 June 1999, he received the Order of Merit from Her Majesty Queen Elizabeth II. He was the first Catholic bishop to receive this civil honour, which is entirely in the gift of the sovereign. He went to Buckingham Palace from his sick bed to receive the award from Her Majesty. He had been diagnosed in April 1999 with inoperable abdominal cancer, which he wrote in a letter to the priests of his diocese, was "not in its early stages". He spoke of the great gift from God he had received of being able to fully prepare for death. The Cardinal telephoned Fr. Timothy Wright the Abbot of Ampleforth to give him the news, so that the brethren would know as soon as the Westminster clergy knew. "Timothy, its cancer". Abbot Timothy replied "Life is much better on the other side than it is here, and I am delighted for you". The Cardinal continued "So many people burst into tears when I tell them, I find it very disturbing".

On 17 June 1999, Cardinal Basil Hume died peacefully at the hospital of St. John and St. Elizabeth. With him when he died were one of his nephews, William Charles; his private secretary, Fr. Jim Curry; Fr. Liam Kelly from the Bishops' Conference of England and Wales; and a nurse. Fr. Curry had just anointed the Cardinal and he died peacefully to the sound of his friends and family praying for him.

Fr. Kelly speaking to *The Tablet* said "On the day of his death, the Cardinal was agitated and restless in the morning but this was controlled as the day went on. Some members of his family came to see him in the afternoon, and then left. After that William, Jim a nurse and myself stayed with him. After 5p.m. his breathing changed. We told the Cardinal that he was being anointed, and we began to pray for him. During the prayers, he gave a sigh and a sharp intake of breath. One of the final prayers we said before he died was: 'Go forth, Christian soul' It was a privilege for us to have been there". He died at 5.20 p.m.

Cardinal Hume's funeral took place on 25 June 1999 at Westminster Cathedral. The chief celebrant was Cardinal Edward Cassidy, Pope John Paul II's envoy. Concelebrating were five cardinals and over five hundred priests and bishops, among a congregation of around two thousand. The Cardinal's body was received into the cathedral the previous evening, and a service of Solemn Vespers was celebrated. The Rt. Rev. Vincent Nichols, Auxiliary Bishop and Diocesan Administrator of Westminster, preached at the Solemn Vespers and the Rt. Rev. John Crowley, Bishop of Middlesbrough, delivered the homily at the funeral Mass.

During his sermon, Bishop Vincent Nichols said: "In the words of the Holy Father, we have lost 'a shepherd of great spiritual and moral character'. We have lost a lovely, gentle courteous friend. And, as tributes from far and wide indicate, we have lost 'a father to all'. So we, in the cathedral, are part of a great company, widespread and diverse, which prays to God for him tonight: prayers of thanksgiving and of supplication. Yet, even at this moment, the Cardinal is prompting and guiding us. For the Gospel text we have just heard (Luke 23:42-46) was his choice for the Solemn Vespers. He wanted us to listen to these words. He asks us, still, to be attentive, in mind and heart, for in these words the Lord is speaking.

"This Gospel text is a conversation, an exchange between two people at the point of death. Yet it is a dialogue of life. The words declare the great truth: that life triumphs over death; that goodness is more powerful than wrong-doing; and that the path of life comes to its fullness in the mystery of the cross – the crosses on which hung two men who gasped these dying words.

"The first to speak, in our passage, is a thief: the good thief. But many might ask, 'What can make a good thief good?' The Cardinal knew the answer to that question. He knew that, deep down, there is good in every person. But it is entangled with our wrong-doing. In a sense there is a thief in all of us: we take short cuts; we extract from others what they do not want to give; we deprive them of our best. The Cardinal knew that to bring out the goodness in us one quality is needed: honesty or openness; openness to others, openness to the truth and, ultimately, a humble openness to God. Throughout his life this was the quality he sought in people, whatever their role in life. If such openness was present, then the dialogue of life could begin. If not, there was nowhere to go. Hanging on the cross, the good thief had this quality in plenty. He reached out: 'Jesus', he said, 'Remember me when you come into your kingdom'.

"Every day of his life, the Cardinal echoed this prayer. In times of trouble, when he agonised over what to do or to say, he would bring his burdens to the Lord. His fundamental serenity, which was not shaken either by sickness or by the angel of death, came from·the Lord. He relied not on any assumption of his own goodness, which he did not trust, nor on his own abilities, which he constantly played down, but on knowing that as long as he tried to do the will of God, then peace would be found.

"I promise you', said Jesus, 'today you will be with me in paradise'. But then, with the sun eclipsed, a darkness came over the whole land. The veil of the Temple was torn, and Jesus cried out. This Gospel dialogue of life ends in chaos. The natural order is in disarray; the symbols of stability are shaken. Out of the depth of the chaos comes the clarion call: 'Father, into your hands I commit my spirit'.

"I heard that just a few weeks ago, as the nausea and pain of his illness began to take hold, the Cardinal was sitting quietly in his study. One of the priests from the cathedral passed by. He called him in. Gently, the Cardinal spoke to him of his disquiet and how, at that moment, he could no longer read, or pray. 'All I can do', he said, 'is just sit here and look at this crucifix'.

"Cardinal Hume taught us much in his life. He taught us even more in the manner of his dying. He taught us how to live, and die, by faith. His lesson is quite simple: even when we are in darkness, in distress, or feeling forlorn, we are to keep our eyes on the cross and our hearts with the Lord".

Bishop John Crowley in his homily said: "To his family and some lifelong friends he was George or Basil, to others Your Eminence, but to most of us he was just Father. The Cardinal answered to many titles. 'How would you prefer to be addressed' said one of his priests in 1976. Back came the surprising reply 'I can cope with just about anything short of 'hey you!'

"But to all of us, whatever we called him, Cardinal Hume was an outstanding spiritual leader, a man we shall achingly miss, and for whose life we are so grateful to God. Our first thoughts in love today are for his family, for his own personal household and staff next door – particularly the Sisters of Mercy – the priests of Westminster Diocese, where he had come to feel so much at home, his monastic brethren, and his many friends. Because he was not just admired but loved, the Cardinal's death has provoked a lot of sadness, a shaking amount of personal grief all over the place.

"But our main task today is to say, 'thank you God, for giving us a shepherd after your own heart'. It is already clear that through his life, and in the manner of his dying, God has amazingly blessed us, and far beyond the boundaries of Church or religious belief.

"In a quite extraordinary as it seems that everyone thought of him as a personal friend. Among the sacks full of letters which engulfed Archbishop's House when his terminal illness became known, a sizeable proportion of them actually began with the words, 'I am not a member of your Church', or, 'I am not a believer'. But each letter bore its witness to a man of God who had touched peoples' hearts in a remarkable way. That universal appeal was somehow symbolised when Her Majesty the Queen conferred upon the cardinal the Order of Merit. How moved he was by the graciousness of that gesture.

"For thirty-five years as monk and for twenty-three years as archbishop, Cardinal Hume centred himself on God. And from that store of wisdom he fed us. He addressed head-on the God-shaped emptiness which is within everyone. Without ever seeking it, he became a reassuring light for perhaps millions of people in this country and beyond. And, all the while, his deeply Benedictine soul guided him towards balance – the middle ground, the common good – but he did it without ever compromising truth; whether it be in the dialogue between Churches, between different faiths, or within his own Church.

"In their two very different ways, Archbishop Worlock and Cardinal Hume kept our Church out of the clutches of extremists – right and left – and far away from those who, by harsh judgements, might easily crush the broken reed. Both pastors were conscious of those on the outside, of those feeling abandoned by the Church. Their Christ-like instinct was to count the stragglers in, and never out.

"When the doctors first told him of his advanced cancer, he went straight to the hospital chapel where he sat praying for half an hour. 'I had preached so often on the seven last words of Jesus from the cross', he said, 'now it was wonderful to find they were such a part of me'. Throughout that initial period of waiting for death he found, to his delight, that his prayer was amazingly sweet, full of consolation. But then, to quote him, 'the curtain came down', and it was back to the darkness of faith. 'But I wasn't worried', he said, 'because I knew what was behind that curtain'.

"In those last few days here on earth he came to a fresh understanding of the Our Father. It was he said, like discovering its inner meaning for the very first time. 'It's only now that I begin to glimpse how everything we need is contained right there in the Lord's own prayer'. In the presence of a friend he then prayed the opening three sentences of the Our Father, adding each time a tiny commentary of his own, To sit there with him and to listen to what he said was to understand afresh all that he stood for. It was to be the recipient again, in a wonderfully privileged way, of his most special gift. As few others have done he raised our minds and hearts right up into the presence of God.

"Humanly speaking it would have been so lovely to have him lead us into the millennium. The year 2000 would also have been the golden jubilee of his priesthood, But that was not to be. Someone else wil now break open the Jubilee door into this cathedral. Someone else will celebrate the Christmas Mass which ushers in the great Jubilee of Christ's birth, 2000 years ago. He won't begrudge them that, because for him now a new future beckons. All his life he had been a pilgrim, searching restlessly for glimpses of God. 'It is your face, O Lord, that I seek. Hide not your face' (Psalm 26/27).

"Now that journey is over. He is safely home behind the curtain, face to face. Our deep love for him and our enourmous sense of gratitude for the gift he was, provokes a final question: if such was the gift, what must God be like, the giver of that gift?"

The burial took place immediately after the Requiem Mass. The Cardinal, at his own request, was buried in the chapel of St. Gregory and St. Augustine, which is also dedicated to the ancient bishops and saints of northern England. A mosaic of St. Benedict looks down on the tomb.

The community at Ampleforth held a traditional thirty-day period of prayer after the death of Cardinal Hume. Prayers were offered for the cardinal, as an expression of fraternal charity by his fellow monks. Intercessions were said during Matins during the thirty-day period. A requiem Mass was said on the third, seventh and thirtieth day following the Cardinal's death, and each year on the anniversary of his death. During the thirty-day period, a place was set for Cardinal Hume when the monks gathered for meals. A crucifix was put on the table in the place he would have occupied if he was visiting the community.

Following Cardinal Hume's death, the most senior auxiliary in Westminister was Bishop James O'Brien who would have taken over the diocese, but he was too ill. Under the code of canon law the cathedral chapter met and chose as diocesan administrator, Bishop Vincent Nichols. The Pope was advised of this decision by the papal nuncio to Great Britain, Archbishop Pablo Puente. The Archbishop then sent a *Terna,* or list of three names of suitable candidates for the vacant See to the Pope.

In November 1999, Archbishop Michael Bowen of Southwark was elected president of the Bishop's Conference of England and Wales for a period of one year. In recent years the office of president has always been held by the Archbishop of Westminster. A similar situation occurred after Cardinal Heenan's death in 1975.

Juxtaposed with Cardinal Hume's reign at Westminster was that of Archbishop Derek Worlock's at Liverpool, who died on 8 February 1996 after a long fight against cancer. He was with Cardinal Hume, a leading figure in the Catholic Church for more than a quarter of a century.

Derek Worlock was born on 4 February 1920 in London, he preceeded his twin sister Patricia by twenty-five minutes. His parents Harford and Dora Worlock had been devout Anglicans. While they were engaged to be married they both decided to become Catholics and received instructions from Father Gavin a Jesuit priest at Farm Street. Harford, a political journalist, was greatly influenced by the writings of Cardinal Newman. Dora worked for the Suffrage Society, both parents were very active in politics.

When Derek was nine he decided that he wanted to be a priest. By this time the family had moved from London to Winchester where Harford Worlock had been appointed Conservative agent for the Winchester constituency. In 1934 Derek sought permission to enter a seminary. However, Bishop Cotter of Portsmouth would only accept candidates who were Irish or from Irish extraction. Instead, with the help of Bishop Joseph Butt the Auxiliary Bishop of Westminster, he entered the seminary of St. Edmund's. He was ordained by Archbishop Griffin, newly installed at Westminster, on 3 June 1944.

His first parish was Our Lady of Victories Kensington, he was only there for just over a year as Archbishop Griffin asked Derek to join his staff in the summer of 1945 as second secretary. This was to be the start of his long service as secretary to three Cardinals. In 1947 he succeeded Monsignor Collingwood as first secretary and principal assistant to Cardinal Griffin, the pace of work under Cardinal Griffin was always hectic. This was a period of re-organisation of the Church in England and Wales, the Cardinal initiated an all out drive to bring the Church out of the shadows or 'out of the cata-combs' as he put it. During his years with Cardinals Griffin and Godfrey there emerged a growing self confidence and the Church expanded. Social issues were uppermost on the agenda, ecumenical work was not seen as important. Vatican II was to change all that, and would also change the priorities of Derek Worlock.

He played a significant role at Vatican II as a *peritus,* an expert adviser, especially for his expertise regarding the lay apostolate. He had for several years worked very closely with a group of laymen who he referred to as 'The Team'. He honed some of his practical experiences with this team. When he moved from Archbishop's House to Stepney, as parish priest, he brought with him qualities of leadership and organisation which he had perfected at the highest echelons of the Church. In addition he had a genuine pastoral concern for all his people, both lay and clergy.

Stepney was the parish of East End dockers, where poverty still prevailed. He was practical not patronising, his motivation was to implement the modernising of the Church at parish level according to the *aggiornamento* of Pope John XXIII. Despite his accent and upper class background, the East Enders were very loyal to him and responded to his sincerity and care. He instituted parish council meetings consulting with lay people for ideas and suggestions. He considered his time at St. Mary and St. Michael's parish as the happiest period of his life.

In the autumn of 1965 Derek Worlock was appointed Bishop of Portsmouth. He did not have the time to consolidate the initiatives he had started. He had given to the people of Stepney the vision to live out the ideals offered by Vatican II. Portsmouth welcomed the new bishop, at the age of forty-five one of the youngest in the hierarchy. He was consecrated on 21 December 1965, the feast of St. Thomas the Apostle, in St. John's Cathedral as the sixth Bishop of Portsmouth. Cardinal Heenan presided at the Mass, and Archbishop Cowderey of Southwark preached. There were 2000 people, 280 priests, sixteen archbishops and bishops in attendance. In the evening there was a reception for Bishop Worlock in Portsmouth's Guildhall, attended by the Lord Mayor of the city and the Mayor of Winchester, along with many bishops, priests and leaders of other Churches.

He made it clear to the priests and people of the diocese he intended to fully implement all of the wide-ranging agenda of the Vatican Council. He intended following the clear lines laid down in each of the conciliar decrees as they affected the life of the diocese. This principle was to form his policy for many years ahead. He established a pastoral centre at Park Place, near Havant. This became a focal point and source of unity for the diocese and as a training centre. He set up a properly constituted Diocesan Pastoral Council fed by parish and deanery councils. He cherished the role of the laity and the ideals of Christian unity.

In 1969 he celebrated the Silver Jubilee of his ordination to the priesthood. That same year, an extraordinary Synod of Bishops was convened in Rome as a direct result of the controversies surrounding *Humanae Vitae*. The Pope was demanding solidarity from his bishops at the same time developing the theme of collegiality.

When Cardinal Heenan died after a painful illness, there was again the traditional speculation about who would go to Westminster. Many saw Bishop Worlock as the ideal choice, an establishment candidate of great experience, once a conservative traditionalist, but now converted, following Vatican II, to a liberal, with almost socialist tendencies. The Westminster clergy were less enthusiastic mistrusting his bureaucratic reputation.

Liverpool was also vacant following the retirement of Archbishop Beck. Bishop Worlock clearly would have liked to go back to Westminster. He was very disappointed when he received the news that he was to go to Liverpool and the largely unknown Abbot of Ampleforth, Basil Hume, was to go South to Westminster.

He wrote a pastoral letter to the clergy and people of Portsmouth diocese dated 14 March 1976, the Second Sunday of Lent:

"At the summons of Pope Paul, I must leave you now to take charge of the Archdiocese of Liverpool. I have always marvelled that the first apostles succeeded in travelling so far with the good news of Jesus Christ. They were, as we say, travelling men. A bishop, as successor of the apostles, must be the same. For the last ten years I have travelled from parish to parish, trying to help you to live according to the Gospel. Now I am asked to leave you and travel to another part of the country, though with the same Gospel. I cannot disguise my sadness at leaving you. But as an apostle it is my task to keep going, never to cease to take the message of the Gospel wherever it is most needed".

The Liverpool reputation for hospitality and good nature showed when he was installed at the Metropolitan Cathedral on 19 March, the feast of St. Joseph patron of the archdiocese and the Universal Church the event was televised by Granada Television. Archbishop Worlock wanted to focus especially in the early days, on the morale of the priests, participation of the laity, Chritian unity and liturgical renewal.

His years in Liverpool, despite his initial disappointment would be filled with great excitement and achievement. One of the jewels, was his association with David Sheppard. Bishop David Sheppard had already established ecumenical relations with Archbishop George Beck. The Anglican Bishop and the new Catholic Archbishop were to take the ecumenical partnership to staggering new heights.

The two bishops had met when they presented the *Epilogue* on television. Now they were both in Liverpool, they were intent on developing a better understanding of each other. They formed a double-act which caught the public mood, they were seldom out of the public lime light. They also formed an alliance with Dr. John Newton, the Methodist District Chairman and Moderator of the Free Churches. They were affectionately known as 'The Liverpool Three'. They initiated a new era of Church understanding and they brought about the signing of a Covenant of Unity by the six Merseyside Church leaders. The 'Call to Partnership' took the local Church communities into a new mode of working and praying together. The very first Holy Week after Worlock's arrival, Anglicans and Catholics met in the church at Hough Green, Widnes, shared by Catholics and Anglicans, to meditate on the Stations of the Cross. The 'Liverpool Three' in the years that followed travelled the length and breadth of the country preaching the message of 'Churches Together'.

In September 1977, the National Conference of Priests had proposed that a national Pastoral Congress be held to bring together the people, religious and clergy to discuss key issues in the life of the Church. The bishops endorsed the idea and Archbishop Worlock was asked to coordinate the planning, with the help of Bishop David Konstant and Bishop Leo McCartie. The Archbishop and Cardinal Hume were anxious to have the Congress accepted by Rome.

Derek Worlock saw the Congress as having similarities with the Vatican Council, with planning being all important. He was closely involved with the Congress at every step. Many thought the Congress was one of Archbishop Worlock's greatest achievements, and won the support of every bishop for the Congress document *The Easter People*. From the Congress came the decision to invite the Pope to Britain to endorse what had taken place. The visit, as history records, despite all the expected difficulties including the short war with Argentina, was a triumph for everyone. Other Churches too, warmed to the personality of Pope John Paul II.

In 1989 the Hillsborough ground of Sheffield Wednesday Football Club was the scene of horrific disaster. Ninety-six people died as a result of overcrowding. The Archbishop went to Hallamshire Hospital the next morning to visit the injured and bereaved. This visit enabled Derek Worlock to obtain the insight to the tragedy and find words of comfort that would help people to come to terms with it.

At the end of July 1995 he began an extended stay in the Lourdes Hospital in Mossley Hill. Earlier in July, he had suffered a collapse and spent two weeks in bed at home. He had no strength in his legs and he had several falls attempting to get around unaided. The illness that gripped him was mortal. He slipped between lucidity and periods of confusion. It was decided to take a brain scan in the Royal Hospital. This revealed two brain tumours that were inoperable. He returned to the Lourdes Hospital very dejected. He realised he only had a short time to live.

With radiotherapy and regular doses of steroids there followed a period of remission, a time of grace and the opportunity to prepare himself for the end. However, on the 8 February 1996, just before dawn he passed away surrounded by the love and care he had always hoped would be there for him at the end. He could perhaps hear the prayers and sense the presence of so many friends around his bedside.

On the day of the funeral, the day he had been due to go to Buckingham Palace to receive the Companion of Honour from the Queen, Cardinal Hume, in his moving panegyric said that instead of "Waiting in the ante-chamber of the palace to see Her Majesty he was now in the ante-chamber of heaven preparing to meet the Majesty of God face to face".

Extracts from: *Cardinal Hume A Portrait* edited by Tony Castle
Published by William Collins Sons & Co. Ltd., London
Ampleforth and its Origins by Abbot Justin McCann OSB and
Dom Columba Carey-Elwes OSB
published by Burns Oates & Washbourne, London
The Worlock Archives by Clifford Longley
published by Geoffrey Chapman, London
Briefing (vol 29 special issue July 1999) used with permission
Briefing is the official monthly journal of the Catholic Bishops of Great Britain
The Tablet (the Cardinal Hume obituary issue dated 26 June 1999)
published by The Tablet Publishing Company, London
Archbishop Derek Worlock His Personal Journey by John Furnival and Ann Knowles
published by Geoffrey Chapman, London

Chapter Eighteen

Cardinal
Cormac Murphy-O'Connor

ORMAC Murphy-O'Connor was installed as the tenth Archbishop of Westminster on 22 March 2000. The millennium year marked the 150th anniversary of the restoration of the Catholic hierarchy by Pope Pius IX.

The Murphy-O'Connors came from County Cork. Cormac's grandfather was a vinter, the family business was founded early in the 19th Century. The family name was created two hundred years ago when a Miss McSweeney married a Mr Murphy. She had two sons by her first marriage who went on to become priests, and one of them became the first Bishop of Hyderabad in India. Following her husband's death, Mrs Murphy married a Mr O'Connor and became Mrs Murphy-O'Connor. There have been numerous priests called McSweeney, Murphy and O'Connor who can trace their roots back to Miss McSweeney.

Cormac's parents emigrated to Liverpool. His father Patrick was a doctor and worked for a while in Liverpool before moving to Reading where he practiced as a GP. They had six children, all of whom were born in Reading. Although a busy doctor, Cormac's father was dedicated to parish life and founded the St. Vincent de Paul Society in Reading. He was awarded a papal knighthood in recognition of his work among the poor in Reading. Their mother Ellen founded the Union of Catholic Mothers in the town and was a school governor.

Young Cormac had a talent for both music and sport, but as a very young boy he had decided to become a priest. Two of his brothers, Patrick and Brian were already students at the English College in Rome and Cormac joined them. He was ordained in October 1956 and was appointed curate at Corpus Christi parish in Portsmouth. His love of music and sport endeared him to parishioners and continued when he moved to Sacred Heart parish in Fareham in 1963.

In 1966 Cormac was appointed private secretary to Bishop Worlock of Portsmouth. He worked closely with Bishop Worlock and in those pioneering post Vatican II days Portsmouth was the first diocese to set up a pastoral centre specifically for the training of lay people. As Worlock's secretary, Cormac was asked to steer the first National Conference of Priests at Wood Hall Pastoral Centre, Wetherby in 1970.

After a brief spell as parish priest of Immaculate Conception parish in Southampton in 1970, he was appointed rector of the English College in Rome. In 1977 Cormac, by now Monsignor Cormac Murphy-O'Connor, hosted the historic visit of the Archbishop of Canterbury, Dr. Donald Coggan, to Pope Paul VI.

In December 1977, Cormac was ordained the third Bishop of Arundel and Brighton. He sought to build good relationships with other Christian Churches. He believes that ecumenism is simply a question of the denominations listening to each other, praying together and working together. He believes unity will come in time and has often described ecumenism as "Like a road with no exit". He says that Christian unity is the restoration of the one Church that in many ways already exists.

Addressing the Anglican Synod at Chichester in 1978, Bishop Cormac stressed that the purpose of ecumenism: "Is not just for the Churches to come together, but rather that together they may give witness to Christ. How important it is to remember that, in the area of ecumenism, it is no longer the objective to convert the other to one's own private view. The purpose of our meeting each other is not that the other turns from his wrong or wicked ways, but rather that each one of us should. The conversion we demand is our own, and that is painful.

"The scope of ecumenism is not a merger of companies, with limits on how the merger will go. It is rather like a road which someone enters and from which he discovers there is no going back. It is a road we enter together and not one taken for our own sakes, but for the sake of all men. We enter it because we have experienced a vision and a union with Christ. And we have a deep belief that the Church exists to serve all people and not just those who belong to it".

In 1983, Bishop Cormac was appointed co-chairman along with the Anglican Bishop of Birmingham Mark Santor of ARCIC II, the second Anglican-Roman Catholic International Commission. The first ARCIC had grown directly out of the historic meeting between Archbihop Michael Ramsey and Pope Paul VI in 1966. Over the following thirty years the commission considered the doctrine of the Eucharist, ministry and ordination, and authority in the Church.

When the Church of England introduced the ordination of women priests, many Anglican clergymen began converting to Roman Catholicism. Some asked about the possibility of becoming Catholic priests. Bishop Cormac was instrumental in discussions with Rome that allowed these men, some married with children, to be ordained. Some of these men became priests of Arundel and Brighton diocese.

Despite the sensitive nature of these ordinations Bishop Cormac's relationship with Church of England leaders was not diminished. The Archbishop of Canterbury George Carey awarded him the Lambeth degree of Doctor of Divinity in recognition of his work for Christian unity and particularly for Anglican-Roman Catholic relations.

In 1986, Lord Longford in his book *The Bishops* had described the then Bishop of Arundel and Brighton as "Often tipped as the natural successor to Cardinal Hume as Archbishop of Westminster". On 13 February 2000, *The Sunday Times* announced that Pope John Paul had appointed him to the post. Two days later on the 15 February the formal announcement was made that Cardinal Hume's successor was to be Cormac Murphy-O'Connor.

At the same time Pope John Paul II, appointed Bishop Vincent Nichols to the archbishopric of Birmingham. The Catholic Church in England and Wales now has a trio of strong archbishops, Cormac Murphy-O'Connor, Vincent Nichols and Patrick Kelly of Liverpool. Together they make a formidable combination.

The response to Bishop Murphy-O'Connor's appointment was warm and positive. The Archbishop of Canterbury, Dr George Carey, spoke of his pleasure at the appointments of both Murphy-O'Connor and Nichols: "I have come to know both men well, and regard them with great esteem", he said. He personally awarded Murphy-O'Connor the first Lambeth Doctorate in Divinity given to a Roman Catholic bishop since the Reformation, in appreciation of his work as co-chairman of ARCIC.

One of Murphy-O'Connor's colleagues on ARCIC, Rev. John Muddiman, of Mansfield College, Oxford, said: "He's a humane, lovely person with a lot of sense. He's entirely orthodox and devoted to the Holy Father, but he is also his own person, and he will be immediately attractive on television as a spokeman for the Catholic Church. He is a caring pastor and has an instant rapport with ordinary folk. In the evening he will sit down   at the piano and sing old Irish songs. But at the same time he is friends with the Royal Family and knows his way around the Establishment".

One of Arcbishop-elect Cormac Murphy-O'Connor's first television appearances was on the BBC *Breakfast with Frost*. Bishop Cormac said he wanted to continue Cardinal Hume's mission to bring Catholicism into the centre of public life in Britain. The repeal of the 1701 Act of Settlement which prevents the heir to the throne from marrying a Catholic, was "a question which needs to be looked at", he said. "There is a strong part of me that would say that an heir to the crown should be free to marry whoever he wishes, whatever denomination, and there must be freedom here".

Bishop Cormac also supported the Archbishop of Canterbury's recent call for there to be a correlation between personal morality and public life. "The moral life of any person affects his or her integrity and I think people have a right in a public figure to recognise that the person they are going to trust in public life is a man or woman of trustworthiness", he said. While everybody had "sins and faults", he thought that Archbishop Carey's point was that "you cannot divorce the integrity of a person from their public life".

In the interview the Bishop Cormac also said that while he was "compassionate" to people having difficulties, he upheld the Vatican's teaching on abortion, contraception and priestly celibacy. On the topic of Christian unity, he said that the ordination of women in the Church of England posed a "real obstacle" to progress.

The onslaught against Christian values appeared to reach new heights during the year of his appointment. The Government were intent in bringing in the repeal of Section 28 of the Local Government Act, which prohibited local authorities from promoting homosexuality in schools.

The Catholic Education Service and the Church of England Board of Education offered a joint statement informing the Secretary of State for Education and Employment, David Blunkett, what they hope to see in the guidance he has promised to give schools on education about sex and relationships:

1. Pupils should be taught from an early age to understand human sexuality and to respect themselves and others. They should be given accurate information. This will enable them to understand difference and help to remove prejudice.

2. Human sexuality (is a gift of God and) finds its perfect expression within loving life-long marriage. Any other physical sexual expression falls short to some degree of that ideal. It follows that human sexuality is not fulfilled in self-gratification or in promiscuous or casual relationships.

3. Traditional (Christian) marriage should be promoted as the fundamental building block of society and of family life as as the proper context for the nurture of children.

4. Pupils have a right to develop without being subject to any physical or verbal abuse about sexual orientation or the encouragement of sexual activity.

5. Lifelong celibacy can be fulfilling. In this way of life an individual's sexual instincts may be channelled into generous love and service to others.

6. Lifelong human friendships are an important gift and should be honoured and cherished.

7. Human beings fall short of the ideal, but the admission of failure can bring forgiveness and reconciliation. People can change their behaviour.

Couples working through problems within marriage can find deeper love and strengthened character.

Cormac Murphy-O'Connor was installed as Archbishop of Westminster on Wednesday 22 March. The installation Mass began with the reading of the apostolic letter of appointment by the papal nuncio, Archbishop Pablo Puente. The provost of Westminster Cathedral, Mgr. Frederick Miles, formally installed the Archbishop in the cathedral, and Bishop Vincent Nichols, Archbishop-elect of Birmingham, placed the crosier in his hands. The new Archbishop was then greeted by the presidents of the ecumenical body Churches Together in England, including the Archbishop of Canterbury, Dr George Carey.

Archbishop Murphy-O'Connor has specialised in work for Christian unity, and in his homily he restated this commitment. "The road to Christian unity", he said, "is like a road with no exit, a pilgrimage of grace we make together". More and more, he added, "all of us who profess Jesus Christ must speak with one voice to give witness to him in this strange and wonderful new world in which we live".

The Archbishop ended his sermon by thanking the Church for all it had given him. "I know that the Church must always be reformed and that it is composed of saints and sinners", he said. But he added that the Church had always been "the heart of my soul, the model of my spiritual being. It is to Christ's Church that I give my loyalty and my love. So I continue as a pilgrim traveller, always teaching, yes, but always listening and always looking for the road ahead".

As the year 2000 drew to its close and with the approach of Christmas – the true focal point to all the Millennium celebrations – MP's voted on 19 December to approve human stem-cell cloning for medical research. The decision, after a free vote to allow 'therapeutic cloning' of embryos by extending 10 year old guidelines placed Britain at odds with the rest of Europe. The European Parliament had recently condemned the practice.

The amendment to the 1990 legislation, in order to allow cloning of human embryos up to 14 days old, was passed by a two-thirds majority in the House of Commons. The Lords subsequently approved the amendment. Scientists will be allowed to create human embryos using the cloning techniques which produced Dolly the sheep.

The Catholic hierarchy in Britain strongly deplored the proposals. The Church of England's Board for Social Responsibility argued on the eve of the vote that research "may be thought to be morally acceptable". Archbishop Cormac Murphy-O'Connor urged the House of Lords to overturn the amendment.

New parliamentary legislation also allowed from the first day in January 2001, the sale of the 'morning after pill'. The Church fought a lost cause battle over the legalisation of abortion. This development was the pharmaceut-ist's ultimate gift to the public's obsessional neurosis and pursuit of sexual gratification. Even some of the tabloid press were revolted by the an-nouncement. A *Daily Express* columnist compared the announcement to Herod's slaughter of the innocents. A secular television commentator spoke against the Government's lack of moral leadership, and the "drive by the pharmaceutical industry to promote an ever-increasing range of products which encouraged casual and indiscriminate sexual behaviour". This along with the constant media bombardment promoting sexual activity as a rec-reational, on demand, designer activity, "influences younger people, even pre-pubescent, to experiment with sex". The unfettered individualism and "trivialisation of sex, without any reference to its real meaning, which is in the context of marriage and of children, could result in dire consequences for young girls and potential gynaecological problems in the future, which pose a serious threat to the health and fertility of women".

The ethos of Western liberalism which enshrines values such as sexual equality, human rights and freedom of choice also challenges ideas about marriage. More than half of all weddings in England and Wales are now civil ceremonies. The Church regards Christian marriage as symbolic and sacra-mental and paramount to the stability of family life.

Stories of sexual abuse became more commonplace and within a few months of Archbishop Murphy-O'Connor's appointment he was faced with severe criticism over a paedophile he had allowed, when he was Bishop of Arundel and Brighton in the early 1980's to continue to work as a priest in a limited ministry at Gatwick Airport. The Archbishop gave a series of inter-views on television and radio, he stressed that if the strict procedures for child protection that were now in place had been in operation in 1985 then the situation would have been handled differently. Speaking on BBC TV's *One o'clock News,* the Archbishop said that in the 1980's "the addiction of paedophilia was just not known" in the way it was now.

Other cases received publicity, including the scandal in the archdiocese of Cardiff. Archbishop Ward was severely criticized in the press and on BBC TV's *Panorama.* The Archbishop, in spite of advice he had received in a confidential letter from Bishop Christopher Budd of Plymouth, had ac-cepted Joe Jordan for ordination. Jordan had been cleared by Sheffield Crown Court of indecently assaulting a boy at Don Valley High School, Doncaster, where he was a teacher. Jordan approached the Plymouth dio-cese to be accepted for training for the priesthood. Bishop Budd thought it safe for Jordan to begin training as a priest but within three years he had changed his mind.

Jordan however told Bishop Budd early in 1995 that he had decided to continue his training as a student of the archdiocese of Cardiff. Jordan was ordained priest by Archbishop Ward in January 1998. During the following eighteen months he indecently assaulted two boys. In December of 1998 Fr John Lloyd, who was Archbishop Ward's press spokesman and adviser, was found guilty at Chester Crown Court of eleven charges of indecent assault and two other more serious charges. Other cases involving Lloyd came to light following the trial. His crimes were thought to be so grave that in October 1999 he was forcibly laicised by the Pope.

The Archbishop himself was arrested by police in London in connection with the alleged sexual assault of a girl thirty years ago. The case against him was completely without foundation, and he was released without charge.

Archbishop Murphy-O'Connor, in September 2000, set up an independent committee to examine and review arrangements made for child protection and the prevention of abuse within the Catholic Church in England and Wales. The nine-strong committee is headed by Lord Nolan, the Law Lord and former chairman of the Committee on Standards in Public Life, which investigated corruption in Parliament.

The National Conference of Priests at their annual meeting in September 2000, expressed their "sorrow and sense of shame" over Catholic clergy found guilty of sexually abusing children. They also debated the current seminary system and the need to reform and reorganise the existing system.

Another public relations disaster was the Vatican Declaration *Dominus Jesus* a document intended as a note for the presidents of Bishops' Conferences. Although claimed to be an internal directive from the Congregation for the Doctrine of the Faith, the Declaration was leaked to the world press.

With ecumenical progress, not only between Christian Churches but also with inter-faith dialogue, the threat of relativism had to be addressed and the Congregation was uncompromising with its Declaration. In Britain especially, hurt was felt by Anglicans with the Declaration's denial that Churches without a valid episcopate and Eucharist can be called Churches at all in "the proper (or full) sense".

The term sister Churches emerged as an expression which appeared in important Vatican documents especially in relation to dialogue between the Catholic Church and the Orthodox Churches. This led to the use of the expression to indicate the Catholic Church on the one hand and the Orthodox Church on the other. The view of the Congregation is that this usage leads people to think that in fact the one Church of Christ does not exist, but may be re-established through the reconciliation of the two sister Churches.

A particular censure was applied to the improper use of this expression to the relationship between "the Catholic Church on the one hand, and the Anglican Communion and non-Catholic ecclesial communities on the other. In this sense, a 'theology of sister Churches' or an 'ecclesiology of sister Churches' is spoken of, characterised by ambiguity and discontinuity with respect to the correct original meaning of the expression as found in the documents of the magisterium".

The Congregation stated emphatically: "It must always be clear, when the expression *sister Churches* is used in this proper sense, that the one, holy, Catholic and apostolic universal Church is not *sister* but *mother* of all the particular Churches. Catholics are required to profess that there is a historical continuity – rooted in the apostolic succession – between the Church founded by Christ and the Catholic Church. The Declaration quotes the statement of the Second Vatican Council that the "Church of Christ subsists in the Catholic Church, governed by the successor of Peter and by the bishops in communion with him". The English phrase 'subsists in' is a translation of the original Latin *subsistit in*. This expression was used by the Second Vatican Council "to harmonise two doctrinal statements: on the one hand, that the Church of Christ despite the divisions which exist among Christians, continues to exist fully only in the Catholic Church, and on the other hand, that outside her structure, many elements can be found of sanctification and truth – that is, in those Churches and ecclesial communities which are not yet in full communion with the Catholic Church".

The Declaration distinguishes between Churches which have the apostol;ic succession and a valid Eucharist, and those which "have not preserved the valid episcopate and the genuine and integral substance of the Eucharistic mystery". In the former "the Church of Christ is present and operative" even though "they do not accept the catholic doctrine of the primacy which, according to the will of God, the Bishop of Rome objectively has and exercises over the entire Church". But the latter class which emerged from the Reformation the Declaration says, "are not Churches in the full sense" (the official English translation says "in the proper sense", the Latin however is sunsu proprio) however "those who are baptised in these communities are, by baptism, incorporated in Christ and thus are in a certain communion, albeit imperfectly, with the Church".

What the Christian faithful may not do is "to imagine that the Church of Christ is nothing more than a collection – divided, yet in some way one – of Churches and ecclesial communities, nor are they free to hold that today the Church of Christ nowhere really exists, and must be considered only as a goal which all Churches and ecclesial communities strive to reach". But the Declaration acknowledges, quoting again from the Second Vatican Council's decree on ecumenism, that "these separated Churches as such, though we believe they suffer from defects, have by no means been deprived of significance and importance in the mystery of salvation. For the spirit of Christ has not refrained from using them as means of salvation which derive their efficacy from the very fullness of grace and truth entrusted to the Catholic Church".

We are all victims of history and in Britain, perhaps more than any other country, the work for Christian unity provides the greatest challenge. The Catholic view is that the Anglican episcopy does not have true apostolic succession. A modern parallel emerges with the decision by the Methodist Church, in the Autumn of 2000, to consider its acceptance of bishops in the effort to become re-united with the Church of England. How will these new bishops be consecrated? Some no doubt will be women. In 1784, faced with the refusal of the Bishop of London to ordain men to lead the American Methodists, and to the grave consternation of his brother Charles, John Wesley ordained them himself. This action, more than any other, made a complete break of the Methodist movement with the Church of England inevitable.

The genuine goodwill felt between Catholic and Anglican ecumenists, and the enthusiasm to achieve real progress towards unity, resulted in an over optimistic sharing of the Eucharist. This was countered in 1998 by the Bishops' Conference issuing the teaching document *One Bread One Body*. "The Catholic Church claims, in all humility to be endowed with all the gifts with which God wishes to endow His Church. The one, holy, Catholic and apostolic Church of Christ is to be found in its fullness, though imperfectly, in the visible Catholic Church as it is here and now . . . Other Christians do not share everything in common with us, and so are not in full communion with the Catholic Church, but we understand all people who believe in the Lord and have been properly baptised as being in some kind of communion with the Catholic Church, although this communion is imperfect".

The debate between ecumenists continues, but however one feels about the apparent insensitivity of the statements and the bad press and controversy they caused, deep down there is a growing acceptance that what has been said was necessary to re-focus on the realities of Catholic doctrine. Many sincere ecumenists had allowed their vision to become blurred. Cardinal Hume spoke about these issues (see page 309) when he said we should face honestly and courageously the obstacles that lay ahead. That as Roman Catholics we must make our position absolutely clear and that the Anglican Church has to make up its mind what it really believes because the spectrum is too wide. He also said that reconciliation of ministries cannot be cheaply bought, or sought for simple convenience, The progress of reconciling ministries will be long and arduous.

One of the reasons for producing this book was to recognise and celebrate the anniversary of the restoration of the hierarchy in England and Wales, during the Jubilee Year 2000. Bishops of England and Wales gathered in Westminster Cathedral in May to sing the *Te Deum* at the tomb of Cardinal Wiseman. The Mass in Westminster Cathedral took place on the feast of the Beatified Martyrs of England and Wales, and began with the bishops lighting candles in the martyrs' chapel. The principal celebrant at the Mass was Cardinal Godfried Danneels, Archbishop of Malines-Brussels, who attended as the special envoy of Pope John Paul II. The Cardinal read out a message from the Pope to Catholics in England and Wales. The congregation included members of both Houses of Parliament and numerous diplomats.

The homily was given by Dom Aidan Bellenger, a Benedictine monk of Downside Abbey. He recalled some of the events at the restoration. The coming to maturity of the English Catholic Church should be celebrated in the year 2000 with "sincere gratitude" rather than triumphalism, Dom Aidan said. He charted the development of the English Church from St. Gregory's monastic model, which was "a Christian alternative to barbarism", to the "clerical" vision of Pius IX and the bishops of 1850, who saw the hierarchy as a "bastion of Church order". At the beginning of the third millennium, he went on, the role of the Catholic hierarchy could be something new again: "a leadership of service and listening, perhaps, rather than of power and domination".

But that did not mean that the Church should be weak and invisible: rather, it should be a "counter-culture, always avoiding the siren voices of establishment and respectability". New forms of media offered new opportunities for the Church "to confront the modern world with the eternal truths of Christianity and to experience a third spring". While it was difficult, "in a world of political correctness and spin", for the Church to be noticed, especially in terms of its whole teaching, rather than the obvious single issues, this could be done. If the Church was now "more humble", and "rather chastened at times", this did not mean it was no longer a Church of proclamation.

Queen Elizabeth in her Christmas 2000 television broadcast to the Nation and Commonwealth spoke of the need to renew and strengthen the spiritual dimension of the lives of all people. She spoke of her own deep faith and commitment to the Christian life, and of her responsibility and eventual accountability to God.

+ + +

On 21 February 2001, Pope John Paul II held his eighth and largest consistory, in which he appointed forty-four new cardinals. The ceremony was held in St. Peter's Square. Among the new cardinals was Archbishop Cormac Murphy-O'Connor. The ceremony was held on the anniversary of the birth of John Henry Newman. The Pope recalled the words of Newman to Pope Pius IX when he was made cardinal: "The Church should do no other than pursue its mission, in faithfulness and peace, to remain always calm and firm, waiting on the salvation of God".

The new Cardinal Archbishop of Westminster said he was "very content" to be the tenth Archbishop of Westminster as well as the fourth former rector of the English College in Rome to be created cardinal. He said receiving his red hat was an honour for him personally, for the Church in England and Wales, and for all his predecessors.

Extracts from: *Archbishop Cormac and the 21st Century Church* by Nick Baty
published by Fount, Harper Collins, London
The Tablet published by the Tablet Publishing Co. Ltd., London
A Celebration of Christianity in our Countryside by Mary Creaser and Elizabeth Glover
published by The Diocese of Bradford/PBK Publishing, Keighley

Epilogue

T
HE new century heralds new opportunities for the Church but perhaps more than any other age, dangers confront and challenge the very fabric of Christian life, not only the clergy, but every Christian young and old in all walks of life should be prepared for this challenge. Fortunately the laity today are more educated and aware of canon law and moral theology than ever before. Since Vatican II when Pope John XXIII opened the windows of the Church to breathe more freely, values among the faithful and society in general have changed considerably, Christians now live in a truly hostile environment.

The obsession of modern society with the trivialisation of sex and materialism, which appeals to the base impulses of human nature, entices people away from Christian values. Scandals abound, exposure of Catholic priests, even bishops, with mistresses, some convicted and jailed for child sexual abuse, have filled newspaper headlines and were exposed on television. Divorce and re-marriage is increasing, the vast majority of children educated in Catholic schools cease the practice of religion immediately they leave school. Mass attendance fell to 1,041,728 in 1999, the lowest level since records began in 1959. The level of decline however, is less than half of that which occurred in 1997-1998. Figures from Christian Research shows the decline in active membership of the Catholic Church appears to be slightly less than that in the Church of England, but the Anglican rate of decline also seems to have slowed. The Free Churches are declining at a slower rate still, while the independent Evangelical house churches are increasing in strength as are the Greek Orthodox.

The reality of the Church is tacitly disappearing, without being expressly rejected. Many no longer believe that what is at issue is a reality willed by Our Lord himself. Even with some theologians, the Church appears to be a human construction, an instrument created by us and one which we ourselves can freely re-organise according to the requirements of the moment. In other words, in many ways a conception of the Church is spreading in Catholic thought, and even in Catholic theology, that cannot even be called Protestant in a classic sense. The Church is composed of men who organise her external visage, but behind this, the fundamental structures are willed by God himself, and therefore they are inviolable. Behind the human exterior stands the mystery of a more than human reality, in which reformers, sociologists, organisers have no authority whatever.

If the Church is viewed as a human construction, the product of our own efforts, even the contents of faith in fact, it no longer has an authentic guaranteed instrument through which to express itself. Without a view of the mystery of the Church that is also supernatural and not only sociological, Christology itself loses its reference to the Divine in favour of a purely human structure.

During Vatican II there was great emphasis on the concept of the Church as 'The People of God' which has dominated the post conciliar ecclesiologies. 'The People of God' in scripture is in fact a reference to Israel in its relationship of prayer and fidelity to the Lord. To limit the definition of the Church to that expression suggests an intention not to give expression to the New Testament understanding of the Church in its fullness. The Church receives her New Testament character more distinctly in the concept of 'The Body of Christ' through baptism and the Eucharist.

There are impulses at work such as the movement in Austria 'We are Church' whereby the laity demand an ever increasing voice in the affairs of the Church. Where the feminist movements demand recognition and womens right to ordination. These impulses are also felt in Britain. If the Church is in fact our Church, if we alone are the Church, if her structures are not willed by Christ, then it is no longer possible to conceive of the existence of a hierarchy as a service to the baptised established by Our Lord himself. It is a rejection of the concept of an authority willed by God, an authority therefore that has its legitimation in God and not, as happens in political structures, in the consensus of the majority of the members of an organisation. But the Church of Christ is not a party, not an association, not a club. Her deep and permanent structure is not *democratic* but *sacramental,* consequently *hierarchical.* For the hierarchy based on the apostolic succession is the indispensable condition to arrive at the strength, the reality of the sacrament. Her authority is not based on the majority of votes, it is based on the authority of Christ himself, which he willed to pass on to men who were to be His representatives until His definitive return. Only if this perspective is acquired anew will it be possible to rediscover the necessity and fruitfulness of obedience to the legitimate ecclesiastical hierarchies.

There is a remedy to the crisis in the understanding of the Church, to the crisis of morality, to the crisis of women. The remedy is The Blessed Virgin Mary. The Second Vatican Council confirmed as the culmination of the Dogmatic Constitution on the Church by inserting the mystery of Mary into the mystery of the Church. Fifty years ago the Church proclaimed the dogma of the Assumption of Mary in body and soul to heavenly glory. At the time, the proclamation so uplifted the Catholic Church. Today, perhaps because we do not wish to place unnecessary obstacles in the way of a reunion with our evangelical fellow Christians, many Catholic Marian devotions have lapsed.

Epilogue

We should in this new millennium renew our devotion to Mary the mother of God. We should urgently rediscover the Marian mystery, in the confused period in which we live where truly every type of heretical aberration seems to be pressing upon the doors of the authentic faith. We should now accept that it is necessary to go back to Mary if we want to return to that truth about Jesus Christ, truth about the Church, and truth about man. Mary must be more than ever the pedagogy, in order to proclaim the Gospel to the men of today.

Mary continues to project a light upon that which the Creator intended for women in every age, ours included, or perhaps precisely in our time, in which we know the very essence of femininity is threatened. Through her virginity and her motherhood, the mystery of women receives a very lofty destiny from which she cannot be torn away. Mary undauntedly proclaims the *Magnificat,* but she is also the one who renders silence and seclusion fruitful. She is the one who does not fear to stand under the Cross, who is present at the birth of the Church. But she is also the one who, as the evangelist emphasises more than once: "Keeps and ponders in her heart" that which transpires around her. As a creature of courage and of obedience she was and still is an example to which every Christian – man and woman – can and should look.

Extracts from: *The Ratzinger Report*
Cardinal Joseph Ratzinger interviewed by Vittorio Messori
translated from the authorised German manuscript
by Salvator Attanasio and Graham Harrison
published by Ignatius Press, San Francisco

Selected Bibliography

Baty, Nick *Archbishop Cormac and the 21ˢᵗ century Church*
Fount, Harper Collins

Beck, The Rt Rev George Andrew *The English Catholics 1850-1950*
Burns Oates London

Maziere-Brady, W *Annals of the Catholic Hierarchy*
Thomas Barker, London

Burton, Dr Edwin *The Life and Times of Bishop Challoner*
Longman Green & Co., London

Conroy, Mgr. Kieran, Editor *Briefing*
Catholic Media Office, London

Camm OSB, Dom Bede *William Cardinal Allen*
Burns Oates & Washbourne, London .

Creaser, Mary and Elizabeth Glover *A Celebration of Christianity In Our Countryside*
The Diocese of Bradford/PBK Publishing Ltd., Keighley

De la Bedoyere, Michael *Cardinal Bernard Griffin*
The Rockcliffe Foundation, London

Furnival, John and Anne Knowles *Archbishop Derek Worlock His Personal Journey* Geoffrey Chapman, London

Gillow, Joseph *Bibliographical Dictionary of the English catholics*
Burns & Oates Ltd, London

Greengrass. Mark *The European Reformation 1500-1618*
Longman, London

Gwynn, Denis *100 Years of Catholic Emancipation 1829-1929*
Longman Green & Co., London

Gwynn, Denis *Cardinal Wiseman*
Browne & Nolan, Dublin

Gwynn, Denis *The Second Spring 1818-1852*
The Catholic Book Club, London

Hemphill OSB, Dom Basil *The Early Vicars Apostolic of England*
Burns & Oates, London

Heenan, Cardinal Archbishop John C. *Not The Whole Truth*
Burns Oates & Washbourne, London

Heenan, Cardinal Archbishop John C. *A Crown of Thorns*
Burns Oates & Washbourne, London

Bibliography

Heenan, Dr. John C. *Cardinal Hinsley*
    Burns Oates & Washbourne, London
Heseltine, G. C. *The English Cardinals*
    Burns Oates & Washbourne, London
Hill, Roland *Lord Acton*
    Yale University Press, New Haven and London
Huebsch, Bill *Vatican Council in Plain English*
    Thomas More Publishers, Allen, Texas, USA
Jenkins, Roy *Gladstone*
    Macmillan, London
Jones, Frederick M. CSSR *Alphonsus de Liguori*
    Gill and Macmillan, Dublin
Kennedy, Paul *The Struggle of a Minority*
    PBK Publishing, Keighley
Ker, Ian *John Henry Newman*
    Oxford University Press
Loades, David *Mary Tudor*
    Blackwell, Oxford
Longley, Clifford *The Worlock Archive*
    Geoffrey Chapman, London
Leslie, Shane *Henry Edward Manning*
    Burns Oates & Washbourne, London
Lingard, John *History of England*
    John Duffy & Sons, Dublin and London
Mackie, J. D. *The Early Tudors*
    The Oxford History of England
MacCulloch, Diarmaid *Thomas Cranmer A Life*
    Yale University Press, New Haven and London
Mermet, Theodule Rey CSSR *The Moral Theology of*
    St. Alphonsus Liguori Liguori Publishing, Miso. USA
Messori, Vittorio *The Ratzinger Report*
    Ignatius Press, San Francisco USA
McLelland, Alan and Michael Hodgetts *From Without the*
    Flamnian Gate Dartman Longman & Todd
McCann, Abbot Justin and Dom Columba Carey-Elwes
    Ampleforth and its Origins Burns Oates & Washburne
McBrien, Richard P. General Editor *Encyclopedia of Catholicism*
    Harper Collins Publishers, New York
Newman, John Henry *Apologia*
    Longman Green & Co, London

O'Neil, Robert *Cardinal Herbert Vaughan*
    Burns & Oates London
Paul, Fr. OSFC *The British Church*
    Burns Oates & Washbourne Ltd., London
Phillips, Rev. G. E. *The Extinction of the Ancient Hierarchy*
    Sands & Co London
Reynolds, E. E. *The Roman Catholic Church in England & Wales*
    Anthony Clarke Books, Wheathampstead, Herts.
Sander, Nicholas *The Rise & Growth of the Anglican Schism*
    Burns & Oates, London
Thurston, Herbert J. SJ and Donald Attwater
    Butlers Lives of the Saints
    Thomas More Publishing, Allen, Texas
Tombs, Robert *France 1814-1914*
    Longman, London
Trappes-Lomax, Michael *Bishop Challoner*
    Longman Green & Co., London
Ullathorne, W.B. *The Auotobiography of Archbishop Ullathorne*
    Burns & Oates Ltd., London
Ward, Rev Bernard (later first Bishop of Brentwood)
    The Dawn of the Catholic Revival in England
    Longman & Co. London
Wheeler, William Gordon Bishop Emeritus of Leeds
    In Truth and Love
    Gowland & Co. Southport

Index of Names